Cooking with Jane Austen

The publisher has done its best to make sure the instructions and/or recipes in this book are correct. However, users should apply judgment and experience when preparing recipes, especially parents and teachers working with young people. The publisher accepts no responsibility for the outcome of any recipe included in this volume.

Cooking with
JANE AUSTEN

Kirstin Olsen

FEASTING WITH FICTION

GREENWOOD PRESS
Westport, Connecticut • London

Library of Congress Cataloging-in-Publication Data

Olsen, Kirstin.
   Cooking with Jane Austen / Kirstin Olsen.
       p.   cm.—(Feasting with fiction, ISSN 1552–8006)
    Includes bibliographical references and index.
    ISBN 0–313–33463–3 (alk. paper)
    1. Cookery, English—History.   2. Literary cookbooks.   3. Austen, Jane, 1775–1817—
Knowledge—Cookery. I. Title. II. Series.
TX717.O67   2005
641.5942—dc22   2005006569

British Library Cataloguing in Publication Data is available.

Copyright © 2005 by Kirstin Olsen

Library of Congress Catalog Card Number: 2005006569
ISBN: 0–313–33463–3
ISSN: 1552–8006

First published in 2005

Greenwood Press, 88 Post Road West, Westport, CT 06881
An imprint of Greenwood Publishing Group, Inc.
www.greenwood.com

Printed in the United States of America

∞™

The paper used in this book complies with the
Permanent Paper Standard issued by the National
Information Standards Organization (Z39.48–1984).

10 9 8 7 6 5 4 3 2 1

for Erica

CONTENTS

Contents

PREFACE AND ACKNOWLEDGMENTS

I am forced to confess that, for almost half my life, cooking was of absolutely no interest to me. Despite my mother's diligence in the kitchen and the justified fame of her cinnamon rolls, and despite my father's knack for re-creating almost any restaurant dish he had ever sampled, I felt out of place at the stove or sink. My grandfather managed the Wrigley Building restaurant in Chicago for about twenty years and enjoyed making a wide variety of dishes at home, including beautiful chocolate truffles. My sister, by the age of thirteen, could feel like eating a chicken pot pie and simply make one, pastry and all, without consulting a cookbook. And yet I felt no desire to join this illustrious band of intrepid chefs. Perhaps because I was surrounded by so many talented cooks, I avoided becoming one myself, turning to other pleasures such as those to be found in books and allowing myself merely to be pleased and nourished by the culinary creations of others.

What converted me to the whisk and the saucepan was a combination of financial need and friendship. In college, my meal plan didn't cover food during vacations, and it was too expensive for me to travel home during shorter breaks of a week or less. My parents were struggling to pay my tuition, and the supplementary meal plans were prohibitively expensive. So, rather than ask my parents to pay for my food at those times, I played poker every night, setting aside my initial stake and using my winnings to buy the next day's food. A steady diet of Whatever Was Cheapest at the Convenience Store, however, soon began to lose its appeal. At the beginning of the next vacation, I bought a wooden spoon, a bowl, and a cookbook.

Armed with these primitive tools and the truly paltry contents of a college dorm kitchen intended for the use of forty to fifty students—which may be defined, for this purpose, as everything too blackened, perforated, dented, or ugly to steal—I began to learn to cook. My friends would sign up for "Kirstin's Meal

Plan," which netted me no profit but helped pay for my own food and got me the company of eight to ten other people stranded, carless, in New Jersey. The camaraderie was too much fun to be resisted, and soon I was cooking at every opportunity. I spent the next twenty years hosting dinner parties whenever I could and learning to cook everything from shrimp étouffée to gingerbread cathedrals.

As it happened, at about the same time that I was learning to cook, I was also introduced to the works of Jane Austen by a splendid professor named Margaret Doody. She was firmly of the mind that works of literature were best appreciated when the reader genuinely understood the historical period that produced them. When she taught Austen, she also taught the dance, etiquette, music, food, and clothing of the time, as well as the works of Austen's literary predecessors, women like Frances Burney, Ann Radcliffe, Maria Edgeworth, and Susanna Rowson. Little did I suspect that Professor Doody's lessons would one day converge with my newfound enthusiasm for food. Nor did I suspect that an assignment for a class on Jewish folklore, which involved beating egg whites to stiff peaks with only a fork and my one overused mixing bowl,* would give me a unique sympathy for the eighteenth-century readers of such cookbook instructions as "beat the Whites of five Eggs with a Knife upon a Pewter Dish half an Hour." I certainly would have been delighted to learn that one day my enthusiasm for history, for literature, and for food would all be united in one project.

I hope that the uses for this book will be as varied as my reasons for being fascinated by it. It can be used by Austen scholars and enthusiasts as a window into the author's time. In some cases, Austen's choice of a particular food illuminates her artistic intentions and proves to be far more significant than a casual reading might indicate.

This book can also be used by those who have an affection either for Austen or for the Regency in general. An introductory chapter provides extensive information on the meals of Austen's day, the times they were served, how they were prepared, and how they were presented to the diners. The second chapter offers background on the long-running controversy in England over the introduction of French food, French cooking techniques, and, worst of all (from the perspective of English servants), French chefs. Each chapter also begins with an introduction dedicated to that particular type of food and its place on the English table. (Most of this information first appeared in my book *All Things Austen* [Greenwood, 2005].) Terms and phrases that appear in **bold** type are cross-references to other recipes in this book. Using all of this information, it

---

*The dorm kitchen whisk having been stolen long ago.

is possible to plan a truly remarkable Regency banquet for one's fellow English country dancers, Janeites, or history buffs.

Teachers should also find this book of value. It has application to history classes as well as to literature classes. I've taught both history and English myself, and, in my experience, nothing gets a class engaged like the chance to eat. In the food of a particular time, just as in the clothing and personal artifacts of a time, we approach its people more closely, more intimately, than through the use of documents alone.

Whenever someone attempts to re-create historical recipes, there are choices to be made. Re-creating them with strict historical accuracy is almost impossible, because both the techniques and the ingredients can be difficult to reproduce. To achieve full immersion in the Regency kitchen experience, one would have to kill a chicken, "draw" it (reach in through the anus in order to pull out the internal organs), pluck it, singe it to remove any remaining traces of feathers, and spit-roast it before an open coal hearth. Then the chicken itself would have to be of a breed available in the late eighteenth or early nineteenth century, with a similar fat-to-muscle ratio and a similar flavor. Similar issues exist for almost every ingredient listed in this book.

To be strictly accurate, one would have to eschew the use of nonstick pans, blenders, food processors, electric ovens, refrigerators, canning jars and lids, and a host of other modern conveniences. Personally, I feel that if the legendary cookbook author Hannah Glasse, whose work was reprinted and widely plagiarized throughout most of the eighteenth century, had been given a food processor and a source of power for it, she would have fought off the French army and navy in order to keep it. I don't want to beat egg whites on a pewter dish for half an hour when I have a perfectly good standing mixer that will do the job in three minutes. I have taken the liberty of assuming that you, my reader, will feel the same way.

But, of course, I could be wrong. And therefore I have chosen a middle ground. The recipes I've written are completely modernized, making use of the sort of equipment to be found in most American kitchens. Only in a few cases, such as the recipes for brewing and cheesemaking, are the tools so specialized that they will have to be found and purchased. Even then, the tools specified can be found at any well-stocked brewing or cheesemaking supply store, including many that sell their goods online.

But I recognize that many people will want to see the original recipe. Some will simply want to bask in the language; others will want to examine the original lists of ingredients; a few will be so committed to accuracy that they will want to re-create historical cooking techniques. For these readers, I have included the recipe I followed most closely and its author. The full names of these authors and their works can be found in the bibliography. If nothing else, reading the original recipes, and keeping in mind the unpredictability and difficulty of cooking over an open fire, gives us some sense of what was going on in the kitchen while the Bennets and Musgroves and Bertrams and Dashwoods ate sedately in the dining parlors of Austen's fictional world.

With modern tools, the recipes are considerably easier to prepare. Most take little effort, and most are surprisingly tasty. English cooking has for centuries been reviled, but in this case at least, its reputation was almost entirely unwarranted. Most of my dozens of volunteer tasters approached with apprehension when told they would be tasting 200-year-old English cuisine. But after their first bite or two, most reacted with pleasure and surprise. Even children were enthusiastic about most of the dishes they tried. My own children have asked me to cook some of their favorites again and again, and they were no doubt as surprised by which dishes they liked as I was. (I never in the world, for example, would have expected boiled plum pudding to become a popular request.) An occasional dish turned out to be so foreign to the modern palate that it evoked nothing but disgust, but those were few and far between and are accompanied by suitable warnings in their introductory notes. But even in those cases, we found that while much about Austen's food was familiar, there were places where the past and the present had diverged from each other so widely that they could only stare at each other and shake their heads in confusion.

I have been fortunate not only in being entrusted with this project but also in the people who traveled this odd little path alongside me. Family and friends tasted, offered critiques, and helped cook. They are listed, I hope without omission, at the end of this chapter. I am also extremely grateful to Candace Sy-Costa, who lent me her considerable expertise in preparing some of the meats that are less common today than they were two hundred years—or even fifty years—ago. Every time I see her enter a kitchen, I think of an eighteenth-century distinction between "plain" and "professed" cooks. A plain cook could manage the basic fare of the English table, such as bread, roasted and boiled meats, and boiled vegetables with melted butter sauce. A professed cook, on the other hand, could create complicated "made dishes," dishes with special sauces and elaborate presentation. A professed cook was mistress of every aspect of the culinary arts and as confident with complex dishes as with simple ones. Candace Sy-Costa is a professed cook if ever there was one.

The great pleasure of this project, in addition to its subject matter, has been the company I kept while testing the recipes and writing about them. There is really something quite lovely about setting a table for sixteen, with candles and crystal sparkling down the tidy rows, with soup at the top and ducks at the bottom and a half-dozen dishes in between, and announcing to some of your dearest relatives and friends those words so long out of use, "You see your dinner." There is enormous comfort in having people about you who are willing to go adventuring into the past, whose knowledge of and appreciation of food enriches your own, and who gather around the dinner table to share lively conversation and good humor. I have always agreed with Anne Elliot's assessment of good company as "the company of clever, well-informed people, who have a great deal of conversation," and I have had no greater affirmation of that truth than in the writing of this book.

MEET THE KITCHEN MAID

Candace Sy-Costa learned to cook from her mother, who is from Hong Kong. She grew up in the Philippines, where she expanded her culinary skills, and has lived in a number of places around the world, including Miami, Florida; Santa Cruz, California; and northern England. Her husband's family is Cuban, a circumstance that encouraged her to master Latin cooking as well. A collector of cookbooks and an enthusiast for all things English, she speaks six languages and works as a professional caterer. She volunteered to help on this project out of the goodness of her heart, and on the strict condition that she not be credited in any way. So much for the strict condition.

MEET THE GUINEA PIGS

Chris Anderson
Julia Anderson
Dianna Beardslee
Christina Bodnar-Anderson
Jennifer Carlisle
Alyson Collins
Delia Costa
Edmundo Costa
Nic Costa
Pascal Costa
Rolando Costa
Gwen Davies
Susan Flinspach
Barbara Hanagan
Barbara James

Hannah Katinsky
Matthew Katinsky
Nola Katinsky
Joe Laurence
Alison Mackie
Dave Mackie
Duncan Mackie
Avis Minger
Audrey Nickel
Johanna Nickel
Tony Nickel
Brian Olsen
Dorothy Olsen
Emily Olsen
Erica Olsen

Nancy Olsen   Ivette Tobin
Bob Orser   Perry Tobin
Teri Orser   Rachel Tobin
Magali Ramirez   Sidney Tobin
Laura Rinaldi   Zack Tobin
Rowen Rinaldi   Jack Vevea
Kathleen Roberts   Rosie Vevea
Mark Rubin   Charles Voelkel
Olivia Simmons   Devon Voelkel
Alexa Sinclair   Eric Voelkel
Andrea Sinclair   Margaret Voelkel
Casten Sinclair   Steve Voelkel
Paul Sinclair   Jacob Waring
Ryder Sinclair   Craig Warren
Ed Thompson   Diane Warren
Haven Thompson   Stafford Warren

JANE AUSTEN'S WORKS AND THEIR ABBREVIATIONS

MINOR WORKS (ABBREVIATION FOLLOWED BY *MW*)

Beaut Desc	*A Beautiful Description of the Different Effects of Sensibility on Different Minds*
Cass	*The Beautifull Cassandra: A Novel in Twelve Chapters*
Cath	*Catharine or the Bower*
Clifford	*Memoirs of Mr. Clifford*
Col Let	*A Collection of Letters*
E&E	*Edgar & Emma*
Evelyn	*Evelyn*
F&E	*Frederic & Elfrida*
H&E	*Henry & Eliza*
Headache	*On a Headache*
J&A	*Jack & Alice*
L&F	*Love and Freindship*
Lesley	*Lesley Castle*
LS	*Lady Susan*
Sand	*Sanditon*
Scraps	*Scraps*
Visit	*The Visit: A Comedy in 2 Acts*
Wat	*The Watsons*

NOVELS

E	*Emma*
MP	*Mansfield Park*
NA	*Northanger Abbey*

P	*Persuasion*
P&P	*Pride and Prejudice*
S&S	*Sense and Sensibility*

All page references are to the 3rd edition of R. W. Chapman's *Oxford Illustrated Jane Austen.*

1

INTRODUCTION

Food in Austen's lifetime differed greatly from food consumed in industrialized countries today. From the methods by which it was brought into the household and prepared to the timing, elements, and presentation of the meals themselves, the food was—though containing many of the same components as modern food—alien enough that it would surprise a modern diner in many ways. The quality, quantity, and variety of the food depended, like so much else, on economic and social class, and it could be said that in these respects the fare enjoyed by the poor differed as much from that of the rich as both did from modern food. However, some generalizations can be made, especially if we confine ourselves to the sorts of meals likely to have been consumed by Austen's characters.

ACQUISITION

Food was acquired from various sources, none of them as consistent or as amply supplied as a modern supermarket. Some items were produced on the family farm. There might be livestock that could be slaughtered as needed, a kitchen garden, and fields in which grain was grown. The garden at Steventon, Jane Austen's first home, was an important part of the family economy, and Jane's mother, Mrs. Austen, remained active in the garden at Chawton until old age, wearing a laborer's green frock and digging her own potatoes. During Jane's lifetime, the Chawton garden also yielded plums, strawberries, mulberries, apricots, gooseberries, and currants. Poultry and bees were also kept by the Austen women, as they had been at Steventon, the chief difference between the two establishments being the lack of a dairy.

Beyond the women's sphere, a farm's livestock offered a potential source of fresh meat. In 1798, for example, Jane writes from Steventon of being able "to kill a pig soon," and Mr. Austen also kept sheep, which were sometimes butchered as well. Gentry families like the Austens could afford to slaughter animals on a fairly regular basis, but humbler farms yielded meat only sporadically. A letter to *The Gentleman's Magazine* in 1819, describing the customs of Herefordshire, points out that the gentry and yeomanry of the country have meat on a daily basis, while the peasantry always keep "a pig, to slaughter for winter bacon." While this is part of passage lauding the general well-being of the poorer residents, and coupled with the pronouncement that they do not deign to eat the supposedly inferior barley bread, the use of the singular—"*a* pig"—points to the fact that the "winter bacon" would have been rationed out much more carefully than in more affluent homes.

Some types of meat, particularly among the gentry and aristocracy, would come from the hunting or fishing activities of the family's men. Other items were acquired by purchase from neighbors or by exchanges with family and friends. The Austens and their circle of connections frequently sent each other surplus produce of one type or another. Those who lived near the sea might send fish to inland relatives and receive, in exchange, a return gift of apples or game birds. For example, Jane Austen sent her friends the Fowles at Kintbury eight soles from Southampton and received some poultry in return. A "hamper of apples" was also sent from Kintbury to Henry Austen in October 1808. Parson James Woodforde, a thorough diarist, also engaged in this sort of friendly, informal barter. On August 24, 1790, he reported sending a dozen apricots from one of his trees to the local squire, Mr. Custance, who "sent us back some fine black Grapes which came from Mackay's Hot House, a Gardner at Norwich." On an earlier occasion, in 1784, he sent three dozen apricots to Custance and received in return a "large Piece of fine Parmesan Cheese"—an imported luxury item that made a handsome gift.

Not all such exchanges were purely friendly. Some were rather more mercenary. Woodforde, for instance, sometimes sold his surplus animals to neighbors or to the local butcher (*Sand, MW* 392). On December 22, 1788, he reported paying his yearly butcher's bill (£39 11s.) and receiving from the butcher, Harry Baker, a refund of £1 15s. 8d. for a calf. It seems likely that most farmers would have engaged in similar deals with tradesmen, offering whatever they had in surplus as partial payment for their purchases.

In all these types of exchange, buyers, sellers, and donors alike were at the mercy of the seasons. Increasingly, throughout the eighteenth century, livestock were able to survive the winter, as improved agricultural methods improved the supply of winter fodder; previously, there had been a mass slaughter in late fall or early winter of animals that would otherwise starve. But even if meat was

MONMOUTH STREET MUTTON.

Pat _ Hurra Measter, and what do ye Ax for this here Shoulder of Mutton.
Butcher _ Why that there Leg of Mutton, will be four and sixpence, I cut it from as nice a Ship as any in Smithfield.
*Pat _ Oh botheration, who do ye take me for, blarneying me over, wid your Ship, and your Second hand Mutton, I can buy a New one in Fleet_*
Market for half that, _ So good Morning to your Honor, as the Devil said to the Pope.
Published 16th March 1798, by LAURIE & WHITTLE, 53 Fleet Street London.

Monmouth Street Mutton, Isaac Cruikshank, 1798. Food was bought from a variety of specialty dealers such as the butchers who hung their cuts of meat from open-air hooks. The butcher's emblems were his long, thin knife, which hung from a cord around his waist; his blood-spattered apron; and the tree stump that served him as a cutting block. (Courtesy of the Lewis Walpole Library, Yale University. 798.3.16.2.)

more continuously available to those who could afford it, fruits and vegetables were restricted to their own particular seasons. Preserving and pickling could extend their lifespan, but it was not the same thing as having the fresh items at hand all year long.

Some foods were imported, but these were rarely brought in to extend the season of domestically raised produce. Instead, they were foods that did not grow successfully in England or that were deemed to be better when processed elsewhere. These items included citrus fruits, spices, tea, sugar, and Woodforde's fine piece of Parmesan. Such foods tended to be expensive, their prices reflecting the additional costs of importation, and their consumption indicated relative affluence and, in some cases, genuine wealth. Their presence was certainly not taken for granted.

Still other foods were available year-round, or nearly so, but were subject to spoilage in an age before refrigeration. Eggs fell into this category, as did milk and some of its by-products. Milk had to be processed immediately: skimmed, strained, or preserved as cheese, or the cream churned into butter. Meat, fish, and poultry also suffered from storage difficulties. Dr. Grant's green goose (*MP* 212) is Austen's most notable example of the failure of meat to keep as long as one might wish.

One way of avoiding some of the thorniest issues of supply and demand was to purchase one's food from specialist shops: a butcher (*Sand, MW* 392; *P&P* 331; *MP* 379) who dealt in meat, in large cities perhaps a poulterer (*MP* 212–13) who specialized in birds, a confectioner for sweets and jellies, a baker (*Sand, MW* 392) for bread, a grocer for imported items such as chocolate or tea, a fruiterer for fruit, and so on. Sometimes there was a significant distance between these sorts of specialist retailers and one's home. Parson Woodforde's village was too small to sustain the kinds of good shops his appetite required, so he did most of his shopping in Norwich or sent a servant there on errands.

The Austens, too, patronized various shops and markets. When the Austen women lived at Chawton, there was a market in nearby Alton, but it was not especially impressive, and most of the marketing was done in Winchester or Farnham. Some items, such as tea, were ordered from as far away as London. In earlier years, at Steventon rectory, the marketing took place mainly in Basingstoke. The principal grocer in Basingstoke, the nearest town to Steventon, advertised in 1794 that his wares included "Old Raisin Wine, Confectionery, Perfumery, Stationery, &c. Oils, fine Westmoreland Hams, Burgess's Essence of Anchovies, Mushroom and India Soy, Sauce Royal, Devonshire Sauce, Lemon Ketchup, Olives, Capers, Vinegar &c." As suggested by this list, shopkeepers could offer a wider variety than farm and friends afforded, and they could offer a more consistent and sometimes fresher supply. In some cases, patronizing shops was not a matter of choice; residents of towns, such and Mr. and Mrs. Austen, Jane, and Cassandra, during the years they lived in Bath, often had no other options. Without a farm or a kitchen garden, they were naturally dependent on shops.

The environment in which one bought food was both like and unlike the supermarkets of today. In a supermarket, food is segregated by type: bread, produce, fish, meat, frozen food, and so on. Similarly, food in Austen's day was distributed into different areas by type. This could happen in one of several ways: The food might be available, as described above, in discrete shops—permanent, fully interior spaces, such as a grocer's shop. These shops, with attractive bow windows filled with goods on display, were increasingly replacing the old-fashioned stalls, which were shops open to the street, with the wares arranged on a counter or hanging from hooks. Then there were markets, which might be permanent or temporary, and which were set up in sizable "market towns" (*E&E, MW* 29; *H&E, MW* 34; *Wat, MW* 322; *P* 10). At a market (*NA* 68), one or more days of the week were set aside for the display and sale of all kinds of goods. As in the case of shops, the vendors remained specialists. One went to a butcher for meat, to a fishmonger for fish, to a grocer or chandler for tea and sugar, and to yet another vendor, perhaps a farm woman, for eggs or butter or local cheese. Assembling a meal, especially one of the lavish dinners that the gentry served to company, involved visiting just as many "departments" as going to the supermarket today, but each department required negotiation with a separate sales staff, an inspection of the quality of the goods, a round or two of haggling perhaps, and a financial transaction. Of course, in many cases these multiple errands were simplified by familiarity; the merchant might simply make a notation in his books, rather than demanding cash for every purchase, as in the case of Parson Woodforde and his yearly butcher's reckoning. A merchant might also come to recognize the level of quality demanded by a particular client and make no attempt to deceive or to haggle, and customers learned to avoid merchants whose wares did not suit them. Nonetheless, the process of buying food was far more complex before the days of shopping carts and checkout lines.

The Austens were fortunate in at least one respect. In the years they resided in Bath, the town was blessed with a number of particularly well-stocked shops. Aside from the markets, held on Wednesdays and Saturdays (and on Mondays, Wednesdays, and Fridays for fish), there were respected dealers in meat, fruit, vegetables, fish, milk products, and even imported wines. Pastry cooks sold confections, ices, jellies, and savory snacks that could be eaten in the shop or taken home. Two of the more prominent Bath pastry shops were Molland's in Milsom Street, mentioned in *Persuasion* (174), and Gill's, built between two buttresses of the Abbey Church.

Shops, of course, charged a premium for the variety and convenience they offered; bakers in particular were singled out by public opinion as price-gougers. But cost was not the only consideration when buying from shops. Shops had the advantage of more consistent supply—they usually had fresh mutton, for example, while a self-dependent farm had to kill a sheep every time mutton was wanted or preserve the meat by salting or smoking. Woodforde's fishmonger, Beale, carried sole, crab, lobster, and mackerel, among other commodities, and it is hard to imagine how the parson could have found time to acquire all these items through his own efforts. But the "fresh" meat was usually less fresh than what was killed as needed on a farm, as it had to sit around for a while until someone bought it.

Furthermore, many shops were guilty, intentionally or accidentally, of diluting or adulterating the products they sold. Meat was hard to adulterate, but tainted meat might, by various stratagems, be disguised as fresh. A cask of stale butter might be passed off as fresh by hiding a lump of fresh butter within the cask, and offering tastes from this small lump to prospective shoppers. Bread was whitened with chalk or alum, and many foods, from pickles to milk, ranged from substandard to poisonous in quality. Frederick Accum, writing in 1820, found that mustard powder was brightened with capsicum (chili powder), that potatoes were soaked in water to increase their weight, and that both black and white pepper contained about 16 percent of what he called "factitious pepper": "oil cakes (the residue of linseed, from which the oil has been pressed,) common clay, and a portion of Cayenne pepper, formed in a mass, and granulated by being first pressed through a sieve, and then rolled in a cask." Ground pepper contained a mixture of ground black pepper, cayenne pepper, and the sweepings of the floors of the pepper warehouses.

These were relatively harmless adulterations, but others were more serious. Pickled items were sometimes made in copper vats, which lent color to the food but also made it poisonous. Vinegar was sharpened by the addition of sulphuric acid. Pastry cooks used cherry laurel leaves to lend a bitter-almond flavor to desserts, not knowing, or not caring, that the pleasant almond flavor came from cyanide. Prepared anchovy sauce was colored with a lead compound called "Venetian red," while olive oil was often processed abroad using lead press plates or lead cisterns and then imported by unsuspecting consumers. Clearly, customers had to be cautious.

Nonetheless, they continued to buy not only from shops and market stalls but from a variety of places serving ready-to-eat food. Large towns such as London had cook shops, which, according to J. P. Malcolm in 1810, sold "baked and boiled meat and flour and pease puddings at a very reasonable rate." Coffee shops and public houses also sold food as well as beverages, and for dessert one might stop at a pastry shop for ice cream, tarts, or gingerbread. Food was also "cried," or sold, in the streets. Sometimes street vendors sold food that could be eaten on the spot, a concept that would come as no surprise to anyone who has ever bought a hot dog in New York, but the more foreign concept to modern readers would be the variety of foods for sale that were meant for home use. An 1819 letter in *The Gentleman's Magazine*, intended as a tongue-in-cheek music criticism of street vendors' cries, lists a wide variety of commodities sold door-to-door: potatoes, shrimp, cod, spinach, muffins, periwinkles, smelts, mackerel, radishes "twenty a penny," watercress, salad, cheese, and buns. His list was by no means exhaustive.

PREPARATION

Even the most casual reader of literature or history must be aware that food preparation (*P&P* 44, 65; *MP* 383) was done in the absence of most modern devices. However, the actual methods of preparation are often something of a mystery to them. What sorts of things were cooked in an oven, and to what extent did it resemble a modern oven? How were dishes cooked over an open fire? What equipment was used? Readers often picture a kitchen fire that is either too early or too late—resembling either the giant open hearths of the Renaissance or the cast-iron stoves of the later nineteenth century.

Regency cooking more closely resembled the former model than the latter, though the huge fireplace with its wood fire had given way to a more compact unit with coal for fuel and a metal grate, consisting of several horizontal bars, to keep the coal from falling out. Cooking at such a hearth could be accomplished in a variety of ways. In many homes, the top bar of the grate could swivel so that it fell into a horizontal plane with the second bar, and on these two bars pots or pans could be perched. Sometimes they supported a gridiron, a round grating used for broiling steaks and chops. Meat could be roasted on spits or in portable tin reflector ovens, which contained a drip tray and a three-walled spatter guard to keep grease from soiling the rest of the kitchen. Toasting forks in a variety of shapes were used to toast bread, muffins, sausages, and other food, and "salamanders"—named for a mythical beast that lived in fire—were pieces of metal with one flattened end that could be heated in the fire and passed over food to brown it. Most houses would also have had one or more hooks or swing arms from which kettles could be suspended. These kettles were used not only for making soup and broth but also for boiling meat, vegetables, and puddings, and for providing hot water for coffee and tea. However, hot water was sometimes made instead in a boiler, an iron or copper container with a lid that stood near the fire and had a tap for drawing off the heated water.

A relatively new enthusiasm for efficiency drove the creation of the boiler, as well as the shallower, smaller fireplace, which saved on fuel. The idea was to capture as much heat as possible from the fire, and to this end ovens were sometimes built adjacent to the fire. There were at least three ways of heating an oven, none of which allowed for much control over temperature. The first was, as stated, to build the oven right next to the main fireplace, so as to radiate heat through the wall that separated them. This had the obvious disadvantage of warming only one side of the oven. The second method was to pass a large iron bar through both the fireplace and the oven; the fire heated the bar, which conducted some portion of the heat to the oven. The third method, which was the standard method for detached ovens (such as the ones in the bakehouses of large homes), as well as for many ovens adjacent to fireplaces, was to build and

Printed for & Sold by Carington Bowles. Published as the Act directs 5 Jan. 1785. N.º 69 in S.ᵗ Pauls Church Yard, London.
CORPORAL TRIM's reflections on Mortality in the Kitchen, on the Death of MASTER BOBBY.
"Are we not here now', continued the Corporal, (striking the end of his stick perpendicularly upon the floor, so as to give an idea of health and stability)—and are we not! (dropping his hat upon the ground) gone! in a moment!"

Corporal Trim's reflections on Mortality in the Kitchen, 1785. This detailed depiction of a kitchen includes many of the tools for making and serving food. On the left side are racks of dishes and a table with a salt or flour shaker and drawers for various items. Below the drawers, two saucepans can be seen, and the keen-eyed can also see a pair of pattens below the saucepans. These pattens would have been worn by the kitchen maids to keep their shoes clean on trips to the garden, outhouse, or farmyard.

On the right are the classic tools of fireside cooking: the coal scuttle in the foreground, the bellows hanging on the wall, and the large fireplace with its horizontal coal grate and kettle. Spits and a mechanism for turning them are located above the fireplace, as are lids for pots and pans. To the left of the fireplace hang a large wooden spoon and a characteristic tapered rolling pin. (Courtesy of the Lewis Walpole Library, Yale University. 785.1.3.5.)

light a fire inside the oven and allow it to burn out. The ashes were swept away, and the food, placed inside, was cooked by the residual heat in the bricks or stones that lined the oven. The effects of this cooking technique can be seen in baking recipes of the time, which sometimes instruct the cook to alternate fire and baking several times for foods that required long periods of heat.

The typical oven had its bottom about two and a half feet above the floor and had a diameter of two to three feet and a rounded roof about one and a half to two feet high. The door was occasionally made of oak strapped with iron, but a fully iron door was more common. Cookbook author Francis Collingwood offered advice on oven construction in *The Universal Cook, and City and Country Housekeeper* (1801):

> Every new oven should be built round, and not lower from the roof [that is, no less from the roof of the oven to the floor of the oven] than twenty

Sensual Love—or a Sop in the Pan, Williams, 1807. A somewhat different view of the kitchen, with sauce-boats and a grater visible in addition to the characteristic string of onions, wooden spoon on its fireside hook, and pot on the fire. The unusual feature of this engraving is the clear view it provides of a roasting joint and the dripping pan underneath, used to catch fat for basting and for later use in tallow candles. Pots and pans, again, are piled under the prep table. (Courtesy of the Lewis Walpole Library, Yale University. 807.5.31.1.)

inches, not higher than twenty-four inches. The mouth should be small, with an iron door to shut quite close; by which means it will require less fire, and keep in the heat much better than a long and high-roofed oven, and in course bake every thing better.

At its hottest, the oven was usually used for bread, which was inserted using a "peel," a tool similar to an enormous spatula, made of iron with a wooden handle. Once the bread was removed, items that required lower heat, such as cakes

The Physicians Friend, 1815. A doctor thanks the French man-cook for making such tasty dishes, whose rich ingredients make people sick and thus generate business for the physician. The English kitchen maids look on in disgust. (Courtesy of the Lewis Walpole Library, Yale University. 815.0.2.)

or pies, might be inserted using a peel made entirely of wood. When only a small amount of residual heat remained, the oven might be used for other tasks: allowing dough to rise, drying the icing on a cake, or drying fruit. If none of these tasks needed to be performed, the cook filled the oven with kindling so that the remaining heat would dry out the wood, making the next oven fire easier to light.

A rather dreadful story from *The Gentleman's Magazine* illustrates the limitations of the eighteenth-century oven. Apparently, a small town became convinced that a bout of ill luck had been caused by witchcraft, and that the witchcraft centered on a particular duck. A kitchen maid, eager to purge the bad luck, seized upon the duck and put it into the oven, hoping to kill it by burning alive, the traditional fate of witches. However, the oven's heat was insufficient and, as ovens did, it gradually cooled. When she removed the duck, she found it alive but with all its feathers burnt off. She tried on two subsequent

Eliza Haywood's *A New Present for a Servant-Maid*, Frontispiece, 1771. Most of the tools of the kitchen staff can be seen in this illustration, and each portion of the engraving represents one of the disciplines of an accomplished cook. The center background is devoted to plain cookery: roasting, stewing, and so forth. Above the hearth are racks of spits in various sizes, a mortar and pestle for grinding spices, candlesticks, and shakers of salt and perhaps flour. Over the large coal fire, a huge kettle of soup simmers, suspended from the swing-out crane; below the kettle, a large bird roasts on a spit.

On the left-hand side, a maid works at the second important discipline: baking and pastry making. Her rolling pin is characteristic of the time, gently tapered at each end rather than possessing distinct handles, to prevent the formation of edge lines in the crust. On the right-hand side, another maid holding a skillet consults Haywood's book. She—or at least her part of the kitchen—is probably intended to symbolize preserving and pickling, a crucial area of food preparation in the days before refrigeration. On the table behind her book can be seen two jars of preserves, covered (in the absence of reliable canning supplies) with sheets of thick paper soaked in brandy and tied on with string. (Library of Congress.)

days to kill the duck in the same way—evidence of how much work was involved in building an oven fire and how long it took to cool—and managed, on the third day, to kill it. The correspondent who related this tale mentioned that the woman had been so severely scolded for her cruelty to the animal that she fell into fits and was likely to die. Whether or not the macabre tale is true, its drama depends on the limitations of baking at the time: ovens could only get so hot, their temperature was to some extent erratic, their heat could not be kept constant over long periods of time, and they required great effort to operate, so much so that one round of baking per day was all that could reasonably be accomplished. Indeed, in most houses, baking was done once or twice a week, if at all; an increasing number of households, particularly among the working classes, chose not to bother with the oven at all but instead bought their bread from bakers' shops. (The Austens, when they lived at Steventon, were not among these families; Mrs. Austen made all her own butter, cheese, bread, beer, and wine.)

Economy of effort extended beyond baking to all the cooking done in the house. There was a tendency to do most of the cooking in preparation for dinner—the most substantial meal of the day—and to use the leftovers from dinner to feed the servants and make up cold suppers. This meant that it was exceedingly difficult to scrape together a dinner at the last minute or to scrap one in favor of an invitation to dine elsewhere. Maggie Lane has pointed out that, while last-minute invitations to tea are common in Austen's writings, her characters know better than to offer a last-minute invitation to dinner when the prospective guest's servants are probably already well advanced in their marketing, cutting, chopping, stewing, and broiling. The sorts of activities involved in making a dinner for company among the gentry can be observed in Parson Woodforde's account of a hectic afternoon in 1788 when he had only three hours' notice that distinguished company would be coming to his house for dinner:

> It occasioned rather a Bustle in our House but we did as well as we could—We had not a bit of White bread in House, no Tarts whatever, and this Week gave no Order whatever to my Butcher for Meat, as I killed a Pigg this Week. We soon baked some white bread and some Tartlets and made the best shift we could on the whole. About 5 o'clock Mr. and Mrs. Custance, Lady Bacon and Son, Mr. Taswell and Nephew arrived. . . . We gave the Company for Dinner some Fish and Oyster Sauce, a nice Piece of Boiled Beef, a fine Neck of Pork rosted and Apple Sauce, some hashed Turkey, Mutton Stakes, Sallad &c. a wild Duck rosted, fryed Rabbits, a plumb Pudding and some Tartlets. Desert, some Olives, Nutts, Almonds,

and Raisins and Apples. The whole Company were pleased with their Dinner &c. Considering we had not above 3 Hours notice of their coming we did very well in that short time. All of us were rather hurried on the Occasion.

It was indeed a victory to amass such a splendid dinner in under three hours, even given the fact that Woodforde kept five servants. He does not indicate how many of them were involved in the "Bustle," but one suspects from his tone that at least some of them were pulled from their regular duties to assist with the emergency preparations. Woodforde would also have had the help of his niece Nancy, who served as his housekeeper. And no doubt some of the dishes were already underway for what he assumed would be a simple dinner at home with Nancy. But it was not the sort of excitement one would desire on a regular basis; therefore, dinner invitations were usually issued well in advance. Austen does refer to impromptu or standing dinner invitations, but these are usually offered to one person at a time—Jane Fairfax (*E* 283) or Mr. Bingley (*P&P* 103), for example—and one person could easily be accommodated by stinting the servants a little and feeding them on plainer fare or by substituting a different cold dish at supper for the dinner leftovers.

Once the cooking was finished, there still remained one aspect of preparation to be performed at the table. This was the carving of the meat (*P&P* 163, *MP* 34), an important ceremony, since meat was the centerpiece of every dinner among prosperous people. It was customary for the hostess to sit at the head of the table and for the host to occupy the foot. Meat which came to the table whole was brought to the bottom of the table, where the host would slice it and serve it to his guests. Cookbooks of the time usually include a section on carving, which was a delicate business. Charles Millington, author of *The Housekeeper's Domestic Library; or, New Universal Family Instructor* (1805), included instructions and diagrams for carving, including this advice:

> In carving, never rise from your seat, but have a seat high enough to give a command of the table; so not help any one to too much at a time: distribute the nice parts, if possible, equally among the whole, and do not cut the slices too thick nor too thin.

The carving of a turkey, chicken, or beef or pork roast is familiar to many home cooks today, but the Regency host had a wider array of animals to divide. He might be called upon to cut up a saddle of mutton, a hare, a pheasant, a goose, a haunch of venison (*P&P* 342, *MP* 52), or a pig's or calf's head. Small wonder that the timid Mr. Woodhouse usually relinquishes his place at the bottom of the table (*E* 291); one suspects that the daunting task of carving at Hartfield is taken up either by Mr. Knightley or by the servants.

SERVING

Many members of the household staff were involved in the preparation and distribution of food. In humble homes, many of the tasks would be performed by a kitchen maid or maid of all work, with the dishes being passed around with little ceremony. However, in most of the homes that appear in Austen's novels, there are servants not only to cook the food but to present it. In houses that could afford to keep male servants (*P* 129), this job would be performed by one or more footmen (*S&S* 233, 355; *P&P* 162; *MP* 180; *NA* 213; *P* 219), who carried in the platters from the kitchen with a great show of bustle and efficiency. The footmen also stood between the table and the walls (*MP* 239), ready to assist diners who needed more of anything.

The Dinner, Symptoms of Eating and Drinking, Bunbury, 1800. Liveried footmen wait at table on the far left and far right of the picture, while a butler in mufti pours wine at the sideboard. (Courtesy of the Lewis Walpole Library, Yale University. 800.0.20.)

The dishes were delivered all together, with platters and tureens scattered at the top, bottom, sides, and corners (*E* 218) of the table and extra food, along with wine and glasses, placed on a sideboard (*E* 458). This made for a great show of abundance and wealth, but it was not, perhaps, the most convenient way to serve a variety of dishes. Some occasionally went cold before they could be served (*MP* 239), while others might not reach the diners who wanted them. Nonetheless, the attractive display was too enchanting to be foregone, and there would be no substantial change in the method of service until the second half of the nineteenth century. In the more prosperous households, there would be a "second course"—not merely a second type of food as we would use this term today, but a removal of most or all of the platters and bowls from the first half of the meal, followed by a completely new set of dishes (*E* 218)—more meat, vegetables, sauces, tarts, and so forth. Then, after a decent interval, this food was removed, along with the tablecloth (*S&S* 355), and wine and dessert were served (*Wat, MW* 325; *S&S* 355), the latter being not so much sweets or cakes as small finger foods such as nuts (*E* 28, 35; *P* 86), olives, and dried or fresh fruit.

Other meals were less elaborate. Servants were indeed present to bring in the food (*MP* 344), clear it away, and attend to the needs of those who were eating, but there were fewer types of food to serve, and there was less show and ceremony expected. The family took more responsibility for making the tea, the coffee, the sandwiches, or whatever else was at hand, leaving less for the servants to do.

BREAKFAST

The names and timing of meals differed in some respects from their modern forms. Then as now, breakfast (*LS, MW* 284, 285, 286; *NA* 60, 84, 154, 203, 235, 241; *S&S* 63, 83, 96, 164, 172, 201, 202, 369; *P&P* 31, 33, 41, 61, 215, 266; *MP* 156, 445; *E* 10, 50, 237, 258, 259, 293, 472; *P* 58–60, 95, 102, 107, 145, 229) was the first meal of the day, but for the gentry it came late, usually around 9:00 or 10:00 A.M. All meals, as we shall see, were later for the idle and fashionable than for the old-fashioned (*E* 443, *P* 59) and for the working classes. Elizabeth Bennet's uncle Mr. Gardiner, for example, leaves "soon after breakfast" for a fishing excursion that begins at noon (*P&P* 266). Lydia Bennet, staying with her uncle Gardiner later in the novel, notes, "We breakfasted at ten as usual" (*P&P* 318). Early breakfasts tend to have a specific reason for being eaten at an uncivilized hour. For example, William Price has to leave unusually early in order to join his ship, and he has an early breakfast, completed by 9:30 (*MP* 280), before the rest of the occupants of Mansfield Park; the rest of them then have their breakfast after he's already departed (*MP* 282–83). William and Fanny, on their journey to Portsmouth, leave similarly early in the morning, before the regular breakfast hour (*MP* 374). Another early breakfast is that of Catherine Morland, on the morning of her ignominious departure from Northanger Abbey (*NA* 228); the unfashionable hour at which she is forced to eat, between 6:00 and 7:00 A.M., emphasizes the incivility of her dismissal. The late hour at which breakfast was served among the gentry, however, should not necessarily be taken as evidence that they were late risers or entirely idle before breakfast. Frequently, they rose fairly early and engaged in some activity before breakfast. Jane played piano before the 9:00 breakfasts at Chawton, for example, and when staying elsewhere she might write letters to fill the time. Others took walks to work up an appetite (*S&S* 180, *P* 104). The eldest Austen son, James, did so when he was a curate at Deane, walking a mile on some mornings to visit his father, who was rector at Steventon.

A healthy appetite was often necessary, for breakfasts could be quite lavish, even if they paled in comparison to the variety and quantity offered at dinner. Breakfast in a substantial home might include cold meat (*MP* 282), cheese, fish, eggs (*MP* 282), coffee, tea (*L&F*, *MW* 106), chocolate (by which Austen's contemporaries meant the beverage, cocoa, rather than solid chocolate), rolls, toast, bread (*NA* 241) and butter, and, on occasion, freshly prepared steaks or chops. Sometimes, the heartier elements of the meal were eschewed, and the meal consisted mostly of some form of bread or cake accompanied by tea or another hot beverage. The wedding breakfast of James's daughter Anna Austen in 1814 was, wrote her sister Caroline, "such as the best breakfasts then were: some variety of bread, hot rolls, buttered toast, tongue or ham and eggs," with the festive additions of chocolate and wedding cake. French traveler François de La Rochfoucauld noted a similar, though not identical, menu in 1784:

> The commonest breakfast is at 9 o'clock. . . . Breakfast consists of tea and bread and butter in various forms. In the houses of the rich, you have coffee, chocolate and so on. The morning newspapers are on the table and those who want to do so, read them during breakfast.

An 1819 letter to *The Gentleman's Magazine* about manners in Herefordshire stated that, like their peers across "the whole kingdom," the gentry and nobility of that county "breakfast upon tea, coffee, or cocoa, with cold meat and eggs." The yeomanry, wrote the author, consumed "mostly tea" at their breakfasts. The

College Breakfast, 1783. The most basic elements of breakfast appear here: bread (presumably buttered) and tea, served in handle-less cups. (Courtesy of the Lewis Walpole Library, Yale University. 783.10.21.1.)

anonymous author of the early-nineteenth-century etiquette manual *The Mirror of the Graces* (1811) took issue with the standard breakfast menu, which she claimed made women ugly:

> Their breakfasts not only set forth tea and coffee, but chocolate and *hot* bread and butter. Both of these latter articles, when taken constantly, are hostile to health and female delicacy. The heated grease, which is their principal ingredient, deranges the stomach; and, by creating or increasing bilious disorders, gradually overspreads the before fair skin with a wan or yellow hue.

It is unknown whether English women took her advice and shunned buttered toast (*L&F*, *MW* 106); one suspects that they continued to indulge.

There were, of course, exceptions to the rules about consuming sizable breakfasts. Parson Woodforde, who certainly liked a big breakfast when he could get it, ate only mutton broth on the morning of April 14, 1784, and that at the ungenteel hour of 6:00 A.M. His excuse was the parliamentary elections to be held in Norwich; like William and Fanny Price, he had a good reason to be on the road early.

LUNCHEON AND PICNICS

The next meal was dinner (*Visit, MW* 52; *Lesley, MW* 121; *Cath, MW* 229; *LS, MW* 299, 303; *Wat, MW* 324–25, 339; *Sand, MW* 389; *S&S* 67, 160, 193, 247, 315; *P&P* 45, 54, 342, 344; *NA* 84, 96, 114, 116, 129, 211; *MP* 104, 141, 142, 191, 194, 220–21, 296, 336, 406–7, 412, 469; *E* 6, 14, 50, 108, 209, 213, 226, 290, 303, 344; *P* 39, 54, 95, 98, 137, 140, 219), and it was by far the most significant meal of the day. At one time it had been held around noon, or in the early afternoon, but the association of high status with late mealtimes led to a creeping inflation of the dinner hour. By Austen's day, the upper classes served dinner to their children at about 2:00 or 3:00 P.M., while the adults ate at 5:00 or 6:00. The result was a long gap in the middle of the day when no food was served. The author of *The Mirror of the Graces* was outraged at the "long and exhausting fast . . . , from ten in the morning till six or seven in the evening, when dinner is served up," not because of the hunger and discomfort that resulted, but because it caused delicate women to overeat, overindulge in wine, and ruin their beauty by consuming foods that supposedly increased bodily heat:

> . . . the half-famished beauty sits down to sate a keen appetite with Cayenne soups, fish, French patées steaming with garlic, roast and boiled meat, game, tarts, sweetmeats, ices, fruit, &c. &c. &c. How must the constitution suffer under the digestion of this *melange*! How does the heated complexion bear witness to the combustion within!

For most diners, however, the question was not what eating did to the complexion but what *not* eating did to their enjoyment of midday.

Therefore, as the gap between breakfast and dinner widened, with everyone trying to eat later than their neighbors, it became more common to have a little something between breakfast and dinner. However, this meal, known variously

[Rowlandson Etchings], 1790. This detail from a set of etchings by Thomas Rowlandson shows a picnic party by a river. (Courtesy of the Lewis Walpole Library, Yale University. 790.6.27.1.)

as noonshine, nuncheon, or luncheon, did not became standard during Austen's lifetime. Even in families who regularly indulged in sandwiches, cold meat, or some other light fare around noon, the food was seen as refreshments or a "collation" (*H&E, MW* 38; *E* 367) rather than as a full meal. It was eaten in the drawing room, or wherever the family happened to be gathered, rather than in the dining room, which further deprived it of full mealtime status. It might also be consumed on the road at an inn, when travelers were at the mercy of schedules and of inn location. In such circumstances, they ate when they had the chance, regardless of time and fashion. "Lunching" was not an English verb until the 1830s and did not become an acceptable term among the educated until still later.

On occasion, people chose to take their afternoon meal outdoors, in which case the meal might be referred to as "cold meat," a "cold collation," or a "picnic." The practice of eating outside with packed lunches was also known as "gipsying." All members of the party were supposed to contribute something to the meal, rather like a potluck dinner today, and the result could either be a good-natured sense of communal purpose or an unpleasant contest of display.

DINNER

Dinner was not only the largest meal but also an important marker in the passage of time. It officially ended the morning and began the evening, regardless of when it was scheduled. Morning dress, in which one went walking and paid morning calls, was exchanged for evening dress (*E* 114), which in women's case often meant revealing a little more skin. After all, there were frequently guests before whom to show off. An invitation to someone's house for dinner (*E* 290) was more intrinsically valuable than an invitation to any other meal, because it was at this meal that the full efforts of the household staff were engaged.

The Gentleman's Magazine letter of 1819 on Herefordshire describes the meal simply enough. Among "the nobility and the gentry," dinner is served at 5:00 or 6:00 P.M. and consists of "soup, poultry, butcher's meat, and sweets: the wines, port and sherry." This, the author insists, is true not only in Hereford-shire but everywhere in England. He makes no such claim for the yeomanry, whom he describes as eating "a profusion of butcher's meat" and drinking cider or beer. Laborers ate more or less meat depending on their circumstances. Live-in servants and farm laborers usually ate the same food as their masters, which generally included a fair amount of meat, while poorer tenant farmers and small craftsmen might be able to afford meat only seldom. According to con-temporary accounts, in Hampshire in 1794 live-in farm laborers ate mostly pork and pudding, while in Middlesex in 1795 laborers ate "bread and cheese and pork for breakfast, coarse joints of beef boiled with cabbages and other veg-etables, or meat pies or puddings for dinner, cold pork, bread and cheese, etc. for supper; and with every meal, small beer."

At its simplest—that is, when no company was present—dinner even among the gentry was not an especially lavish display, especially by the standards of the day. Parson Woodforde, when dining alone at home, lists very simple dinners in his diary: "Fryed Soals and cold green Goose for Dinner" and "Giblet Soup and Shoulder Mutton rosted" are two typical entries from July, 1791. Perhaps there were side dishes as well, but as he often lists vegetable or fruit dishes when dining out at friends' houses, it seems likely that the dinner included little more than the meat. A dinner of similar simplicity appeared on Henry Austen's London table in 1813 when he welcomed his sister Jane, his brother Edward, and three of Edward's daughters—in Jane's words, "a most comfortable dinner of soup, fish, bouillée, partridges, and an apple tart, which we sat down to soon after five."

However, dinners for company tended to be as lavish as the host's budget al-lowed (*MP* 221, 239). *The Mirror of the Graces* describes boarding-school girls as constantly competitive for status based on wealth and display, comparing notes on each other's number of servants, houses in London, and "the number of courses habitually served up at table." Most dinners consisted of one "course"—that is, one set of dishes, perhaps only three or four, perhaps as many as twelve or fourteen—placed on the table nearly simultaneously. In such cases, the customary formula was for the host to say, "You see your dinner" (*Wat, MW* 354) in order to inform the company that no second course would be forth-coming, and they might eat all they liked of the present dishes without needing to save room for more. In especially wealthy homes, this first course would be followed by a second course (*P&P* 84, 120, 338). Whether the meal was of one

The Glutton, Rowlandson, 1813. This is a large dinner for one man, though it would have been considered perfectly appropriate for company. Soup and meat are being brought in from the kitchen, and a chicken, some vegetables, and some other little dishes, possibly "made dishes," are already on the table, along with cruets of oil and vinegar, a decanter, and a glass of wine. More wine is being poured into a glass at the sideboard, and several bottles are waiting in a wine bucket at the base of the table. (Courtesy of the Lewis Walpole Library, Yale University. 813.0.13.)

course or two, it was usually followed by dessert (*E* 89, 219). Austen frequently omits a catalogue of the dishes at her fictional dinners, but Parson Woodforde was good enough to note down almost everything he ate on visits, and we can gather, from his lists, the sorts of food that appeared at the tables of the gentry.

At a postbaptismal dinner for one of the squire's children, for example, he describes far more than the standard, simple, family fare:

> We had for dinner a Calf's Head, boiled Fowl and Tongue, a Saddle of Mutton rosted on the Side Table, and a fine Swan rosted with Currant Jelly Sauce for the first Course. The second Course a couple of Wild Fowl called Dun Fowls, Larks, Blamange, Tarts etc. etc. and a good Desert of Fruit after amongst which was a Damson Cheese. I never eat a bit of a Swan before, and I think it good eating with sweet sauce.

Woodforde was always impressed with a generous display of food, and he was positively agog at a banquet held by his bishop in Norwich on September 4, 1783:

> There were 20 of us at the Table and a very elegant Dinner the Bishop gave us. We had 2 Courses of 20 Dishes each Course, and a Desert after of 20 Dishes. Madeira, red and white Wines. The first Course amongst many other things were 2 Dishes of prodigious fine stewed Carp and Tench, and a fine Haunch of Venison. Amongst the second Course a fine Turkey Poult, Partridges, Pidgeons and Sweatmeats. Desert—amongst other things, Mulberries, Melon, Currants, Peaches, Nectarines and Grapes. A most beautiful Artificial Garden in the Center of the Table remained at Dinner and afterwards, it was one of the prettiest things I ever saw, about a Yard long, and about 18 Inches wide, in the middle of which was a high round Temple supported on round Pillars, the Pillars were wreathed round with artificial Flowers—on one side was a Shepherdess on the other a Shepherd, several handsome Urns decorated with artificial Flowers also &c. &c.

Woodforde himself had more limited means. His yearly tithes came to a little under £300, and he made a little more from "surplice fees," or payments for his services at marriages, weddings, and funerals. He could not host dinners of such magnificence, but he liked to entertain his friends. His diary covers many years and a great many dinners, but two examples will suffice. On both occasions, one in June 1781 and the other in January 1790 he entertained the same group— the local squire, Mr. Custance; his wife, Mrs. Custance; and a fellow clergyman, Mr. Du Quesne. In 1781 he offered them a first course of boiled chicken, tongue, boiled leg of mutton with capers, and "Batter Pudding" and a second course of roast duck, peas, artichokes, tarts, and blancmange. For dessert he served almonds, raisins, oranges, strawberries, and wine. In 1790, the specific dishes were altered, but the atmosphere of abundance remained constant; his guests received skate with oyster sauce, pea soup, ham, chicken, the same old boiled leg of mutton with capers, roast turkey, fried rabbit, brawn (a kind of jellied, potted pork—see *P* 134), tarts, and mince pies. He finishes his list with "&c.," so one may safely assume that dessert and wine followed this gargantuan meal.

Woodforde's diary reveals a pattern to his eating: simple dinners at home with a rough average of two meat dishes and two sweet or savory side dishes, contrasted with huge dinners in company, whether at home or in the homes of others. There are a few exceptions to the pattern. One of these is Good Friday. Woodforde rarely stinted himself, but he felt awkward about eating meat or playing cards on Good Friday, and on that day in 1790 he limited himself to "Smelts, boiled Eggs, Fritters and toasted Cheese." Another exception is his annual tithe dinner, usually held in early December. This was an entertainment given to those farmers who had come to pay him their annual tithe. It could be a tense occasion in some places, where farmers resented handing over a significant percentage of their income or produce to a clergyman. The method and timing of payment differed from parish to parish, as, no doubt, did parsons' attempts to soothe their shorn flocks. In Woodforde's case, he collected once a year and got everyone good and drunk to make them feel better about it. His tithe dinners are not heavy on the almonds, raisins, artichokes, or Madeira. He keeps the food plain and plentiful and washes it down with cheap, strong liquor. In 1782, he fed his parishioners salt fish, veal knuckle, pig's face, roast sirloin of beef, the ubiquitous boiled leg of mutton and capers, and "plenty of plumb Puddings," accompanied by wine, rum, strong beer, and ale. The following year, the food was exactly the same, except that the veal knuckle and pig's face were replaced by boiled rabbit. His assessment of what farmers expected must have been fairly accurate, for he reported, "Plenty of Wine, Punch and Strong Beer after Dinner till 10 o'clock. We had this Year a very agreeable meeting here, and were very agreeable—no grumbling whatever." His tithe dinners for other years boast similar menus—no complicated "made dishes" to confuse the common palate, but piles and piles of meat.

Few sources are as exhaustive as Woodforde's diary when it comes to food, but other documents of the time confirm his reports of small, private dinners versus large ones for company. The cookbooks of the time consistently offered suggestions for dishes to be served together in small family meals. Susannah Carter's *The Frugal Housewife, or Complete Woman Cook* (1795) listed several bills of fare for August:

> *Ham* and *fowls* roasted, with gravy sauce: *beans*.
>
> > *Or,*
>
> *Neck* of *venison*, with gravy and claret sauce: *fresh salmon*, with lobster sauce: *apple pie* hot and buttered.
>
> > *Or,*
>
> *Beef a-la-mode*: *green pease*: *haddock* boiled, and fried *soals* or *flounders* to garnish the dish.

However, it was more common to provide extensive bills of fare, perhaps on the theory that housewives could manage to throw three or four dishes together without much assistance. *The French Family Cook* (1793) suggests, for a spring dinner for twelve people, served by five servants, a first course of herb soup, asparagus and green pea soup, "a piece of beef" in the middle of the table, a dish of radishes, and a dish of butter. The soup, radishes, and butter should then be removed, while the beef remains, and four new dishes are placed on the table: "Mutton chops à la ravigotte, dressed with sallad herbs," veal breast with green peas, chicken fricassee, and a "pigeon fricandeau." For the third course—an unusual innovation—the author suggests roast rabbits, a roast fowl, or two large roast chickens, "Three small side dishes, and two sallads." Dessert (*Wat, MW* 325) consists of cherry compote, strawberries, cakes, whipped cream, currant jelly, apricot marmalade, and, in the center of the table, a bowl of "gauffres"; these were a mixture of sugar, egg, cream, lemon, and orange cooked in what sounds very much like a waffle iron. A summer dinner for ten in the same volume called for roasted meat in the middle of the table, a "veal tourt," "a fowl between two plates," rabbit hash, and "sheeps tongues en papillotes" for the first course; a "dish of little cakes," chickens, a leveret, peas, cream à la Madeleine, a salad of lettuce, and a salad of oranges for the second course; and peaches, cherries, plums, cream cheese, cakes, and mulberries for dessert. Sarah Harrison's *The House-keeper's Pocket-book; And Compleat Family Cook* (1748) shows several diagrams indicating not only the dishes to be served but their placement on the table. A typical first-course arrangement shows soup at the top of the table, to be replaced midway through the course by stewed carp; chine of veal at the bottom of the table; salad in the middle; and beans and bacon on one side, fricassee on the other. For the second course, these dishes are replaced, respectively, by partridges or capons, rabbits or wild ducks, tarts, peas or veal sweetbreads, and "Fry'd Patties." On the sideboard, she has neat's tongue or sliced ham, prawns, butter, anchovies, and cheese.

The contrast between this latter type of meal, with its groaning sideboard, and a comparatively simple family dinner (*P&P* 61, 120) is borne out in Austen's brief descriptions. The Coles, true to their delight in showing off their new wealth, invite plenty of company and shower them with a multiplicity of dishes (*E* 88–89), exemplifying the role of dinner hosts. The Grants, too, throw generous dinners (*MP* 239), not so much from a sense of novelty and hospitality as from the demands of Dr. Grant's palate. Small dinners without company, by contrast, are barely sketched, if they are even mentioned at all.

Dinner, even more so than breakfast, was subject to fashionable delay, for postponing this meal advertised one's wealth; a later dinner, and the consequent extension of evening activities into the hours after dark, meant extra expenditure on candles. Only the lowliest workmen still ate dinner at noon, therefore, and among themselves, the gentry, aristocracy, tradesmen, and artisans kept tabs on each other to see who reigned supreme at staving off hunger. The difference of an hour or even half an hour was no trivial matter. Comparing the manners of the modest rectory at Steventon to those of her wealthy brother Edward's house in Kent, Jane wrote in 1798, "We dine now at half after Three, and have done dinner I suppose before you [her sister Cassandra, then visiting Edward] begin. . . . I am afraid you will despise us." Ten years later, she reported, "We never dine now till five."

At least some of her characters betray the same awareness of dinner hours. The genteelly poor Elizabeth Watson, in Austen's unfinished novel *The Watsons*, has to apologize to the fashionable Lord Osborne when he makes a "morning" call at 2:55 P.M. (*Wat, MW* 344) and finds the family's housemaid readying the table for dinner. "I am sorry it happens so," explains Elizabeth, ". . . but you know what early hours we keep" (*Wat, MW* 346).* *The Watsons*, perhaps because it examines the life of a family barely holding on to its gentry status, is the most concerned of all Austen's works with the timing of meals and the social consequences of this timing. The self-consciously trendy Tom Musgrave aspires to "an 8 o'clock dinner" (*Wat, MW* 355) and even implies that he might dine as late as nine (*Wat, MW* 356), an absurdly late hour. When he accidentally lingers late enough for supper at the Watsons', he flees, though he has eaten nothing all evening, simply for the pleasure of "calling his next meal a Dinner" (*Wat, MW* 359).

Musgrave is unusually silly about his mealtimes; most of Austen's characters eat, by early nineteenth-century standards, at a much more reasonable hour. The Dashwoods at Barton Cottage eat at 4:00 (*S&S* 74, 361), as do Catherine Morland, General Tilney, and Miss Tilney when they eat at Henry's Woodston parsonage (*NA* 214). Of course, both *Sense and Sensibility* and *Northanger Abbey* are early novels; as the years went by, the dinner hour crept further and further into evening. As evidence, Diana Parker, a character in the unfinished late novel *Sanditon*, eats at 6:00 (*Sand, MW* 411), though she is not satirized for any pretense to cutting-edge etiquette. Even within a single novel, however, there may be differences of dinnertime based on social stature, London or provincial residence, and adherence to London or rural manners when in the country. (London dinnertimes were generally later.) Henry Tilney, for example,

*The Watsons had their parallels in the real world. In 1789, novelist Horace Walpole wrote that his unfashionable four o'clock dinners were often interrupted by "morning" calls from acquaintances. Another fictional example occurs in the Juvenilia, where Lady Greville not only interrupts someone else's dinner, but forces the unfortunate victim to stand at her coach door in wind and cold (*Col Let, MW* 158–59). The class-conscious Lady Greville would know that even though she herself has not yet eaten dinner, her hostess will be in the middle of that meal; her rudeness in refusing to come in is therefore compounded by the timing of her visit.

may dine at 4:00, but his richer and more ostentatious father dines at 5:00 (*NA* 162, 165).

TEA

Dinner ended with the withdrawal of any ladies to another room while the gentlemen remained in the dining room to talk, drink, and smoke. Some eighteenth-century sideboards were even equipped with chamberpots so that the

Tea, Rowlandson, 1786. The "tea things" are in evidence on this table: the urn for heating water, which dominates the group of dishes; the teapot; the handle-less cups; and the sugar bowl, from which the gentleman on the right is taking a lump of sugar with the aid of tongs. (Courtesy of the Lewis Walpole Library, Yale University. 786.5.15.7.)

gentlemen could relieve themselves without having to exit the room. When they had finished discussing subjects deemed inappropriate or uninteresting to women—politics, financial matters, hunting, bawdy humor, and the like—they rejoined the ladies in the parlor or drawing room (*MP* 334–35), and here tea was served (*Col Let, MW* 150; *Evelyn, MW* 187, 189; *LS, MW* 269; *Wat, MW* 354; *Sand, MW* 390–91, 413; *NA* 118; *S&S* 99; *P&P* 166, 344–45, 346; *MP* 104, 177; *E* 8, 124, 347, 382–83, 434).

Tea was, at this point, neither fully a meal nor simply the pouring of a beverage. Its components varied from household to household, but in the homes frequented by the Austens it included not only tea but coffee as well. The women of the family prepared these beverages, and there was frequently some sort of food offered as well. At its simplest, this was bread and butter, which might take the form of some sort of roll or muffin, toast made in the kitchen, or slices of bread to be toasted at the drawing-room fire (*MP* 383). However, many families chose to provide more than bread. There might be cakes or other sweet offerings.

The time at which tea was served depended on when the family ate dinner. The correspondent who wrote to *The Gentleman's Magazine* about Herefordshire habits in 1819 noted that dinner among the gentry was served at 5:00 or 6:00 and tea between 8:00 and 10:00. The Austen family, when it dined at 3:30, served tea at 6:30. And the fictional Edwardses of Austen's incomplete novel *The Watsons* take their muffin and dish of tea at 7:00 (*Wat, MW* 326).

SUPPER

Supper (*F&E, MW* 8–9; *J&A, MW* 23; *Col Let, MW* 167; *P&P* 84, 348; *MP* 267, 283, 376), too, was dependent on dinner for its schedule, and even for its very existence. Supper as a formal meal, with hot dishes, the tablecloth laid, and everyone sitting around the table, was virtually nonexistent among the fashionable. Dinner had crept later and later, with teatime following about three hours afterward, and the result was that there was no time before bedtime to go through the full ritual that a sit-down meal demanded. Therefore, "supper," when it was eaten at all, became more of a hearty snack—in the words of *The Gentleman's Magazine* letter cited above, it was merely "a tray of cold meat, or a light thing hot." Some people, who took their dinner and tea especially late, eschewed supper altogether (*Wat, MW* 351). Upon reflection, Austen herself realized that the Bennets should have been among those who skipped supper; class-conscious Mrs. Bennet, who routinely speaks of serving two-course dinners and who brags that her daughters are ignorant of the work of the kitchen, would probably have followed fashion in this respect, even if her sister Mrs.

Philips still likes "a little bit of hot supper" (*P&P* 74). Resigned to her mistake, Jane sighed in a letter that "I suppose it was the remains of Mrs. Bennet's old Meryton habits." More likely, the slip was the result of the Austens' old habits. There are several references to suppers in Austen's letters—a supper of tart and jelly with Edward's wealthy benefactress and adoptive mother, Mrs. Knight; another of widgeon, preserved ginger, and black butter served to guests; a third of toasted cheese, served to Jane in 1805 by Edward Bridges because it was her favorite supper food. Clearly, in this respect at least, Austen and some of her circle were content to be well fed and unfashionable.

However, at balls, where the participants might stay active until well after midnight, it was not only acceptable but even obligatory to serve a substantial supper (*S&S* 252; *E* 248, 254–56). Public balls, such as those at Bath's assembly rooms, often served tea (*NA* 21, 25, 59), while private balls tended to have more extensive refreshments. The latter might include cold or hot drinks (as the weather dictated), soup, sandwiches, or more complex dishes. For the guests who merely played cards, sat by the fire, or watched the dancers and gossiped, the supper was a convenience; for those who danced for hours with little intermission, it was a necessity, hence Austen's famous, oft-quoted pronouncement that "A private dance, without sitting down to supper, was . . . an infamous fraud upon the rights of men and women" (*E* 254). However, this is not Austen's only word on the subject. Another reference, this time from *Sense and Sensibility*, makes clear that while food of some kind was a constant, its presentation was variable and depended on the preferences of the hosts and the requirements of fashion. A "mere sideboard collation" (*S&S* 171)—that is, a sort of buffet table, at least in its comparative level of informality—will do for the country, but not for London, where a sit-down meal with footmen in attendance is a necessity.

It should be understood, however, that fashion did not reign entirely supreme in the matter of suppers. While suppers at balls were almost universally fancier and more extensive than family suppers at home, the fact that the aristocracy and their imitators had nominally abandoned supper as a meal did not mean that the rest of the country necessarily followed the trend. Suppers in some form were still necessary for those who ate their dinner on the early side, and the dishes served at supper, though presented with less formality and often eaten cold, could, in many homes, rival the complexity of those served at dinners. Hartfield's supper of "minced chicken and scalloped oysters," gruel, wine, boiled eggs, custard, and wine (*E* 24–25) may be unfashionable, but it is not unique. Austen's Juvenilia provide a concrete example of a simple supper united with an implication that the gentry went in for something a little more lavish:

> "Was your Mother gone to bed before you left her?" said her Ladyship. . . .

"She was just sitting down to supper, Ma'am."

"And what had she got for Supper?" "I did not observe." "Bread & Cheese I suppose." "I should never wish for a better supper," said Ellen. "You have never any reason" replied her Mother, "as a better is always provided for you." (*Col Let, MW* 156–57)

Clearly, Ellen's supper is more akin to Hartfield's chicken and oysters than to Austen's own favorite toasted cheese.

Cookbooks of the time continued to provide bills of fare for suppers, and though dinner remained preeminent, supper was not forgotten by its adherents. Susannah Carter's *The Frugal Housewife, or Complete Woman Cook* (1795) suggested, in its bills of fare, plans for suppers that sound rather like Hartfield's. One supper includes a "white fricassee of chickens," peas, roast duck, and gravy; another suggests roast chickens or pigeons, asparagus, and artichokes with melted butter. *The French Family Cook* (1793) offers pages of supper menus, including the following "Little Family Suppers of Four Articles":

Boiled Chickens. Cold Beef or Mutton Sliced. Pickles. Scolloped Oysters.

Boiled Tripe. Bologna Sausage sliced. Pat of Butter in a Glass. Hashed Hare.

Gudgeons fried. Biscuits. A Pat of Butter. Rasped Beef. Duck roasted.

Roasted Chickens. Potted Beef. Cheesecakes. Sausages, with Eggs poached.

Whitings broiled. Tongue sliced. Biscuits. Calf's Heart.

Veal Cutlet. Tart. Butter. Radishes. Asparagus.

The anonymous author's suppers increase in size; suppers of four articles are succeeded by those of five, seven, nine, and so on. One of the suggestions for a supper of eleven items is buttered lobster, peas, lemon custard, scalloped oysters, cold chicken, roasted sweetbreads, sliced ham, artichokes, two ducklings, raspberry cream in cups, jellies, and a preserved green orange in the middle of the table. It is hard to conceive of this meal fitting on a single tray, and harder still to imagine the only seventeen-item menu doing so; one supposes that these suppers were for balls and other special occasions. Sarah Harrison's menus, in the midcentury *The House-keeper's Pocket-book; And Compleat Family Cook*, are far simpler. She offers a supper of poultry, potted venison, lobster or crab in the shell, and tarts or cheesecakes, to be replaced at the end of the meal by a selection of fruit.

2

FRENCH CUISINE

French cooking, like the French language and French manners, occupied an ambivalent place in English culture. On the one hand, the aristocracy adored all things French and leapt to pay French "man-cooks" far more than they would pay an English woman. Many people further down the social ladder then imitated this vogue for France. On the other hand, there was a good deal of patriotic irritation at Francophilia, and this irritation only increased as wars with France dragged on for most of Austen's life.

Austen herself exemplified the ambiguous attitude toward things French. She had a cousin who was married to a French nobleman, and she herself spoke and read at least some French. Yet she was from one of the most staunchly patriotic classes—the Tory country gentry—and there is some evidence that the older she got the more intransigent she grew against the French. In her novels, we often see her subtly pitting French attitudes against English ones, and in the later novels, at least, we are supposed to see the French-influenced characters (Mary and Henry Crawford and Frank Churchill, for example) as seductive but dangerously immoral.

The battle between French and English only explicitly reaches the dinner table in one of her novels, however. This is *Pride and Prejudice*, in which Darcy's circle is twice identified with French cooking. The first instance brings up the feature of French cooking which was so controversial—sauce. Sauces were integral to French presentation, with the chief meats or vegetables thickly intermingled with their sauce in a ragout. The English style of presentation, on the other hand, was to plop a large piece of meat onto a platter with a comparatively thin sauce spooned around it. To the English, the former method seemed deceptive—*anything* could be hidden in there—and the latter was straightforward and honest. A goose was a goose and looked like a goose. The contrast forms the substance of Elizabeth Bennet's only exchange with Mr. Hurst, Mr.

French Liberty, British Slavery, 1792. At the height of fears about France's revolutionary fervor spreading to England, caricaturists contrasted the plight of the pre-revolutionary French peasants with the prosperity of Englishmen. The French are invariably depicted as gaunt and gnawing on some unappetizing food, while the Englishmen are fat, regaling themselves on bread, beef, and beer. (Courtesy of the Lewis Walpole Library, Yale University. 792.12.21.4.)

French Happiness, English Misery, 1793. The standard iconography of the contrast between French and English is gruesomely augmented by a "List of The Killed and Wounded" near the fireplace, with totals that reveal heavy French losses in the war; a hanged man outside the window, near a severed head on a pike and an aristocrat's infant impaled on spikes; and a cat in the foreground so gaunt that it seems to have been deflated. (Courtesy of the Lewis Walpole Library, Yale University. 793.1.3.1.)

Bingley's brother-in-law, "who when he found her prefer a plain dish to a ragout, had nothing to say to her." (*P&P* 35) With that, Austen dismisses Mr. Hurst from serious consideration, not only because he thinks too much of food, but also because he has chosen the wrong side of the argument.

Elizabeth Bennet could have found plenty of real-world adherents to her cause. Parson Woodforde ate a dinner on August 28, 1783, at which he was deeply impressed by the wealth of his host but wholly unimpressed by the meal. After awestruck descriptions of the host's silk-upholstered chairs and seven-and-a-half-foot by five-and-a-half-foot looking glass, he sat down to a two-course meal with a total of eighteen dishes in which "most of the things [were] spoiled by being so frenchified in dressing." Cookbook author Hannah Glasse had no inherent objection to "frenchified" presentation, and she duly included ragouts in her cookbook, but she was deeply miffed at the lionization of French cooks. Good sauces could be made for far less than French sauces, she claimed, "*but if gentlemen will have* French *cooks, they must pay for* French *tricks.*" In her eyes, French cuisine is nothing but a great fraud perpetrated on the English ruling classes:

> A Frenchman *in his own country will dress a fine dinner of twenty dishes, and all genteel and pretty, for the expence he will put an* English *lord to for dressing one dish. But then there is the little petty profit. I have heard of a cook that used six pounds of butter to fry twelve eggs; when every body knows (that understands cooking) that half a pound is full enough, or more than need be used: but then it would not be* French. *So much is the blind folly of this age, that they would rather be imposed on by a* French *booby, than give encouragement to a good* English *cook!*

Yet that was precisely the situation. Those who could afford it *did* hire French cooks. Few could afford it; Glasse was right about one thing, and that was that French chefs charged their employers handsomely for their services. Mrs. Bennet refers to this practice in one of her assessments of Mr. Darcy's wealth, commenting, "I suppose he has two or three French cooks at least." (*P&P* 342)

French recipes tended to be segregated in English cookbooks. In this cookbook, however, they are presented alongside the English recipes in a spirit of post-Napoleonic reconciliation. Readers wishing to identify them can look for attribution to *The French Family Cook* or to the word "ragout" or "ragoo" in the title of the recipe.

3

BEEF AND VEAL

Beef was the defining food of eighteenth-century England, in the same way that apple pie is identified with America, but to a far greater extent. Roast beef was celebrated in song and pictorial art as the source of British strength and the evidence of British virtue. It was perceived as simple, straightforward, copious, and life-giving, as opposed to the Frenchman's little bits of things—frogs and snails and pretentious sauces—that, according to the propaganda of the day, left him dangerously lean and jealous of the fat and jolly Englishman. Even those who couldn't afford to eat meat very often lauded the Roast Beef of Old England.

For those who could afford meat on a daily basis, beef and veal were popular choices. Parson James Woodforde, who kept an extensive diary of, among other things, his eating habits, frequented noted beef dishes in his meals:

JANUARY 28, 1780	"Calf's Head"
JUNE 8, 1781	"a Tongue" (probably a beef tongue, as sheep's tongues were usually served in groups)
AUGUST 21, 1781	"Veal Collops"
MAY 14, 1782	"part of a Rump of Beef boiled"
NOVEMBER 20, 1782	"a Piece of rost Beef"
DECEMBER 3, 1782	"a Knuckle of Veal . . . a fine Surloin of Beef rosted"
JANUARY 7, 1783	"a hot Tongue" (he specifies that it was hot because it was served at supper, a meal at which most or all the dishes were typically served cold)
APRIL 30, 1783	"a Piece of rosted Beef . . . and hung Beef, grated"

JULY 29, 1783   "a Piece of boiled Beef"

AUGUST 28, 1783   "some stewed Beef with Caper Sauce"

DECEMBER 2, 1783   "a fine large Surloin of Beef rosted"

JULY 2, 1784   "boiled Beef"

NOVEMBER 30, 1784   "a fine Loin of Beef rosted"

AUGUST 29, 1786   "Tripe"

APRIL 17, 1787   "Knuckle of Veal and a Tongue"

DECEMBER 1, 1789   "boiled Beef and rost Beef"

These dishes, and many others like them, were served at Woodforde's home, at the homes of his friends, and at inns. In many cases, he does not bother to note

Fast Day!, 1793. Wartime shortages do not affect a group of parsons in this anti-clerical print, which shows its subjects enjoying brimming glasses of wine, roast potatoes (on the right), a steaming pudding (on the left, next to the decanter), and that sine qua non of the well-stocked table, a giant beef roast. (Courtesy of the Lewis Walpole Library, Yale University. 793.4.19.1.)

the cut of meat used; instead, he comments on the method of preparation—boiled, stewed, roasted—and whether or not he enjoyed it.

His diary tells us how commonplace beef was on the tables of the gentry, but it tells us more than that. Woodforde's descriptions, like other cookbooks, diaries, and letters of the time, reveal the wide range of animal parts that were consumed. Beef was too tasty and too valuable to be wasted. Therefore, people consumed the whole animal, or as close as they could get to it. They ate the head—Hannah Glasse's classic cookbook *The Art of Cookery Made Plain and Easy* contains several animal-head recipes, including "Calf's Head Surprize"—the organs, the knuckles, the neck, the tongue, the udder. Even the bone marrow was scraped out and used in soups and sauces. (While researching this book, I described to an acquaintance how eighteenth-century cooks used to serve tongue and udder together in the same dish. He thought about it for a moment and then said slyly, "That sounds about right.")

❀ THE ROAST BEEF OF OLD ENGLAND ❀

(Glasse)

... after having laboured both Night and Day, in order to get the Wedding dinner ready by the time appointed, after having roasted Beef, Broiled Mutton, and Stewed Soup enough to last the new-married couple through the Honey-moon, I had the mortification of finding that I had been Roasting, Broiling, and Stewing both the Meat and Myself to no purpose. (*Lesley, MW* 112–13)

I shall be able to manage the Sir-loin myself; my Mother will eat the Soup, and You and the Doctor must finish the rest. (*Lesley, MW* 113)

... if she accepted any refreshment, [she] seemed only to do it for the sake of finding our that Mrs. Collins's joints of meat were too large for her family. (*P&P* 169)

*Served cold (*Lesley, MW *128), roast beef could have been served at supper, at breakfast, or at midday as part of a cold collation or a luncheon at an inn. Large cuts of meat were also sometimes boiled; one recipe of Hannah Glasse's called for a round roast to be steeped in saltpeter, salt, and brown sugar for up to twelve days, then cut in various places and the cuts filled with different types of stuffing, including parsley and "fat pork." Then the entire "forced" or stuffed round was boiled for four hours and then thinly sliced. To the modern palate, Glasse's roast beef is considerably tastier than her boiled round.*

To roast a piece of beef about ten pounds will take an hour and a half, at a good fire. Twenty pounds weight will take three hours, if it be a thick piece; but if it be a thin piece of twenty pounds weight, two hours and a half will do it; and so on according to the weight of your meat, more or less. Observe, in frosty weather your beef will take half an hour longer.

Be sure to paper the top, and baste it well all the time it is roasting, and throw a handful of salt on it. When you see the smoak draw to the fire, it is near enough; then take off the paper, baste it well, and drudge it with a little flour to make a fine froth: take up your meat, and garnish your dish with nothing but horse radish.

Never salt your roast meat before you lay it to the fire, for that draws out all the gravy. If you would keep it a few days before you dress it, dry it very well with a clean cloth, then flour it all over, and hang it where the air will come to it; but be sure always to mind that there is no dampness about it; if there is, you must dry it well with a cloth.

MODERN RECIPE

4-lb. round roast   1 T flour

kosher salt

Preheat oven to 425°F. Set the roast on a rack in a roasting pan; if there is fat on the roast, place the fat facing upward. Cover the roast with a piece of parchment paper. Roast until inside temperature on a meat thermometer is at least 130°F (for rare meat).* When roast seems close to done, scatter with kosher salt. When the internal temperature has reached 130°F, sprinkle flour over the roast. Cook until the flour has browned. Let the roast stand for 10 to 30 minutes before carving.

*130°F to 140°F for rare, 140°F to 155°F for medium, 155°F to 170°F for well done.

 BAKED LEG OF BEEF

(Glasse)

> Cook) Here is the bill of fare.
> Chloe reads) 2 Ducks, a leg of beef, a stinking partridge, & a tart.—I will
>   have the leg of beef and the partridge. (*Scraps, MW* 173)

Leg of beef is no longer a common cut in American supermarkets, chiefly because of the "sinews and fat" Glasse mentions as part of the cut. London broil, as superior cut to the leg steak, has been substituted in this recipe, though if you can find a leg of beef, by all means give it a try.

Take a rasher of two of bacon or ham, lay it at the bottom of your stew-pan; put your meat, cut in thin slices, over it; and cut some onions, turnips, carrots, and celery, a little thyme, and put over the meat, with a little all-spice; put a little water at the bottom, then set it on the fire, which must be a gentle one, and draw it till it is brown at the bottom (which you may know by the pan's hissing, then pour boiling water over it, and stew it gently for one hour and a half: if a small quantity, less time will do it. Season it with salt. . . . when it is baked, strain it through a coarse sieve. Pick out all the sinews and fat, put them into a sauce-pan with a few spoonfuls of the gravy, a little red wine, a piece of butter rolled in flour, and some mustard; shake your sauce-pan often, and when the sauce is hot and thick, dish it up, and send it to table. It is a pretty dish.

 ## MODERN RECIPE

1 London broil, sliced crosswise into ¼"-thick pieces

4 slices of bacon, cut in half crosswise

1 large onion, halved and sliced

1 turnip, peeled and cut in 1" dice

2 carrots, peeled and cut crosswise in 1" segments

3 stalks celery, cut crosswise in 1" segments

½ tsp. allspice

⅓ cup water

1½ cups very hot or boiling water

salt to taste

Sauce
½ cup dry red wine

2 T butter

1 T flour

1 T Dijon mustard

On a stove burner at medium-low heat, place a wide and deep sauté pan that can be covered with a lid. Lay the half-strips of bacon in a single layer in the bottom of the pan. Cover with layers of London broil and the vegetables. Sprinkle the allspice and the ⅓ cup water and heat until the liquid in the bottom of the pan begins to sizzle. Add the hot water and cover tightly. Cook at medium-low for 45 minutes, then at low for another 45 minutes.

As soon as the beef is done, make the sauce. Heat 3 T of the meat juice with the red wine over medium heat until it begins to sizzle. Roll the 2 T of the butter in the flour and pinch it a little to incorporate the rest of the flour. The idea here is to distribute the flour over the surface of the butter so that as the butter melts, it thickens the sauce and spreads the flour evenly, without

Continued on next page

> *Continued from previous page*
>
> lumps.* As soon as the butter is melted, add the mustard. Warm the sauce for a few more seconds and serve immediately.
>
> Season the beef and vegetables with salt and serve with the sauce.
>
> *See *Appendix 1: "What's with All the Butter?"*

 FRIED BEEF STEAKS

(Glasse)

You will not dine as you did yesterday, for we have nothing but some fried beef. (*Wat, MW* 341)

And when did you get anything to eat? And what would you like to have now? I could not tell whether you would be for some meat, or only a dish of tea after your journey, or else I would have got something ready. And now I am afraid Campbell will be here, before there is time to dress a steak, and we have no butcher at hand. It is very inconvenient to have no butcher in the street. (*MP* 378–79)

Take rump steaks, pepper and salt them, fry them in a little butter very quick and brown; take them out and put them into a dish, pour the fat out of the frying-pan, and then take half a pint of hot gravy; if no gravy, half a pint of hot water, and put into the pan, and a little butter rolled in flour, a little pepper and salt, and two or three shalots chopped fine; boil them up in your pan for two minutes, then put it over the steaks, and send them to table.

MODERN RECIPE

4 steaks	1 cup beef **broth**
salt	flour
pepper	3 large shallots
5 T butter, *in all*	

Continued on next page

Continued from previous page

In a large skillet over medium to medium-high heat, melt 4 T of the butter until it sizzles and begins to brown. Meanwhile, salt and pepper the steaks on both sides. Add the steaks to the pan and cook until brown on both sides and pink in the middle, about 5 minutes on each side. When they are done, remove them to a warm oven or warming drawer and make the sauce.

Pour the fat out of the skillet, leaving just a trace behind. Return the pan to medium-high heat and add the broth and the chopped shallots. When the broth boils, add a tablespoon of butter rolled in flour. (Mash the flour a little into the butter as you roll it.)* Reduce the sauce to a simmer until the butter is melted and the sauce is fully heated, about 2 minutes. Serve immediately with the steaks.

*See *Appendix 1: "What's with All the Butter?"*

BEEF COLLOPS

(Glasse)

"Collops" were small slices of meat. Cookbook authors rarely used inches to indicate sizes for cutting and slicing; they tended to use vague descriptions, such as "cut them up very fine." When sizes are indicated, they are often comparisons to common objects, such as a walnut or, as in this case, a coin. Almost any kind of steak can be used for this purpose, but the coulotte steaks specified in this version of the recipe yield roughly appropriately-sized pieces when cut crosswise.

Take some rump steaks, or any tender piece, cut like Scotch collops [in Glasse's instructions, the "size of a crown piece but very thin"], only larger, hack them a little with a knife, and flour them; but a little butter into a stew-pan, and melt it, then put in your collops, and fry them quick for about two minutes; put in a pint of gravy, a little butter rolled in flour; season with pepper and salt; cut four pickled cucumbers in thin slices, half a walnut, and a few capers, a little onion shred very fine; stew them five minutes, then put them into a hot dish, and send them to table. You may put half a glass of white wine into it.

MODERN RECIPE

2 coulotte steaks, cut crosswise about ¼" thick	salt
flour	4 dill pickles, finely chopped
5 T butter, *in all*	2 tsp. chopped walnut
½ cup prepared **gravy** and ½ cup beef **broth**, or 1 cup **cullis**	2 tsp. capers
	¼ onion, grated
pepper	½ cup white wine

Pound the slices of steak with the flat side of a kitchen mallet, reducing them to about half their original thickness. Melt 3 T of the butter in a large skillet. Dredge the steak slices in flour and fry them in the skillet over medium heat until browned on both sides, about 2 to 3 minutes each side.

Add the gravy and broth or cullis. Mix the remaining 2 T butter with 1 T flour* and stir this into the sauce until it is completely melted. Immediately add the pickles, walnut, capers, and onion, and season to taste with pepper and salt. Stir in the white wine, heat through, and serve.

*See *Appendix 1: "What's with All the Butter?"*

BEEF HASH

(Glasse, Carter)

> She was so little equal to Rebecca's puddings, and Rebecca's hashes, brought
> to table as they all were, with such accompaniments of half-cleaned plates,
> and not half-cleaned knives and forks, that she was very often constrained
> to defer her heartiest meal, till she could send her brothers in the evenings
> for biscuits and buns. (*MP* 413)

Beef was one of the few foods that, according to Glasse, was available year-round. This no doubt accounts, at least in part, for its popularity. Boiling beef was one of the most common ways of preparing it, perhaps because of the comparatively easy preparation: beef when boiling did not spatter as it did when roasting, nor did it need to be constantly rotated on a spit. Leftover beef, as well as other types of meat, could be quickly prepared as "hashes" by chopping up the cooked meat, reheating it, and adding a simple sauce.

Numerous cookbook authors include recipes for beef hash, which was simply a way of using up the leftovers from a beef roast. My tasters found Glasse's recipe tastier than

Carter's, but Carter's works well if you have not premade any of the standard Regency condiments.

Glasse's Recipe

Cut your beef in very thin slices, take a little of your gravy that runs from it, put it into a tossing-pan with a teaspoon of lemon-pickle, a large one of walnut-catchup, the same of browning, slice a shalot in, and put it over the fire; when it boils, put in your beef; shake it over the fire till it is quite hot, the gravy is not to be thickened, slice in a small pickled cucumber; garnish with scraped horse-radish or pickled onions.

Carter's Recipe

Take the raw part of any piece of roasted beef, and cut it into thin slices, about the length of a little finger, and about the same breadth. Take also a little water, and an equal quantity of gravy; boil it well with a large onion cut in two, pepper and salt, then take a piece of butter rolled in flour, and stir it in the pan till it burns. Put it into the sauce, and let it boil a minute or two. Then put in the sliced beef, but you must only just let it warm through. Some add a few whole capers, mushrooms, walnut pickle, or catchup. Serve this up to table in a soup-dish, garnished with pickles.

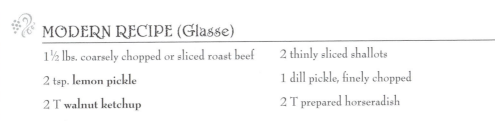

MODERN RECIPE (Glasse)

1½ lbs. coarsely chopped or sliced roast beef	2 thinly sliced shallots
2 tsp. **lemon pickle**	1 dill pickle, finely chopped
2 T **walnut ketchup**	2 T prepared horseradish
2 T **browning**	

In a skillet, heat the lemon pickle, walnut ketchup, browning, and shallots over medium-low heat. Add the roast beef and heat just until warmed through. Place on a serving platter and garnish with the pickles and horseradish.

MODERN RECIPE (Carter)

1½ lbs. chopped or sliced roast beef	pepper and salt to taste
½ cup water	2 T butter rolled in 1 T flour*
½ cup beef **broth**	2 tsp. capers
1 large onion, halved and thinly sliced	1 T **walnut ketchup**

In a large saucepan, bring the water, beef broth, onion, pepper, and salt to a boil. Reduce the heat to medium-low and add the butter and flour. When the butter has melted and the sauce has thickened slightly, add the meat. Heat until warmed through and transfer to a serving bowl. Pour the sauce over the meat and toss in the capers and walnut ketchup or Worcestershire sauce.

*See *Appendix 1: "What's with All the Butter?"*

FRICASSEED TRIPE

(Millington)

LADY H. Sir Arthur never eats Tripe; tis too savoury for him you know my
Lord. (*Visit, MW* 53)

Cut it into pieces about two inches square, put them into the stewpan, with as much wine as will half cover them, a little white pepper, sliced ginger, a blade of mace, a bunch of sweet herbs, and an onion. When stewed a quarter of an hour, take out the herbs and onion, and put in a little shred parsley, the juice of a lemon, half an anchovy cut small, a cup full of cream, and either the yolk of an egg, or a piece of butter. Season it till pleasant to taste, then dish it, and garnish with lemon.

MODERN RECIPE

1½ lbs. tripe	5 sprigs of fresh thyme
1¼ cups white wine	5 sprigs of fresh parsley
pinch of white pepper	1 carrot, coarsely chopped

Continued on next page

Continued from previous page

2 slices of ginger

blade of mace or ½ tsp. ground mace

juice of ½ lemon

1 onion, coarsely chopped

1 cup cream

2 anchovy filets, chopped

2 T of butter rolled in 1 T flour*

Cut tripe into pieces 1" to 2" square. Put them in a saucepan with the wine, white pepper, herbs, carrots, ginger, mace, and onions. Stew over medium heat for about 30 minutes or until the tripe is tender.

When tripe is fork tender, strain out the reduced sauce, and return to the pan with the cooked tripe. Add the chopped parsley, anchovy filets, cream, and floured butter.

Simmer for about 5 minutes over medium-low heat. Season with salt and pepper to taste and serve.

*See *Appendix 1: "What's with All the Butter?"*

❈ NEAT'S TONGUE ❈

(*The French Family Cook*)

We brought a cold Pigeon pye, a cold turkey, a cold tongue, and half a dozen Jellies with us, which we were lucky enough with the help of our Landlady, her husband, and their three children, to get rid of, in less than two days after our arrival. (*Lesley, MW* 119)

The "large pepper" mentioned in the first recipe for tongue was a part of a plant related to the species of plant that produces black pepper. As "large pepper" is no longer commonly used as a condiment, I have substituted a small amount of white pepper to create roughly the same flavor. Cold tongue "salted, smoked, and dried," as the French Family Cook *author describes it, corresponds well to the cured tongue available in many delis as a sandwich meat.*

To dress a Neat's Tongue en Brezole, and other ways

Boil it a little more than half in water, and having taken off the skin, cut the tongue in little thin bits about the size of a half-crown, and put it into a stew-pan with parsley, scallions, and champignons, the whole cut small, large pepper, and sweet oil, and set it over a very slow fire, adding a glass of white wine when it begins to boil, and when it is done a little cullis. If the flavour be not high enough, in serving it add the juice of a lemon.—*A neat's tongue* may be also served with a ragoût of cucumbers and divers other vegetables, and with several different sauces; as sauce à la ravigote, sauce petite, &c. for which see the article of Sauces. It may also be served cold as a dish in the second course, salted, smoked, and dried.

To serve a Neat's Tongue with a Gratin*

Take a neat's tongue, and having first parboiled it, throw it into your pot and let it boil with any sort of meat till the skin will easily come off; then cut it into pieces, and shred small some parsley and scallions, five or six leaves of tarragon, three shallots, a few capers, and an anchovy; then mix a handful of grated crumb of bread with a bit of butter half the size of an egg, and a part of the herbs you have shred, and arrange the whole in a dish for table, placing half the slices of tongue first, and over them the remainder of the herbs; then arrange the slices of tongue that remain in a second layer, seasoning them with salt and large pepper, and moisten the whole with three or four spoonfuls of broth and half a glass of wine. Let it boil till it forms a gratin in the bottom of the dish; and when you serve it, add a little broth, merely as a sauce to it.

*That which sticks to the bottom of a dish when any thing has been dressed in it.

MODERN RECIPE

For tongue en Brezole	For tongue with a gratin
1 raw beef tongue	1 raw beef tongue
2 T olive oil	1 cup chopped parsley
3 cups chopped mushrooms	5 or 6 scallions
¾ cup chopped scallions	1 tsp. dried or 2 tsp. fresh tarragon
¾ cup chopped parsley	2 tsp. capers
6 oz. white wine	1 anchovy filet
1 lemon	2½ T butter, *in all*
¼ tsp. white pepper	⅓ cup bread crumbs
3 T beef **broth** or **cullis** (optional)	3 shallots
	salt
	white pepper
	½ cup wine

Continued on next page

Continued from previous page

For either type of tongue

Boil the tongue in a large pot of water until the skin peels off easily, about three hours. To determine whether the skin will come off easily, let the tongue cool out of the water until it can be handled, then slit the skin somewhere with a sharp knife and peel the skin away from the slit. (Do not try to peel from the cut edge of the skin; this part tends to cling longer than the rest and can be cut away, once the rest of the skin has been removed.) Reserve the water in which the tongue was boiled, and slice the tongue into thin strips. Then cut the strips into bite-size pieces.

For tongue en Brezole

Heat the olive oil in a large pan over medium heat and sauté the mushrooms and scallions together for about 1 minute. Add the tongue, parsley, and white wine and stir until the liquid begins to sizzle. Add the white pepper and 3 T of the water in which the tongue was boiled; instead of the boiling liquid, you may add 3 T of beef broth or of pre-prepared cullis. Add the juice of 1 lemon. Heat thoroughly and serve hot.

For tongue with a gratin

Sauté the scallions, parsley, capers, tarragon, shallots, and anchovy in 1 T butter. Mix the remaining butter with the bread crumbs. At this point you have two choices.

You may add the tongue to the pan, stirring all the ingredients together and spreading them in an even layer. Sprinkle salt and pepper to taste across the top of the layer. Then add 3 T of the tongue's cooking liquid and the ½ cup of wine and cook until most of the liquid is gone and the bottom of the layer has browned nicely. Then add 2 T more of the tongue's cooking liquid and serve.

Or you can mix the cooked vegetables with the butter and bread crumbs in a bowl. Spread half this mixture across the bottom of a stovetop-safe serving dish, and cover it with half the tongue slices. Spread the rest of the butter mixture over these slices, and then add a second layer of meat. Sprinkle with salt and white pepper, pour in the cooking liquid and wine, and cook on the stovetop until the liquid is mostly evaporated and the bottom is nicely browned. Add 2 T cooking liquid, heat, and serve.

MINCE PIE

(Glasse)

I fancy she was wanted about the mince pies. For my part, Mr. Bingley, I always keep servants that can do their own work; *my* daughters are brought up differently. (*P&P* 44)

I reduced the amount of fat in this recipe, though I left enough in to bind the ingredients. I also decreased the amount of currants, which results in a slightly less sweet and more balanced flavor. The cooked currants are, however, surprisingly mild in flavor. Less sweet than raisins, they do not overwhelm the other ingredients as much as you might suspect from the appearance of the prepared filling. Nonpareils and sweetmeats were small sweet items such as bits of candied citrus peel. They have been omitted from this recipe, but you can add them if you wish to experiment. This pie keeps extremely well in the refrigerator and can be eaten hot or at room temperature. The crust is resistant to moisture but not too tough.

Take about a pound of very tender beef, two pounds of suet, and about two pounds of currants; cloves and mace to your taste; lemon-peel and the juice of two good lemons, white wine and red sufficient to moisten the meat; add some chopped nonpareils, and sweetmeats (if you please); beat the spice with a little salt, and sweeten with moist sugar to your taste.

MODERN RECIPE

1¼ lbs. skirt steak, finely chopped, browned, and the fat drained off

1 lb. lard or suet cut into ¼" dice

1½ lbs. currants

1 apple, peeled, cored, and chopped into ¼" dice

zest and juice of two lemons

½ cup wine

1 tsp. kosher salt

1 T brown sugar

1 recipe **good crust for great pies**

Preheat oven to 350°F. Mix all ingredients in a large bowl. Roll out the crust about ³⁄₁₆" to ¼" thick and cover the bottom and sides of 2 pie pans, trimming away the excess. Prick the crust in a few places around the bottom and sides. Fill the crusts with mincemeat. Roll out the leftover

Continued on next page

Continued from previous page
crust and cut two circles a little larger than the upper diameter of the pie pans. Place these top crust over the pans, trim away any excess, and pinch the upper and lower crusts together all the way around the rim. Cut 3 vents in the top crust, each about 1½" long, with a sharp knife. Bake until top crust is nicely browned and liquid begins to bubble and ooze at the sides and/or vents, about 60 to 90 minutes.

FRIED COWHEEL AND ONION

(Bradley)

CLOE. I shall trouble Mr Stanly for a Little of the fried Cowheel & Onion.
STANLY. Oh Madam, there is a secret pleasure in helping so amiable a
   Lady—. (*Visit, MW* 53)

Cowheel turns out to be a nearly impossible dish to find in cookbooks of Austen's era, though dishes that sound somewhat similar are easy to come by. Veal knuckles are fairly common, and many of the recipes for veal knuckles include onions. However, Austen's terminology implies that we are in search of a foot, or part of a foot, rather than a joint of some kind. The OED defines cowheel as "The foot of a cow or ox stewed so as to form a jelly," or a dish made from this jelly, but this definition presents the food historian with a few difficulties. The first, Austen's union of gelatin and onions, is not quite as bizarre as it seems; savory jellies were an old tradition in English cooking, and though they were being superseded in popularity by sweet jellies, it is not necessarily out of the question to unite jelly and onions in a single dish. However, Austen specifically refers to the cowheel as "fried," and fried gelatin is indeed hard to imagine. Furthermore, jellies are almost always referred to as being made from calves' feet, not those of cows or oxen. More importantly, the concept of fried gelatin is simply not present in the cookbooks of Austen's day. Therefore, she must have meant something else.

One has to return to much earlier cookbooks to find this dish, which by Austen's day was very humble fare. (In fact, part of the humor of the relevant scene comes from the fact that a knight or baronet, his wife, and their genteel company are served a series of homely dishes, including tripe, red herring, pork liver, and suet pudding.) A recipe for "Cow-Heel" appears in Richard Bradley's The Country Housewife and Lady's Director *(1736), and a somewhat altered recipe, under the name "Fried Ox Feet," resurfaces in John Farley's* The London Art of Cookery *(1783). Both versions meet*

Austen's requirements. They use the feet of adult cattle rather than of calves, they are fried, and they include onions.

After the problem of identification has been solved, however, the modern cook faces the difficulty of actually finding a cow or ox foot. This is virtually impossible unless one has slaughtered the cow oneself. In this version, the more widely available short ribs of beef, which, like the feet, offer a relatively small proportion of meat to bone and other tissue, have been substituted. Bradley presents two ways of preparing this dish, one in which the beef and onions are simply dredged in flour and fried in butter, and one in which the onions are stewed in a sauce. I have opted for the first method of preparation, as it the simpler preparation and therefore fits Austen's purposes as a humble dish.

Take out the Bones, and clean it, cut it to pieces, and wash it; then flour it, and strew over it a little Pepper and Salt, then fry it brown in Hog's-Lard, made very hot in the Pan. Prepare at the same time some small Onions boiled whole, till they are tender, and pull off as many of the Coats or Skins, till you see them pure white; then make a Sauce of Gravey, some White-Wine, Nutmeg, and a little whole Spice, with a little Salt and Pepper, and thicken it with burnt Butter. Let your Onions, when they are skin'd, be made hot in Milk, and lay them whole in the Dish, with the Cow-Heel, and pour the Sauce over the whole. Some who have strong Stomachs will slice Onions, and flouring them well, fry them with the Cow-Heel, but this must be fry'd in Butter.

❦ MODERN RECIPE (Farley)

6 beef short ribs

flour for dredging

pepper and salt to taste

½ large white onion, cut into two quarters and thinly sliced crosswise

4 T butter

Cut the bones away from the short rib meat and slice the meat on the diagonal into thin strips about ⅛" wide. Dip the meat and onions in a bowl of flour. Heat the butter in a large skillet over medium-high heat. Add the meat and onions, sprinkle with salt and pepper, and cook until the meat is browned and the flour coating begins to turn golden, about 5 to 7 minutes. Serve immediately.

 MODERN RECIPE (Bradley)

1¼ lbs. pearl onions	2 cups milk
1 lb. beef short ribs	¼ cup **cullis** or **gravy**
¾ c. flour	¼ cup white wine
1 T kosher salt	pinch each nutmeg, salt, and pepper
2 tsp. black pepper	3 T butter
¼ lb. lard	

Bring a pot of water to boil. Meanwhile, trim the ends off the pearl onions and peel them. When the water boils, add the onions and boil until tender, about 10 minutes. Drain off the water but leave the onions in the pot.

Trim the bones and thick fat away from the short ribs. Cut the remaining meat into strips about ¼" thick.

In a small bowl, mix the flour, pepper, and salt. Toss the meat strips in the flour and shake off excess. Heat the lard on high heat in a large skillet until it melts and begins to sizzle. Add the beef strips and cook until nicely browned on both sides, about 2 to 3 minutes each side. Drain the pieces of meat on paper towels and keep warm.

Add the milk to the pot containing the onions and warm over medium-low heat. Meanwhile, make the sauce. Heat the cullis or gravy, wine, nutmeg, salt, and pepper over low heat. In a separate pan, heat the butter until it begins to brown. Add it to the sauce.

To serve, drain off the milk from the onions and stir the onions and beef strips together in a serving bowl. Pour the sauce over the beef and onions and serve immediately.

BEEF ALAMODE

(Glasse)

Rostock Market makes one's mouth water, our cheapest Butcher's meat is double the price of theirs;—nothing under 9[d] all this Summer, & I believe upon recollection nothing under 10[d].—Bread has sunk & is likely to sink more, which we hope may make Meat sink too. (Letter from Jane to Francis Austen, September 25, 1813)

The sheer number of ingredients in this recipe, its French-influenced name, and the relatively "high" or strong spicing, all reveal it to be a fancy dish, the sort that would have been served at a fine dinner party rather than in a humble home.

Take a small buttock, or leg-of-mutton-piece of beef, or a clod, or a piece of buttock beef, also two dozen of cloves, as much mace, and half an ounce of all-spice beat fine; chop a large handful of parsley, and all sorts of sweet herbs fine (cut fat bacon as for beef à la Daub, and put it into the spice, &c. and into the beef the same); put it into a pot, and cover it with water; chop four large onions very fine, and six cloves of garlic, six bay-leaves, and a handful of champignons or fresh mushrooms; put all into the pot with a pint of porter or ale, and half a pint of red wine; put in some pepper and salt, some Cayenne pepper, a spoonful of vinegar, strew three handfuls of bread raspings, sifted fine, over all; cover the pot close, and stew it for six hours, or according to the size of the piece; if a large piece, eight hours; then take the beef out and put it in a deep dish, and keep it hot over some boiling water; strain the gravy through a sieve, and pick out the champignons or mushrooms; skim all the fat off clean, put it into your pot again, and give it a boil up; if not seasoned enough, season it to your liking; then put the gravy over your beef, and send it to table hot; or you may cut it in slices if you like it best, or put it to get cold, and cut it in slices with the gravy over it; for when the gravy is cold, it will be in a strong jelly.

N.B. This makes an excellent dish, but many of the ingredients, such as the garlic, mushrooms, &c. may be left out.

MODERN VERSION

1 chuck roast, about 3 lbs.	3 bay leaves
1 tsp. ground cloves	1 cup button mushrooms
1 tsp. ground mace	2 cups beer
2 tsp. ground allspice	1 cup red wine
1 cup coarsely chopped parsley	1 tsp. black pepper
1 T mixed dried herbs such as oregano, marjoram, thyme, and sage; or 2 T fresh mixed herbs	1½ tsp. salt
	½ tsp. cayenne pepper
4 slices bacon	1 T vinegar
2 large onions, finely chopped	¾ cup bread crumbs
3 cloves garlic, minced	

Continued on next page

Continued from previous page

Place the beef roast in a deep covered pot or Dutch oven. Sprinkle the cloves, mace, and allspice over the meat. In a small bowl, mix the parsley and other herbs. Toss the bacon slices in the herbs, lay them over the meat, and sprinkle the leftover herbs in the pot. Add the onions, garlic, bay leaves, mushrooms, beer, and wine. Then add enough water to just cover the meat. Add the pepper, salt, cayenne, vinegar, and bread crumbs and stir gently to just mix the ingredients. Cover tightly. Bring the liquid to a boil over medium heat, then reduce the heat to medium-low and simmer gently for 4 to 6 hours or until the meat is very tender.

Remove the beef from the pot and keep warm. Skim the fat from the sauce and strain the sauce. Adjust the seasonings and serve the beef on a platter and the sauce in a gravy boat.

Unlike many Regency meat dishes, which cry out to be served immediately, this is one that reheats well or, as Glasse hints, can be served cold as a sandwich meat. Refrigerating the sauce in advance of the serving time also simplifies the process of skimming off the fat.

PORTUGAL BEEF

(Glasse)

Chestnuts, as anyone knows who has had the misfortune to peel a lot of them at once, are a royal pain to work with. Fortunately, some well-stocked groceries and online suppliers carry prepeeled, canned chestnuts. These have one principal disadvantage, which is that they are somewhat soft. However, this is not a serious problem for this recipe and actually makes them easier to use; they can simply be crumbled with your fingers rather than chopped.

Austen's audience was accustomed to contrasts of color and texture in food. This dish, with its dark fried beef, tender stewed beef, and rich sauce, would not have offered much contrast of color, but would certainly have provided diners with several contrasting textures. The tasters who sampled this dish found it very appetizing, both on the night it was first served and afterward as leftovers in sandwiches.

Take a rump of beef, cut it off the bone, cut it across, flour it, fry the thin part brown in butter, the thick end stuff with suet, boiled chesnuts, an anchovy, an onion, and a little pepper. Stew it in a pan of strong broth, and when it is tender, lay both the fried and stewed together in your dish; cut the fried in two and lay on each side of the stewed, strain the gravy it was stewed in, put to it some pickled gerkins chopped, and boiled chestnuts, thicken it with a piece of butter rolled in flour, a spoonful of browning, give it two or three boils up, season it with salt to your palate, and pour it over the beef. Garnish with lemon.

MODERN RECIPE

1 rump roast, 3 to 4 lbs.	4 T butter
1 cup beef suet, finely chopped	2 dill pickles, finely chopped
¾ cup finely chopped or crumbled chestnuts	½ cup whole peeled chestnuts
1 anchovy filet, finely chopped	2 T butter rolled in and mixed with 1 T flour*
1 onion, finely chopped	
pepper to taste	1 T **browning**
2 cups beef **broth**, or **cullis**	salt to taste
flour	lemons for garnish (optional)

Cut about a fifth of the roast off one end and about a fifth off the other end. Keep these pieces cool in the refrigerator while you prepare the center section.

Set the center section on one cut edge and make a slit through the interior of the piece of meat. The cut should be made as if you intended to cut the meat in half, but should stop about 1" away from each edge. (See diagram.) Place the meat on a piece of plastic wrap or parchment paper and open it around the cut so that it forms a wide "O."

In a medium-sized bowl, mix the suet, chopped chestnuts, anchovy, onion, and pepper. Stuff the interior of the "O" with this mixture. Using the plastic wrap or parchment paper to keep the stuffing from falling out the bottom, lift the stuffed meat into a covered pot just large enough to hold it comfortably. Lay the beef in the pan

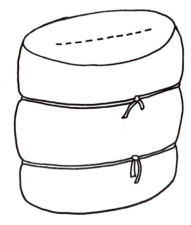

Slit diagram for Portugal beef. (KO)

with the bottom side down (in other words, meat-side-down, as opposed to stuffing-side-down). Pour in the broth and heat over medium until the liquid begins to boil. Reduce heat to medium low, cover, and simmer gently until meat is tender (about 1 to 1½ hours).

When the stewed meat nears completion, melt 4 T butter in a skillet over medium heat and dredge the reserved pieces of beef in flour. Fry the meat in the butter, turning every few minutes until all sides are nicely browned. Remove to a serving platter and keep warm.

When the stewing beef is done, place it on the center of the serving platter between the two fried sections of the roast. Continue to keep warm.

Strain the sauce, return it to the pot over medium-low heat, and add the pickles and whole chestnuts. When the pickles and chestnuts are warm, add the butter rolled in flour and stir until

Continued on next page

Continued from previous page

the butter is melted and the sauce begins to thicken. Add the browning and raise the heat to medium. Season with salt to taste. When the sauce begins to bubble, pour it around the beef on the serving platter, garnish with lemon quarters if desired, and serve immediately.

See Appendix 1: "What's with All the Butter?"

❧ BEEF FRICANDO ❧

(Raffald)

A veal fricando was made in almost exactly the same way. It began with steaks ½"
thick and used similar seasonings and garnishes. The half lemon can be augmented by
a little lemon pickle if you like.

Cut a few slices of beef five or six inches long and half an inch thick, lard it with bacon, dredge it well with flour and set it before a brisk fire to brown. Then put it in a tossing pan with a quart of gravy, a few morels and truffles, half a lemon, and stew them half an hour. Then add one spoonful of catchup, the same of browning and a little Chyan. Thicken your sauce and pour it over your fricando. Lay round them forcemeat balls and the yolks of hard eggs.

❧ MODERN RECIPE

1 London broil steak, about 1½ lbs.	half a lemon
6 slices bacon	1 T **walnut ketchup** or **mushroom ketchup**
flour for dredging	1 T **browning**
4 cups **gravy**	½ tsp. cayenne pepper
6 morels	1 recipe **force-meat balls**
2 truffles, sliced	6 hard-boiled egg yolks

Continued on next page

Continued from previous page

Slice the steak crosswise into ½"-thick slices. Lay the bacon slices over the bottom of a skillet (preferably nonstick) over medium-high heat. Dredge the beef slices in flour and lay them on top of the bacon. Brown the beef on both sides, about 3 minutes per side.

Discard the bacon. Place the beef in a saucepan with the gravy, morels, truffles, and lemon. Cover and simmer over medium-low heat for 30 minutes.

Uncover, add the ketchup, browning, and cayenne, and stir over medium heat until the sauce thickens, about 5 to 10 minutes. Transfer to a serving platter and garnish with the force-meat balls and egg yolks.

THE INSIDE OF A COLD SIRLOIN OF BEEF

(Glasse)

Another fatty, delicious dish brought to you courtesy of the eighteenth century. This one was a big hit with the tasters. The anchovy, which I thought would be noticeable in the sauce, faded very much into the background; if you want a distinct anchovy flavor in the sauce, I suggest using a whole filet or even one and a half.

Cut out all the inside (free from fat) of the sirloin in pieces as thick as your finger and about two inches long, dredge it with a little flour, and fry it in nice butter of a light brown, then drain it, and toss it up in rich gravy that has been well seasoned with pepper, salt, shallot, and an anchovy; just before you send it up, add two spoonfuls of vinegar taken from pickled capers; garnish with fried oysters, or what you please.

MODERN RECIPE

2 to 3 lbs. of previously roasted beef (Glasse calls for sirloin, but we used a roast round of beef, which was much cheaper and still tasted terrific.)

1 stick (8 T) butter

flour

pepper to taste

2 cups beef stock (if unsalted, add salt to taste)

2 large shallots, coarsely chopped

Continued on next page

Continued from previous page

½ anchovy filet, coarsely chopped

capers or fried oysters (optional)

2 T liquid from a jar of capers

Slice the beef roast ½" to ¾" thick. Trim these slabs into strips ¾" wide and about 2" long; trim off any gristly, fatty, or burned bits; reserve any of these bits that are not too fatty. Toss the beef pieces in the flour and set aside.

Put the beef stock in a small saucepan and add the shallots, anchovy, pepper, salt (if using), and any reserved beef trimmings. Simmer for 20 to 30 minutes, reducing the liquid slightly.

Melt the butter in a large nonstick skillet and add the beef slices. If they are sticky, toss them again in flour and shake off any excess before frying. Turn the beef slices until they are browned on all sides.

While the beef is browning, strain the sauce and keep warm. You may some of the leftover flour to thicken it if you like.

Place beef in a mound in the center of a platter. Stir the caper liquid into the sauce and pour the sauce onto the platter around the beef slices. Garnish with capers or fried oysters at the edges of the platter.

❀ FRICASSEE OF SWEETBREADS ❀

(Millington)

The baked apples and biscuits, excellent in their way, you know; but there was a delicate fricassee of sweetbread and some asparagus brought in at first, and good Mr. Woodhouse, not thinking the asparagus quite boiled enough, sent it all out again. (*E* 329)

The sweetbreads are the thymus glands of immature animals such as calves. When prepared properly, they have a rich, buttery taste. This recipe tastes very good in combination with the **stewed cabbage***.*

Scald the sweetbreads and cut them into slices. Beat up the yolk of an egg very fine, with a little flour, pepper, salt, and nutmeg. Dip the slices of sweetbread into this, and fry them of a nice light brown. Then thicken a little good gravy with some flour; boil it well, and add catsup or mushroom powder, a little juice of a lemon, and Cayenne pepper. Put the sweetbreads into this, and when they have stewed in it about five minutes, put the whole into the dish, and serve it up. Garnish with sliced lemon.

MODERN RECIPE

2 lbs. sweetbreads	**Sauce**
2 egg yolks plus 1 whole egg beaten together	1½ cups **gravy**
½ T flour	1 tsp. lemon juice
¼ tsp. ground nutmeg	¼ tsp. cayenne pepper
butter for frying	dash of **walnut ketchup** or pinch of **mushroom powder**
chopped parsley for garnish	

Scald sweetbreads in boiling water and quickly remove them to a bowl of ice water after. (Some modern cookbooks suggest scalding the sweetbreads in milk; this is really for maintaining a white color only and is not strictly necessary.) Take out as much of the white membranes as possible with a sharp paring knife or kitchen scissors. After all the sweetbreads have been thus cleaned, place them together in a small deep pan (such as a loaf pan) with a weight on them to squeeze out as much water as possible. Let it rest in this fashion for at least 1 hour. Slice the sweetbreads.

Melt 1 T butter in a skillet over medium heat. Beat the egg yolks and whole egg well; then stir in the flour, nutmeg, and salt and pepper to taste. Dip the sweetbreads into this batter and fry them in the butter. When the sweetbreads have turned a golden brown on both sides, remove and set aside. Be careful not to overcook them or they can become tough, rubbery, and even chalky to the taste. Work in batches, melting 1 T butter for frying each batch.

Meanwhile, make the sauce. Mix all ingredients in a saucepan, heat through, and adjust seasonings. Add the sweetbreads and garnish with chopped parsley.

 VEAL CUTLETS

(Farley)

Mrs. Jennings . . . was . . . only disturbed that she could not make them choose their own dinners at the inn, nor extort a confession of their preferring salmon to cod, or boiled fowls to veal cutlets. (*S&S* 160)

Cut your veal into pieces about the thickness of half a crown, and as long as you please. Dip them in the yolk of an egg, and strew over them crumbs of bread, a few sweet herbs, some lemon-peel, and a little grated nutmeg, and fry them in fresh butter. While they are frying, make a little gravy, and when the meat be done, take it out, and lay it in a dish before the fire; then shake a little flour into the pan, and stir it round. Put in a little gravy, squeeze in a little lemon, and pour it over the veal. Make use of lemon for your garnish.

MODERN RECIPE

2 lbs. veal scallopini	½ T finely grated lemon zest
2 egg yolks	½ tsp. grated nutmeg
1 cup bread crumbs	4 T butter
1 tsp. dried or 2 tsp. chopped fresh oregano	¾ cup beef **broth** or **cullis**
1 tsp. dried or 2 tsp. chopped fresh parsley	1 T flour
½ tsp. dried or 1 tsp. chopped fresh marjoram	1 lemon

Cut the veal into pieces about 2" to 3" square. Pound them with a kitchen mallet until they are about half their original thickness.

In one bowl, beat the egg yolks lightly with a fork. In another, mix the bread crumbs, herbs, lemon zest, and nutmeg. Dip the veal slices in the egg yolk and then coat them with the bread-crumb mixture.

In a skillet, melt the butter over medium heat. Fry the veal slices in a single layer until well browned on both sides (about 5 minutes per side). Remove to a platter and keep warm.

Add the beef broth to the skillet. When it is warm, sprinkle the flour over the surface of the liquid and whisk until smooth. Squeeze the lemon, strain the seeds, and add the lemon juice to the sauce. Pour the sauce around the veal slices on the platter and serve immediately.

❈ MINCED VEAL ❈

(Raffald)

We spent a very pleasant Day, and had a very good Dinner, tho' to be sure the Veal was terribly underdone, and the Curry had no seasoning. I could not help wishing all dinner-time that I had been at the dressing it—. (*Lesley, MW* 121)

Cut your veal in slices, then cut it in little square bits, don't chop it. Put it into a saucepan with two or three spoonfuls of gravy, a slice of lemon, a little pepper and salt, a good lump of butter rolled in flour, a teaspoonful of lemon pickle, and a large spoonful of cream. Keep shaking it over the fire till it boils, but don't let it boil above a minute, if you do it will make your veal eat hard. Put sippets round your dish and serve it up.

MODERN RECIPE

2 lbs. veal, cut into ½" to ¾" cubes (either uncooked or previously cooked can be used)

3 T beef broth

1 slice of lemon

½ tsp. pepper

1 tsp. salt

3 T butter rolled in and mixed with 1½ T butter*

1 tsp. **lemon pickle**

1½ T heavy whipping cream

¾ cup water (optional)

4 T butter

several pieces of white bread, about the size of a third of a sandwich slice

In a skillet, melt the butter over medium-high heat. As soon as it starts to sizzle, add the slices of bread, frying them golden brown on both sides. These are the "sippets." Set these aside.

Put all the ingredients in a saucepan over medium-low heat. If you are using uncooked veal, add the optional water. Cook for 5 minutes if using cooked veal or 15 minutes if using uncooked. Remove the lemon slice, arrange the sippets around the edge of a dish, and pour the minced veal in the center.

*See *Appendix 1: "What's with All the Butter?"*

PETIT PASTIES

(Glasse)

These miniature pasties would have been used as a garnish around a meat or fish dish. They are also excellent on their own with a variety of condiments such as chutney, steak sauce, Caribbean jerk sauces, and virtually any sauce normally served as an accompaniment to meat.

Make a short crust, roll it thick, make them about as big as the bowl of a spoon and about an inch deep; take a piece of veal, enough to fill the patty, as much bacon and beef-suet, shred them all very fine, season them with pepper and salt, and a little sweet herbs; put them into a little stew-pan, keep turning them about, with a few mushrooms chopped small, for eight or ten minutes; then fill your petty-patties and cover them with some crust; colour them with the yolk of an egg, and bake them. Sometimes fill them with oysters for fish, or the melts of the fish pounded, and seasoned with pepper and salt; fill them with lobsters, or what you fancy. They make a fine garnishing, and give a dish a fine look: if for a calf's head, the brains seasoned is most proper, and some with oysters.

 MODERN RECIPE

1 recipe **puff paste**	1 T chopped fresh tarragon
1 lb. ground veal	1 T chopped fresh oregano
3 slices thick-cut bacon, finely chopped	½ cup chopped fresh parsley
1½ tsp. salt	3 or 4 brown or white button mushrooms, finely chopped
½ tsp. black pepper	3 egg yolks

Prepare the puff paste and set aside under a kitchen towel. Preheat the oven to 400°F.

In a bowl, combine the veal, bacon, salt, pepper, tarragon, oregano, parsley, and mushrooms. Brown this mixture in a large skillet over medium heat, stirring frequently and breaking up any clumps of ground veal. When the veal is cooked thoroughly (about 10 minutes), drain off the fat.

Roll out the puff paste between ⅛" and ¼" thick. Using a cookie cutter or a knife, cut several 3" circles of pastry. Place a tablespoon of filling in each one, fold it over to form a semicircle, and pinch the seal closed. Place the pasties on a baking sheet lined with parchment paper or a non-stick liner.

Brush the pasties with egg yolk and cook at 400°F until golden-brown, about 15 to 20 minutes. Serve warm or at room temperature, but don't leave them out at room temperature for more than a couple of hours.

SCOTCH COLLOPS À LA FRANÇOISE

(Glasse)

She says there was hardly any veal to be got at market this morning, it is so uncommonly scarce. (*NA* 68)

Take a leg of veal, cut it very thin, lard it with bacon, then take half a pint of ale boiling, and pour over it till the blood is out, and then pour the ale into a bason;

take a few sweet herbs chopped small, strew them over the veal, and fry it in butter, flour it a little till enough, then pour it into a dish, and pour the butter away, toast little thin pieces of bacon and lay round, pour the ale into the stew-pan with two anchovies, then beat up the yolks of two eggs and stir in, with a little nutmeg, some pepper, and a piece of butter; shake all together till thick, and then pour it into the dish. Garnish with lemon.

MODERN RECIPE

2 lbs. veal scallopini	flour
8 slices bacon	2 anchovy filets
1 cup beer	2 egg yolks, lightly beaten
1 tsp. dried or 2 tsp. chopped fresh oregano	¼ tsp. nutmeg
1 tsp. dried or 2 tsp. chopped fresh parsley	½ tsp. black pepper
1 tsp. dried or 2 tsp. chopped fresh marjoram	1 lemon for garnish (optional)
5 T butter, *in all*	

Cut the veal slices into pieces 1½" to 2" square and pound with a kitchen mallet until the slices are very thin. Lay the veal and bacon in a skillet in alternating layers.

In a small saucepan, bring the beer to a boil and pour it over the veal and bacon. Let sit for 10 minutes, then pour the liquid off into a bowl. Set the bacon slices aside.

Mix the oregano, parsley, and marjoram. Pat this mixture onto both sides of the veal slices.

Melt 4 T of the butter in a large skillet over medium heat. Add the veal slices in a single layer, working in multiple batches if necessary. Brown the slices on both sides (about 1 to 2 minutes per side) and remove them to a plate, sprinkling both sides lightly with flour. When all the veal is cooked, wipe the remaining butter out of the pan and add the bacon, frying over medium heat till crisp. Remove the veal to the center of a platter. Crumble the bacon lightly and arrange the pieces in a ring around the veal. Keep the platter warm while you prepare the sauce.

Wipe the bacon grease out of the skillet and add the reserved beer and anchovies. Heat over low heat 5 minutes, then add the egg yolks, whisking them rapidly to keep them from solidifying. Add the nutmeg, pepper, and 1 T butter, shaking the pan gently until the butter is completely melted. Pour the sauce around the bacon and veal and garnish with lemon, if desired.

❁ FORCE-MEAT BALLS ❁

(Glasse)

Cooks made several different types of forcemeat, which was then used in one a several ways. It could be used as a stuffing or as a layer in a multilayer dish; one recipe uses it between the leaves of a boiled cabbage. Forcemeat was also used to make round or cylindrical decorations for other dishes—eighteenth-century meatballs.

Take half a pound of veal, and half a pound of suet, cut fine, and beat in a marble mortar or wooden bowl; have a few sweet herbs and parsley shred fine, a little mace dried and beat fine, a small nutmeg grated, or half a large one, a little lemon-peel cut fine, a little pepper and salt, and the yolks of two eggs; mix all these well together, then roll them in little round balls, and some in little long balls; roll them in flour, and fry them brown. If they are for any thing of white sauce, put a little water in a sauce-pan, and when the water boils put them in, and let them boil a few minutes, but never fry them for white sauce.

❧ MODERN RECIPE

1½ lbs. ground veal	¼ tsp. mace
1 anchovy filet, minced*	¾ tsp. nutmeg
½ cup bread crumbs*	zest of one lemon
1 egg yolk*	½ tsp. pepper
1 tsp. tarragon	1 tsp. salt
½ tsp. sage	flour
1 tsp. thyme	butter or water for cooking
2 T parsley	

Mix all ingredients together in a mixing bowl. If you are using the forcemeat as a stuffing or layer, proceed as directed in the other recipe. If you are using the forcemeat as a garnish, roll the meat into balls about 1" in diameter or into tubes about ¾" thick and 2" long. Roll in flour and fry in butter (for dishes served with a brown sauce) or boil (for dishes served with a white sauce).

*Glasse does not include this ingredient in her principal recipe for force-meat balls, but she does include it in the forcemeat for her **chicken pie**. Consider it optional.

 PANFRETTES

(The French Family Cook)

Cut slices of veal about the size of two fingers, and at least as long as three; beat them with a cleaver till they are no thicker than a crown-piece, and put upon every slice some stuffing made of veal, or any kind of meat you choose, beef suet, a little parsley, scallions, and a shalot. When the whole is minced, add the yolks of two eggs, half a kitchen spoon full of brandy, salt and pepper; spread it over the veal and roll it, cover each piece with a thin slice of bacon, and tie it; then put them upon the spit covered with paper, and when they are enough, grate bread over them, and brown them at a clear fire: serve them with a clear gravy sauce agreeably seasoned.

MODERN RECIPE

8 thin slices veal	1 large shallot, minced
1 lb. bacon	2 egg yolks
1 lb. ground veal	1 T brandy
3 oz. chopped beef fat	½ tsp. salt
1 cup chopped parsley	½ tsp. pepper
¾ cup finely chopped scallions	¼ cup bread crumbs

Preheat oven to 425°F. Flatten the veal slices with a mallet. Combine all the other ingredients except the bacon and the bread crumbs in a mixing bowl. Lay a slice or two of bacon side by side on a plate or other work surface, folding the bacon over if necessary so that it is about as long, or a little longer, than the longest edge of one of your slices of veal. Lay the veal on top, and cover the veal almost all the way to the edges with a layer of the ground-veal mixture. Starting at one of the short sides, roll up the bacon, veal, and stuffing, jelly-roll-fashion, and set it in a baking dish or pan. (The original recipe recommended tying the panfrettes with string, but I found this step to be unnecessary. You only need to do this if your rolls show signs of unwrapping themselves.)

Bake the panfrettes until they are well browned and cooked through, about 25 minutes. Then scatter the bread crumbs over them and cook for another 5 minutes.

4

MUTTON AND LAMB

Beef may have been the most prized of all meats, but England was a wool-producing nation with a long history of raising sheep. Jane's father was among the many farmers who kept a flock of sheep, and mutton was frequently served at Steventon Rectory. Mutton appears frequently in the diaries of Parson Woodforde, usually at dinner, which was the meal he most often described:

JANUARY 28, 1780	"a Saddle of Mutton rosted on the Side Table"
MARCH 8, 1780	"some hash Mutton"
MAY 17, 1781	"a Neck of Mutton boiled"
MAY 14, 1782	"a Leg of Mutton rosted with sweet Sauce"
DECEMBER 3, 1782	"a Leg of Mutton boiled and Capers"
AUGUST 5, 1783	"a Saddle of Mutton tosted"
NOVEMBER 30, 1784	"a Leg of Mutton boiled and Capers"
DECEMBER 19, 1785	"a Saddle of Mutton"
JUNE 2, 1786	"a Leg of Mutton rosted"
NOVEMBER 7, 1788	"Saddle Mutton roasted"
FEBRUARY 29, 1788	"Mutton Stakes"
JANUARY 1, 1790	"a boiled Leg of Mutton and Capers"
JULY 14, 1791	"Shoulder Mutton rosted"

He also mentions eating lamb, though it appears less frequently than mutton:

JANUARY 7, 1783	"a fore Qr. [quarter] of London Lamb"
APRIL 30, 1783	"a Leg of Lam[b] boiled"
MAY 26, 1784	"a fore Qr. of Lamb rosted"
JULY 2, 1784	"Lamb-Stakes" (as part of a cold supper)
JUNE 10, 1786	"a fore Qr of Lamb"
APRIL 17, 1787	"a fine Fore Quarter of Lamb"

The primary reason for the less frequent appearance of lamb is its availability. "House lamb," lamb specially raised in pens, was available from November to March, while "grass lamb," young lamb still drinking milk from a pasture-fed ewe, was only available from April to September. Grass lamb was younger, more

The Dinner Spoil'd!, 1799. A husband proclaims the meat "not fit to eat" and grumbles, "These are the blessed effects of boiling Mutton in a cloth!" Boiling meat in a cloth was, however, a standard practice and was supposed to keep the color pale—something Austen's contemporaries found aesthetically appealing. (Courtesy of the Lewis Walpole Library, Yale University. 799.10.1.3.)

tender, and fed on the ewe's richer spring milk; thus this meat was more desirable. Woodforde and his friends tended, not surprisingly, to prefer the grass lamb, and it is in the spring that most of his references to eating lamb occur. Mutton, on the other hand, was available year-round.

In the United States, it is extremely difficult to find mutton, as consumers tend to prefer lamb. Readers in Britain or New Zealand will find it easier to locate mutton, but as mutton was simply unavailable to me, I have substituted lamb for mutton in all of the recipes below while retaining the original titles and wording of the historical recipes.

❁ BROILED MUTTON CHOPS ❁

(Farley)

... after having roasted Beef, Broiled Mutton, and Stewed Soup enough to last the new-married couple through the Honey-moon, I had the mortification of finding that I had been Roasting, Broiling, and Stewing both the Meat and Myself to no purpose. (*Lesley, MW* 112–13)

Take a loin of mutton, and cut chops from it about half an inch thick, and cut off the skin, and part of the fat. Rub your gridiron with suet as soon as it be hot, and lay on your chops. Keep turning them often, and take care that the fat which falls from them do not make the fire blaze and smoke your chops. Put them into a dish as soon as you think they be done, and rub them with butter. Slice a shalot very thin into a spoonful of water, and pour it on them with a spoonful of mushroom ketchup, and a little salt.

❧ MODERN RECIPE

6 lamb loin chops	2 T water
2 T butter	1 T **mushroom ketchup**
1 shallot, thinly sliced	½ tsp. salt

Heat the broiler or a barbecue grill. Grill or broil the lamb chops on each side to desired degree of doneness. Meanwhile, heat the water, shallot, mushroom ketchup, and salt together in a small pan. Serve the sauce in a small dish alongside the chops.

❀ SPLIT LEG OF MUTTON AND ONION SAUCE ❀

(Raffald)

I see a Leg of Mutton. (*L&F, MW* 100)

We none of us want to hear the bill of fare. A friendly meeting, and not a fine dinner, is all we have in view. A turkey or a goose, or a leg of mutton, or whatever you and your cook chuse to give us. (*MP* 215–16)

Split the leg from the shank to the end, stick a skewer in to keep the nick open, baste it with red wine till it is half roasted. Then take the wine out of the dripping pan and put to it one anchovy, set it over the fire till the anchovy is dissolved. Rub the yolk of a hard egg in a little cold butter, mix it with the wine, and put it in your sauce boat. Pour good onion sauce over the leg when it is roasted and serve it up.

MODERN RECIPE

1 leg of lamb	1 hard-boiled egg yolk
2 cups red wine	2 T butter
1 anchovy filet	1 recipe **onion sauce**

Preheat the oven to 450°F. If the leg of lamb still has the bone in, remove the bone. Once the leg is boneless, cut the meat along one side so that the piece will lie relatively flat. Place the meat on a rack in a roasting pan and pour 1 cup of the red wine over the meat. Roast for 30 minutes, basting with the pan juices every 10 minutes, and adding ⅓ of the remaining red wine at each basting.

Remove the roasting pan from the oven and drain off the pan juices. Put the juices in a saucepan and return the leg of lamb to the oven, roasting until the inner temperature registers 140°F to 160°F on a meat thermometer.

Meanwhile, add the anchovy to the pan juices and heat over medium-low. With a fork, mash the hard-boiled egg yolk together with the butter. Add the butter-egg mixture to the saucepan and stir until the butter is thoroughly dissolved.

Serve the lamb on a platter and the sauce in a sauceboat. In a separate sauceboat, serve **onion sauce**.

SHOULDER OF MUTTON SURPRISED

(Farley)

One shoulder of mutton, you know, drives another down. (*S&S* 197)

Put a shoulder of mutton, having first half boiled it, into a tossing-pan, with two quarts of veal gravy, four ounces of rice, a little beaten mace, and a teaspoonful of mushroom powder. Stew it an hour, or till the rice be enough, and then take up your mutton, and keep it hot. Put to the rice half a pint of cream, and a piece of butter rolled in flour. Then shake it well, and boil it a few minutes. Lay your mutton on the dish, and pour your gravy over it. You may garnish with either pickles or barberries.

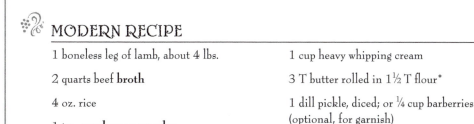

MODERN RECIPE

1 boneless leg of lamb, about 4 lbs.	1 cup heavy whipping cream
2 quarts beef **broth**	3 T butter rolled in 1½ T flour*
4 oz. rice	1 dill pickle, diced; or ¼ cup barberries (optional, for garnish)
1 tsp. **mushroom powder**	

Bring a large pot of water to a boil. Add the lamb and cook for 20 minutes. Remove the lamb and place it in a somewhat smaller pot (preferably nonstick) along with the beef broth, rice, mace, and mushroom powder. Bring the liquid to a boil over high heat, then reduce to medium-low and cook, covered, for 1 hour. Remove the lamb from the pot and set it on a serving platter.

Skim the remaining sauce. Add the cream and the floured butter to the sauce and warm over medium-high heat for 5 minutes. Pour the sauce over and around the lamb and garnish, if desired, with pickles or barberries.

*See *Appendix 1: "What's with All the Butter?"*

MUTTON KEBOBBED

(Glasse)

. . . it all ended, at last, in his telling Henry one morning, that when he next went to Woodston, they would take him by surprize there some day or other, and eat their mutton with him. (*NA* 209)

Take a loin of mutton and joint it between every bone; season it with pepper and salt moderately, grate a small nutmeg all over, dip the chops in the yolks of three eggs, and have ready crumbs of bread and sweet herbs, dip them in, and clap them together in their former shape again, and put it on a small spit; roast it before a quick fire, set a dish under, and baste it with a little piece of butter, and then keep basting with what comes from it, and throw some crumbs of bread and sweet herbs all over it while roasting; when it is enough take it up, lay it in the dish, and have ready half a pint of good made gravy and what comes from the mutton; take two spoonfuls of catchup, and mix a tea-spoonful of flour with it and put to the gravy, stir it together and give it a boil, and pour over the mutton.

MODERN RECIPE

5 lamb loin chops	1 tsp. dried or 2 tsp. chopped fresh parsley
pepper and salt to taste	1 tsp. dried or 2 tsp. chopped fresh thyme
1 tsp. grated nutmeg	4 T butter
3 egg yolks	1 cup **gravy** or **cullis**
1 cup bread crumbs	2 T **walnut ketchup**
1 tsp. dried or 2 tsp. chopped fresh oregano	1 tsp. flour

Preheat oven to 450°F. Salt and pepper the lamb chops on both sides.

In a bowl, mix the egg yolks and nutmeg. In another bowl, mix the bread crumbs, oregano, parsley, and thyme. Dip each chop in the egg yolk mixture, moistening it on all sides. Then coat it with the bread crumb mixture.

Place the chops in a roasting pan lined with aluminum foil. Arrange them standing up, largest to smallest, and pin them together by running 2 or 3 skewers through the line of chops. (If you use only one skewer, the chops will not turn properly.)

Continued on next page

Continued from previous page

Place the roasting pan in the oven and roast the chops until the underside is well browned, about 10 to 15 minutes. Melt the butter and drizzle some of it over the chops as they cook. Rotate the skewered row of chops to place a new side at the bottom and continue to roast until that side is browned, about 10 to 15 minutes more, and baste again with the remaining butter and the pan juices. Rotate once more and cook the last side, about 10 to 15 minutes. The inside of the innermost chop should register 140°F to 145°F on a meat thermometer.

When the chops are done, remove them to a serving platter and carefully extract the skewers, leaving the chops closely aligned in a row. Pour any pan juices into a saucepan and add the gravy or cullis, walnut ketchup, and flour, whisking until the flour is smoothly incorporated into the sauce. Heat the sauce until it begins to simmer, and then pour it into a sauceboat and serve alongside the platter of chops.

MUTTON HASH

(Carter)

Her father asked him to do them the honour of taking his mutton with them, and Fanny had time for only one thrill of horror, before he declared himself prevented by a prior engagement. (*MP* 406)

Samphire was a kind of coastal plant, mentioned in the works of Shakespeare and eaten in several parts of England. For the purposes of this dish, almost any type of greens will do. This hash, like all hashes, was an excellent way of using up the remains of a roast.

Take mutton half roasted, and cut it in pieces as big as a half-crown; then put into the sauce-pan half a pint of red wine, as much strong broth or gravy, (or water, if you have not the other) one anchovy, a shallot, a little whole pepper, some nutmeg grated and salt to your taste; let these stew a little, then put in the meat, and a few capers and samphire shred; when it is hot through, thicken it up with a piece of fresh butter rolled in flour; have toasted sippets ready to lay in the dish, and pour the meat on them. Garnish with lemon.

MODERN RECIPE

1½ to 2 lbs. cooked lamb or mutton	½ tsp. grated nutmeg
1 cup red wine	salt to taste
1 cup **broth**, **gravy**, or **cullis**	1 T capers
1 anchovy filet	½ cup leafy greens, roughly chopped
1 shallot, minced	2 T butter rolled in 1 T flour*
1 tsp. black peppercorns	lemon wedges for garnish (optional)

Cut the lamb or mutton into pieces about 1" square and ⅛" to ¼" thick.

In a saucepan over medium-low heat, warm the wine, broth or gravy, anchovy, shallot, pepper, nutmeg, and salt. Cook for about 10 minutes to let the flavors blend and to allow the anchovy to dissolve.

Add the sliced meat, capers, and greens. Cook just until all the ingredients are heated through. Then stir in the butter rolled in flour. Lay pieces of toasted bread on a platter. When the butter has melted and the sauce is thickened, pour the hash onto the toast. Garnish with lemon wedges, if desired.

*See *Appendix 1: "What's with All the Butter?"*

LOIN OF MUTTON À LA CONTI

(The French Family Cook)

In the moment of parting, Edmund was invited by Dr. Grant to eat his mutton with him the next day; and Fanny had barely time for an unpleasant feeling on the occasion, when Mrs. Grant, with sudden recollection, turned to her and asked for the pleasure of her company too. *(MP* 215)

Take a loin of mutton, and lift up the skin that is underneath; then take a quarter of a pound of streaked bacon well interlarded, and two anchovies washed: cut them ready for larding, and shred two shalots, parsley, scallions, half a laurel leaf, and three or four leaves of tarragon, very fine, and dip the bits of bacon and anchovies into it: lard the mutton with them, and stew it with all the herbs that remain, a glass of white wine, and the same quantity of broth, three hours over a slow fire. When it is done skim off the fat, and thicken the sauce over the fire with a little flour and butter, and serve it with the mutton.

MODERN RECIPE

Lamb loin or boned leg	1 bay leaf
¼ lb. bacon	1 tsp. dried tarragon
2 anchovy filets	1 cup white wine
2 shallots, finely chopped	1 cup beef broth
¾ cup chopped parsley	1 T flour
3 scallions, chopped, both green and white parts	2 T butter, slightly softened

In a medium-sized bowl, mix the shallots, parsley, scallions, and tarragon. Place pieces of bacon and the two anchovies, one by one, into the bowl to coat both the bacon and the anchovies with the herb mixture. Place the lamb in a deep pot with a lid and drape the bacon and anchovies over the lamb. Pour the wine and broth into the pot, add the bay leaf to the liquid, and cover tightly. Cook over medium-low heat until the internal temperature reaches 140°F to 160°F, depending on the desired degree of doneness (about 2 hours). Make sure that there is always liquid in the pot, and add more wine and broth if the liquid evaporates.

When the lamb is done, remove it to a warmed serving platter. Pour off the remaining liquid from the pot, skim off the fat, and pour the liquid into a small saucepan. Mix the 2 T butter with the 1 T flour* and melt the butter in the cooking liquid. This will thicken the sauce, and the mixing of the flour with the butter will prevent lumps from forming.

*See *Appendix 1: "What's with All the Butter?"*

ROAST SADDLE OF MUTTON

(Glasse)

. . . they were overtaken by Mr. John Knightley returning from the daily visit to Donwell, with his two eldest boys, whose healthy, glowing faces shewed all the benefit of a country run, and seemed to ensure a quick dispatch of the roast mutton and rice pudding they were hastening home for. (*E* 109)

Mr. Weston . . . made use of the very first interval in the cares of hospitality, the very first leisure from the saddle of mutton . . . . (*E* 119)

It is entirely possible that you won't be able to find mutton, let alone the saddle of mutton. (If you live in the United States, it will be practically impossible.) Therefore, this recipe has been adapted for a boneless leg of lamb. The "roast saddle" got the most enthusiastic taster reviews of all the lamb recipes included in this book.

It is the two chumps of the loins. Cut off the rump, and carefully lift up the skin with a knife: begin at the broad end, but be sure you do not crack it nor take it quite off; then take some slices of ham or bacon chopped fine, a few truffles, some young onions, some parsley, a little thyme, sweet marjoram, winter-savory, a little lemon-peel, all chopped fine, a little mace and two or three cloves beat fine, half a nutmeg, and a little pepper and salt; mix all together, and throw over the meat where you took off the skin, then lay the skin on again, and fasten it with two fine skewers at each side, and roll it in well-buttered paper. It will take two hours roasting: then take off the paper, baste the meat, strew it all over with crumbs of bread, and when it is of a fine brown take it up. For sauce take six large shalots, cut them very fine, put them into a saucepan with two spoonfuls of vinegar and two of white wine; boil them for a minute or two, pour it into the dish, and garnish with horse-radish.

 ## MODERN RECIPE

1 boneless leg of lamb, about 4½ to 5½ lbs.	pinch of ground cloves
3 slices lean bacon, finely chopped	½ tsp. ground nutmeg
⅓ cup diced mushrooms or truffles	1 tsp. black pepper
½ cup finely chopped onion	1 tsp. salt
½ cup finely chopped fresh parsley	½ cup bread crumbs
1 T finely chopped fresh thyme	6 large shallots
1 T finely chopped fresh marjoram	2 T white vinegar
½ T dried savory	2 T white wine
zest of 1 lemon	4 T grated fresh horseradish
2 tsp. ground mace	

Preheat oven to 425°F.

Working with a small, sharp knife, lift up the skin on the leg of lamb, leaving it intact on three sides to form a "pocket."

Continued on next page

Continued from previous page

In a bowl, mix the ingredients from the bacon to the pepper and salt. Stuff this mixture under the skin of the lamb. Wrap the lamb in two pieces of parchment paper—one running around it lengthwise and one running around it crosswise. Loosely tie the parchment paper in place with kitchen twine. Place the lamb in a small roasting pan and the pan in the oven and cook until the inner temperature reaches 140°F to 150°F, about 1½ to 2 hours.

Remove the paper and sprinkle the lamb with the bread crumbs. Return to the oven until the bread crumbs are brown, about 5 minutes.

Meanwhile, make the sauce. Mix the shallots, vinegar, and wine in a small saucepan and bring to a boil over medium heat. Boil for 1 minute.

Set the lamb on a serving platter and garnish with the shallot sauce and grated horseradish.

A HARRICO OF MUTTON

(Glasse)

. . . they had to listen to the description of exactly how little bread and butter she ate for breakfast, and how small a slice of mutton for dinner . . . . (*E* 168)

I mean to have some haricot mutton to-morrow. (Letter by Jane Austen, November 17, 1798)

Take a neck or loin of mutton, cut it into thick chops, flour them, and fry them brown in a little butter; take them out, and lay them to drain on a sieve, then put them into a stew-pan, and cover them with gravy; put in a whole onion and a turnip or two, and stew them till tender; then take out the chops, strain the liquor through a sieve, and skim off all the fat; put a little butter in the stew-pan and melt it, with a spoonful of flour, stir it well till it is smooth, then put the liquor in, and stir it well all the time you are pouring it, or it will be in lumps; put in your chops and a glass of Lisbon; have ready some carrot about three quarters of an inch long, and cut round with an apple-corer, some turnips cut with a turnip-scoop, a dozen small onions all blanched well; put them to your meat, and season with pepper and salt; stew them very gently for fifteen minutes, then take out the chops with a fork, lay them in your dish, and pour the ragoo over it. Garnish with beet-root. The wine may be omitted.

🌿 MODERN RECIPE

8 loin lamb chops or boneless leg of lamb sliced 1" thick	1 T flour
flour	1 cup port
5 T butter, *in all*	1 carrot, trimmed, peeled, and cut crosswise ¾" long
1½ cups beef **gravy**	12 small boiling onions, peeled
1 onion, trimmed, peeled, and quartered	pepper and salt to taste
1 turnip, trimmed and peeled	

Dip the lamb chops in flour. Melt 4 T of the butter in a deep-sided skillet or pot over medium-high heat. Working in two batches if necessary, brown the chops on both sides, about 3 minutes per side.

When all the chops are browned, set them aside on a plate and put the gravy, onion, turnip, 1 T butter, flour, and port into the pot. Stir over medium-low heat until warm, then put the chops back in, along with the carrot, onions, pepper, and salt. Cover and cook over medium-low heat for 15 minutes.

❁ LAMB CHOPS LARDED ❁

(Glasse)

It was now the middle of June, and the weather fine; and Mrs. Elton was growing impatient to name the day, and settle with Mr. Weston as to pigeon-pies and cold lamb, when a lame carriage horse threw every thing into sad uncertainty. (*E* 353)

Cut the best end of a neck of lamb into chops, and lard one side, season them with beaten cloves, mace and nutmeg, a little pepper and salt; put them into a stew-pan, the larded side uppermost; put in half a pint of gravy, a gill of white wine, an onion, a bundle of sweet herbs, stew them gently till tender; take the chops out, skim the fat clean off, and take out the onion and sweet herbs; thicken the gravy with a little butter rolled in flour, add a spoonful of browning, a spoonful of catchup, and one of lemon-pickle. Boil it up till it is smooth, put in the chops larded side down, stew them up gently for a minute or two; take the chops out and put the larded side uppermost in the dish, and the sauce over them. Garnish with lemon and pickles of any sort; you may add truffles and morels and pickled mushrooms in the sauce, if you please; or you may do the chops without larding.

MODERN RECIPE

2 to 2½ lbs. lamb chops	½ tsp. dried or 1 tsp. fresh chopped parsley
5 slices bacon	½ tsp. dried or 1 tsp. fresh chopped rosemary
¼ tsp. ground cloves	½ tsp. dried or 1 tsp. fresh chopped marjoram
¼ tsp. ground mace	2 T butter rolled in 1 T flour*
¼ tsp. ground nutmeg	1 T **browning**
½ tsp. black pepper	1 T **walnut ketchup**
1 tsp. salt	1 T **lemon pickle**
1 cup **gravy** or **cullis**	lemon for garnish (optional)
½ cup white wine	Pickled vegetables such as onions, mushrooms, or small gherkins for garnish (optional)
1 onion, quartered	

In a small bowl, mix together the cloves, mace, nutmeg, pepper, and salt. Rub this mixture onto all sides of the lamb chops. Lay them in a pot with a lid and place the bacon on top of the chops. Add the gravy or cullis, wine, onion, and herbs to the pot. Bring to a boil over medium heat and reduce the heat to medium-low. Cover and simmer gently until the chops are tender and fully cooked.

Remove the chops and bacon to a platter and skim the fat from the sauce. Add the butter rolled in flour, browning, walnut ketchup, and lemon pickle. Raise the heat to medium again and bring the sauce to a boil. Then pour the sauce into a sauceboat and serve alongside the chops.

*See *Appendix 1: "What's with All the Butter?"*

5

PORK

Pork was in many ways the most versatile and the least glamorous of the three most popular meats. It could be prepared in all the same ways as beef and mutton: boiled, baked, spit-roasted, stewed, minced in pies, salted, smoked, and so on. It also kept particularly well, when smoked and cured as ham or bacon. As bacon, indeed, it was the staple meat of the working classes; a "flitch" or large piece of bacon hung in many homes, where pieces could be hacked off as needed. Village shops also sold bacon in small quantities for those too poor to keep a substantial quantity on hand. Bacon featured in a popular annual contest, in which one English town offered a flitch of bacon to any couple who claimed to be perfectly happily married.

Parson James Woodforde often dined on pork of one variety or another. He enjoyed "Piggs Face," ham, beans and bacon, "Piggs Pettytoes," roast neck of pork, "fry" (fried internal organs of some sort, the exact identity of which varied), brawn (collared, boiled, and potted boar's flesh) and various cuts of boiled pork, including the neck. Other diners enjoyed pork sausages, in which meat and fat were mixed with eggs, wine, or water; sausages sold by butchers were often soaked in salt water, partly for the sake of preservation and partly to help the sausages maintain their weight. Some sausages were formed in links, using intestinal casings; others were made into a skinless paste, stored in pots, and taken out as needed. The paste was shaped into skinless links the length of a finger, dipped in flour or egg, and fried in suet.

CHRISTMAS IN THE COUNTRY.

Christmas in the Country, 1791. Pranks, kissing under the mistletoe, and the drinking of punch and wine were all part of Christmas merrymaking. So was the consumption of pork products such as brawn. The brawn cannot be seen in this image, but hams hang from the ceiling at the upper left. (Courtesy of the Lewis Walpole Library, Yale University. 791.1.1.2.)

 ROAST HAM

(Glasse)

... in the summer he was for ever forming parties to eat cold ham and chicken out of doors. (*S&S* 33)

My Mother and I . . . joined in heartfelt lamentations on the dreadful Waste in our provisions which this Event must occasion, and in concerting some plan for getting rid of them. We agreed that the best thing we could do was to begin eating them immediately, and accordingly we ordered up the cold Ham and Fowls, and instantly began our Devouring Plan on them with great Alacrity. (*Lesley, MW* 113–14)

The curing of hams is a complex business, worthy of a book in itself, and while I longed to explain the ins and outs of building a smokehouse, selecting curing salts, and proper smoking, there simply wasn't enough space in this volume. My readers will have to be content with using ham in other recipes rather than making their own hams from scratch, as Mrs. Austen often did. Those who cannot be content may investigate the bibliography, where they will be directed to more comprehensive information about the making of hams.

Take of the swerd, or what we call the skin, or rind, and lay it in lukewarm water for two or three hours; then lay it in a pan, pour upon it a quart of canary, and let it steep in it for ten or twelve hours. When you have spitted it, put some sheets of white paper over the fat side, pour the canary in which it was soaked in the dripping-pan, and baste it all the time it is roasting; when it is roasted enough pull off the paper, and dredge it well with crumbled bread and parsley shred fine; make the fire brisk, and brown it well. If you heat it hot, garnish it with raspings of bread: if cold, serve it on a clean napkin, and garnish it with parsley for a second course.

Or thus: take off the skin of the ham or gammon, when you have half-boiled it, and dredge it with oatmeal sifted very fine, baste it with butter, then roast it gently two hours; stir up your fire, and brown it quick; when so done, dish it up, and pour brown gravy in the dish. Garnish with bread raspings, if hot; if cold, garnish with parsley.

 ## MODERN RECIPE

1 ham, about 4 to 7 lbs.	3 cups sherry

Place the ham in a bowl and pour the sherry over it. Marinate it, refrigerated, for up to 6 hours, turning it in the sherry every hour.

Preheat the oven to 450°F. Drain off the sherry from the ham and place it in a deep skillet over high heat. When it begins to boil, carefully light a match and light the fumes. Continue to boil the sherry until the flame dies down, about 5 minutes. (*Note*: This is an important step. If you don't do this, the sherry can ignite in the oven and explode, blowing the oven door open and possibly causing damage or injury.) Pour the sherry into a roasting pan and place the ham, skin side up, in the roasting pan as well.

Roast the ham, basting it with the pan juices every half hour. Roast until the internal temperature reaches 160°F, about 1 to 2 hours, depending on the ham's size.

❧ HAM PIE ❧

(Glasse)

Lady Lucas, who had been long yawning at the repetition of delights which she saw no likelihood of sharing, was left to the comforts of cold ham and chicken. (*P&P* 100)

This is a classic Regency meat pie, in which the pastry, tasty though it is, serves chiefly as a casing for the stewing of essentially bland meats. One advantage of this method of preparation is that the meat, while virtually unspiced, stays remarkably juicy. The pastry is incredibly sturdy. Not only does it not leak, but it stays intact even after sitting out for quite a while. Once, after making this enormous pie, I lifted the entire bottom section out in one piece—tricky more because of the quantity of juice inside the crust rather than because the crust itself gave any sign of yielding under the weight. The recipe is also interesting for its method of distributing the fat throughout the pastry. Whereas now we would almost certainly blend in cold butter or shortening and then add cold water, here the liquid is heated first. I have added the liquid in two stages in order to produce a more consistent result.

Take some cold boiled ham and slice it about half an inch thick, make a good crust, and thick, over the dish, and lay a layer of ham, shake a little pepper over it, then taste a large young fowl clean picked, gutted, washed, and singed; put a little pepper and salt in the belly, and rub a very little salt on the outside; lay the fowl on the ham, boil some eggs hard, put in the yolks, and cover all with ham, then shake some pepper on the ham, and put on the top-crust; bake it well, have ready when it comes out of the oven some very rich beef gravy, enough to fill the pie; lay on the crust again, and send it to table hot: if you put two large fowls in, they will make a fine pie; but that is according to your company, more or less; the larger the pie the finer the meat eats; the crust must be the same you make for a venison pasty; you should pour a little strong gravy into the pie when you make it, just to bake the meat, and then fill it up when it comes out of the oven; boil some truffles and morels and put into your pie, which is a great addition, and some fresh mushrooms or dried ones.

MODERN RECIPE

2 lbs. cooked ham

black pepper and kosher salt

1 chicken, about 3 to 3½ lbs.

4 eggs, hard-boiled

½ cup **gravy** or **cullis**

6 oz. brown mushrooms such as brown button mushrooms or portobellos, cut in slices about 1" wide and ¼" thick

1 recipe of "**a good crust for great pies**"

Preheat the oven to 400°F.

Make the pastry. Set aside about ⅓ of the pastry and cover it to keep it from drying out. Flour a board or smooth countertop and roll the remaining ⅔ of the dough out into a very large circle, about ¾" to 1" thick. Lay the layer of dough on top of a large pan. (I used a 13" × 2" deep-dish pizza pan). If the dough is disinclined to come off the board or countertop easily, sprinkle a little flour on top, and a little more under it as you loosen it, folding back the portion of the dough that has already been gently loosened from the board or countertop. When a little more than half the dough has been loosened, you should be able to slide your pan under it gradually as you loosen the rest. You should not need to grease the pan in which you assemble the pie.

Once the pastry has been draped over the pan, press it into the corners of the pan. Let the pastry drape over the top edges of the pan and trim it with a sharp knife, leaving about 1" of pastry hanging over the top all the way around. Any extra pastry can be placed with the rest that you set aside.

Cut the ham into ½" thick slices and lay them in a single layer in the pastry. Sprinkle some pepper over the ham. Remove the giblets from the chicken, wash it inside and out, and pat it dry. Rub the inside of the chicken with pepper and salt and the outside with about a teaspoon of kosher salt. Lay the chicken in the center of the pie, on top of the ham.

Halve the hard-boiled eggs and remove the yolks. You can reserve the whites for another purpose or do what I do and feed them to the kids clamoring to know how long that enormous pie is going to take to cook. Place the egg yolks around the chicken, scatter the mushrooms around the chicken as well, and pour in the gravy or cullis. If you have any ham left over, lay the remaining slices on top of the mushrooms and egg yolks, leaning them against the sides of the chicken.

Roll out the reserved pastry ¾" to 1" thick. Lay the sheet of pastry over the pie and trim the edges so that about ¾" to 1" extends beyond the top edge of the pan and rests loosely on the edges of the bottom crust. Do not pinch the top and bottom crust together.

Place the pie in the center of the oven. After about 1 hour, you can remove the pie from the oven and, using a spatula or two, carefully lift one side of the top crust. Test the chicken's temperature at the inner thigh. It should register 180°F on a meat thermometer. If it does not, replace the pie in the oven. The pie may take as much as 2 hours to bake. If the crust begins to brown too fast around the edges or on top, cover the affected areas with aluminum foil or parchment paper.

Continued on next page

Continued from previous page

To serve, take the entire pie to the table with a separate large platter next to it. Using spatulas (or your hands, if you feel extra confident and showy), lift off the top crust and expose the steaming filling. The chicken can be carved and portions of the remaining filling served out; the top crust can be cut up on its platter and doled out in small portions to your guests.

Note: The assumption was that more gravy would be added to the pie just before serving, and you may certainly do this, but my experience with this particular pie is that it requires no added liquid at the end. The juices present in the chicken, ham, mushrooms, gravy, and in the crust itself make a rich broth that requires little amendment.

❁ LIVER AND CROW ❁

(Ellis)

MISS F. Take away the Liver & Crow & bring in the suet pudding. (*Visit, MW* 53)

This dish presents us with some difficulties, for none of the major cookbook authors of the later eighteenth century seem to have included a recipe for it. Indeed, since they frequently plagiarize from one another, adding a handful of original recipes to enliven a new cookbook, and slightly rewording hundreds of others culled from competitive cookbooks, the researcher encounters the same frustratingly similar description over and over. Hannah Glasse writes of bacon hogs, "The liver and crow is much admired fried with bacon; the feet and ears are both equally good soused." Charles Millington and John Farley phrase it in precisely the same words. This is typically the only reference to the dish in standard eighteenth-century cookbooks, which explains why some critics have been perplexed by the reference to "crow" in the above quotation, thinking it perhaps to be a reference to the actual bird—or to some sort of bird, at any rate. Clearly, liver and crow was a well-known dish to Austen's contemporaries, so well known that an explanation of its preparation seemed unnecessary.

In order to find a full recipe for the dish, we need to go back to the mid-eighteenth century, to a useful book by William Ellis, The Country Housewife's Family Companion *(1750). This volume is only in part a cookbook; in many other respects it is a complete guide to being a farm wife, with extensive sections on keeping the dairy and curing cattle of disease, caring for poultry, processing wheat and storing flour, and doctoring the family and servants. There is an explicit emphasis on frugality, and many of the recipes are specifically identified as being for "poor people," while only one is directed at "the gentry." French names for styles of preparation, always an indicator of fashion, are absent, but perhaps the strongest evidence that this was a cookbook for the working classes was the almost total reliance on pork as meat. There are plenty of directions for preparing bacon, brawn, and pig's innards, but only a handful of recipes for beef and mutton, and the references to beef are entirely about using calf guts. The presence of not one but two recipes for liver and crow in this volume confirms our suspicions about the dishes in* The Visit *being deliberately chosen for their humorous incongruity on a genteel table.*

Ellis offers two ways of preparing the pig's liver and its "crow"—its intestines or its mesentery (a piece of tissue adjacent to the stomach and intestines). Either method was quick and used few ingredients, just the sort of meal a woman might cook after she had spent a tiring day helping to slaughter a bacon hog.

An obvious problem for the modern cook is how to get one's hands on pig liver and mesentery. Unless you have an extraordinarily well-connected butcher, or happen to raise pigs yourself, you will find this difficult to do. In deference to this difficulty, I have substituted thin strips of pork sirloin, which work very well. Should you find yourself unexpectedly in possession of actual *liver and crow, you may, of course, cleave to the original historical recipe.*

The sauce dictated in this recipe is very simple and tastes especially good with many other Regency recipes, including that for **veal cutlets**.

The liver, the crow, and the sweet-bread, is the first meat we dress of a hog, for this sort is fit for frying as soon as it is cut out; our farmers wives therefore make no more to do in dressing this, than to cut the liver, the crow, and the sweet-bread, in pieces about two or three inches square, and fry them in the same fat the crow yields; and if they prove too thick she cuts them thinner. When fry'd enough, it is eaten with mustard for an agreeable dinner to a whole family.—A second way to fry liver and crow is, to cut the liver into short thick pieces, because being short and thick they will fry the tenderer, but the sweet-bread and crow rather long ways, about the same bigness; then soak the pieces of liver first in scalding water, and while this is doing, make a composition with eggs, water, flower, salt, shred sage, pepper, and grated bread; in which dip all the pieces of meat, and fry them in lard or butter, over a quick fire. For sauce, melt butter, and mix it with sugar and mustard.

MODERN RECIPE

1¼ lbs. thinly sliced pork sirloin	**Sauce**
2 eggs	2 T butter
¼ cup water	1 T sugar
¼ cup flour	4 T prepared mustard
2 T finely chopped fresh or 1 T dried sage	
2 T bread crumbs	
¼ lb. lard	

In a bowl, mix the eggs, water, flour, sage, and bread crumbs. Melt the lard in a skillet over medium heat.

Dip the pork slices into the batter and fry in the lard until golden brown on both sides, about 3 to 4 minutes per side. Drain on paper towels and keep warm.

Meanwhile, melt the butter in a small saucepan and blend in the sugar and mustard. Stir over medium-low heat for 2 to 3 minutes, then serve alongside the pork.

BRAWN

(Beeton, Ellis)

On one side was a table, occupied by some chattering girls, cutting up silk and gold paper; and on the other were tressels and trays, bending under the weight of brawn and cold pies, where riotous boys were holding high revel; the whole completed by a roaring Christmas fire, which seemed determined to be heard, in spite of the noise of the others. (*P* 134)

Brawn was preserved pork, noted both for its longevity and for the thick rind that surrounded it. It was made from a bacon hog, an adult and frequently enormous pig, whose legs would be cured as hams, whose sides would become bacon, and whose head and jellied feet became brawn. Such hogs were traditionally slaughtered in November, and the brawn, which could keep for weeks or even months, became a Christmas staple.

When it was steeped in brine, wine, ale, or verjuice (the soured juice of unripe grapes), brawn became "souse," referred to in a 1799 letter of Jane's to Cassandra regarding the killing of a pig from the farm the Austens leased at Cheesedown:

My father furnishes him [their youngest brother Charles, who was going to sea as a second lieutenant] with a pig from Cheesedown; it is already killed and cut up, but it is not to weigh more than nine stone; the season is too far advanced to get him a larger one. My mother means to pay herself for the salt and the trouble of ordering it to be cured by the spar[er]ibs, the souse, and the lard.

This letter was written in late January, so the really big bacon hogs would all have been slaughtered already, hence Jane's reference to the pig's comparatively small size.

The problem with reproducing brawn in a modern kitchen is the lack of the essential parts of the pig. Try going into a modern grocery store and asking for pig's head, pig's belly, and ox feet; the people behind the butcher's counter are liable to look at you with a mixture of dismay, pity, irritation, and bewilderment. Don't you know, they will be asking themselves (and sometimes you), that such bits get made up into sausage? Therefore, the modern cook is forced to improvise.

First, forget the belly. Unless you're butchering the pig yourself, you're not going to find something like it. This unfortunately means no rind—and the rind was generally how Regency shoppers judged the freshness of brawn that they purchased rather than made at home. Second, forget the head (and possibly the feet). It's a rare butcher indeed these days who will supply you with ox or calf feet, or even with unpickled pigs' feet. You'll need to substitute another meat rich in fat and connective tissue; I've chosen spareribs (not the expensive baby back ribs, just plain old cheap spareribs) and beef short ribs.

Almost every cookbook author of the time included at least one recipe for brawn or "mock brawn." The difference between the two was that true brawn was made with the haunches of the pig, while mock brawn was made with less desirable pieces and usually with a little beef thrown in as well. In each, the meat was boiled until it could be easily pulled off the bone, chopped finely, rolled up somehow, and then pressed until it was hard. Seasoning varied. John Farley simply cured the head and belly in saltpeter and then stored the whole brawn in a salt-and-water brine. Hannah Glasse made collared swine's face, a similar dish, with salt and pepper. William Ellis, writing in the mid-eighteenth century, used pepper, cloves, mace, nutmeg, and salt, and Mrs. Beeton, writing in 1865, used nearly identical spices.

Methods of rolling the mock brawn varied as well. The belly itself, "tapes," sheet tin, and earthenware pots were all used to keep the brawn compressed into the proper shape. By Beeton's time, special brawn tins were available for the purpose. Modern cooks may use a variety of containers for pressing the brawn. A coffee can, a large canister, even a sturdy plastic storage bowl, can all be employed. The trick is not so much the container as having the proper "follower." The follower is a flat disc that just barely fits into the brawn container. Weights will be piled on top of this follower in order to compress the brawn, and if the follower is too small, bits of meat will seep

out around the edges. In a pinch, a small plate or saucer can be used, but a flat follower is best.

The pressing of the brawn raises another problem for modern cooks. Housekeepers
in Austen's day pressed the brawn at room temperature, albeit at a cool room temperature. They assumed that the salt or saltpeter used in preparing the brawn would act as
a preservative. This was probably true to some extent, but it was necessity rather than
preference that kept them from refrigerating their brawn. Leaving any meat out at
room temperature for extended periods of time makes me nervous, even if it is part of a
traditional method of preparation. When I make brawn, therefore, I do only the first
part of the pressing at room temperature and the remainder in the refrigerator for the
sake of safety.

In the following recipe, I have chosen to adhere most closely to Isabella Beeton's instructions. Even though her cookbook was published decades after the Regency, its directions are the most specific and do not rely on the use of the belly as a wrapping. I
have also included, for the purposes of comparison, William Ellis's recipe, which was directed to country housewives.

Beeton's Recipe

To a pig's head weighing 6 lbs. allow 1½ lb. lean beef, 2 tablespoonfuls of salt,
2 teaspoonfuls of pepper, a little cayenne, 6 pounded cloves. Mode—Cut off
the cheeks and salt them, unless the head be small, when all may be used. After
carefully cleaning the head, put it on in sufficient cold water to cover it, with
the beef, and skim it just before it boils. A head weighing 6 lbs. will require
boiling from 2 to 3 hours. When sufficiently boiled to come off the bones easily, put it into a hot pan, remove the bones, and chop the meat with a sharp
knife before the fire, together with the beef. It is necessary to do this as quickly
as possible to prevent the fat settling in it. Sprinkle in the seasoning, which
should have been previously mixed. Stir it well and put it quickly into a brawn-
tin if you have one; if not, a cake-tin or mould will answer the purpose, if the
meat is well pressed with weights, which must not be removed for several hours.
When quite cold, dip the tin into boiling water for a minute or two, and the
preparation will turn out and be fit for use.

Ellis's Recipe

. . . take two buttocks, and hang them up two or three days, then take them down
and dip them in hot water, pluck off the skin, and dry them very well with a
clean cloth. When you have so done, take lard (that is to say, the flair of a hog)
cut it in pieces as big as your little finger, and season it very well with pepper,
cloves, mace, nutmeg, and salt; put each of them into an earthen pot; then add a

pint of claret wine, and a pound of mutton suet, and so close it with paste. Let the oven be well heated, and so bake them. You must give time for their baking, according to the bigness of the haunches and the thickness of the pots; they commonly allot seven hours for the baking of them. Let them stand three days, then take off the cover, and pour away all their liquor; then have clarify'd butter, and fill up both the pots to keep it for use. It will thus keep very well two or three months.—This is to be cut out in slices at pleasure, and eaten with vinegar or mustard is excellent.

 ## MODERN RECIPE

6 lbs. pork spareribs	2 tsp. black pepper
1½ lbs. beef short ribs	¼ tsp. cayenne pepper
2 T kosher salt	½ tsp. ground cloves

Place the pork ribs and beef ribs in a large stock pot and cover with water. Bring the water to a boil and reduce the heat slightly, boiling the ribs for 2½ hours, and adding more water as necessary to keep the meat covered. As the meat boils, skim off the foamy scum that rises. (A small fine-mesh strainer works best for this.) Meanwhile, mix the spices together in a small bowl.

Remove the meat from the pot, pull it off the bones, and chop or pull it into small pieces. The broth in which it was cooked can be cooled, skimmed of fat, and used as a broth or stock for soups. (Beeton specifically recommended it for making pea soup.)

Toss the chopped meat with the spices, mixing thoroughly. Place the meat mixture in a container and place the follower on top. Balance a sturdy mug or ramekin on top of the follower and a plate on top of that. Then place something heavy on top of the plate. The cup or ramekin allows the meat to be compressed below the top of the container.*

Press the brawn for 1 hour in a cool room. Then move the pressing apparatus to a refrigerator and continue to press for several hours. When pressing is complete, remove the follower and weights and cover the brawn container. Refrigerate overnight.

Remove the brawn from its container, warming the outside of the container if necessary to loosen the brawn around the edges. If this fails, run a knife around the sides of the container. Slide the brawn out of its container and onto a serving platter. Slice and serve cold or at room temperature with vinegar and/or mustard.

*The pressing of brawn, in the absence of a special brawn tin, requires a little improvisation and care. When I make brawn, I use a ramekin on top of my follower, a wide plate on that, and a heavy canister filled with 10 pounds of rice centered on the plate. I've also used a plastic-and-metal cheese press, which works extremely well, but which requires an investment in a special tool—not necessarily what everyone would want to do.

❈ PORK CHOPS ❈

(Farley)

> Now we have killed a porker, and Emma thinks of sending them a loin or a leg; it is very small and delicate—Hartfield pork is not like any other pork—but still it is pork—and, my dear Emma, unless one could be sure of their making it into steaks, nicely fried, as our's are fried, without the smallest grease. (*E* 172)

Mr. Woodhouse's claim that "Hartfield pork is not like any other pork" sounds fanciful and even a little mad to modern ears. Our livestock breeds have grown so standardized that the idea of one pig tasting substantially different from another is almost inconceivable. But in the early nineteenth century, there were strong differences between animals from region to region, and even from farm to farm.

Emma's father is a bit daft about one thing, though, and that is the idea of frying anything in the Regency period "without the smallest grease." Steaks of all kinds were fried in large quantities of butter—partly to keep them from sticking to the pan, partly for the sake of flavor, and partly for the sake of the cook, whose perquisites included the right to sell leftover dripping fat. The more butter she used, the more was "left over" in the pan, and the richer she got. This leaves two possibilities. Either Mr. Woodhouse, by "grease," means the pork fat on the steak or chop itself, or he means broiling (grilling) rather than frying. In other words, he is referring either to a fried but very lean chop, or to a grilled chop, whose only added grease would be the suet rubbed on the gridiron to prevent the steaks or chops from sticking. For the sake of thoroughness, I include two recipes from John Farley's The London Art of Cookery *which, between them, address both possibilities. The first is for broiled pork chops (not steaks, as Mr. Woodhouse would have it) and follows the general lines for mutton chops (half-inch-thick chops, frequent turning, and avoidance of too much smoke from the fire). The second is actually a portion of a recipe for beef steaks, as Farley does not include a recipe for fried pork. His techniques for frying, however, are consistent enough from one dish to another to allow for a little culinary license.*

Broiled Pork Chops

The same rules we have laid down for broiling mutton, will hold good with respect to pork chops, with this difference only, that pork requires more broiling than mutton. As soon as they be enough, put a little good gravy to them, and strew a little sage, rubbed fine, over them, which will give them an agreeable flavor.

Fried Beef Steaks

. . . take rump steaks, pepper and salt them and fry them in a little butter very quick, and brown: then put them into a dish, and pour the fat out of the frying pan. Take half a pint of hot gravy, half a pint of hot water, and put into the pan. Add to it a little butter rolled in flour, a little pepper and salt, and two or three shalots chopped fine. Boil them up in your pan for two minutes, and pour it over the steaks. . . .

MODERN RECIPE

4 pork chops	3 T chopped fresh sage
salt and pepper	3 T butter
½ recipe **gravy**	

Heat the butter in a large skillet over medium heat. Salt and pepper the chops on both sides. Lay the chops in the skillet and cook until browned on both sides and cooked all the way through, about 5 to 7 minutes per side. Lay the chops on a warmed serving platter, pour a little gravy around them, and sprinkle the chopped sage on top.

ROAST PORK LOIN

(Glasse)

". . . Now we have killed a porker, and Emma thinks of sending them a loin or a leg; it is very small and delicate—Hartfield pork is not like any other pork—but still it is pork—and, my dear Emma, unless one could be sure of their making it into steaks, nicely fried, as our's are fried, without the smallest grease, and not roast it, for no stomach can bear roast pork—I think we had better send the leg—do you not think so, my dear?"

"My dear papa, I sent the whole hind-quarter. I knew you would wish it. There will be the leg to be salted, you know, which is so very nice, and the loin to be dressed directly in any manner they like." (*E* 172)

My dear sir, if there is one thing my mother loves better than another, it is pork—a roast loin of pork. (*E* 175)

A *"porker"* differed from a bacon hog in age. While bacon hogs were allowed to live comparatively long lives, so that they could grow huge, porkers were killed young, in early adulthood, to yield more tender meat. The meat was also put to different purposes. The legs that became hams on a bacon hog became loin and salted leg on a porker. The killing season for porkers also differed from that of bacon hogs: Hannah Glasse gives the season as September to March, with the sole exception of the month of November. This omission is not an error; November was the traditional month for butchering bacon hogs, and plenty of pork products would have been available at that time without any need for killing porkers.

The principal cookbook authors of Austen's time do not spend much time discussing the proper way to roast a loin of pork. They spare their attention for the far more glamorous business of killing, dehairing, gutting, and roasting an entire pig. However, Glasse and her many imitators suggest skinning and roasting a hindquarter of pork, the very part given to the Bateses. Minus the leg (which the Bateses plan to salt and boil later), this equals the loin.

Glasse's recipe has many deficiencies. One is the uncharacteristic absence of any spice, salt, butter, or flour on the roasting meat. Another is a flagrant disobedience to her own rule of fifteen minutes per pound of meat. It is hard to imagine that any hindquarter of a *"large roasting pig"* could weigh a paltry two pounds. Therefore, I have included a second recipe of hers, even though it specifically applies to the leg rather than to the hindquarter.

At the time of the year when house-lamb is very dear, take the hind-quarter of a large roasting pig, take off the skin and roast it, and it will eat like lamb with mint-sauce, or with a salad, or Seville orange. Half an hour will roast it.

Roast a leg of pork thus: take a knife, as above, and score it; stuff the knuckle part with sage and onion, chopped fine with pepper and salt: or cut a hole under the twist, and put the sage, &c. there, and skewer it up with a skewer. Roast it crisp, because most people like the rind crisp, which they call crackling. Make some good apple-sauce, and send up in a boat; then have a little drawn gravy to put in the dish. This they call a mock goose.

MODERN RECIPE

1 pork loin | **Salad, apple sauce**, or orange wedges (optional)

Preheat oven to 450°F. Lay the pork in a roasting pan and cook until the inside temperature reaches 160°F. Serve with salad, apple sauce, or orange wedges.

❀ RAGOUT OF PORK CHOPS ❀

(The French Family Cook)

"We consider our Hartfield pork," replied Mr. Woodhouse—"indeed it certainly is, so very superior to all other pork, that Emma and I cannot have a greater pleasure than"—

"Oh! my dear sir, as my mother says, our friends are only too good to us. . . ." *(E* 173–74)

*My version of this recipe omits the sweetbreads and poultry livers, but feel free to reinsert them. See the recipe for **fricasseed sweetbreads** for instructions about preparing sweetbreads.*

Cut a loin or neck of fresh pork into chops, and stew it with a little broth, a bunch of herbs, pepper and salt: have ready a veal sweetbread, parboiled, and cut into large dice; put it into a stew-pan, with mushrooms, the livers of any kind of poultry, and a little butter; set it over the fire, with a little flour, a glass of white wine, some gravy, and as much broth, adding salt and whole pepper, a bunch of parsley, scallions, a clove of garlic, and two cloves; let the whole boil, and reduce to a strong sauce, and serve it over the chops: or do the chops in the same manner as the ragout, and when full half done, add the sweetbread, livers and mushrooms.

❧ MODERN RECIPE

5 loin pork chops	2 T flour
½ cup **broth** or **cullis**	1 cup white wine
½ tsp. dried sage	½ cup **gravy**
½ tsp. dried oregano	½ cup chopped fresh parsley
pepper and salt to taste	2 scallions, thinly sliced
6 to 8 mushrooms	1 clove garlic, peeled and coarsely chopped
2 T butter	2 whole cloves

Place all the ingredients in a large, deep skillet over medium heat. When the liquid boils, reduce the heat slightly and cover tightly. Cook for 15 to 20 minutes and serve.

❧ BOILED LEG OF PORK ❧

(Rundell)

I was only gone down to speak to Patty again about the pork . . . for my mother was so afraid that we had not any salting-pan large enough. (*E* 173)

That's right, my dear, very right. . . . They must not over-salt the leg; and then, if it is not over-salted, and if it is very thoroughly boiled, just as Serle boils our's, and eaten very moderately of, with a boiled turnip, and a little carrot or parsnip, I do not consider it unwholesome. (*E* 172)

I shall not attempt calling on Mrs. Goddard, for I really do not think she cares for any thing but *boiled* pork: when we dress the leg it will be another thing. (*E* 177)

Some markets sell pieces of salt pork, and these can be boiled according to the second half of the recipe. If you cannot find salt pork, you can make it according to the first half of the instructions below. Rundell does not specify whether curing salts (such as sodium nitrate and sodium nitrite) or ordinary table salt are to be used in the preparation of her leg. Many recipes for preserving meat from this time period call for saltpeter, while others call for ordinary salt. The references to the whiteness of the meat would seem to indicate the use of ordinary salt, but I've prepared it both ways just in case.

Salt it eight or ten days; when it is to be dressed, weigh it: let it lie half an hour in cold water to make it white: allow a quarter of an hour for every pound, and half an hour over, from the time it boils up; skim it as soon as it boils, and frequently after. Allow water enough. Save some of it to make peas-soup. Some boil it in a very nice cloth, floured; which gives a very delicate look. It should be small and of a fine grain.

Serve peas-pudding and turnips with it.

❧ MODERN RECIPE

1 small pork roast, about 2 to 3 lbs.	1 T meat curing mix per pound or ½ cup kosher salt per pound

Continued on next page

Continued from previous page

Salting

If you choose to cure the meat, rub 1 T meat curing mix per pound over the surface of the pork. Seal it in a plastic bag and refrigerate at 36°F–40°F for 8 to 10 days.

If you choose to use ordinary salt, rub kosher salt liberally over the surface of the pork. Place it in a plastic bag with the remaining salt and refrigerate for 8 to 10 days. Shake and turn the bag once a day to redistribute the salt around the meat.

Cooking

Remove the pork from the bag and rinse off the excess salt. Place the pork in a bowl of cold water and refrigerate it for ½ hour. Drain off the water and rinse the pork again.

Bring a large pot of water to a boil on the stove. Add the pork, return the water to a boil, and skim off any foam that rises to the surface. Cook, skimming occasionally, for 30 to 45 minutes (15 minutes per pound). Serve with **boiled turnips**.

BEANS AND BACON

(Glasse)

Our Dinner was Mackerell at Top, Soup at Bottom removed for a Neck of Venison, one Chicken on one Side, and Beans and Bacon on the other; Pease and Cherry Tart succeeded. (Letter of Jane Austen's uncle, James Leigh Perrot, July 4, 1806)

The bacon in this recipe was probably leaner than American bacon and would have been served as a single chunk of meat. This version assumes the use of either American or leaner Canadian or English-style bacon, but chopped into smaller bits to facilitate both the cooking and the eating. I have incorporated the butter and parsley into the dish, but feel free to serve them on the side, as Glasse indicated.

When you dress beans and bacon, boil the bacon by itself and the beans by themselves, for the bacon will spoil the colour of the beans. Always throw some salt into the water, and some parsley, nicely picked. When the beans are enough, (which you will know by their being tender,) throw them into a cullender to drain. Take up the bacon and skin it; throw some raspings of bread over the top, and if you have an iron, make it red hot and hold over it, to brown the top of the bacon; if you have not one, hold it to the fire to brown; put the bacon in the middle of the dish, and the beans all round, close up to the bacon, and send them to table, with parsley and butter in a bason.

MODERN RECIPE

1 lb. green beans, trimmed and cut crosswise in half

4 slices bacon, coarsely chopped

2 T bread crumbs

2 T butter

2 T chopped parsley

Bring two pots of water to boil over high heat. Put the bacon in one and the beans in the other. Boil each for about 5 minutes and remove from the heat.

Preheat the broiler. In a small saucepan, melt the butter and add the parsley. Arrange the beans in an ovenproof skillet and put the bacon in the middle. Scatter the bread crumbs over the whole dish and drizzle on the butter and parsley.

Pass the skillet of beans and bacon under the broiler until they brown slightly, about 1 to 2 minutes.

PORK SAUSAGE

(Farley)

My Mother sends her Love to Mary, with Thanks for her kind intentions & enquiries as to the Pork, & will prefer receiving her Share from the two *last* Pigs. (Letter from Jane to Cassandra, January 24, 1813)

Sausages in Austen's day were not always stuffed into intestines and cured. Some, like these, were shaped by hand and fried right away.

Take six pounds of young pork, free from skin, gristles, and fat. Cut it very small, and beat it in a mortar till it be very fine. Then shred six pounds of beef suet very fine, and free from all skin. Take a good deal of sage, wash it very clean, pick off the leaves, and shred it very fine. Spread your meat on a clean dresser or table, and then shake the sage all over it, to the quantity of about three large spoonfuls. Shred the thin rind of a middling lemon very fine, and throw them over the meat, and also as many sweet herbs as, when shred fine will fill a large spoon. Grate over it two nutmegs, and put to it two teaspoonfuls of pepper, and a large spoonful of salt; then throw over it the suet, and mix all well together. Put it down close in a pot, and, when you use it, roll it up with as much egg as will make it roll smooth. Make them of the size of a sausage, and fry them in butter or good dripping. Be sure that the butter in the pan be hot before you put them in, and keep rolling them about. When they be thoroughly hot, and are of a fine light brown, then take them out and serve them up. Veal eats well done in this manner, or veal mixed with pork. If you choose it, you may clean some guts, and fill them with this meat.

MODERN RECIPE

1¼ lbs. ground pork	1 tsp. dried thyme
½ lb. lard or suet, finely chopped	½ tsp. nutmeg
2 T finely chopped fresh sage	¼ tsp. black pepper
zest of one lemon	1 tsp. salt
1 tsp. dried oregano	1 egg
1 tsp. dried marjoram	6 T butter

Mix all ingredients except the butter in a mixing bowl. Combining them with your hands works better than combining them with a spoon. Take clumps of this mixture, about ¼ cup at a time, and roll them into sausage links no thicker than 1" in diameter.

Melt the butter in a skillet and fry the sausages in the butter over medium heat. Fry, turning, until browned on all sides and cooked through, about 3 minutes per side.

6

POULTRY

The care of poultry was a woman's job, supervised by the lady of the house or by a designated servant. In many homes, the poultry-yard was a profitable concern, with surplus eggs and fowls being sold at market. In others, the goal was simply to meet the needs of the individual household.

The flesh of domestic fowl was widely consumed. Whole birds were roasted or boiled; shredded meat from chickens, ducks, geese, and turkeys was also "dressed," or prepared, in various ways. It might be baked into thick-crusted pies, potted, pickled, or stewed. Parson Woodforde ate poultry as much as he ate red meat. In his many diary entries that attest to this fact, he notes such dishes as "boiled Fowl," "three nice Spring Chicken rosted," "a Couple of Chicken boiled," "a couple of Ducks rosted," "a Goose," "a green Goose rosted," "4 Spring Chickens boiled," "a couple of Fowls rosted," "a boiled Turkey and Oyster Sauce," "a fine Turkey Poult," "some hashed Turkey," and "a prodigious fine, large and very fat Cock-Turkey rosted." On numerous occasions,

A Jord–n for the Duke's Chamber, Dent, 1791. A detail from a print satirizing the relationship between the actress Dorothea Jordan and the duke of Clarence shows a kitchen maid with a large bird on a spit. (Courtesy of the Lewis Walpole Library, Yale University. 791.11.1.1.)

there was more than one poultry dish in a given meal. For example, at a baptismal dinner in 1780 hosted by the local squire, he ate not only "boiled

Morning, or the Man of Taste, 1802. Breakfast, with its muffins and dishes of tea, is interrupted by the French cook with a lobster and a freshly killed duck. (Courtesy of the Lewis Walpole Library, Yale University. 802.4.5.1+.)

Le Gourmand, J. Nixon and Isaac Cruikshank, 1791. The gourmand of the title consumes a goose. (Courtesy of the Lewis Walpole Library, Yale University. 791.7.24.1+.)

Fowl," but also "a couple of Wild Fowl called Dun Fowls, Larks," and "a fine Swan rosted with Currant Jelly Sauce."

Chickens appear to have been the most common of the domestic fowl, while ducks might be either domestic or wild. Of the larger birds, geese were more popular than turkeys, the latter of which were thought to be flavorless and tough. However, there was no bias against turkey at Steventon, where Mrs. Austen raised them and where the bird was sometimes served at Christmas. At Michaelmas, goose was the preferred bird; a popular proverb promised prosperity to those who ate "goose on Michael's day." Such Michaelmas geese would have been "stubble" geese, older geese fattened on the gleanings of shorn grainfields. The other kind of goose was a "green" goose, named not for its color but for its youth and inexperience. Green geese were killed at about three or four months of age and were eaten in the spring. Both geese and turkeys were driven to London on foot for the vast city market.

✿ ROAST CHICKEN ✿

(*The French Family Cook*, Farley)

. . . we ordered up the cold Ham and Fowls, and instantly began our Devouring Plan on them with great Alacrity. (*Lesley, MW* 113–14)

. . . in the summer he was for ever forming parties to eat cold ham and chicken out of doors. . . . (*S&S* 33)

Lady Lucas, who had been long yawning at the repetition of delights which she saw no likelihood of sharing, was left to the comforts of cold ham and chicken. (*P&P* 100)

Roast birds of various kinds were an extremely popular dish. This was due in part to simplicity of preparation and in part, as the above quotations indicate, to the ease with which roast poultry could be served at room temperature or used up in leftovers and "made dishes." Every well-equipped kitchen had several spits for roasting geese, ducks, "fowls" (largish birds of any sort), chickens, and small game birds. The spits were turned by a junior servant, a child, or, in some cases, by a dog who ran on a wheel to generate the necessary force. The standard procedure was to dredge the birds with flour and then baste them periodically with butter. Sometimes there was a stuffing, sometimes not; a sauce of some kind was generally thought necessary, even if it was merely a broth thickened with butter and flour and seasoned with salt and pepper. The two recipes below differ only in the stuffings and sauces; the method of roasting the bird itself is consistent.

Farley's Recipe

Having cleansed and dressed your large fowls, put them down to a good fire, singe, dust, and baste them well with butter. They must be near an hour at the fire. Make your gravy of the necks and gizzards, and when you have strained it, put in a spoonful of browning. Take up your fowls, pour some gravy into a dish, and serve them up with egg sauce.

THE FRENCH FAMILY COOK's Recipe

Singe and draw them, and put a little grated bacon, the liver minced, some shred parsley and scallions, and a very little salt, into the body, and sew it, that nothing falls out. Put it over the fire in a stew-pan, with the skimmings of the pot, a few minutes, and roast it, covered with thin slices of bacon and paper: do not let the fire be too fierce, lest it should discolour your fowl, which should be (if for a side-dish) of a pale colour. When it is done, dish and serve it with any of the following sauces or ragouts: For which see the chapter upon sauces.*

Sauce à la Ravigotte,	Sauce à la Carpe,
Sauce à la Espangole,	Sauce à la Italienne,
Sauce à la Sultane,	Sauce aux petits oeufs,
Sauce à l'Allemande,	Sauce piquante,
Sauce à l'Angloise,	Sauce à la Reine.
Sauce blanche, with capers and anchovies;	

RAGOUTS

OF	OF
Truffles,	Crawfish,
Mushrooms,	Pistachios,
Morelles,	Fat Livers,
Small onions,	Girkins,
Cucumbers,	Oysters.
Chards,	

The French Family Cook lists a number of sauces that could be served with roast chicken, but many of the sauces are extremely similar to one another. A representative sampling of them may be found in Chapter 15: "Sauces and Spices."

MODERN RECIPE

The French Family Cook	*Farley*
1 chicken	1 chicken
flour	flour
4 T butter, melted	4 T butter, melted
1 chicken liver, minced	chicken giblets and neck
2 slices bacon, minced	1 T **browning**
¼ cup finely chopped parsley	2 T butter rolled in 1 T flour*
2 scallions, white and green parts, minced	1 recipe **egg sauce**
½ tsp. kosher salt	
1 recipe **sauce à la** _____	

Preheat oven to 450°F. Remove the giblets, rinse the chicken and pat it dry. Set it on a roasting rack in a roasting pan and dredge it lightly with flour.

For THE FRENCH FAMILY COOK's Recipe

In a small bowl, mix the chicken liver, bacon, parsley, scallions, and salt. Stuff this mixture inside the bird.

For Both

Baste it with the melted butter and set it in the center of the oven. Check it and baste it every 15 minutes. Remove it from the oven when the temperature at the inner thigh reaches 190°F, about one hour.

For Farley

While the chicken is roasting, place the neck and giblets in a saucepan with 1½ cups of water. Bring to boil, reduce heat to a simmer, cover, and cook for 45 minutes. Strain out the solids, skim off the fat, and add the floured butter and browning. Stir until the butter melts, then keep warm until the chicken is ready to serve.

*See *Appendix 1: "What's with All the Butter?"*

POTTED HAM AND CHICKEN

(Glasse)

I took down the remains of The Ham & Chicken. . . . (Lesley, MW 114)

Take as much lean of a boiled ham as you please, and half the quantity of fat, cut it as thin as possible, beat it very fine in a mortar, with a little oiled butter, beaten mace, pepper, and salt, put part of it into a China pot, then beat the white part of a fowl with a very little seasoning; it is to qualify the ham; put a lay of chicken, then one of ham, then chicken at the top, press it hard down, and when it is cold, pour clarified butter over it; when you send it to the table, cut out a thin slice in the form of half a diamond, and lay it round the edge of your pot.

 ## MODERN RECIPE

½ lb. cooked ham	½ tsp. mace
¼ lb. lard	1 tsp. pepper, *in all*
½ lb. cooked chicken	1½ tsp. salt, *in all*
1 stick (¼ lb.) butter plus 2 T, *in all*	

Melt 2 T of the butter. In a food processor, puree this butter along with the ham, the lard, the mace, and ½ tsp. each of the pepper and salt. Turn the mixture out into a bowl and wipe the food processor clean.

Put the chicken, ½ tsp. pepper, and 1 tsp. salt into the food processor and puree.

Melt the remaining 1 stick of butter and pour off the clear melted butter, leaving the milk solids behind. Spoon a layer of ham into a ramekin or other container and make it smooth and flat with the back of the spoon. Then add a layer of pureed chicken, then a second layer of ham, then finally a second layer of chicken. Pour clarified butter over the second layer of chicken and refrigerate.

The potted meat can be eaten on its own or spread on **sandwiches**.

❊ PULLETS À LA SAINTE MENEHOUT ❊

(Glasse)

We both loved Reading. She preferred Histories, & I Receipts. She loved drawing Pictures, and I drawing Pullets. (*Lesley, MW* 129)

"Drawing" a fowl meant extracting the insides—the guts and other organs—before cooking. It was one stage in the preparation of a bird, which also included plucking off most of the feathers and singeing off the rest by passing the bird briefly before the fire. A "pullet" was a hen of intermediate age. A young female hen was called a chicken until she began to lay eggs, after which she was a pullet until her first moult. After the moult, she was technically a fowl.

This particular recipe is especially tasty; my daughter Emily liked it so much that she asked for it as the centerpiece of her eleventh-birthday dinner. Kids like the flavor, and adults appreciate the tenderness of the meat. The beef slices are also very tasty; Glasse makes no mention of what to do with them after the sauce is made, but I thought they were too good to go to waste. Admittedly, it's not a low-fat dish, as the chicken skin is kept on and the sauce is not skimmed—but if you're looking for low-fat cuisine, you're in the wrong country in the wrong century. There's a reason the gentry got gout!

After having trussed the legs in the body, slit them along the back, spread them open on a table, take out the thigh-bones, and beat them with a rolling-pin; then season them with pepper, salt, mace, nutmeg, and sweet herbs; after that take a pound and a half of veal, cut it into thin slices, and lay it in a stew-pan, of a convenient size, to stew the pullets in; cover it, and set it over a stove or slow fire; and when it begins to cleave to the pan, stir in a little flour, shake the pan about till it be a little brown; then pour in as much broth as will stew the fowls, stir it together, put in a little whole pepper, an onion, and a little piece of bacon or ham; then lay in your fowls, cover them close, and let them stew half an hour; then take them out, lay them on the gridiron to brown on the inside; then lay them before the fire to do on the outside; strew them over with the yolk of an egg, some crumbs of bread, and baste them with a little butter; let them be of a fine brown, and boil the gravy till there is about enough for sauce; strain it, put a few mushrooms in, and a little piece of butter rolled in flour; lay the pullets in the dish, and pour in the sauce. Garnish with lemon.

N.B. You may brown them in an oven, or fry them, which you please.

MODERN RECIPE

2 chickens, each approximately 4 lbs.	1 T flour
1 T kosher salt	3 cups chicken broth
½ tsp. black pepper	2 tsp. black peppercorns
¼ tsp. mace	1 large onion, quartered
¼ tsp. nutmeg	3 slices bacon, uncooked
1 tsp. marjoram	2 egg yolks
1 tsp. tarragon	¼ cup dry bread crumbs
¼ tsp. sage	3 T melted butter
1½ lbs. thinly sliced veal or beef	1 pint white mushrooms, stems removed
	lemons for garnish

Remove the giblets from the chickens. Wash and dry them. Cut each chicken open from neck to tail on the back side and remove the spine. (Removing the spine is not strictly necessary, but it makes the bird a little prettier.) From the inside, find the thigh bone and cut it out, leaving the surrounding flesh as intact as possible. One method is to cut along the bone, reach in around the bone, and twist it at both ends, hard, to detach it from the joints. Turn the chickens over and pound them to tenderize and flatten. You can use a tenderizing mallet if you like; we followed Glasse's suggestion and whacked them with a rolling pin, which was surprisingly fun, especially for kids. Beware, however, of small flying chicken bits.

In a bowl, mix the salt, pepper, mace, nutmeg, marjoram, tarragon, and sage. Spread the spice mixture over both sides of each chicken.

Put a roasting pan that is safe for the stovetop across two burners set between medium and medium-low heat. When the pan is hot, lay the pieces of veal or beef in a single layer across the bottom of the pan. When they begin to brown, sprinkle the flour over them and turn them over. Preheat the broiler or, if you choose to use a charcoal grill for browning the chicken, light your coals. (All the rest of the instructions will presume you are using the broiler rather than the grill.) If using the broiler, place your rack below the top position, so that the chicken will be about 3" away from the heating coil.

When both sides of the meat slices are browned, add the stock, pepper, onion, and bacon to the pan. We placed the onion at the corners of the pan and the bacon slices in the middle. Place the chickens in the pan, skin side up, and cover tightly. Simmer on the stove, between medium and medium-low heat, for 30 minutes or until the thickest part of the leg registers at about 160°F on a meat thermometer.

Continued on next page

Continued from previous page

Line a broiler pan with foil and arrange the flattened chickens on the top rack of the broiler pan, skin side up. Broil for about 7 minutes or until lightly browned. Flip the chickens skin side down and broil for another 7 minutes. While the chickens broil, bring the sauce in the roasting pan to a boil. Boil until reduced by about half and strain into a bowl or sauce boat. Reserve the beef or veal slices, bacon, and onions and keep warm. In the same roasting pan, sauté the mushrooms.

Turn the chickens over once more (the tricky part here is keeping the chickens, which should now be very tender, from falling apart as you turn them), baste with the egg yolk, sprinkle with the bread crumbs, and drizzle with the melted butter. Return to the broiler for about 3 more minutes or until the bread crumbs are golden brown and the egg yolk has been fully cooked.

On a large platter, arrange the mushrooms on one side, the beef slices, bacon, and onions on the other. (Alternatively, make up two platters, one for each chicken, with the mushrooms on one side of one platter and the beef or veal mixture on the other.) Place the chickens on the platter(s) and spoon the sauce around the chickens. Garnish with lemon wedges or slices.

BOILED FOWLS

(Raffald)

Mrs. Jennings . . . was . . . only disturbed that she could not make them choose their own dinners at the inn, nor extort a confession of their preferring salmon to cod, or boiled fowls to veal cutlets. (*S&S* 160)

Recipes for birds often indicate that the legs should be partially stuffed inside the body cavity. One recipe for a mock bird, made of chicken "forcemeat," retains the legs and places them inside the sculpted carcass. The optional instructions below call for the legs to be pushed into the chicken's body—just in case you'd like to know how this was done.

I found this technique for cooking chicken odd at first and unlikely to work. However, it actually works quite well. In fact, it remains the method for cooking Hainanese chicken, a dish originating in Singapore. The chicken requires relatively little cooking time and turns out juicy and tender. The pale skin of the bird, which was so attractive to eighteenth-century diners and remains so attractive in parts of Asia, makes it a little unusual for those used to roast chickens with their crispy, brown skins. However, the technique is worth keeping in mind for modern dishes, such as stir-fry, where the chicken would be skinned and shredded or sliced anyway.

When you have plucked your fowls, draw them at the rump, cut off the head, neck, and legs, take the breastbone very carefully out. Skewer them with the end of their legs in the body, tie them round with a string, singe, and dust them well with flour. Put them in a kettle of cold water, cover it close, set it on the fire. When the scum begins to rise take it off, put on your cover, and let them boil very slowly twenty minutes. Take them off, cover them close, and the heat of the water will stew them enough in half an hour. It keeps the skin whole, and they will be both whiter and plumper than if they had boiled fast. When you take them up drain them, pour over them white sauce or melted butter.

MODERN RECIPE

1 chicken, 4 to 5 lbs.   1 recipe **white sauce** or **melted butter**

flour

Bring a large pot of water to a boil over high heat.

Remove the giblets from the chicken. Rinse it and pat it dry inside and out. Reach into the body cavity and, with a small, sharp knife, make an incision on the inside of the area where the thigh meets the body. You are not trying to cut all the way through to the outside of the bird, just creating a point through which you can reach under the skin of the thigh and drumstick. On the outside of the bird, cut all the way around the skin at the end of the drumstick so that the skin can be pulled up and over the end of the bone.

Reaching in from the inside of the bird, loosen the skin all the way around the thigh and drumstick. Pull the leg into the body cavity and push the loose tube of skin in after it. Repeat with the chicken's other leg.

Dust the chicken lightly with flour. Add it to the boiling water. Boil, uncovered, 20 minutes. Turn off the heat, cover the pot, and let the bird sit in the hot water for 30 minutes. At the end of 30 minutes, test the temperature at the inner thigh. It should register between 180°F and 190°F.

Serve with white sauce or melted butter.

MINCED CHICKEN

(Glasse)

... with the real good-will of a mind delighted with its own ideas, did she then do all then honours of the meal, and help and recommend the minced chicken and scalloped oysters with an urgency which she knew would be acceptable to the early hours and civil scruples of their guests. (*E 24*)

Hashes were made out of various kinds of meat, but Glasse's only recipe for minced chicken is entitled "To mince Veal or Chicken for the Sick, or weak People." Mr. Woodhouse, at whose home this dish is served, seems to qualify on both counts. Its bland flavorings sound as if they would have appealed to his unadventurous tastes.

Mince a chicken, or some veal, very fine, take off the skin; just boil as much water as will moisten it, and no more, with a very little salt, grate a very little nutmeg; then throw in a little flour over it, and when the water boils put in the meat; keep shaking it about over the fire a minute; then have ready two or three very thin sippets, toasted nice and brown, laid in the plate, and pour the mincemeat over it.

 ## MODERN RECIPE

1½ to 2 cups of leftover cooked chicken, chopped

½ cup water

½ tsp. salt

pinch of nutmeg

1 T flour

4 T butter

several pieces of white bread, about the size of a third of a sandwich slice

In a skillet, heat the water, salt, and nutmeg to a boil over medium; add the flour and then the chicken. Heat until the chicken is thoroughly warmed, about 5 minutes, stirring occasionally.

In a separate skillet, melt the butter over medium-high heat. As soon as it starts to sizzle, add the slices of bread, frying them golden brown on both sides. These are the "sippets" of Glasse's recipe. Arrange the sippets on a platter and spoon the chicken in the center.

 # FOWLS À LA BRAISE

(Raffald)

Eliz[th] called briskly after Nanny "to tell Betty to take up the Fowls." (*Wat, MW 346*)

Many of the recipes of Austen's time call for ingredients that can no longer be found except, in some cases, on farms and in slaughterhouses. This one, for example, calls for a "veal caul"—that is, the amniotic sac of a newly born calf. Its principal purpose was to hold the layers of the dish together. In this version of the recipe, the veal caul has been replaced by parchment paper for containment and a little beef to replace any lost flavor.

Skewer your fowl as for boiling with the legs in the body, then lay over it a layer of bacon cut in pretty thin slices. Then wrap it round in beet leaves, then in a caul of veal, and put it into a large saucepan with three pints of water, a glass of Madeira wine, a bunch of sweet herbs, two or three blades of mace, and half a lemon. Stew it till quite tender, take it up and skim off the fat. Make your gravy pretty thick with flour and butter and strain it through a hair sieve, and put to it a pint of oysters, a teacup full of thick cream. Keep shaking your tossing pan over the fire, and when it has simmered a little, serve up your fowl with the bacon, beet leaves and caul on, and pour your sauce hot upon it. Garnish with barberries or red beetroot.

MODERN RECIPE

1 chicken, 4 to 5 lbs.	½ tsp. mace
6 slices bacon	half a lemon
3 beets with their greens	3 T butter rolled in and mixed with 1½ T flour*
1 lb. thinly sliced beef or veal	
6 cups water	2 cups oysters in their shells
1 cup Madeira	¾ cup heavy whipping cream
2 sprigs each fresh thyme, sage, and tarragon	

Pull the chicken's legs into the body as in the recipe for **boiled fowls**. Drape the slices of bacon over the outside of the chicken.

Rinse the beet leaves and wrap them around the outside of the chicken and bacon. Wrap parchment paper around the outside of this, and tie it in place with kitchen twine. Put the chicken into a large pot or Dutch oven and add the beef, water, Madeira, herbs, mace, and lemon. Bring the liquid to a boil, reduce it to a simmer, cover the pot, and stew for 1½ to 2 hours.

Continued on next page

Continued from previous page

Meanwhile, trim, peel, and boil the beets until they are tender. Slice them ¼" thick and set them aside. Shuck the oysters and refrigerate them until you are ready to finish the sauce.

Unwrap the chicken, check at the inner thigh to make sure the temperature registers between 180°F and 190°F, and set the chicken on a serving plate to keep it warm.

Strain the remaining liquid in the pot, return it to the pot, and raise the heat to medium. Add the floured butter; cook, stirring occasionally, for 5 minutes. Add the oysters and cream, lower the heat to medium-low, and cook for another 5 minutes, lowering the heat if the sauce shows any signs of returning to a boil. Pour the sauce around the chicken on the platter, garnish with the slices of beets, and serve immediately.

*See Appendix 1: "What's with All the Butter?"

FOWL EN QUADRILLE

(*The French Family Cook*)

This makes a showy and very tasty dish.

Cut a fowl in quarters, and stew it between thin rashers of bacon, with a truffle, a slice of ham, a bunch of parsley, scallions, two shalots, half a laurel-leaf, some leaves of basil, a clove, a little salt and whole pepper, and a glass of white wine. When the stew is done, mince, separately, the truffle, the ham, the yolk of an egg boiled hard, and some capers. Then skim the fat off, strain the sauce; thicken it over the fire with a bit of butter, about the size of a walnut, rolled in flour, and put it in the dish; put the four quarters of the fowl in the dish; covering the first with the minced ham, the second with the hard egg, the third with the truffle, and the fourth with the capers.

MODERN RECIPE

1 large roasting chicken (5 to 6 lbs.)—whole or cut up	1 lb. thick-cut bacon
	1 large or 3 small truffles

Continued on next page

3 thin slices of ham	1 tsp. salt
1 cup chopped parsley	1 tsp. black peppercorns
4 scallions	1 cup white wine
2 shallots	1 egg
1 bay leaf	2 T capers
¼ cup chopped fresh basil	2 T butter
1 whole clove	1 T flour

This dish can be made on the stovetop or in the oven at 350°F.

Cut the chicken into quarters if it is whole. In a pot with a lid, lay half the bacon in a single layer. Arrange the chicken pieces in a single layer on top, and lay the other half of the bacon over the chicken. Near one quarter of the chicken, place the truffles in the pan; near another quarter, lay the slices of ham; and place the parsley, scallions, shallots, bay leaf, basil, clove, and peppercorns around the remaining two quarters. Sprinkle the salt evenly over the chicken pieces, and pour in the white wine. Cover tightly and stew in the oven or on medium-low heat on the stovetop until tender and thoroughly cooked, about 1 hour.

Meanwhile, hard-boil the egg: Place the whole egg in a saucepan of water and bring to a boil. When the water boils, reduce heat to a simmer and cook 12 minutes. Place the egg in cold water, crack the shell, and run under cold water again. Peel off the shell. Cut egg in half and remove the yolk. Finely chop the yolk, and discard the white.

Remove the chicken quarters to a serving platter and keep warm. Remove the truffles from the pan, slice them thinly, and scatter them over the chicken quarter near which they cooked. Do the same for the ham and the quarter near which it was cooked. Sprinkle the egg yolk over the third quarter and the capers over the fourth. Keep the platter warm while making the sauce.

Strain the liquid that remains in the chicken pot. Return it to the pot or to a small saucepan and heat over medium heat. Roll the butter in the flour, pinching it as necessary to mix it with the flour. Add the floured butter to the sauce and melt it to thicken the sauce. As soon as the butter is melted and evenly distributed, pour the sauce around the chicken in the platter and serve immediately.

❀ CHICKEN-SURPRIZE ❀

(Glasse)

If a small dish, one large fowl will do; roast it, and take the lean from the bone; cut it in thin slices, about an inch long, toss it up with six or seven spoonfuls of cream, and a piece of butter rolled in flour, as big as a walnut. Boil it up and set it to cool; then cut six or seven thin slices of bacon round, place them in a patty-pan, and put some force-meat on each side; work them up in the form of a French roll, with a raw egg in your hand, leaving a hollow place in the middle; put in your fowl. and cover them with some of the same forcemeat, rubbing them smooth with your hand and a raw egg; make them of the height and big-ness of a French roll, and throw a little fine grated bread over them. Bake them three quarters or an hour, in a gentle oven, and place them on your mazarine, that they may not touch one another; but place them so that they may not fall flat in the baking; or you may form them on your table with a broad kitchen knife, and place them on the thing you intend to bake them on. You may put the leg of a chicken into one of the loaves you intend for the middle. Let your sauce be gravy, thickened with butter and a little juice of lemon. This is a pretty side-dish for a first course, summer or winter, if you can get them.

MODERN RECIPE

1 chicken (raw or preroasted), about 4 lbs. be-fore cooking

6 to 8 thin slices of ham

½ cup cream

2 T butter, in all

flour

bread crumbs

1 recipe **gravy**

1 T lemon juice

Roast the chicken, if it's not preroasted at the store. Remove and reserve the drumsticks and wings. Take 1 tablespoon of the butter and flour it on all sides; I find it helps to pinch it in two with my fingers, mix it with flour, and re-form it into a lump, flouring the outside; this distributes the flour a little more evenly.

Shred the rest of the chicken finely and warm it in a pan with the cream and your floured ta-blespoon of butter. Bring to a boil, then turn off the heat and set it aside. Preheat oven to 300°F.

Trim the ham if necessary to pieces about 6" long and 4" wide. They can be a little more square than this, but they shouldn't be longer than 6". Place each slice of ham in your hand and smear one side of it with forcemeat, about ¼" thick. Turn it over and place about ¼ cup of chicken in the center of the slice of ham. Fold the ham and forcemeat around the chicken into a ball, adding more forcemeat if necessary to seal the opening. Smooth the ball and place, sealed side down, in a ramekin or in one compartment of an oversize muffin tin.

When all the ham and forcemeat has been used up, sprinkle the shaped "muffins" with bread crumbs. Cook at 300°F for about 30 to 40 minutes, or until the forcemeat is cooked all the way

Continued on next page

Continued from previous page

through. You may want to remove them from the muffin tins when they are about ⅔ done, placing them on a cookie sheet to brown the sides.

Meanwhile, warm the gravy. Shortly before serving, reheat the reserved wings and drumsticks and stir the lemon juice into the gravy. Thicken the gravy by adding another piece of butter, prepared in flour like the first one.

Arrange the chicken wings and drumsticks around the edges of a platter. Spoon the gravy into the center of the platter and arrange the "muffins" in the gravy. If you like, you can serve any leftover shredded chicken in a separate dish.

CHICKEN PIE

(Glasse)

We both loved Reading. She preferred Histories, & I Receipts. She loved drawing Pictures, and I drawing Pullets. No one could sing a better Song than She, and no one make a better Pye than I. (*Lesley, MW* 129)

Meat pies in Austen's day were bland, even by the standards of the modern British shepherd's pie. They tended simply to insinuate a thick pastry crust between the pan and the meat, using the pastry as a kind of edible stewpot. One of the advantages of this method of preparation was that the pie could be removed from the pan and stored in its pastry casing for later use, freeing the pan for other uses in the meantime.

A variety of methods of preservation were used for meats in Austen's day, and not all of them were the sort we would be willing to use today. Some meats, such as ham, bacon, and certain cuts of beef, were cured using a mixture of salts and saltpeter. "Collared beef," for example, one of Glasse's recipes, used "two ounces of salt-petre, two ounces of sal-prunella, two ounces of bay-salt, half a pound of coarse sugar, and two pounds of white salt" to make a brine for curing flank steak. The meat sat in this "pickle" for eight days and was then seasoned, rolled, and tied up with cloth and "beggar's tape." Then it was boiled, pressed with weights, sliced, and served cold.

Beef might also be potted, meaning that it was seasoned, sometimes cured with additives, aged, and pounded into a paste. It was then sealed in earthen pots with a thick layer of clarified butter to keep out air. A wide variety of meats were potted, including ham, beef, veal, and shrimp. Veal and tongue might be pounded smooth, mixed gently together, and potted as "marble veal." Meat was also smoked, salted, and dried.

Most meat pies had a "raised" crust—that is, shaped like a clay vessel out of very stiff, virtually inedible, dough. In many cases, they were made in two pieces. The bottom of the crust would be shaped and filled, and the top of the crust built as a separate, detachable piece. The cooking would take place with very little liquid inside the crust, and then gravy would be added at the very end, to keep the crust from disintegrating in the oven.

Some pies were enormous. Glasse's "Yorkshire Christmas Pie" uses a bushel of flour for the crust and includes a boned turkey, goose, fowl, partridge, and pigeon, stuffed one inside the other, as well as a hare, woodcocks, moor fowl, and other game birds. "These pies are often sent to London in a box, as presents," she says; "therefore the walls must be well built."

I have left this pie at its fairly prodigious original size. You may make the pie in a normal 9" pie pan by halving the quantities of the first seven ingredients.

Make a puff-paste crust, take two chickens, cut them to pieces, season them with pepper and salt, a little beaten mace, lay a force-meat made thus round the side of the dish: take half a pound of veal, half a pound of suet, beat them quite fine in a marble mortar, with as many crumbs of bread; season it with a very little pepper and salt, an anchovy with the liquor, cut the anchovy to pieces, a little lemon peel cut very fine and shred small, a very little thyme, mix all together with the yolk of an egg; make some into round balls, about twelve, the rest lay round the dish; lay in one chicken over the bottom of the dish, take two sweet-breads, cut them into five or six pieces, lay them all over, season them with pepper and salt, strew over them half an ounce of truffles and morels, two or three artichoke-bottoms cut to pieces, a few cock's-combs, (if you have them,) a palate boiled tender and cut to pieces; then lay on the other part of the chicken, put half a pint of water in, and cover the pie; bake it well, and when it come out of the oven, fill it with good gravy, lay it on the crust, and send it to table.

 ## MODERN RECIPE

1 recipe **force-meat balls**, fried	3 boiled artichoke hearts, quartered
1 recipe **puff paste**	2 tsp. pepper, *in all*
2 chickens, cut in pieces	3 tsp. salt, *in all*
2 veal sweetbreads	1 tsp. ground mace
¼ oz. truffles, thinly sliced	1 recipe **gravy** (optional)
6 to 8 small morels	

Continued on next page

Continued from previous page

Preheat oven to 350°F. Roll out the puff paste ¼" thick and line the bottom and sides of a 12" × 2" round pan with it. Trim the crust so that it extends ½" beyond the rim of the pan. Do not prick the bottom or sides of the crust as you might for a modern pie; it will not be necessary and will impair the ability of the crust to seal in the meat juices.

Mix 1 tsp. of the pepper, 2 tsp. of the salt, and the mace, and use this to rub the chicken pieces. Lay half the chicken pieces in the pie crust along with the forcemeat balls.

Cut up the sweetbreads and season them with the remaining 1 tsp. of pepper and 1 tsp. of salt. Lay the pieces around the chicken pieces and forcemeat balls. Scatter the truffle slices, morels, and quartered artichoke hearts around the pie, then lay on the other half of the seasoned chicken pieces. Pour in 1 cup of water.

Roll out a crust ¼" thick and lay it on top of the pie, cutting it with a ½" overhang so that it matches the bottom crust. Do not, however, pinch the top and bottom crusts together. You will need to be able to lift up the top crust at the end of the cooking time.

Bake 1¼ hours. Be careful of meat juices as you remove the pan from the oven; they will tend to want to sneak out between the top and bottom crusts and burn you (or just make a mess on the floor!).

If you're using the gravy, heat it, stirring occasionally, for 5 minutes over medium heat. Lift up the top crust and pour the gravy over the filling, then replace the top crust.

❈ FOWL À LA BECHAMEL ❈

(The French Family Cook)

It is usual to make this dish with a fowl that has been already roasted, and served at table. Cut it up, or, which is better, when it is almost entire, take all the meat from the bones, and cut it into thin slices: then put into a stew-pan a pint of cream or a gill of milk, and when it boils thicken it with a bit of butter, half the size of an egg, mixed up with flour, adding salt, pepper, two shalots, half a clove of garlic, parsley, and scallions, and let it boil gently half an hour: when it is reduced to the consistence of a sauce, strain it, and put in the fowl to warm, not suffering it to boil. If the sauce should not be quite enough thickened, add the yolk of an egg beat up: when you serve it, add a few drops of vinegar.

MODERN RECIPE

1 roasted chicken, cut up

2 cups cream

2 T butter rolled in and mixed with 1 T flour*

salt and pepper to taste

2 shallots, minced

1 small clove garlic, minced or pressed

¼ cup finely chopped parsley

2 thinly sliced scallions

1 egg yolk (optional)

½ tsp. white vinegar

In a large saucepan, bring the cream to a boil over medium heat. Add the floured butter, salt, pepper, shallots, garlic, parsley, and scallions, and reduce the heat to a simmer. Cook for 30 minutes, then add the chicken pieces and cook until the chicken is warmed through. Do not let the sauce return to a boil.

If the sauce seems thin, beat an egg yolk and slowly add about ½ cup of the hot sauce to it in a bowl, whisking constantly to keep the egg from cooking. Then add this sauce with the egg yolk to the main saucepan. Add the vinegar and serve.

*See *Appendix 1: "What's with All the Butter?"*

ROAST DUCK

(Farley)

Cook) Here is the bill of fare.
Chloe reads) 2 Ducks, a leg of beef, a stinking partridge, & a tart.
(*Scraps, MW* 173)

Kill and draw your ducks; then shred an onion, and a few sage leaves. Season these with salt and pepper, and put them into your ducks. Singe, dust, and baste them with butter, and a good fire will roast them in twenty minutes; for the quicker they are done the better they will be. Before you take them up, dust them with flour, and baste them with butter to give them a good frothing, and a pleasing brown. Your gravy must be made of the gizzard and pinions, an onion, a tea-spoonful of lemon-pickle, a few pepper corns, and a large blade of mace, a spoonful of ketchup, and the same of browning. Strain it, pour it into your dish, and send it up with onion sauce in a bason.

MODERN RECIPE

1 duck	1 tsp. **lemon pickle**
2 onions, *in all*	½ tsp. peppercorns
¼ cup chopped fresh sage	½ tsp. mace
2 tsp. salt	1 T **walnut ketchup** or **mushroom ketchup**
1 tsp. pepper	1 T **browning**
2 T flour	1 cup **broth**
4 T melted butter	

Preheat oven to 450°F.

Remove the giblets and neck from the duck, rinse it inside and out, and pat it dry. Place it on a rack in a roasting pan.

Chop or grate the onions. Mix about 1 cup of the onion with the sage, salt, and pepper, and stuff the duck with it. Skewer the duck closed. Set the remaining onion aside.

Baste the duck with a little of the melted butter and put it in the oven. Roast, basting occasionally, until the temperature at the inner thigh reaches 180°F, about 1½ hours.

Meanwhile, make the sauce. Place the giblets, neck, leftover onion, lemon pickle, peppercorns, mace, ketchup, browning, and broth in a small saucepan, and simmer gently for 30 minutes. Remove the giblets and neck and discard.

When the duck is fully cooked, dust it with the flour, drizzle any remaining butter over it (or drizzle the pan juices if there's no butter left), and let the flour and butter brown for about 5 minutes more.

Remove the duck to a platter and serve the sauce on the side.

DUCKS À LA MODE

(Raffald)

She was going to the butcher's, she told me, on purpose to order in some meat on Wednesday, and she has got three couple of ducks, just fit to be killed. (*P&P* 331)

I skipped the boning and resewing of the ducks in this set of instructions, as it seemed unlikely to me that modern cooks would want to engage in such a time-consuming pro-

cess. If you want to be truly authentic, however, feel free to adopt Raffald's technique. The taste is largely the same in both cases, although the slicing of the ducks afterward is considerably easier if they are boned.

Slit two ducks down the back and bone them carefully. Make a forcemeat of the crumbs of a penny loaf, four ounces of fat bacon scraped, a little parsley, thyme, lemon peel, two shallots or onions shred very fine, with pepper and salt and nutmeg to your taste, and two eggs. Stuff your ducks with it and sew them up, lard them down each side of the breast with bacon, dredge them well with flour and put them in a Dutch oven to brown. Then put them into a stewpan with three pints of gravy, a glass of red wine, a teaspoonful of lemon pickle, a large one of walnut and mushroom catchup, one of browning, and one anchovy, with Chyan pepper to your taste. Stew them gently over a slow fire for an hour. When enough, thicken your gravy and put in a few truffles and morels, strain your gravy and pour It upon them. You may a la mode a goose the same way.

MODERN RECIPE

2 ducks	flour
10 oz. (by weight) fresh bread crumbs	6 cups beef or chicken **broth**
¼ lb. bacon	1 cup red wine
½ cup parsley	1 tsp. **lemon pickle**
1 tsp. dried thyme	1 T **walnut ketchup**
zest of two lemons	1 T **mushroom ketchup**
½ cup grated onion	1 T **browning**
½ tsp. black pepper	1 anchovy filet
1 tsp. kosher salt	¼ tsp. cayenne pepper or more to taste
½ tsp. grated nutmeg	2 T butter softened slightly and rolled in and mixed with 1 T flour*
2 eggs	
4 T butter	optional: truffles and morels

Rinse and pat the ducks dry. In a large bowl, mix the bread crumbs, parsley, thyme, lemon zest, onion, pepper, salt, nutmeg, and eggs. (Your hands will work better for this than a spoon, as in-

Continued on next page

Continued from previous page

deed they will for most "forcemeats.") Loosely stuff the birds with the forcemeat (meat stuffing) and sew or skewer the cavity closed. Make a slit in the thick skin, following the center line of the breast, about 3" long, and loosen the skin on either side of the breast with your fingers. Insert bacon into each side of the breast of each duck, between the skin and the meat.

Heat 4 T of butter in a large pot over medium-high heat. Dredge the ducks thoroughly with flour and, when the butter is sizzling, brown the ducks, one at a time, on all sides. Drain off the fat and return the ducks to the pot, along with the broth, wine, lemon pickle, ketchups, browning, anchovy, and cayenne. Cover and cook over medium-low heat until the meat is tender, about 1½ to 2 hours.

Remove the ducks to a serving platter and keep warm. Skim the fat from the cooking liquid and add the butter mixed with flour to thicken the sauce. (If this quantity of butter is insufficient to thicken the amount of sauce remaining, add more butter and flour in similar proportions until your sauce is the consistency of gravy or thick cream.) Pour a little sauce around the ducks on the platter and serve the rest in a sauceboat. Optional: garnish the platter with truffles and morels.

*See Appendix 1: "What's with All the Butter?"

WILD DUCKS HASHED

(Farley)

> I am usually at the fire cooking some little delicacy for the unhappy invalid—Perhaps hashing up the remains of an old Duck, toasting some cheese or making a Curry which are the favourite dishes of our poor friend. (*Beaut Desc, MW* 72)

This is a great way to use up leftover duck after one of your wild Regency dinner parties. It's also a practical and easy way to serve duck for dinner without being trapped in the kitchen. Make the duck and cut it up a day ahead; the total prep time after that is only about ten minutes, and the browning in the sauce makes it taste as if you worked all day on the dish. Since you can skin the cooked duck before mixing up the dish, too, it cuts down a great deal on the fat content. My mother, who has always avoided duck because she believed it was greasy, adored this dish.

Having cut up your duck as for eating, put it in a tossing-pan, with a spoonful of good gravy, the same of red wine, and an onion sliced exceedingly thin. When it has boiled two or three minutes, lay the duck in the dish, and pour the gravy over it. You may add a teaspoonful of caper liquor, or a little browning; but remember that the gravy must not be thickened.

MODERN RECIPE

1 cooked duck, cut up into serving pieces	3 T red wine
1 onion, thinly sliced	1 tsp. liquid from a jar of capers
3 T broth	1 T **browning**

Place a nonstick skillet with a lid over medium heat. Add all the ingredients, cover, and cook until the liquid boils. Reduce the heat slightly and simmer for about 3 minutes. Place the duck pieces on a warm serving platter and pour the sauce over it.

❀ ROAST STUBBLE GOOSE ❀

(Raffald)

Mrs. Martin was so very kind as to send Mrs. Goddard a beautiful goose: the finest goose Mrs. Goddard had ever seen. Mrs. Goddard had dressed it on a Sunday, and asked all the three teachers, Miss Nash, and Miss Prince, and Miss Richardson, to sup with her. (*E* 28–29)

A stubble goose was an older bird, fattened on the harvest gleanings and served, traditionally, at Michaelmas. In Elizabethan times, it had been served with mustard and vinegar, but by Austen's time the standard accompaniment was applesauce.

To roast a Stubble Goose

Chop a few sage leaves, and two onions very fine; mix them with a good lump of butter, a teaspoonful of pepper and two of salt. Put it in your goose, then spit it and lay it down, singe it well, dust it with flour; when it is thoroughly hot baste it with fresh butter. If it be a large one it will require an hour and a half before a good clear fire. When it is enough, dredge and baste it, pull out the spit, pour in a little boiling water.

To make Sauce for a Goose

Pare, core, and slice your apples. Put them in a saucepan with as much water as will keep them from burning. Set them over a very slow fire, keep them close covered till they are all of a pulp, then put in a lump of butter, and sugar to your taste. Beat them well and send them to the table in a china basin.

MODERN RECIPE

1 goose	2 tsp. salt
3 T chopped fresh sage	flour
2 onions, finely chopped	melted butter for basting
3 T butter, softened	1 recipe **apple sauce**
1 tsp. pepper	

Preheat oven to 450°F.

Remove the giblets and neck from the body cavity of the goose. Wash the goose, pat it dry, and set it on a rack in a roasting pan. Mix the sage, onion, 3 T butter, pepper, and salt in a bowl and pack this stuffing into the body cavity. Skewer or sew the cavity closed. Generously sprinkle flour over the goose.

Roast the goose until the temperature at the inner thigh is 180°F (between 1 and 1½ hours), basting with butter every 20 to 30 minutes.

Serve with apple sauce.

ROAST GREEN GOOSE

(Raffald)

... though Dr. Grant is most kind and obliging to me, and though he is really a gentleman, and I dare say a good scholar and clever, and often preaches good sermons, and is very respectable, I see him to be an indolent selfish bon vivant, who must have his palate consulted in every thing, who will not stir a finger for the convenience of any one, and who, moreover, if the cook makes a blunder, is out of humour with his excellent wife. To own the truth, Henry and I were partly driven out this very evening, by a disappointment about a green goose, which he could not get the better of. (*MP* 111)

When your goose is ready dressed, put in a good lump of butter, spit it, lay it down, singe it well, dust it with flour, baste it well with fresh butter. Baste it three or four different times with cold butter, it will make the flesh rise better than if you were to baste it out of the dripping pan. If it is a large one it will take three quarters of an hour to roast it. When you think it is enough, dredge it with flour, baste it till it is a fine froth and your goose a nice brown. Dish it up with a little brown gravy under it, garnish with a crust of bread, grated, round the edge of your dish.

sauce:

Take some melted butter, put in a spoonful of the juice of sorrel, a little sugar, a few coddled gooseberries, pour it into your sauce boats and send it hot to the table.

MODERN RECIPE

1 goose

flour

butter for basting

Sauce

3 T butter

3 T finely chopped sorrel or 1 tsp. lemongrass paste

1 tsp. sugar

1 small can gooseberries

Preheat oven to 450°F.

Remove the giblets and neck from the body cavity of the goose. Wash the goose, pat it dry, and set it on a rack in a roasting pan. Generously sprinkle flour over the goose.

Roast the goose until the temperature at the inner thigh is 180°F (between 1 and 1½ hours), basting with butter every 20 to 30 minutes.

Meanwhile, make the sauce. Melt the butter over low heat. Add the sorrel or lemongrass paste, sugar, and drained gooseberries, and keep warm until the goose is ready to serve.

🌸 GOOSE WITH MUSTARD 🌸

(The French Family Cook)

"Very well, very well," cried Dr. Grant, all the better. I am glad to hear you
have any thing so good in the house. But Miss Price and Mr. Edmund
Bertram, I dare say, would take their chance. We none of us want to hear the
bill of fare. A friendly meeting, and not a fine dinner, is all we have in view.
A turkey or a goose, or a leg of mutton, or whatever you and your cook
chuse to give us." (*MP* 215–16)

Take a young tender goose, mince the liver, and mingle it with two shallots, half a
clove of garlic, parsley and scallions, cut small, a laurel-leaf, thyme and basil,
shred fine, a piece of butter, salt and whole pepper; put it into the goose, and having sewed, roast it, basting it from time to time with a little butter, holding a plate
under, to preserve what falls. When the goose is almost done, mix a spoonful of
mustard in the butter, and continue basting it, throwing on grated bread till it be
well covered. Let it remain at the fire till it be of a fine colour, and serve it with a
sauce made with a full spoonful of mustard, a spoonful of vinegar, a small glass of
gravy or broth, salt and whole pepper, and thickened over the fire with a bit of butter, half the size of an egg, rolled in flour: serve it in the dish with your goose.

🍇 MODERN RECIPE

1 goose

2 shallots, minced

1 clove garlic, minced or pressed in a garlic
press

½ cup fresh chopped parsley

2 minced scallions, both white and green
parts

1 bay leaf

½ tsp. dried thyme

1 T fresh chopped basil

2 T butter

salt and pepper to taste

flour

butter for basting

Sauce

2 T Dijon mustard or 1 T reconstituted dry
yellow mustard

2 T white vinegar

6 oz. broth

salt and pepper to taste

2 T butter rolled in 1 T flour*

Continued on next page

Continued from previous page

Preheat oven to 450°F.

Remove the giblets and neck from the body cavity of the goose. Reserve the liver. Wash the goose, pat it dry, and set it on a rack in a roasting pan. Finely chop the liver and mix in a bowl with the shallots, garlic, parsley, scallions, thyme, basil, butter, and bay leaf. Stuff the goose with this mixture. Skewer or sew the cavity closed. Generously sprinkle flour over the goose.

Roast the goose until the temperature at the inner thigh is 180°F (between 1 and 1½ hours), basting with butter every 20 to 30 minutes.

Meanwhile, make the sauce. Heat the mustard, vinegar, broth, salt, and pepper in a small saucepan over medium-low heat. When the goose is ready to serve, add the floured lump of butter, stir until it melts, then continue to heat the sauce for about 2 more minutes.

See Appendix 1: "What's with All the Butter?"

❊ ROAST TURKEY ❊

(Farley)

Dinner came, & except when Mrs R. looked at her husband's head, she continued gay & flippant, chiding Eliz^th for the profusion on the Table, & absolutely protesting against the entrance of the roast Turkey—which formed the only exception to "You see your dinner".—"I do beg & entreat that no Turkey may be seen today. I am really frightened out of my wits with the number of dishes we have already." (*Wat, MW* 353–54)

A turkey or a goose, or a leg of mutton, or whatever you and your cook chuse to give us. (*MP* 215–16)

Turkey and oysters were considered particularly well suited to each other. This turkey is served with an oyster sauce, while other turkey recipes, such as Elizabeth Raffald's recipe for boiled turkey, included not only oyster sauce but also an oyster stuffing. Raffald's boiled turkey featured a stuffing or "forcemeat" of oysters, bread crumbs, butter, cream, eggs, lemon peel, nutmeg, pepper, and salt. Then the turkey was to be boiled, with an emphasis on keeping the skin "very white." Then the bird was served with an accompanying oyster sauce and a garnish of "lemon and barberries." A white-skinned bird no longer sounds very appetizing, but Farley's roast turkey recipe remains quite tasty.

Having dressed your turkey, according to the prepatory directions already given for boiling it, . . . truss its head down to the legs, and make your forcemeat, which must be thus prepared. Break a penny loaf into crumbs, shred a quarter of a pound of beef suet very fine, a little sausage meat or veal minced and pounded, and season to your taste with pepper, salt, and nutmeg. Mix up all together lightly with three eggs and stuff it into the craw. Spit it, dust it with flour, and baste it several times with cold butter, which will froth it much better than the hot contents of the dripping-pan, and make the turkey more plump. When it be properly done, renew the frothing in the same manner as before, and dish it up. A middling sized turkey must be down at the fire an hour and a quarter. Pour into your dish your sauce, such as you will find under the section on Sauces. Serve it up garnished with lemon and pickles.

MODERN RECIPE

1 fresh turkey	3 eggs
10 oz. (by weight) fresh white bread crumbs	flour
½ lb. ground veal or pork	butter for basting
1 tsp. black pepper	lemon wedges and pickled vegetables (optional)
1 tsp. salt	
1 tsp. ground nutmeg	1 recipe **oyster sauce**

Preheat oven to 450°F. Remove the giblets from the turkey, wash the turkey, and pat it dry. The giblets may be reserved for making **giblet soup**. In a bowl, mix the bread crumbs, ground meat, eggs, and spices, and use this stuffing to fill the neck cavity. If there is stuffing left over, use it inside the body cavity. Remember not to pack the stuffing in too tightly, as the bread will absorb liquid and expand during cooking.

Scatter some flour over the turkey, brush it with melted butter, and put it in the oven, reducing the heat immediately to 350°F. Cook it for 15 minutes per pound or until a meat thermometer registers a temperature of 180°F when inserted into the inner thigh. Every 30 to 60 minutes, scatter more flour over the turkey and brush it with melted butter.

Remove turkey from oven and cover for 15 minutes to allow the juices to settle. Place the turkey on a serving platter, garnishing it if you like with lemons and pickled vegetables such as pickled mushrooms or pickled beets. Serve oyster sauce on the side.

❀ TURKEY PINIONS WITH SMALL ONIONS AND CHEESE ❀

(*The French Family Cook*)

LORD F. I wish we had any Desert to offer you. But my Grandmother in her Lifetime, destroyed the Hothouse in order to build a receptacle for the Turkies with it's materials . . . . (*Visit, MW* 54)

This is a tasty recipe, but finding six or eight turkey wings, unburdened by the rest of the turkey, can be a challenge in most supermarkets. I have adapted it for turkey breast, which is a good deal easier to find. It is also a good way to use up miscellaneous leftovers from a whole roast or boiled turkey.

Take six or eight pinions which you have scalded, parboiled and picked, and put them into a stew-pan with a bunch of parsley and scallions, two cloves, half a laurel-leaf, and a little basil; or moisten them with a glass of white wine and as much broth, and let them stew over a slow fire for half an hour; then put in at least a dozen of small onions, having boiled them a quarter of an hour in water and taken off the skins, a little salt and whole pepper; let them stew till they are done, and then take them out of the stew-pan to drain; strain the sauce through a sieve, and if there be too much, reduce it over the fire, and thicken it with a bit of butter about the size of an egg mixed with flour; then take the dish you send to table, and put a little sauce into it, and over that half a handfull of gruyere cheese grated; dish the pinions (with the small onions between) upon it, and then pour over the remaining sauce; cover it with more grated cheese, and put the dish upon your stove that the sauce may simmer till it is quite consumed; then brown it with a salamander and serve it hot.

❀ MODERN RECIPE

1 small turkey breast or 3 cups miscellaneous turkey bits, cooked through or parboiled	1 small bay leaf
½ cup fresh parsley	2 tsp. fresh or 1 tsp. dried basil
4 scallions	¾ cup white wine
2 whole cloves	¾ cup chicken broth
	12 small boiling onions

Continued on next page

Continued from previous page

1 tsp. kosher salt	3 T butter rolled in and mixed with 1½ T flour*
1 tsp. peppercorns	½ cup grated Gruyère cheese

Coarsely chop the parsley. Thinly slice the scallions, white and green parts alike. Cut the turkey into pieces no bigger than 3" long and 1" wide. (They can be quite a bit smaller; the original recipe called for picking the flesh off wings, which would not have yielded especially large chunks of meat.)

In a saucepan, combine the turkey, parsley, scallions, cloves, bay leaf, basil, white wine, and broth. Simmer these over medium-low heat, covered, for 30 minutes.

Meanwhile, bring a medium saucepan of water to a boil. Trim the tops and bottoms from the small onions and add them to the boiling water. Boil 15 minutes and slip off the outer layer of skin. Add the onions, salt, and peppercorns to the saucepan with the turkey in it and cook until the onions are tender.

Pour the turkey and onion mixture through a strainer. If the remaining sauce is very thin, reduce it a little over medium heat. If it is too thick, add a little more wine or broth. Add the floured butter to bring it to the consistency of gravy.

Pour half the sauce into a stovetop-safe and oven-safe serving platter or dish. (If you don't have such a platter, a casserole dish or other oven-safe serving dish will work reasonably well. Simply cook the turkey, uncovered, for a few minutes at 400°F.) Sprinkle the Gruyère cheese over this, and then add the turkey and onions. Pour the remaining sauce on top. Place the serving dish on the stovetop and cook over medium-low heat until the sauce bubbles and thickens a little more and the cheese melts. Then use a crème brulée torch or the broiler to brown the top of the food a little.

*See *Appendix 1: "What's with All the Butter?"*

❀ TURKEY LEGS À LA CRÈME ❀

(The French Family Cook)

We brought a cold Pigeon pye, a cold turkey, a cold tongue, and half a dozen Jellies with us. (*Lesley, MW* 119)

. . . what is worse, cook has just been telling me that the turkey, which I particularly wished not to be dressed till Sunday, because I know how much more Dr. Grant would enjoy it on Sunday after the fatigues of the day, will not keep beyond to-morrow. . . . (*MP* 212)

This is a very tasty dish that does not really require the suggested sauce of "gravy . . . with salt and whole pepper."

If they have been already served at table, do not lard them, but otherwise lard them with fat bacon, and do them as follows: Put a bit of butter, about as big as an egg, mixed with a spoonfull of flour, into a stew-pan, with salt, pepper, scallions, a clove of garlic, two shalots, thyme, basil, three cloves, a laurel-leaf, a few coriander seeds, and a gill of milk, and stew them over the fire till they boil; then put in the legs of your turkey, and let them boil very gently; when they feel tender, take them out, and leave them to drain: then take the fat off the stew, dip the legs into it, and cover them with grated bread; broil them over a slow fire, and baste them gently with the remainder of the fat. Then put half a glass of gravy into a stew-pan, with salt and whole pepper, and toss it up, to serve with the turkey legs.

MODERN RECIPE

4 turkey legs	2 shallots
4 slices of bacon	1 tsp. dried thyme
3½ T butter	2 T fresh thinly sliced basil
1 T flour	3 whole cloves
1 tsp. salt	1 bay leaf
½ tsp. pepper	1 tsp. coriander seed
4 scallions, both white and green parts, chopped	½ cup milk
	¼ cup bread crumbs
1 clove garlic	

Put the butter, flour, salt, pepper, scallions, garlic, shallots, thyme, basil, cloves, bay leaf, coriander, and milk into a wide-lidded pot on the stove over medium-high heat.

Lift up the skin of the turkey legs and insert one slice of bacon into each leg between the meat and the skin.

When the liquid in the pot begins to bubble, add the turkey legs, cover the pot, and reduce the heat to medium-low. Simmer until the turkey legs are tender, about 45 minutes to 1 hour, depending on their size.

Continued on next page

Continued from previous page

Meanwhile, preheat the broiler and prepare a broiling pan. When the turkey legs are done, remove them from the pot on the stove, place them on the broiling pan, and scatter the bread crumbs over them. Cook under the broiler on the middle rack of your oven just until the bread crumbs are browned, about 30 seconds to 1 minute. Remove to a warm serving platter and pour the sauce from the pot around the legs.

TURKEY À LA POELE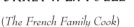

(The French Family Cook)

Mrs. Weston's poultry-house was robbed one night of all her turkies. . . . (*E* 483)

We shall be delighted to see Edward on Monday—only sorry that you must be losing him. A Turkey will be equally welcome with himself. (Letter from Jane to Cassandra, December 2, 1815)

Take a turkey ready prepared for dressing, press it a little upon the breast to make it flat, and truss the feet in the carcase; put it into a stew-pan with a bit of butter or bacon at the bottom, parsley, scallions, champignons, and garlic, all shred small. Set it over the fire a few minutes, and then put it into another stew-pan with salt and whole pepper; cover the breast with thin slices of bacon, add a glass of white wine and the same quantity of broth, and stew it over a slow fire; then take off the fat, and put a little cullis into the sauce to thicken it. A young fowl or chicken may be done in the same manner.

MODERN RECIPE

1 small turkey, about 9 to 10 lbs.	6 cloves garlic, minced or pressed
8 slices bacon	1 T salt
1 cup chopped parsley	1 T peppercorns
1 cup chopped scallions	1 cup white wine
¾ lb. mushrooms, finely diced	1 cup **broth**

Continued on next page

Continued from previous page

Place the turkey in a large pot or Dutch oven with 4 slices of the bacon under it and 4 slices on top. Add the other ingredients to the pot, scattering them to distribute them fairly evenly. Bring the liquid to a boil, then cover the pot and reduce the heat to medium-low. Cook for 2 hours or until the temperature at the inner thigh registers 180°F to 190°F.

7

GAME

The gentry of Austen's day were fond of hunting, and they brought their bags home for both personal consumption and gifts for friends. Jane's letters record several gifts of game, including venison, pheasants, a hare, rabbits, and "4 brace of birds," being sent from her brother Edward's estates to various recipients. Most of Austen's male relatives are known to have hunted, a privilege reserved for landowners and their invited guests, though Austen herself, like almost all women of her time, did not hunt.

Preparation of game was an iffier proposition than preparation of beef or chicken. For one thing, the supply was extremely seasonal. Hannah Glasse gives the seasons for game animals as follows:

Dottrel	September to December
Duck (wild)	July to December
Hare	September to February
Larks	September to December
Leveret	April to August
Partridge	July to February
Pheasant	July to February
Pigeon (tame)	January to February
Pigeon (wild)	February to May, August to December
Plovers	June to August
Rabbit (tame)	February to March
Rabbit (wild)	All year
Snipe	October to February
Teal	September to December
Venison (buck)	June to September

Venison (doe)	October to January
Wheat-ears	June to August
Widgeon	October to December
Wildfowl (misc.)	January to February
Woodcock	October to February

Elizabeth Raffald, in *The Experienced English Housekeeper*, prints a similar list. The table is not necessarily a strict account of what would have been eaten when, as there were external restrictions not reflected in Glasse's list. Partridge hunting, for instance, began on September 1, so the real season for eating partridge did not begin until that day. Glasse's list does reflect, however, the fact that some game animals were available for more of the year than others.

Secondly, eating game depended to some extent on luck. Though genteel hunters often had servants, gamekeepers, and huntsmen to assist them, it was still possible to venture out and come back empty-handed, or with a small enough bag that it hardly warranted serving to company. Farming game oneself diminished the risk; Mrs. Austen's relatives at Stoneleigh, a sizable estate, raised rabbits and pigeons as well as the more conventional types of poultry.

Game was also variable. The age and experience of an animal could make it tastier or tougher, and the cook had to weigh such considerations carefully. John Farley, cook of the London Tavern, acknowledges this in his directions for marketing in *The London Art of Cookery*. His entry on woodcocks will suffice as an example:

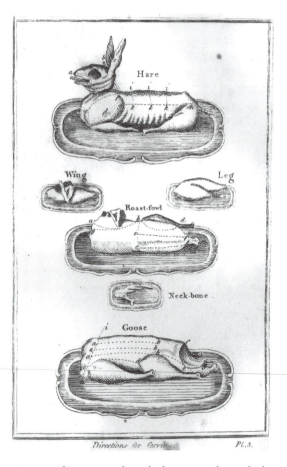

Directions for carving a hare, fowl, or goose, from Charles Millington's *The Housekeeper's Domestic Library; or, New Universal Family Instructor*, 1805. (Library of Congress.)

A woodcock is a bird of passage, and is found with us only in the winter. They are best about a fortnight or three weeks after their first appearance, when they have rested after their long passage over the

The Rabbit Merchant, 1810. A door-to-door rabbit seller, touting the quality of his goods, has apparently just described them to his potential customer as sweet and fresh. The old lady responds by spreading the rabbit's legs and sniffing to see if the meat smells rotten, a common technique used by shoppers. "Sweet indeed," she says, "why it smells Quite Strong." "Yes Ma'am," replies the rabbit seller, "and so would you were you held in the same position." (Courtesy of the Lewis Walpole Library, Yale University. 810.0.4.)

ocean. If they be fat, they will feel firm and thick, which is a proof of their good condition. Their vent will be also thick and hard, and a vein of fat will run by the side of the breast; but a lean one will feel thin in the vent. If it be newly killed, its feet will be limber, and the head and throat clean; but the contrary, if stale.

Shopping instructions in various cookbooks also indicate how to tell, by feathers, beak color, and so forth, how old a particular bird was when it was killed. This could be important for the cook, as a bird's age affected its probable toughness and therefore the cooking method or time most suited to its preparation.

Despite all the difficulties involved in serving game, it remained popular in the sorts of homes about which Austen wrote. Parson Woodforde, whose occupation, income, and social class place him firmly within, though near the bottom of, the world she depicted, frequently dines on game. A pattern emerges from his diary entries. Venison is a rare treat, eaten on grand occasions, such as a magnificent dinner at the bishop's, where it forms part of the first course. Wildfowl are much more common and, like rabbits, usually form part of the second course. Intriguingly, some of his birds are consumed out of the seasons specified by Glasse and Raffald, indicating either that their lists are inaccurate or that some game birds were reared specifically to be eaten out of season. Leaving aside the question of cookbook accuracy, the second possibility is quite likely. Tame pigeons, ducks, rabbits, and pheasants, for example, were raised to supplement the supply of their wild cousins. Woodforde does not usually state the source of his meat, only its species, so in many cases he may have been eating a domesticated bird.

He consumed a wide variety of game. At dinners at the local squire's house, he ate "a couple of Wild Fowl called Dun Fowls," larks, roast pigeon, roast hare, roast pheasant, and roast snipe. At others' homes he was served partridges, pigeons, pigeon pie, roast hare, "a very fine Leveret rosted," and fricasseed rabbit. Game was also served on his own table. At various times, he offered his guests pigeons, wild duck, "a fine hare," fried rabbit, roast rabbit, "a Couple of Rabbitts smothered with Onions," and roast partridge. At his annual tithe dinners, when he offered his parishioners ample food and drink to ease the sting of their tithe payments, he traditionally served boiled rabbit and onion along with the beef, mutton, and puddings. When dining alone, also, he ate game: "one Partridge rosted, & Pigeon Pye," "a Couple of Widgeon," and boiled rabbit, among other dishes. One of his most game-intensive meals was a supper at the King's Head inn in Norwich, when he supped with the family that owned the inn and had "the best Supper I ever met with at an Inn.—Hashed Fowl, Veal Collopes, a fine Woodcock, a Couple of Whistling Plovers, a real Teal of the small kind and hot Apple Pye."

✿ ROAST PHEASANT ✿

(Farley, *The French Family Cook*)

... the housekeeper, after a great many courtesies on the subject of pheasants, had taken her to the dairy, told her all about their cows, and given her the receipt for a famous cream cheese. ... (*MP* 104)

Dr. Grant is ill ... he did not eat any of the pheasant to-day. He fancied it tough—sent away his plate. ... (*MP* 171)

Pheasants were not a common domestic fowl, even in Austen's day, but then Sotherton, the home of the aforementioned housekeeper and her exotic poultry, is an unusually fine estate. Pheasants were much admired for their plumage, and were therefore presented in a manner different from most game birds. They were spitted with the head on and the neck and head plumage wrapped in paper to keep the feathers from burning. The long, striped tail feathers were set aside and stuck into the bird's rump before it was served. Several other kinds of game bird, including woodcock and snipe, were served with the heads still attached, but in most cases the feathers were not preserved. Sometimes birds were positioned so that the bill touched the breast, so that the bird appeared to be sleeping on the platter.

Farley's Recipe

Dust them with flour, and baste them often with fresh butter, keeping them at a good distance from the fire. A good fire will roast them in half an hour. Make your gravy of a scrag of mutton, a tea-spoonful of lemon pickle, a large spoonful of ketchup, and the same of browning. Strain it, and put a little of it into the dish; serve them up with bread sauce in a bason, and fix one of the principal feathers of the pheasant in its tail.

THE FRENCH FAMILY COOK's Recipe

Roast them either drawn or larded, or with a stuffing made with the livers minced, with grated bacon, parsley and scallions shred fine, pepper and salt, and covered with slices of bacon and paper; serve them with sauce à la Provençale, or any other sauce in the fashionable taste. They may be served also in patty hot or cold, or in a tureen.

MODERN RECIPE (Farley)

1 pheasant	1 tsp. **lemon pickle**
flour	1½ T **walnut** or **mushroom ketchup**
melted butter	1½ T **browning**
¾ cup lamb or beef broth	

Preheat the oven to 450°F. Remove the giblets from the bird. Wash the pheasant and pat it dry, then dredge it lightly in flour and lay it in a roasting pan lined with foil. It does not necessarily need to be on a rack; the pheasant is not a fatty bird and will not produce lakes of drippings.

Continued on next page

Continued from previous page

Baste the bird with melted butter and roast until the temperature at the inner thigh reaches 180°F, about 30 to 45 minutes, depending on the size of your bird. If the skin begins to brown too quickly, reduce the heat to 425°F and cover the pheasant loosely with parchment paper. Check the bird every 10 to 15 minutes and baste with melted butter.

Meanwhile, make the gravy by heating the broth, lemon pickle, walnut or mushroom ketchup, and browning in a small saucepan. This will not be a particularly thick gravy, although the version made with mushroom ketchup will be somewhat thicker and more peppery than that made with walnut ketchup. Serve the pheasant on a platter and the sauce in a sauceboat.

MODERN RECIPE (THE FRENCH FAMILY COOK)

1 pheasant

6 strips of bacon, *in all*

¼ cup chopped fresh parsley

2 finely chopped scallions, white and green parts

pepper and salt

Preheat the oven to 450°F. Remove the giblets from the bird. Wash the pheasant and pat it dry, then lay it in a roasting pan lined with foil. It does not necessarily need to be on a rack; the pheasant is not a fatty bird and will not produce lakes of drippings.

Finely chop the giblets (but not the neck) and 3 strips of the bacon. Mix these in a small bowl with the parsley, scallions, and a little salt and pepper. Stuff the pheasant with this mixture. Lay the remaining 3 strips of bacon across the pheasant.

Roast until the temperature at the inner thigh reaches 180°F, about 30 to 45 minutes, depending on the size of your bird. If the skin begins to brown too quickly, reduce the heat to 425°F and cover the pheasant loosely with parchment paper.

BRAISED PHEASANT

(Farley)

Dinner was soon followed by tea and coffee, a ten miles' drive home allowed no waste of hours, and from the time of their sitting down to table, it was a quick succession of busy nothings till the carriage came to the door, and Mrs. Norris, having fidgetted about, and obtained a few pheasant's eggs and a cream cheese from the housekeeper, . . . was ready to lead the way. (*MP* 104–5)

*I left the sweetbread out of this recipe, but you may add it in again if you wish. Just look at the recipe for **fricasseed sweetbreads** for notes on preparing sweetbreads.*

Having put a layer of beef all over your pan, a layer of veal, a little piece of bacon, a piece of carrot, an onion stuck with cloves, a blade or two of mace, a spoonful of pepper, black and white, and a bundle of sweet herbs, lay in the pheasant. Then lay a layer of beef, and a layer of veal, to cover it. Set it on the fire for five or six minutes, and then pour in two quarts of boiling gravy. Cover it close, and let it stew very softly an hour and an half. Then take up your pheasant, and keep it hot. Let the gravy boil till it be reduced to about a pint, and then strain it off, and put it in again. Put in a veal sweetbread, first being stewed with the pheasant. Then put in some truffles and morels, some livers of fowls, artichoke bottoms, and asparagus tops, if you have them. Let these simmer in the gravy about five or six minutes, and then add two spoonfuls of ketchup, two of red wine, and a little piece of butter rolled in flour, with a spoonful of browning. Shake all together, put in your pheasant, let them stew altogether, with a few mushrooms, about five or six minutes more. Then take up your pheasant, and pour your ragoo all over, with a few forcemeat balls. Garnish with lemon. You may lard it, if you think proper so to do.

MODERN RECIPE

¾ lb. thinly sliced beef	1 pheasant, washed and patted dry
2 slices bacon	2 quarts **broth**
½ carrot, peeled	2 truffles
1 onion, quartered	6 to 8 morels
2 tsp. whole cloves	2 poultry livers (or the giblets and neck of the pheasant)
½ tsp. blade mace	
½ T black pepper	2 cooked artichoke hearts, quartered
½ T white pepper	20 asparagus tips
2 sprigs fresh rosemary	2 T **walnut ketchup** or **mushroom ketchup**
2 sprigs fresh marjoram	2 T red wine
2 sprigs fresh tarragon	1 T butter rolled in and mixed with ½ T flour*
	1 T **browning**

Continued on next page

Continued from previous page

6 to 8 mushrooms

lemon wedges for garnish (optional)

force-meat balls for garnish (optional)

Lay out the beef slices in a single layer to cover the bottom of a wide pot or Dutch oven. Lay the bacon over the beef. Arrange the carrot and onion around the edges of the pot and sprinkle in the cloves, mace, pepper, and fresh herbs. Set the pheasant in the middle of the pot and lay any extra beef on top. Pour in the broth and bring the liquid to a boil over medium heat. Then reduce the heat to medium-low, cover the pot, and simmer for 1½ hours.

Remove the pheasant from the pot and keep it warm. Raise the heat to medium-high and reduce the liquid in the pot by half, stirring occasionally. Strain the liquid, return it to the pot, and add the truffles, morels, livers or pheasant giblets and neck, artichoke hearts, and asparagus tips. Reduce the heat to medium or medium-low and simmer 5 minutes.

Add the walnut or mushroom ketchup, red wine, floured butter, and browning. Stir and cook for 1 minute.

Return the pheasant to the pot, add the mushrooms, and cook for 5 more minutes. Then place the pheasant on a serving platter and ladle the contents of the pot around it. Garnish, if you wish, with forcemeat balls and/or lemon wedges.

*See *Appendix 1: "What's with All the Butter?"*

PIGEONS IN A RAGOUT OF CRAWFISH

(*The French Family Cook*)

. . . the two Ladies sat down to Supper on a young Leveret, a brace of Partridges, a leash of Pheasants and a Dozen of Pigeons. (*F&E, MW* 8–9)

Take three or four middling-sized pigeons, scalded and drawn; split them a little upon the back, to enlarge the breast, and stew them with a little broth, and a glass of white wine, a bunch of parsley, scallions, a clove of garlic, two cloves, salt and pepper: when they are done, put some mushrooms into a stew-pan, with a bit of butter, half the size of an egg, and a dozen of craw-fish picked, and set them over the fire; shake in a little flour, and moisten them with the broth of the pigeons, strained through a sieve; let the ragout boil till the sauce be nearly consumed, and add the yolks of three eggs beat up, with cream, a little grated nutmeg, and shred parsley, and thicken it, without boiling, over the fire. Then having drained and dished your pigeons, serve the ragout of crawfish over them.

MODERN RECIPE

2 pigeons, rinsed and patted dry	salt and pepper to taste
2 cups **broth**	8 oz. mushrooms, sliced or diced
1 cup white wine	2 T butter rolled in and mixed with 1 T flour*
½ cup chopped fresh parsley plus 1 T, *in all*	½ cup crawfish meat
3 chopped scallions	3 egg yolks
1 clove of garlic, peeled	2 T cream
2 whole cloves	⅛ tsp. ground nutmeg

Cut the pigeons along the spine so that they lie flatter. Place them in a stew pot with the broth, wine, parsley, scallions, garlic, cloves, salt, and pepper, and stew covered over medium to medium-low heat for 20 to 30 minutes.

Remove the pigeons from the pan and keep them warm. Strain the liquid that remains in the pot and return it to the pot along with the mushrooms, floured butter, and crawfish. Boil until the sauce is reduced by half. Reduce the heat to low.

In a heatproof mixing bowl, mix the egg yolks, cream, and nutmeg. Add a little of the hot sauce to this mixture, stirring well. Repeat, adding more sauce to the egg yolk mixture, until you have about a cup of liquid. Then add this back to the pot along with the pigeons and keep warm until ready to serve.

*See *Appendix 1: "What's with All the Butter?"*

PIGEON PIE

(Glasse)

We brought a cold Pigeon pye, a cold turkey, a cold tongue, and half a dozen Jellies with us, which we were lucky enough with the help of our Landlady, her husband, and their three children, to get rid of, in less than two days after our arrival. (*Lesley, MW* 119)

It was now the middle of June, and the weather fine; and Mrs. Elton was growing impatient to name the day, and settle with Mr. Weston as to pigeon-pies and cold lamb, when a lame carriage horse threw every thing into sad uncertainty. (*E* 353)

... tho' I constantly applauded even every Country-dance, She play'd, yet not even a pidgeon-pye of my making could obtain from her a single word of approbation. This was certainly enough to put any one in a Passion; however, I was as cool as a Cream-cheese. . . . (*Lesley, MW* 129)

Eighteenth-century pies can be quite surprising to modern cooks. They often have very stiff, dense crusts that were meant as quasi-edible pie pans rather than as part of the dish; they mix meats in sometimes startling ways; and, as in this dish, they often leave the bones in, expecting the cautious diner to remove them as he ate.

Make a puff-paste crust, cover your dish, let your pigeons be very nicely picked and cleaned, season them with pepper and salt, and put a good piece of fine fresh butter, with pepper and salt in their bellies; lay them in your pans, the necks, gizzards, livers, pinions, and hearts, lay between, with the yolk of a hard egg and beef-steak in the middle; put as much water as will almost fill the dish, lay on the top-crust and bake it well; this is the best way to make a pigeon-pie; but the French fill the pigeons with a very high force-meat, and lay force-meat balls round the inside, with asparagus-tops, artichoke-bottoms, mushrooms, truffles and morels, and season high; but that is according to different palates.

MODERN RECIPE

½ recipe **puff paste**

1 pigeon, rinsed and patted dry

1 T butter

1 tsp. salt

1 tsp. black pepper

1 hard-boiled egg yolk

½ lb. beef steak, sliced ¼" thick

Preheat oven to 350°F. Lay out the bottom crust in a pie pan. Mix the butter with the pepper and salt and stuff the lump of seasoned butter inside the pigeon. Place the pigeon in the center of the pie and crumble the egg yolk around it. Arrange the slices of beef around the pie between the pigeon and the sides of the pastry. Pour in ½ cup water, lay on the top crust, and bake for 1 hour and 40 minutes.

It is helpful to follow the eighteenth-century model of simply laying on the top crust, without pinching the top and bottom crusts together. Cut both the bottom and top of the crust so that they hang slightly beyond the edge of the pie pan, and do not attach them. After 1½ hours or so of cooking, remove the pie from the oven, carefully lift up the top crust with a spatula, and check to see that the pigeon is thoroughly cooked. If it is not, you can simply replace the "lid" and continue baking.

❀ PIGEONS WITH FINE HERBS ❀

(The French Family Cook)

Then, there is a dove-cote, some delightful stewponds, and a very pretty canal; and every thing, in short, that one could wish for. . . . (*S&S* 197)

Many country estates had a "dove-cote," or house for semitame pigeons. Encouraging pigeons to breed on one's land was a risky decision, as the birds might eat grain. Worse still, they might eat the neighbors' grain, thus starting or exacerbating local tensions. However, it was tempting to have a ready supply of small birds for the table, and many farmers, including Colonel Brandon in the above quotation, maintained a dove cote. There were therefore a good many recipes and methods of presentation for pigeon. "Pigeons Transmogrified" were pigeons seasoned with pepper and salt, boiled for an hour and a half in puff pastry wrapped in cloth, and served with gravy. "Pigeons in Fricando," by contrast, were larded with bacon and stewed slowly with leeks and either mutton broth or veal gravy. "Pigeons in a Hole," another of Hannah Glasse's recipes, featured birds baked in a batter of eggs, flour, and milk, while still another Glasse recipe called for boiling the pigeons with their heads intact, then stuffing them inside hollowed-out cucumber ends as if they were still in their eggs, each with a sprig of barberries in its mouth.

Scald four pigeons that have been kept till they are high-flavoured, truss them, and let them boil up in water; slit the back a little, to make them lie flat, and put them into a stew-pan, with the livers minced, a bit of butter rolled in flour, salt, whole pepper, champignons, shallots, parsley, scallions, half a clove of garlic, the whole shred fine, half a laurel-leaf, thyme, and basil, shred to a powder: let it simmer half an hour over a slow fire, and then put in half a glass of white wine and as much broth. When the whole is done skim off the fat, and serve it as thick sauce.

❀ MODERN RECIPE

4 squabs	2 cups sliced button mushrooms
2 T butter rolled in 1 T flour*	3 thinly sliced shallots
½ tsp. kosher salt	1 cup chopped fresh parsley
1 tsp. black peppercorns	1 clove garlic

Continued on next page

Continued from previous page

1 bay leaf   1 tsp. dried basil or 2 tsp. fresh sliced basil

1 tsp. dried thyme

Wash and dry the pigeons and reserve the giblets. Bring a pot of water to a boil. Parboil the pigeons, one or two at time if necessary, for 5 minutes. Cut them up the back along the spine and flatten them. Place the pigeons in a large pan on the stovetop, laying them in a single layer. Add the floured butter, salt, peppercorns, mushrooms, shallots, parsley, garlic, bay leaf, thyme, and basil. Cover the pigeons and set on the stove at medium-low for ½ hour.

*See Appendix 1: "What's with All the Butter?"

ROAST PARTRIDGE

(Glasse)

Cook) Here is the bill of fare.
Chloe reads) 2 Ducks, a leg of beef, a stinking partridge, & a tart.—I will
                  have the leg
                  of beef and the partridge.
                         exit Cook.
                  And now I will sing another song.
SONG
I am going to have my dinner,
After which I shan't be thinner,
I wish I had Strephon
For he would carve the partridge
if it should be a tough one.

Chorus) *Tough one, tough one, tough one,*
             For he would carve the partridge if it should be a tough one.
             (Scraps, *MW* 173–74)

. . . the two Ladies sat down to Supper on a young Leveret, a brace of Partridges, a leash of Pheasants and a Dozen of Pigeons. (*F&E, MW* 8–9)

When birds were roasted, eighteenth-century cooks generally left the legs outside the body and fixed them to the rest of the body with skewers. When birds were boiled, however, the legs were dealt with in various fashions. Sometimes they were cut off and placed, thighs inward, inside the body cavity of the bird. Sometimes they were turned toward and under the wings.

Let them be nicely roasted, but not too much; baste them gently with a little butter, and dredge with flour, sprinkle a little salt on, and froth them nicely up; have good gravy in the dish, with bread-sauce in a boat, made thus: take about a handful or two of crumbs of bread, put in a pint of milk or more, a small whole onion, a little whole white pepper, a little salt, and a bit of butter, boil it all well up; then take the onion out, and beat it well with a spoon; or take poivrade-sauce in a boat, made thus: chop four shalots fine, a gill of good gravy, and a spoonful of vinegar, a little pepper and salt; boil them up one minute, then put it in a boat. Twenty minutes is enough to roast them.

MODERN RECIPE

2 partridges	**Sauce**
flour	4 shallots
butter	½ cup **gravy**, beef **broth**, or **cullis**
	1 T white vinegar
	pepper and salt to taste

Preheat oven to 450°F. Remove the giblets from the partridges, rinse them, and pat them dry. Dredge them lightly in flour, sprinkle them with salt, and lay them in a baking pan. Baste them with butter and roast them until tender and fully cooked, about 25 to 30 minutes.

Meanwhile, make the poivrade sauce. Finely mince the shallots and heat them over medium-low heat in a small saucepan with the gravy, broth, or cullis. Add the vinegar and salt and pepper to taste. When the partridges are ready, raise the heat and bring the sauce to a boil. Boil for 1 minute and serve the sauce alongside the birds in a sauce boat.

 **PARTRIDGE IN PANES**

(Raffald)

They would make me sit near the fire, & as the partridges were pretty high, Dr Richards would have them sent away to the other end of the Table, that they might not offend Mr Watson—which I thought very kind of him. (*Wat, MW* 344)

The most common culinary meaning of "high" was "heavily spiced." This dish of Raffald's, a so-called "made dish" because it was more complex than a whole bird cooked and sent up with sauce, is not particularly "high" but might have seemed so to an eighteenth-century palate.

Half roast two partridges and take the flesh from them. Mix it with the crumbs of a penny loaf steeped in rich gravy, six ounces of beef marrow or half a pound of fat bacon scraped, ten morels boiled soft and cut small, two artichoke bottoms boiled and shred small, the yolks of three eggs, pepper, salt, nutmeg, and shred lemon peel to your palate. Work them together and bake them in moulds the shape of an egg, and serve them up cold or in jelly. Garnish with curled parsley.

 ## MODERN RECIPE

2 partridges	3 egg yolks
½ cup bread crumbs	½ tsp. pepper
¼ cup **cullis**	½ tsp. salt
½ lb. bacon, finely chopped	½ tsp. nutmeg
10 morels or button mushrooms	zest of one lemon
2 artichoke hearts, cooked (and, if canned, rinsed clean of canning liquid)	parsley for garnish

Preheat the oven to 450°F. Roast the partridges for 15 minutes and let them cool. Reduce the oven heat to 350°F. Meanwhile, bring a small pot of water to a boil and add the morels or mushrooms. Cook until the fungi are soft, then drain and finely dice them.

When the partridges are cool enough to handle, pull all the meat off the bones and finely shred it. In a bowl, mix the partridge meat, bread crumbs, cullis, and bacon. Finely chop the artichoke hearts and add them, too, along with the remaining ingredients except for the parsley.

Form the meat mixture into small meatballs and place them on a pan to bake. (A nonstick mini-muffin pan works best, but a cookie sheet lined with parchment paper will do.) Bake the meatballs until cooked through and nicely browned, about 10 to 15 minutes depending on their size. Garnish with parsley and serve at room temperature.

STEWED PARTRIDGES

(Glasse)

. . . even Mr. Darcy acknowledged, that the partridges were remarkably well done; and I suppose he has two or three French cooks at least. (*P&P* 342)

Truss your partridges as for roasting, stuff the craws, and lard them down each side of the breast; then roll a lump of butter in pepper, salt, and beaten mace, and put it into the bellies, sew up the vents, dredge them well and fry them a light brown; then put them into a stew-pan with a quart of good gravy, a spoonful of Madeira wine, the same of mushroom catchup, a tea-spoonful of lemon-pickle, and half the quantity of mushroom powder, one anchovy, half a lemon, a sprig of sweet marjoram; cover the pan close and stew them half an hour, then take them out and thicken the gravy, boil it a little and pour it over the partridges, and lay round them artichoke-bottoms boiled and cut in quarters, and the yolks of four hard eggs, if agreeable.

MODERN RECIPE

4 partridges	1 T **mushroom ketchup**
1½ sticks (12 T) butter, *in all*	1 tsp. **lemon pickle**
flour	½ tsp. **mushroom powder**
2 tsp. black pepper	1 anchovy filet
1 tsp. kosher salt	½ lemon
1 tsp. ground mace	1 tsp. dried or 2 tsp. chopped fresh marjoram
1 quart beef **broth**	8 artichoke heart quarters for garnish (optional)
1 T Madeira	4 hard-boiled egg yolks for garnish (optional)

Remove the giblets from the partridges, rinse them, remove any feathers, and pat them dry. In a small bowl, combine the pepper, salt, and mace. Cut four 1-tablespoon pats of butter and roll each in the pepper, salt, and mace mixture. Mash any leftover spices into the butter pats, dividing them equally among the 4 pats. Place 1 lump of seasoned butter inside the body cavity of each partridge. Skewer the partridges closed.

Continued on next page

Continued from previous page

Set the partridges in a large covered pot in a single layer. Pour in the remaining ingredients except for the artichoke hearts and egg yolks. Bring the liquid to a boil over medium heat, then cover the pot, reduce the heat to medium-low, and stew the partridges for half an hour.

Remove the partridges to a serving platter and keep warm. Raise the temperature of the pot to medium again and cook the sauce briskly for about 5 minutes or until it begins to thicken. Pour the sauce around the partridges and arrange the artichoke hearts and hard-boiled egg yolks around the partridges, if you are using these garnishes.

❀ ROAST LEVERET ❀

(The French Family Cook)

. . . the two Ladies sat down to Supper on a young Leveret, a brace of Partridges, a leash of Pheasants and a Dozen of Pigeons. (*F&E, MW* 8–9)

*Leveret, or young hare, is hard to find in the United States. Rabbit is, however, widely available online and from well-stocked groceries. I served both this recipe and the more traditionally English **boiled rabbit with onion sauce** at a Bastille-Day Regency dinner where French-style and English-style dishes were pitted against each other. The roast leveret won the taste test almost unanimously, the one dissenting vote being cast by a woman who read about rabbit with onion sauce decades ago and had always wondered wistfully what it might taste like.*

Skin it, take out the entrails, and put it over the fire a few minutes, with butter or fat; then lard and roast it, and when it is done serve it with sauce and vinegar, and pepper and salt, which should be served in a sauce-boat apart. If you would introduce it as a side dish, when it is done and cold, cut it into small slices, and serve them in a thick pepper sauce, or in shallot sauce, or different sorts of these sauces.

 MODERN RECIPE

1 rabbit, cut in serving pieces   2 slices of bacon

3 T butter

Continued on next page

Continued from previous page

Shallot Sauce
1 cup finely chopped shallots

2 cups beef broth

¾ cup vinegar

½ tsp. pepper

1 tsp. salt

Preheat oven to 400°F. In a large pan, melt the butter over medium-high heat and add the rabbit pieces, browning them on all sides. Place the pieces in a roasting pan and cook until tender and well browned, about 50 minutes.

Meanwhile, place all the ingredients for the shallot sauce in a saucepan and bring to a boil, then reduce heat and simmer for 30 minutes.

 # BOILED RABBIT WITH ONION SAUCE

(Raffald)

Austen does not mention rabbit, but this was a popular dish, served at Parson Wood-forde's annual tithe dinner for several years running. The bizarre presentation, with the jawbones sticking out of the eyes like horns, was a common feature of recipes for rabbit. Unfortunately (or perhaps fortunately) most rabbit sold by butchers is missing the head, so this detail cannot be recreated unless you hunt the rabbit yourself.

When you have cased your rabbits, skewer them with their heads straight up, the fore legs brought down, and the hind legs straight. Boil them three quarters of an hour at least, then smother them with onion sauce made the same as for boiled ducks. Pull out the jaw bones, stick them in their eyes, put a sprig of myrtle or barberries in their mouths, and serve them up.

 ## MODERN RECIPE

1 rabbit, cut into serving pieces

onion sauce

In the water used for boiling the onions for the onion sauce, boil the rabbit pieces until tender (about 45 minutes). Serve warm with onion sauce on the side and with a little of the sauce poured over the rabbit.

❈ STEWED HARE ❈

(Raffald)

I got that Man a Hare from one of Sidney's friends. . . . (*Sand, MW* 412)

When you have paunched and cased your hare, cut her as for eating. Put her into a large saucepan with three pints of beef gravy, a pint of red wine, a large onion stuck with cloves, a bundle of winter savory, a slice of horseradish, two blades of beaten mace, one anchovy, a spoonful of walnut or mum catchup, one of browning, half a lemon, Chyan and salt to your taste. Put on a close cover and set it over a gentle fire and stew it for two hours. Then take it up into a soup dish and thicken your gravy with a lump of butter rolled in flour. Boil it a little and strain it over your hare. Garnish with lemon peel cut like straws and serve it up.

❧ MODERN RECIPE

1 onion, peeled	1 anchovy
20 whole cloves	1 T **walnut ketchup**
1 rabbit, cut up into serving pieces	1 T **browning**
3 14-oz. cans beef stock	half a lemon
2 cups red wine	½ tsp. cayenne pepper
1" piece of horseradish root or 1 T prepared horseradish	1 tsp. salt
½ tsp. mace	2 T butter rolled in 1 T flour*

Push the sharp end of each clove into the onion. Place the clove-studded onion and all the other ingredients (except for the butter rolled in flour) in a wide, fairly deep pot with a lid. Cover the pot and cook over medium heat for 2 hours, stirring occasionally.

Remove the rabbit pieces to a serving dish and keep warm. Discard the onion. Add the floured butter to the remaining liquid, stir the sauce until it thickens, strain, and pour over the rabbit pieces.

*See *Appendix 1: "What's with All the Butter?"*

❀ HAUNCH OF VENISON ❀

(Millington)

The venison was roasted to a turn-and everybody said, they never saw so fat a haunch. (*P&P* 342)

The soup would be sent round in a most spiritless manner, wine drank without any smiles, or agreeable trifling, and the venison cut up without supplying one pleasant anecdote of any former haunch. (*MP* 52)

Spit the haunch, lay over it a large sheet of paper, and then a thin common paste, with a paper over that. Tie it fast, to keep the paste from dropping off; if the haunch be large, it will take four hours roasting. As soon as it is done, take off the paper and paste, dredge it well with flour, and baste it with butter. As soon as it is of a light brown, dish it, with brown gravy, or currant jelly sauce, and send up some in a boat.

❀ MODERN RECIPE

1 venison roast	butter
flour	

Preheat oven to just under 450°F. Place the roast in a roasting pan and cover the pan loosely with parchment paper. Roast until inner temperature is 140°F to 150°F, about 15 to 20 minutes per pound. Let stand 10 minutes, then carve and serve.

❀ VENISON PASTY ❀

(Farley)

Spread a Cloth in the dining Parlour, and carry in the venison pasty—.
(*Evelyn, MW* 182)

This recipe does not yield small pasties like those eaten in England today, but one large pie. The pie's purpose was not so much to provide a delectable crust as to serve as a convenient box in which to store the meat. The enormous amount of butter called for by

Farley was also intended to seal the meat and its juices in a layer of fat to assist in preservation. Modern cooks would be well advised not to rely on crust and butter, however; store your leftovers in the refrigerator.

Having boned a breast or shoulder of venison, season it well with pepper, salt and mace. Lay it in a deep dish, with the best part of a neck of mutton, cut in slices, and laid over the venison. Pour in a large glass of red wine, put a coarse paste over it, and bake it two hours in an oven. Then lay the venison into a dish, and pour the gravy and a pound of butter over it. Make a good puff paste, and lay it near half an inch thick round the edge of the dish. Then roll out the lid, which must be somewhat thicker than the paste on the edge of the dish, and lay it on. Then roll out another lid pretty thin, and cut it in flowers, leaves, or whatever form you please, and lay it on the lid. If your pie should not be immediately wanted, it will keep in the pot it was baked in, eight or ten days; but in that case, keep the crust on, to prevent the air getting into it.

MODERN RECIPE

1 shoulder of venison	1 lb. thinly sliced lamb
1 tsp. pepper	1½ cups red wine
½ T salt	1 recipe **puff paste**
1 tsp. mace	½ lb. butter

Preheat oven to 350°F. Mix the salt, pepper, and mace in a small bowl and rub them over the venison. Place the venison in a small lidded oven-safe pot, add the wine, cover it, and let it stew in the oven for 2 hours. Let the venison stand and cool, still covered, for about 20 minutes. Raise the oven temperature to 400°F.

Meanwhile, make the puff pastry, roll it out between ¼" and ½" thick, and use it to line a 10" springform pan. Let the pastry extend beyond the upper edge of the pan by about ½". Reserve the remainder of the pastry and keep under plastic wrap to prevent it from drying out.

Remove the venison from the pot and finely chop it. Cut the butter into small pieces and lay the chopped venison and butter in the pastry-lined pan. Pour in the liquid from the stew pot.

Roll out the remaining pastry and make a top for the pie, between ¼" and ½" thick. Pinch the top and sides of the pastry together. If there is any pastry left over, roll it out ¼" thick and use cookie cutters to cut out shapes to arrange around the top of the pie.

Place the pie in the oven and bake until the crust is a deep golden brown.

8

SEAFOOD

As an island nation, Britain had plenty of access to good fish. Improving transportation times meant that saltwater fish could maintain their freshness farther and farther inland, much to the delight of the populace. This meant, however, that stewponds, where the gentry had bred freshwater fish, fell somewhat out of favor, as it was believed that freshwater fish had a less pleasant taste than ocean varieties. (However, when Mrs. Austen visited Stoneleigh in 1806, she noted that the magnificent estates had, among its other attractions, ponds that produced excellent fish.) Of course, fish could always be salted, in which case perishability was less of a concern, but salt fish were even less desirable than fish from stewponds.

Carp was the classic stewpond fish. Its ubiquity in the mid-eighteenth century was reflected in the fact that Hannah Glasse included nearly three pages of recipes for carp, devoting as much space to it as to eels and cod, the other seafood she discusses in great detail. Many of her recipes are extremely interesting; in one, for example, two unscaled carp are steeped in boiling vinegar and served with horseradish and sweetened cream. In another, the carp are stewed in a sauce made of their own blood, stale beer, and more than a dozen other ingredients, while half the roe of the fish is mixed with egg yolk, nutmeg, and lemon zest, shaped into patties, fried, and served with triangular toasts. A third recipe, which she describes as "a top dish for a grand entertainment," stews carp or tench in water and red wine and seasons them with walnut ketchup, mushroom powder, cayenne pepper, onion, cloves, mushrooms, and horseradish. However, by the time Maria Rundell wrote in 1806, carp occupied much less of the space devoted to seafood. Salmon, herring, lobsters, and oysters, as well as other saltwater delicacies, each receive more attention than carp.

While the variety of game consumed in the eighteenth century might be surprising to modern home cooks, the variety of fish is a little less so, if only be-

Frying Sprats, Gillray, 1791. One simple method of preparing small fish was to lay them on a gridiron over the fire. (Courtesy of the Lewis Walpole Library, Yale University. 791.11.28.2.)

cause we usually have access to so many kinds of fish in our supermarkets. Hannah Glasse, who tends to be fairly comprehensive on such matters, lists recipes for turbot, carp, tench, cod, mackerel, weavers, salmon, herring, water-sokey, eels, lampreys, pike, haddock, sturgeon, skate, sole, crab, lobster, prawns, shrimp, crayfish, oysters, mussels, scallops, smelts, whitebait, and miscellaneous small and flat fish. John Farley and Elizabeth Raffald follow her lead, though Farley lists trout among his fish.

Parson Woodforde's diary confirms that many species of fish were eaten. Though he does not list fish in his meals as often as meat, poultry, and game, seafood does appear fairly regularly. On one evening in May, 1781, he had four guests for dinner and served them, among other dishes, a "great Pike which was rosted and a Pudding in his Belly, some boiled Trout, Perch, and Tench, Eel and Gudgeon fryed." The pike, whose size apparently "astonished" his guests, was so large that it had to be set out on two large dishes and "part of the Kitchen Window shutters." Woodforde was less ambitious at his annual tithe dinners for his parishioners, where he typically served "Salt Fish." On other occasions, for company, he served pike, "fryed Soals," mackerel, "Skaite and Oyster Sauce," and smelts. Though he was something of an outdoorsman—he loved hunting hare, for instance—he appears not to have caught most of his own fish, preferring to deal with a Mr. Beale, who worked as a fishmonger in nearby Norwich. We encounter periodic reports that he has sent a servant to Norwich for fish, and on one occasion in 1789 he buys "a fine Crab" directly from a fisherman. (It weighed four pounds and cost Woodforde a shilling.) At the homes of others, Woodforde ate a similar array of seafood. He mentions "fresh Salmon and Oyster Sauce," crabs, perch, trout, more "fryed Soals," carp, stewed tench, pike, mackerel, "Soals" with lobster sauce, and boiled skate.

Woodforde's catalogue confirms the instructions of the major cookbook authors, who frequently specify the use of seafood in sauces and stuffings. Oysters often form the basis of "forcemeat," sausages, and sauces, while anchovies in small quantities are added to sauces for their intense flavor. Poultry and fish were the dishes most likely to be garnished with seafood-based sauces.

Oysters were beloved in other contexts as well. London cookshops sold cheap oysters to the working classes, just as later in the nineteenth century oysters would be sold by street vendors as a snack. Oddly, during the eighteenth century, it was fashionable to buy green oysters. The oysters of certain Essex rivers developed coatings of algae around September, and when their odd appearance became appealing to diners, oystermen began "breeding" green oysters by catching regular oysters and steeping them in salt marshes for a few weeks until they acquired a dark green tint to their shells. Less reputable dealers saved time and trouble by dyeing the oysters with copperas or other poisonous green dyes.

❀ STEWED OYSTERS ❀

(Raffald)

I shall retreat in as much secrecy as possible to the most remote corner of the House, where I shall order a Barrel of Oysters, & be famously snug. (*Wat, MW* 335)

As Tom Musgrave was seen no more, we may suppose his plan to have succeeded, & imagine him mortifying with his Barrel of Oysters, in dreary solitude. . . . (*Wat, MW* 336)

Oysters were a popular snack in the eighteenth and nineteenth centuries. They were sold on street corners in cities and were often devoured in their fried and pickled forms. Both high and low society adored them. This recipe, for stewed oysters, makes a good side dish at a Regency banquet.

When you have opened your oysters, put their liquor into a tossing pan with a little beaten mace. Thicken it with flour and butter, boil it three or four minutes, toast a slice of white bread and cut it into three-cornered pieces. Lay them round your dish, put in a spoonful of good cream, put in your oysters and shake them round in your pan. You must not let them boil, for if they do it will make them hard and look small. Serve them up in a little soup dish or plate. *N.B. You may stew cockles, muscles or any shellfish the same way.*

 MODERN RECIPE

2 8-oz. cans whole shelled oysters

½ tsp. mace

2 T butter rolled in 1 T flour*

6 slices white bread, cut diagonally in half and toasted

2 T heavy whipping cream

Place a colander over a bowl and pour the oysters into the colander. Then put the liquid into a saucepan along with the mace and bring it to a boil. Boil for 3 minutes, meanwhile toasting the white bread and laying 2 triangular slices at the edge of each of 6 soup bowls. Add the floured butter to the liquid, which will thicken the sauce as it melts. Once the butter is melted, reduce the heat to a simmer and add the cream and oysters. When the oysters are warmed through, pour the oysters and sauce into the bowls and serve.

*See *Appendix 1: "What's with All the Butter?"*

 SCALLOPED OYSTERS

(Glasse)

. . . the supper-table, which always closed such parties . . . was all set out and ready, and moved forwards to the fire, before she was aware. . . . [W]ith the real good-will of a mind delighted with its own ideas, did she then do all then honours of the meal, and help and recommend the minced chicken and scalloped oysters with an urgency which she knew would be acceptable to the early hours and civil scruples of their guests. (*E* 24)

Put them on a gridiron over a good clear fire, let them remain till you think they are enough, then have ready some crumbs of bread rubbed in a clean napkin, fill you shells and set them before a good fire and baste them with butter; let them be of a fine brown, keeping them turning to be brown all over alike; but a tin does them best before the fire. They eat much the best done this way, though most people stew the oysters first in a sauce-pan, with a blade of mace thickened with a bit of butter, and fill the shells, then cover them with crumbs, and brown them with a hot iron; but the bread has not the fine taste of the former.

🌸 MODERN RECIPE

10 whole oysters, shells on	2 T dry bread crumbs
4 T butter	pinch of ground mace

Preheat the broiler. Melt the butter and add the mace, stirring until the spice is evenly distributed. Shuck the oysters, removing one shell and arranging them on a baking sheet on the remaining shell. Scatter the bread crumbs over the oysters and drizzle them with the butter. Broil until the bread crumbs are nicely browned, about 2 to 4 minutes. Serve immediately.

🌸 FRIED SOLE 🌸

(Raffald)

Isabel had seen the World. She had passed 2 Years at one of the first Boarding schools in London; had spent a fortnight in Bath & had supped one night in Southampton.

"Beware my Laura" (she would often say) "Beware of the insipid Vanities and idle Dissipations of the Metropolis of England; Beware the unmeaning Luxuries of Bath & of the Stinking fish of Southampton." (*L&F, MW* 78–79)

Invite him to dinner, Emma, and help him to the best of the fish and the chicken. . . . (*E* 14)

Austen was to become well acquainted with the "Stinking fish of Southampton," as she, her mother, and her sister Cassandra were to live there for three years, from 1806 to 1809, with her brother Frank and his wife, Mary. While residing there, in February 1808, they sent "four pairs of small soals" to friends in Berkshire, so sole seems an appropriate fish to choose in connection with this quotation.

Skin your soles as you do eels, but keep on their heads, rub them over with an egg and strew over them breadcrumbs. Fry them over a brisk fire in hog's lard a light brown. Serve them up with good melted butter, and garnish it with green pickles.

MODERN RECIPE

4 sole filets	3 T lard or butter
1 egg, beaten	1 recipe **melted butter**
½ cup bread crumbs	1 kosher dill pickle, chopped

Melt the lard or butter in a skillet over medium heat. Dip the filets in the egg and then in the bread crumbs and fry until the flesh is firm and opaque, about 5 minutes each side. Put the melted butter sauce in a small dish on a platter. Arrange the filets around the dish of butter and garnish with the chopped pickle.

 # BROILED SALMON

(The French Family Cook)

Mrs. Jennings . . . was . . . only disturbed that she could not make them choose their own dinners at the inn, nor extort a confession of their preferring salmon to cod, or boiled fowls to veal cutlets. (*S&S* 160)

Cut it in slices, steep it in a little sweet oil, or good butter, salt and pepper, and broil it; basting it while doing with the oil. When done, serve over it any of these sauces or ragouts directed for the turbot . . . : you may also serve it done with court-bouillon . . . with the same sauces.

Serve it for a first dish; do not take off the scales, but, when done, put it upon a napkin dry, with green parsley round it.

To serve it as a side dish, take off the scales; the court-bouillon, in which it should be boiled, is made with white wine, soup maigre, roots, onions shread, a bunch of sweet herbs, salt, pepper and a bit of butter. Every sort of fish with court-bouillon is done in the same manner.

Sauces: espagnole, hachee, au vin le champagne; ragouts: cresses, little eggs, salpicon, oysters, truffles or champignons.

MODERN RECIPE

| 2 large salmon filets or 3 salmon steaks | ½ tsp. salt |
| ½ cup olive oil | ½ tsp. pepper |

Mix the olive oil, salt, and pepper in a bowl. Dip the salmon into the marinade, coating all sides. Place the salmon into the bowl, cover, and refrigerate for 1 hour, turning the pieces and recoating them with any extra marinade after ½ hour.

Heat a grill or preheat the broiler. The fish will cook best if the heat is not too intense, so if using the broiler make sure the rack you use is in the middle of the oven. If using a grill, grill the fish off to one side of the coals. Brush the grill (or a broiler pan, if using the broiler) with oil. Grill or broil the salmon until tender and until the fish loses its glossy translucent quality, about 5 to 10 minutes depending on the size of the pieces. If using filets, cook with the skin side down. If using steaks, carefully flip the steaks halfway through the cooking time.

SALMON BOILED IN WINE

(Farley)

I am not without hopes of tempting Mrs Lloyd to settle in bath;—Meat is only 8^d per pound, butter 12^d & cheese 9½^d. You must carefully conceal from her however the exorbitant price of Fish;—a salmon has been sold at 2^s: 9^d p^r pound the whole fish. (Letter from Jane to Cassandra, May 5, 1801)

Take some slices of bacon, fat and lean together, a pound of veal cut thin, and a pound and a half of beef. Strew over them some pepper and salt, and put them in a deep stew-pan; then a fine piece of fresh salmon, cut out of the middle. Put it into the stew-pan upon the other ingredients, and pour in as much water as will just cover it, and no more. Set it over a gentle fire till the salmon is almost done, then pour the water entirely away, and put in two quarts of white wine, with an onion cut in pieces, some thyme and sweet marjoram stripped from the stalks. Let them stew gently, and while they are doing, cut a sweetbread into thin slices; then cut the slices across, and stew them in a saucepan with some rich veal gravy. When they be enough, add a quarter of a pint of essence of ham. Take up the salmon, lay it in the dish, and pour the sweetbread and its sauce over it.

MODERN RECIPE

2 salmon steaks	1 small onion, quartered and sliced
4 slices bacon	1 tsp. dried or 2 tsp. chopped fresh thyme
1 lb. thinly sliced beef or veal	1 tsp. dried or 2 tsp. chopped fresh marjoram
3 cups white wine	½ cup strong ham broth

In a wide pot, lay the bacon strips in a single layer. Cover them with a single layer of beef or veal, and lay the salmon steaks on top of the beef in the center of the pot. Pour in enough water to barely cover the salmon. Gently simmer about 30 minutes.

Pour off the water and add the wine, onion, thyme, and marjoram, and continue to simmer the salmon until it is tender and just barely pinker than the surrounding flesh when pierced in the center with a small sharp knife, about 10 minutes more. Add the ham broth, heat through, and serve.

COD EN DAUPHIN

(The French Family Cook)

> . . . good lord! how unlucky! there is not a bit of fish to be got to-day. Lydia, my love, ring the bell. I must speak to Hill, this moment. (*P&P* 61)

Cod was one of the most popular salt-water fish of Austen's day. Herrings had once reigned supreme, but with a new tax on salt they were no longer profitable to preserve, and fishermen often threw back a significant percentage of their catch.

Scale and gut a fresh cod, sear and dry it, and steep it two hours in sweet oil, with salt, whole pepper, parsley and scallions whole, a clove of garlic, and a laurel-leaf: then take an iron skewer and run it through the cod: begin at the eyes, bring it out at the middle of the body, and finish at the tail, to give your cod the form of a dolphin. Put it upon a baking-dish, and having basted it with the oil and herbs, stew it in an oven; when it is done, draw out the skewer, and dish it with a ragout made thus: Take the soft roes of three carp, parboil them with the heads of some asparagus, put the whole in a stew-pan, with a good bit of butter, some champignons, and a bunch of parsley and scallions; turn it a few times over the fire, put in a little flour, and wet it with a glass of white wine and some good vegetable soup. When your ragout is done, and the sauce reduced and agreeably seasoned, add the yolks of three eggs beat up with cream; thicken the sauce upon the fire, and serve it over the cod; do not put in your asparagus heads till the ragout is almost finished.

MODERN RECIPE

2 lbs. ling cod	6 to 8 mushrooms, diced
1 cup olive oil	2 scallions, thinly sliced
1½ tsp. salt	⅓ cup finely chopped parsley
1 tsp. black peppercorns	2 T caviar
⅓ cup chopped parsley	2 T flour
3 scallions, halved crosswise	¾ cup white wine
1 garlic clove, gently crushed	½ cup vegetable broth
1 bay leaf	salt and pepper to taste
20 asparagus tips	3 egg yolks
3 T butter	½ cup heavy whipping cream

In a bowl, mix the oil, salt, peppercorns, parsley, scallions, garlic, and bay leaf. Add the fish and turn to coat it on all sides. Marinate the fish in the refrigerator for at least 1 hour.

Preheat the oven to 350°F. Lift the fish out of the marinade, shake off any excess, place it in a baking dish, and bake 30 minutes.

Meanwhile, make the ragout. Bring a saucepan of water to a boil and add the asparagus. Boil two minutes, then remove the asparagus and dunk it in ice water to stop the cooking.

In a saucepan, melt the butter over medium-low heat. Add the mushrooms, scallions, parsley, and caviar. Whisk in the flour, then add the wine and vegetable broth. Raise the heat to medium and simmer briskly until the sauce is reduced by about a third. Add salt and pepper to taste and reduce heat to low.

In a small bowl, whisk together the cream and egg yolks. Stir this mixture into the ragout, let the ragout thicken, and add the asparagus tips. When the asparagus tips are warmed through, transfer the cod to a serving platter and spoon the ragout around and over the cod.

COD WITH ONIONS

(The French Family Cook)

> Mrs. Jennings ... was ... only disturbed that she could not make them choose their own dinners at the inn, nor extort a confession of their preferring salmon to cod, or boiled fowls to veal cutlets. (*S&S* 160)

Cut five or six onions in bits, put them upon the fire with some butter and let them remain some time, frequently stirring them, till they begin to be coloured; then put in [a] little flour, and stir them over the fire till they are well browned; then add a spoonful of vinegar, some salt, whole pepper, and a little broth. The onions being well done, and the sauce thickened, put in the cod, boiled, and in flakes; let it simmer in the sauce, and before you serve it up, add a bit of butter.

MODERN RECIPE

5 onions, chopped	1 tsp. salt
8 T butter, *in all*	1 tsp. black peppercorns
3 T flour	½ cup **broth**
1 T white vinegar	2 lbs. cod or other white fish

Melt 6 T of the butter in a large skillet and add the onions. Cook over medium-low heat until the onions are translucent, about 10 minutes, then raise the heat to medium and cook until the onions begin to turn pale brown, about 5 minutes more.

Scatter the flour over the onions and cook 5 more minutes, stirring frequently. Add the vinegar, salt, pepper, and broth, and cook 5 more minutes, uncovered.

Meanwhile, bring a pot of water to a boil. Add the fish and cook until the fish is firm and opaque, about 5 minutes (more or less, depending on the thickness of your filets). Drain the fish, break it into relatively small pieces, and add it with the remaining 2 T butter to the pan of onions, stirring for a few minutes to combine the ingredients and allow the flavors to mingle.

❀ BUTTERED CRAB OR LOBSTER ❀

(Glasse)

At Devizes we had comfortable rooms and a good dinner, to which we sat down about five; amongst other things we had asparagus and a lobster, which made me wish for you, and some cheesecakes. (Letter from Jane to Cassandra, May 17, 1799)

I used Dungeness, and I used three because modern crabs tend not to be as large as those caught in Austen's time; more efficient fishing methods mean that most seafood is being caught younger and younger, and thus smaller.

Take two crabs or lobsters, being boiled, and cold, take all the meat out of the shells and bodies, mince it small, and put it all together into a sauce-pan; add to it a glass of white wine, two spoonfuls of vinegar, a nutmeg grated, then let it boil up till it is thoroughly hot: then have ready half a pound of fresh butter, melted with an anchovy, and the yolks of two eggs beat up and mixed with the butter; then mix crabs and butter all together, shaking the sauce-pan constantly round till it is quite hot; then have ready the great shell either of a crab or lobster; lay it in the middle of your dish, pour some into the shell, and the rest in little saucers round the shell, sticking three-corner toasts between the saucers and round the shell. This is a fine side-dish at a second course.

❧ MODERN RECIPE

3 precooked crabs or 3 cans crab meat or 3 lobster tails	½ lb. butter
	1 anchovy, chopped
1 cup white wine	2 egg yolks, beaten
2 T white vinegar	2 slices white bread, toasted and cut in half diagonally
1 tsp. nutmeg	

If you are using whole cooked crabs, remove the legs from the crabs and crack the legs and claws, removing the meat. Pry off the top shell at its back hinge; I found it helpful to insert something into the joint first. A knife might work, but I used a closed pair of scissors. Remove the top shell carefully; try to keep the best-looking one for your platter and reserve that one in a saucepan of

Continued on next page

Continued from previous page

salted water. Underneath the shell is a lot of goo, mouth parts, gills, etc.; remove and discard these. You will be left with the bottom part of the crab, which has an indentation at the front and an obvious midline. Take one side of the crab in each hand and break it along this midline, then pick out the crab meat, which is separated by tough, bony membranes. (It's not unlike picking cloves out of a head of roasted garlic.)

OR,

For canned crab meat, open cans. Drain crab meat. Easier than the goo-filled crab shell, huh? The down side is that you don't get a spiffy shell as decoration for the platter. But you may be able to live with that.

OR,

For the lobster tails, boil the tails until the shell is bright red and the flesh is firm and opaque, about eight to ten minutes. Cool the tails and insert a fork under the lower (and thinner) part of the shell, prying it up to snap the lower shell into pieces that you can pull away. Try to preserve the upper shells intact if you can; you can use them to decorate the platter later. Scrape out the meat and shred into small pieces.

Melt the butter and anchovy in a saucepan over low heat. Turn off the heat and allow the butter to cool but not solidify.

Heat the crab or lobster meat, wine, vinegar, and nutmeg in another saucepan over medium-high heat.

Turn on the heat under your saucepan of salted water and boil the reserved crab shell, if using whole crabs.

When the crab or lobster meat is hot and the liquid begins to boil, add the egg yolks to the *butter* mixture and stir thoroughly. Stir the butter mixture into the meat and shake the saucepan to mix the butter and meat together.

If you are using whole crabs: On a large platter, spoon about 1½ cups of the crab mixture. Cover with the boiled crab shell. Put the rest of the crab meat into two small bowls and place these on the platter. Between the crab shell and the bowls, at the edges of the platter, arrange the toast triangles. Serve immediately.

If you are using lobster tails, space the shells evenly around the platter with the open ends facing inward and about 2" to 3" apart. Place one of the four toast triangles in the middle of the platter. Mound the lobster meat in the center of the platter, on top of this piece of toast, and covering the open end of the tails. Pour the sauce over and around the meat and arrange the toast slices in between the lobster tails.

🌸 POTTED SHRIMP 🌸

(Raffald)

*Austen's contemporaries would have saved a variety of meats in this manner and would
have stored them for far longer than we would consider safe today. To stay on the safe
side, refrigerate potted meats and use them within three days.*

Pick the finest shrimps you can get. Season them with a little beaten mace, pepper and salt to your taste, and with a little cold butter pound them all together in a mortar till it comes to a paste. Put it down in small pots and pour over them clarified butter.

MODERN RECIPE

1 lb. cooked small shrimp

¼ lb. butter, cut into pieces

1 tsp. mace

½ tsp. black pepper

½ tsp. kosher salt

¼ lb. clarified butter

Put the shrimp, ¼ lb. chopped butter, mace, pepper, and salt into a food processor and process until it forms a smooth paste. Spoon the paste into ramekins, leaving no air bubbles, and cover with a ¼" thick layer of clarified butter. To use the shrimp, scrape off the clarified butter, and spread the mixture on bread (see **sandwiches**).

🌸 STEWED PRAWNS, SHRIMP, OR CRAWFISH 🌸

(Glasse)

Pick out the tails about the quantity of two quarts; take the bodies, give them a bruise and put them into a pint of white wine, with a blade of mace; let them stew a quarter of an hour, stir them together, and strain them; then wash out the sauce-pan, put to it the strained liquor and tails: grate a small nutmeg in, add a little salt, and a quarter of a pound of butter rolled in flour; shake it all together, cut a pretty thin toast round a quartern loaf, toast it brown on both sides, cut it into six pieces, lay it close together in the bottom of your dish, and pour your fish and sauce over it; send it to table hot. If it be craw-fish or prawns, garnish your dish with some of the biggest claws laid thick round. Water will do in the room of wine, only add a spoonful of vinegar.

⚜ MODERN RECIPE

1 lb. prawns, shrimp, or crawfish	½ tsp. salt
1 cup white wine	¼ lb. butter rolled in and mixed with ¼ cup flour*
¼ tsp. mace	
½ tsp. nutmeg	1 slice toasted **English bread**

Place the shellfish, wine, and mace in a saucepan over medium-low heat. Cover and cook for 15 minutes. Add the nutmeg, salt, and floured butter and cook for 5 more minutes.

Cut the toast into six pieces, arrange them in a serving dish, and pour the shellfish and sauce over them.

*See *Appendix 1: "What's with All the Butter?"*

 **FRIED HERRING**

(Raffald)

> MISS F. I am afraid Mr Willoughby you take no care of yourself. I fear
> you don't meet with any thing to your liking.
> WILLOUGHBY. Oh! Madam, I can want for nothing while there are red her-
> rings on table. (*Visit, MW* 53)

Herrings are a seasonal fish, and it can be hard to locate whole fresh herrings at your local supermarket. Any smallish saltwater fish, however, can be substituted; I generally use whole sardines.

Scale, wash, and dry your herrings well. Lay them separately on a board and set them to the fire two or three minutes before you want them, it will keep the fish from sticking to the pan; dust them with flour. When your dripping or butter is boiling hot put in your fish a few at a time, fry them over a brisk fire. When you have fried them all, set the tails up one against another in the middle of the dish. Then fry a large handful of parsley crisp, take it out before it loses its colour, lay it round them, and parsley sauce in a boat. Or if you like onions better, fry them, lay some round your fish, and make onion sauce for them. Or you may cut off the heads after they are fried, chop them and put them into a saucepan with ale, pepper, salt and an anchovy. Thicken it with flour and butter, strain it, then put it in a sauce boat.

MODERN RECIPE

6 to 12 whole small fish such as herrings or sardines, scaled

flour for dredging

8 T butter

1 cup fresh parsley, *not* chopped

Sauce
liquid from the fish

6 oz. ale

pepper and salt to taste

1 anchovy filet, minced

3 T butter rolled in and mixed with 1½ T flour*

Rinse the fish and set them in a colander over a bowl to drain for 10 minutes. Meanwhile, fill a bowl with flour and melt the butter in a large skillet over medium heat. When the fish have sat for 10 minutes, dredge them in the flour and fry them in the butter until nicely browned, about 4 to 8 minutes per side, depending on the size of the fish.

Set the fish aside on paper towels to drain, and keep them warm. Pour the butter into a small saucepan and raise the heat to medium-high.

Pour the liquid from the draining fish into a saucepan along with the ale, salt, pepper, anchovy, and floured butter. Cook over medium heat until the butter is melted and the sauce just begins to bubble, about 5 minutes.

Toss the handful of parsley into the hot butter and fry it just until it starts to turn crisp, about 1 minute. Remove it and drain it on paper towels.

Place the fish on a platter with their tails meeting in the center. Place the parsley on top of the touching tails, strain the sauce, and serve it in a sauce boat.

*See *Appendix 1: "What's with All the Butter?"*

9

EGGS AND DAIRY

In most homes, gentry and working-class alike, women had charge of the dairy (*P&P* 163; *MP* 104) and the poultry-yard (*P&P* 163; *MP* 104). Here, their tasks included milking, cheese making, butter making, feeding chickens or other fowls, and gathering eggs. In the dairy, according to cookbook author Charles Millington, daily labor included not only the gathering and the processing of milk, but also the scrupulous care and cleaning of the dairy utensils:

Doctor Syntax and the Dairy Maid, Rowlandson, 1813. Most of the tools of the dairy can be seen here, including the tall cheese press behind and to the left of Doctor Syntax; the wide, shallow pans for new milk; and the butter churn. (Courtesy of the Lewis Walpole Library, Yale University. 813.4.1.4.)

They should be well washed every day in warm water, and afterwards rinced in cold, and must be entirely cool before they are used. If, however, any kind of metal vessels are improperly retained in the dairy, they must be scalded every day, and well scrubbed and scoured.

Mrs. Austen superintended the dairy at Steventon, though she does not seem to have done the actual work.

For those women who bought their cheese, eggs, and butter at market, it was important to be a careful shopper. Butter merchants, according to the most popular cookbooks of the day, would disguise bad butter as good by having a good lump hidden in the cask and offering tastes from that portion only or by having a thin layer of good butter over a cask of bad. Cheese might be infested with worms, mites, or maggots, and housewives were cautioned to make sure the entire rind of the cheese was intact, "for, though the hole in the coat may be but small, the perished part within maybe considerable." The freshness of eggs was to be judged by their temperature, by holding them up to a candle to see if the yolk appeared solid and the white clear, or by placing them in cold water, where

John Farley assured his readers that an "addled or rotten" egg would float. Eggs could be stored for a while in bran, straw, hay, sawdust, ashes, or salt, but Farley advised that "the sooner an egg is used, the better it will be."

It was always preferable to produce dairy products at home, where their quality could be strictly controlled. Milk (*P* 135), in particular, was valued when it came straight from the cow. However, the milk available for sale in London, cried in the streets by milkwomen with a pail hanging from each end of a pole slung across their shoulders, was especially notorious. Watered down, thin, and blue (*MP* 439), often contaminated by germs, it was avoided by anyone who had a choice. Mrs. Austen, who had had a small herd of dairy cows at Steventon, no doubt missed them after the family moved to Bath and then on to Southampton and Chawton. At Chawton, Cassandra lamented, "We have not now so much as a

Spring and Winter, Dighton, 1785. The milkmaid with her characteristic pails and yoke. (Courtesy of the Lewis Walpole Library, Yale University. 785.10.9.1.)

cow." Recollections from the 1820s, not many years after Jane's death, have the Austen's manservant fetching milk from Edward's larger nearby estate, Chawton House, with Cassandra's dog Link carrying the pail in his mouth.

Most of the milk consumed in the eighteenth century was cows' milk. Earlier centuries had relied to some extent on the milk of goats and sheep, but this dependence seems to have waned by Austen's day. However, the milk of asses was a delicacy treasured by invalids, who found it easier to digest than cows' milk (*Sand, MW* 393, 401). It is worth remembering that pasturage for dairy cows was less consistent than today, and the unfortunate dairymaid might discover, upon milking, that her cows had been eating cabbage or turnips, which would give the milk a bad odor.

Many cookbooks offered suggestions about the proper running of a dairy. Charles Millington, in *The Housekeeper's Domestic Library; or, New Universal Family Instructor* (1805), provides extensive instructions. According to him, freshly collected milk should cool in the pail if the weather was warm, but if the weather was cold, the separation of the cream should be hastened by adding a small amount of boiling water. The milk stood in pails or wide, shallow pans in a cool part of the dairy for up to twenty-four hours in warm weather, thirty-six or forty-eight in cool weather, and the separated cream was churned every day if possible. Millington urges his housekeepers to churn at least twice a week in the summer. Churning was to be done early in the morning, when cool weather would help the butter solidify; this phenomenon could be assisted by keeping a pump churn partially submerged in cold water. When the butter had formed, it was removed from the churn with the hands and kneaded in cold water. A knife was drawn through it at every possible angle to draw out dirt or hair that might have blown into the milk pans. Finally, the butter was salted and either made into decorative shapes or simply packed into containers; Millington warns against using lead containers, as it was well known by the early nineteenth century that lead was poisonous. Earthenware pots or wooden casks were preferred in most dairies, and partially filled containers would be layered with salt and filled up the next time butter was made.

Churning was still often done with the old-fashioned vertical churn, in which a handle was raised up and down to agitate the cream. However, in the later eighteenth century, another style became popular. In this type of churn, known as a barrel churn, the barrel was horizontal, with interior paddles turned by two distinct handles.

Milk for drinking was taken from the pans after the cream had been skimmed off to make butter. The buttermilk that remained in the churn after the butter was made was also drunk as a beverage. Alternatively, the whole or skim milk could be processed with rennet and made into cheese. Distinctive regional pasturage, local bacteria, and a lack of pasteurization no doubt gave cheese a much different flavor than it has today; some artisan cheeses probably come close to approximating the intensity and variety of flavors. The rennet was derived from a calf's stomach bag, pickled in brine or salted, dried, and used a piece at a time as needed. A section of the bag would be boiled to yield the rennet.

Cheese made in the summer, when cows were pastured on fresh grass, was the richest of all. Full of milkfat, it had a yellow hue, and accordingly, housewives shopping for cheese looked for the golden tinge. It did not take cheese makers long to learn how to simulate the appearance of summer cheese; they simply added saffron, annatto, or marigold petals to the mixture. Their deception lives on in the artificial coloring applied to many cheeses, including much cheddar. The same trick was applied to butter sold at markets and in chandlers' shops, using marigold petals or carrot juice as a food coloring.

Domestic cheeses included Stilton, Cheshire, North Wiltshire, and cheddar; imported cheeses, which were more expensive and had to be purchased from grocers and other specialty food dealers, were led in popularity by Parmesan. Parson Woodforde received a gift of Parmesan cheese from a neighbor and was impressed by its quality. On another occasion, he made a point of serving a particular kind of cheese that had been admired earlier by one of his guests. Cheese was always well liked at all levels of society, and everyone who could afford to buy it ate it.

❀ SOLOMON-GUNDY ❀

(Farley)

Mr Rob. Mascall breakfasted here; he eats a great deal of Butter. (Letter from Jane to Cassandra, October 12, 1813)

This is not exclusively a dairy dish, nor is it featured in Austen's works, but it is an interesting dish, and it seems silly either to exclude butter from this section or to give a recipe for churning butter. (If you need one, here's your recipe: Put heavy whipping cream in your food processor and hit "ON." Wait a while. When there's butter in the bowl, hit "OFF." Pour off the liquid and add salt to taste.) Solomon-Gundy, also known as "Salmagundy," certainly has butter as a key ingredient and makes, as one of our sources might have said, a pretty side dish for a grand table. It's essentially the Regency equivalent of an antipasto plate. Its essence is the contrast between colors, textures, and flavors.

Take a handful of parsley, two pickled herrings, four boiled eggs, both yolks and whites, and the white part of a roasted chicken. Chop them separately, and exceedingly small. Take the lean of some boiled ham scraped fine, and turn a china bason upside down in the middle of a dish. Make a quarter of a pound of butter into the shape of a pine apple, and set it on the bason's bottom. Lay round your bason a ring of shred parsley, then a ring of yolks of eggs, then Whites, then ham, then chickens, and then herrings till you have covered your bason, and disposed of all the ingredients. Lay the bones of the pickled herrings upon it, with their tails up to the butter, and let their heads lie on the edge of the dish. Lay a few capers, and three or four pickled oysters round the dish.

MODERN RECIPE

¼ lb. butter	1 roasted chicken
1 cup coarsely chopped parsley	1 large slice ham, finely chopped
1 jar pickled herring	1 T capers
4 hard-boiled eggs	4 oysters, raw or pickled

Line a small bowl as smoothly as possible with plastic wrap. Soften the butter and spread it in the bottom of the bowl, filling in all air spaces. Refrigerate the butter until it is hard, then lift the butter out using the plastic wrap. Invert the butter in the center of a serving platter, remove the plastic wrap, and smooth the surface of the butter if necessary using the back of a spoon run under hot water. Using a knife, make several parallel lines across the surface of the butter, about ⅛" deep and about ¾" apart. Then make a series of identical lines perpendicular to the first set, giving the butter a "pineapple" appearance.

Arrange the parsley in a ring around the butter. Cut the hard-boiled eggs in half, remove the halved yolks from each section, and pick any flakes of yolk off the whites. Arrange the yolks, cut side down, at even intervals around the outside of the parsley, and arrange the whites, cut side down, between them. Make a ring of ham around the eggs. Shred the meat of the chicken and arrange this in a ring around the ham.

Place the bits of herring in a ring around the chicken, placing the four oysters at even intervals within the row of herring. Scatter capers over the herring-and-oyster ring.

✿ EGGS EN SURTOUT ✿

(The French Family Cook)

Mrs. Norris, having fidgetted about, and obtained a few pheasant's eggs and a cream cheese from the housekeeper, . . . was ready to lead the way. (*MP* 104–5)

Mrs. Norris obtained her pheasants' eggs to hatch, not to cook (MP 106); the eggs in question in this dish would have been hens' eggs.

Boil half a pound of bacon, cut into thin slices, and fry some bits of bread in butter: put three spoonfuls of cullis into your dish, garnish the rim with the fried bread; break some eggs into the middle, cover them with the rashers of bacon, and do them over a slow fire.

 ## MODERN RECIPE

½ lb. bacon

3 slices of bread, cut or broken into chunks about 1" × 2" (the recipe for **french bread** works well for this, even when stale)

4 T butter

5 eggs

3 T **broth** or **cullis**

Preheat the broiler and have a shelf situated near the bottom of the oven. Boil the bacon in a large saucepan, making sure that the water does not boil over, for 5 minutes. Melt the butter in a skillet and add the pieces of bread, turning them frequently, until they are browned all over. Arrange the pieces of bread around the edges of a frying pan with an oven-safe handle. Pour the broth into the pan, and then crack the eggs into the middle of the pan. Arrange the bacon slices on top of the eggs and broil until the bacon is browned and the eggs are firm, about 5 to 10 minutes depending on your broiler and the distance of the pan from the heating element.

✿ FARCED EGGS ✿

(Glasse)

However when he once got to Devizes he was determined to comfort himself with a good hot Supper and therefore ordered a whole Egg to be boiled for him & his Servants. (*Clifford, MW* 43)

Mrs. Bates, let me propose your venturing on one of these eggs. An egg boiled very soft is not unwholesome. Serle understands boiling an egg better than any body. I would not recommend an egg boiled by any body else—but you need not be afraid—they are very small, you see—one of our small eggs will not hurt you. (*E* 24)

... there her uncle kindly left her to cry in peace, conceiving perhaps that the deserted chair of each young man might exercise her tender enthusiasm, and that the remaining cold pork bones and mustard in William's plate, might but divide her felings with the broken egg-shells in Mr. Crawford's. (*MP* 282)

Hard-boiled eggs were made no differently than they are today, but they were used and eaten somewhat differently. When eaten on their own, they were often opened with egg scissors, scissor-handled silver or pewter tools with spiked blades that sliced off the top of the egg. Eggs were also sometimes boiled so as to create one huge egg; the yolks of five or six eggs were mixed gently together, tied in a bladder to form a round shape, and boiled till they solidified. Then the hardened yolk ball was placed inside an oval bladder filled with the whites. This second bladder was boiled and removed, leaving an ostrich-egg-sized "boiled egg" that could be sliced open as the centerpiece of an egg-based dish. Sometimes the illusion was assisted by running a cord through the yolks before they were boiled, and then using this thread to center the yolk inside a wooden mold for cooking the whites.

Hard-boiled eggs were also a common ingredient in sauces. Usually, only the yolks were used, adding a sulphurous flavor to certain dishes. The recipe below uses both the yolks and whites; Glasse finishes the dish by using the kitchen fire-shovel as a salamander.

Get two cabbage-lettuces, scald them, with a few mushrooms, parsley, sorrel, and chervil; then chop them very small with the yolks of hard eggs, seasoned with salt and nutmeg; then stew them in butter, and when they are enough, put in a little cream, then pour them into the bottom of a dish; take the whites and chop them very fine with parsley, nutmeg, and salt; lay this round the brim of the dish, and run a red-hot fire-shovel over it, to brown it.

✣ MODERN RECIPE

1 head of cabbage	3 hard-boiled eggs, whites and yolks separated from each other
½ lb. button mushrooms	
6 T finely chopped fresh parsley, *in all*	salt
¼ cup each finely chopped fresh sorrel and chervil (optional)*	½ tsp. nutmeg, *in all*
	5 T butter
	¼ cup cream

Bring a large pot of water to boil on the stove. Quarter the cabbage and parboil it for 4 minutes. Remove the cabbage and let it drain. Add the mushrooms to the boiling water and parboil them for 2 minutes. Remove those also and let them drain. (The eggs can be hard-boiled in the same water.)

Finely chop the cabbage and mushrooms. Over medium-low heat, cook the cabbage, mushrooms, parsley, sorrel and chervil,* hard-boiled egg yolks, and ¼ tsp. nutmeg in the butter, and add salt to taste. Cook until the cabbage is somewhat softened but not limp, about 10 minutes. Add the cream and transfer the mixture to an oven-safe serving dish.

Chop the hard-boiled egg whites and toss them with ¼ tsp. nutmeg and salt to taste. Arrange this mixture around the rim of the cabbage mixture. Using a kitchen torch or the broiler, lightly brown the top surface of the food and serve.

*If you cannot find sorrel or chervil, add ¼ cup finely chopped romaine lettuce and 1 T fresh lemon juice.

❂ OMELETTES ❂

(Raffald, Farley)

The Dr. was very fond of eating, and would have a good dinner every day; and Mrs. Grant, instead of contriving to gratify him at little expense, gave her cook as high wages as they did at Mansfield Park, and was scarcely ever seen in her offices. Mrs. Norris could not speak with any temper of such grievances, not of the quantity of butter and eggs that were regularly consumed in the house. (*MP* 31)

Raffald's Recipe

Put a quarter of a pound of butter into a frying pan. Break six eggs and beat them a little, strain them through a hair sieve. Put them in when your butter is hot and strew in a little shred parsley and boiled ham scraped fine with nutmeg, pepper and salt. Fry it brown on the under side. Lay it on your dish but don't turn it, hold a hot salamander half a minute over it to take off the raw look of the eggs. Stick curled parsley in it and serve it up. *N.B. You may put in clary and chives or onions if you like.*

Farley's Recipe

Beat up six eggs with cream, boil some of the largest and finest asparagus, and when boiled cut off all the green in small pieces. Mix them with the eggs, and put in some pepper and salt. Make a slice of butter hot in a pan, put them in and serve them on buttered toast.

MODERN RECIPE (Raffald)

½ stick butter (4 T)	1 cup finely diced ham
6 eggs	¼ tsp. nutmeg
½ cup chopped fresh parsley	½ tsp. pepper

Melt the butter in a large ovenproof skillet on the stove over medium heat. Beat the eggs well in a bowl and add the parsley, ham, nutmeg, and pepper. (Raffald suggests using salt as well, but I found the salt in the ham adequate; the addition of more salt simply made the omelette too salty.)

When the butter is hot, pour the egg mixture into the skillet. Reduce the heat to medium-low and cook until firm on the bottom side, about 5 minutes. Brown the top with a kitchen torch or the broiler.

There are multiple ways to finish the ham omelette. Raffald used a "salamander," just a piece of metal that could be heated and passed over food to brown it. One way to make the omelette is to use a reduced amount of butter (4 T versus Raffald's quarter pound), a nonstick skillet, and a kitchen butane torch of the kind used for browning crème brulée. The other way is to use an ovenproof skillet, which will usually not feature a nonstick coating, and to pass the omelette under the broiler to brown its top side. In this case, it is necessary to use more butter (¼ lb.) to keep the omelette from sticking to the pan.

MODERN RECIPE (Farley)

6 eggs	½ tsp. pepper
¼ cup cream	½ tsp. salt
6 asparagus stalks	2 T butter
	buttered toast (optional)

Beat the eggs well in a bowl with the cream, salt, and pepper. Bring a pot of water to a boil, boil the asparagus stalks for 5 minutes or until just tender, and place them in a bowl of cold water to stop them from growing limp and overdone. Cut the asparagus stalks crosswise into ¼" pieces and mix them into the eggs.

Heat the 2 T butter over medium heat in a nonstick skillet. Add the eggs and cook just until the bottom is firm, about 3 minutes. Slide a spatula under the omelette and fold it in half. Cook until nicely browned on the bottom side, about 2 to 3 minutes. Flip the omelette and cook till the other side is browned as well, about 2 to 3 minutes more.

Serve with buttered toast, if desired.

EGGS EN ALLUMETTES

(*The French Family Cook*)

The anonymous author of this work thought eggs were good for more than eating. They served various medical purposes as well. "The yolks of new-laid eggs beat up in warm water," he wrote, "is called hen's milk, and, taken going to bed, is good for a cold: the fine skin within the shell, beat and mixed with the white, is excellent for chopped lips; and the shell, burnt and pounded, for whitening the teeth: taken in wine, it is good for stopping a spitting of blood."

As for this recipe, "allumettes" are matchsticks, which tells us how these little bits of egg should be sliced.

Beat up the yolks of eight eggs with a kitchen-spoonful of brandy; set them over the fire in a dish, and when well done and cold, cut them into allumettes, and dip them into a batter about the consistence of thick cream, made with flour mixed with white wine, a spoonful of oil, and some salt: fry and glaze them with sugar and a salamander.

MODERN RECIPE

8 egg yolks

1 T brandy

6 T butter, *in all*

½ cup white wine

¼ cup plus 3 T flour

1 T oil

½ tsp. kosher salt

1 T sugar

Preheat the broiler. (If you have a butane kitchen torch, the sort used for browning crème brulée, you may brown the sugar with this instead of with the broiler. This method is preferable, as it allows you far more control over the browning and helps avoid the formation of burned spots.)

Beat the egg yolks and brandy well in a small mixing bowl. Melt 2 T butter in a small nonstick skillet over medium-low heat. When it is melted, pour in the eggs and cook very gently until the yolks have solidified. The goal is not to brown or flip the yolks but to cook them into a firm sheet.

Remove the pan from the heat and let the eggs cool. Slice them into strips ¼" wide and about 3" long.

Mix the flour, white wine, oil, and salt in a small mixing bowl. Melt 4 T of butter over medium-high in the same nonstick skillet you used for cooking the yolks. Dip the "matchsticks" of yolk and brandy into the wine batter and fry them on both sides in the butter. When they are golden brown, remove them to a pan—a metal pie pan works well—and scatter them with sugar.

Place the pan under the broiler briefly to brown the sugar (or brown with a butane kitchen torch).

EGGS AND SPINACH

(The French Family Cook)

*The same author included recipes for eggs browned in butter, pepper, salt, and vinegar, and for eggs poached in a sauce of minced ham, **cullis**, **broth**, vinegar, pepper, and salt. This recipe, oddly, mingles spinach, eggs, and some unexpectedly sweet flavors. Two thirds of my tasters found the slightly sweet flavor appealing; one third were unimpressed.*

Take some spinach boiled in water, well squeezed and pounded, and strain it through a strainer, with some good cream; beat up six eggs with it, and strain it a second time; then add some sugar, macaroons pounded, orange-flower water, and a few grains of salt; put it into your dish for table, and set it over a slow fire, letting it remain till a light gratin is formed at the bottom.

MODERN RECIPE

4 cups fresh leaf spinach, washed, stems removed	1½ T marzipan or one small almond macaroon, crumbled
6 eggs, beaten	1 tsp. sugar
¼ cups cream	1 tsp. orange-flower water
	pinch salt

Bring a pot of water to a boil. Add the spinach and boil 3 minutes. Rinse the spinach with cold water, squeeze out the excess moisture, and run it through a food mill or food processor to make a fine paste.

In a bowl, mix the spinach, eggs, cream, marzipan or macaroon, sugar, orange-flower water, and salt. Pour the mixture into a large nonstick skillet and set it over low heat until the bottom is set and nicely browned, about 25 minutes.

Heat a second nonstick skillet of the same size or a little larger. Place the larger skillet, upside down, over the eggs and spinach. Holding the skillet handles together, quickly flip the eggs and spinach from one skillet to the other and cook over low to medium-low heat until the other side of the food is lightly browned and the eggs are set all the way through, about 10 more minutes.

❀ CREAM CHEESE ❀

(Millington, Hunter)

. . . the housekeeper, after a great many courtesies on the subject of pheasants, had taken her to the dairy, told her all about their cows, and given her the receipt for a famous cream cheese. . . . (*MP* 104)

Mrs. Norris, having fidgetted about, and obtained a few pheasant's eggs and a cream cheese from the housekeeper, . . . was ready to lead the way. (*MP* 104–5)

There Fanny, you shall carry that parcel for me—take great care of it—do not let it fall; it is a cream cheese, just like the excellent one we had at dinner. Nothing would satisfy that good old Mrs. Whitaker, but my taking one of the cheeses. (*MP* 105)

This was certainly enough to put any one in a Passion; however, I was as cool as a Cream-cheese. . . . (*Lesley, MW* 129)

Freshly made cream cheese has a unique, tangy flavor and a rich texture. The authors of cookbooks in Austen's time sometimes used a combination of milk and cream thickened with rennet and sometimes used cream alone. Modern cream cheeses, too, can be made of either milk and cream or cream only, and can be made at room temperature or with the addition of a little stovetop heat. Therefore, I had a little latitude in determining what sort of recipe to use.

The authors of old cookbooks all concurred in recommending warm weather for the manufacture of this cheese, which implies that they did not cook the curd but allowed it to ripen at the temperature of the dairy or kitchen. The "famous cream cheese" of Sotherton was probably an all-cream cheese, as cream was the richest, least prevalent, and therefore most desirable product of the dairy. Sotherton, a massive old estate, seems to have had the best of everything, and its seems logical to assume that this applied to its dairy products as well as to its poultry and orchards. The following recipe reflects these bits of evidence.

Millington's Recipe

Take twelve quarts of new milk and a quart of cream, put them together with two spoonsfuls of rennet, (or less, according to its strength) just warm; and when it has stood still till the curd is produced, lay a cloth in the vat (which must be made of a proper size for the cheese) cut out the curd with a skimming dish, and put it into the vat till it is full, turning the cheese-cloth over it; and as the curd settles, lay more on till you have laid on as much as will make one cheese. When the whey is drained out, turn the cheese into a dry cloth, and then lay a pound weight upon it; at night turn it out into another cloth, and the next morning salt it a little; then having made a bed of nettles or ash-leaves to lay it on, cover it with the same, shifting it twice a day for about ten days, when it will be fit for use.

Hunter's Recipe

Make a frame of old oak (for fir would give a taste) 8½ inches long, 3 inches deep, 3 inches wide within, and open at the top and bottom. Take a quart, or more, of cream from the vessel before it is stirred for churning, and place a piece of linen cloth in the frame, sufficiently large to hang over the edge. This will act as a siphon to drain off the whey, as no pressure whatever must be used for that purpose. Then pour the cream into the frame or mould, and set it on a dish, a table, or a few rushes. Change the cheese daily into a clean dry cloth, till it begin to adhere to it, when it will be in a proper state to be coated once a day, with fresh leaves of the stinging nettle. After this, it will soon be ripe for use.

OBS[ervation].

This kind of cheese can only be made in summer, when there is a sufficient degree of heat to ripen it. Besides, the cream is the richest at that season. Some persons prefer this kind of cheese in its sour state, before it has become perfectly ripe. Others again object to its richness when made of all cream, and recommend a mixture of cream and milk, made into a curd with rennet.

MODERN RECIPE

½ gallon heavy cream

2 tsp. noniodized salt

1 packet direct-set or 4 oz. prepared mesophilic starter

Sterilize all utensils.

Warm the cream to room temperature (72°F to 76°F). Add the starter and stir. Cover the container and let the cream sit overnight at 72°F to 80°F. In the morning, the cream will be very thick.

Sterilize a colander and line it with butter muslin, a very tightly woven form of cheesecloth. Pour the thickened cream into the muslin and tie the corners of the muslin together, forming a bag.

Hang the bag over a bowl, allowing the liquid and thinner cream to drip away. One way to hang the bag is to suspend it from a chopstick or pencil with each end of the chopstick or pencil resting on something tall, such as a stack of books. I find it easier to place the bowl under an upper cabinet and hang the bag from the cabinet knob or handle. Let the bag drain for about 12 hours.

Turn the cheese into a bowl and add salt. Cool it in the refrigerator and cut into sections. These sections can then be wrapped in plastic wrap and stored in the refrigerator or frozen.

STILTON CHEESE

(Millington)

. . . he was only giving his fair companion an account of the yesterday's party at his friend Cole's, and that she was come in herself for the Stilton cheese, the north Wiltshire, the butter, the cellery, the beet-root and all the dessert. (*E* 88–89)

Stilton, a strong-flavored blue cheese, was famed throughout England. One report in the first half of the eighteenth century stated that it was flavored with mace; another, a description by Daniel Defoe, said that it was "brought to table with the mites or maggots round it so thick that they bring a spoon with them for you to eat the mites with as you do the cheese." Like all cheeses of the time, it would have been made with unpasteurized milk, and bacteria within the milk would have accomplished its transformation into cheese; today the same process is hastened by chemical additives. Alexander Hunter advised his readers to age Stilton cheese for two years, but you can taste yours after a few months—or just buy it at the supermarket if you do not want to invest in cheese-making supplies!

Take the night's cream, and put it into the morning's new milk, with the rennet; when the curd is produced it must not be broken, as is done with other cheese, but take it out with a soil dish altogether. And place it in the sieve to drain gradually, and, as it drains, keep gradually pressing it till it becomes firm and dry; then place it in a wooden hoop, and afterwards keep it dry on boards, turning it frequently, with cloth binders round it, which are to be tightened as occasion requires; but the dairy-maid must not be disheartened if she does not succeed perfectly in her first attempt. In some dairies the cheese, after being taken out of the wooden hoop, is bound tight round with a cloth, which cloth is changed every day, until the cheese become firm enough to support itself; after the cloth is taken off, it is rubbed every day all over for two or three months, with a brush, and if the weather is damp or moist, twice a day; and even before the cloth is taken off, the top and bottom is well rubbed every day.

MODERN RECIPE

2 gallons whole milk

2 cups heavy whipping cream

⅛ tsp. blue mold (*P. roqueforti*)

2 oz. mesophilic starter (or 1 packet direct-set mesophilic starter)

¼ tsp. liquid rennet dissolved in ¼ cup distilled water

1 T cheese salt

Continued on next page

Continued from previous page

Make sure all utensils are very clean!

Pour the cream and milk into a large pot and heat to 86°F. (This step is most reliable if done in a double boiler.)

Turn off the heat, add the mold and starter, cover the pot and let sit for ½ hour. Then add the rennet and water and stir gently and thoroughly for five minutes. Cover again and let sit for 90 minutes at 86°F, heating again slightly if necessary to maintain the temperature.

Line a large colander with cheesecloth and set it in a bowl. (You may need two such setups if the colanders are small.) Lift out the curds (the solidified, cheesy milk) with a slotted spoon and set them in the colander(s). The curds will be fairly soft. When you can no longer get a good spoonful of curds from the pot, set it aside. You can either discard the liquid (whey) left over, or use it as liquid for baking bread.

Let the soft curds sit in the colanders for 90 minutes. Do not pour off the whey that seeps into the bowls. Then empty the liquid from the bowls and gather the ends of the cheesecloth, closing the "bag" containing the curds and twisting to extract some moisture. Let the bag sit, pouring off liquid from the bowl as necessary, and occasionally tightening the bag, until the curds have stopped dripping.

Tie the bag ends closed and place it on a clean cheese board or cutting board. Place another board on top and put a weight on top of the top board. (A five-pound bag of sugar or flour works well.) Let the bag sit under 5 to 8 pounds of weight overnight at 68°F to 70°F.

The next morning, empty the curds into a bowl and mix them gently with the salt. The salted curd should be lumpy rather than perfectly smooth and uniform. Sanitize a two-pound cheese mold, cheese boards, and cheese mats, either by boiling or by washing in a no-rinse sanitizing solution such as iodophor. Place a mat on a board, the mold on the mat, and the curds in the mold. Then place another mat and board atop the cheese mold. Flip the mold and boards upside-down frequently for the first day, then a few times a day for the next four days.

Sterilize a metal skewer and poke holes into the cheese all around the sides at about 1" intervals. These holes will allow the blue mold to grow inside the cheese.

Move the cheese to a cool and humid place and let it sit on a cheese mat for at least a month and preferably 3 or 4 months.

❀ NORTH WILTSHIRE CHEESE ❀

. . . he was only giving his fair companion an account of the yesterday's party at his friend Cole's, and that she was come in herself for the Stilton cheese, the north Wiltshire, the butter, the cellery, the beet-root and all the dessert. (*E* 88–89)

Wiltshire was well known in Austen's time as dairy country, and the local cheesemakers achieved extraordinarily consistent results. As a result, their cheese was quite popular, and Val Cheke estimates that, in 1798, 5,000 tons were produced. The cheese was typically a hard cow's-milk cheese, similar in flavor to a cheddar or Cheshire cheese. None of my eighteenth- and nineteenth-century sources included a recipe for this sought-after cheese, but the Lackham (Wiltshire) Museum of Agriculture and Rural Life (www.lackhamcountrypark.co.uk) has a recipe based on eighteenth-century production methods. The following recipe is adapted from their instructions.

MODERN RECIPE

2 gallons whole milk

1 packet direct-set mesophilic starter

1 tsp. liquid rennet diluted in ¼ cup cool unchlorinated water

1 T noniodized salt

3 drops annatto-based cheese coloring (optional)

Sterilize all utensils with hot water or a sterilizing solution such as Iodophor.

Warm the milk in a double boiler to 85°F to 90°F. Add the starter, stir gently and thoroughly, cover, and let sit at 85°F for 1 hour. Add coloring, if desired, and rennet solution, stirring gently and thoroughly. Cover and let sit at 85°F to 90°F for another hour, or until a solid curd forms and breaks cleanly when cut with a knife.

Cut the curd into ½" chunks and gradually raise the temperature of the curds and whey to 100°F over the course of about half an hour—no more than 2 degrees every 5 to 6 minutes. Stir the curds from time to time for about half an hour after the mixture has reached 100°F. The curds will gradually shrink. Remove the pot from the hot water and let it sit for a few minutes. Line a sterilized colander with cheesecloth and place in a large sterilized bowl or roasting pan. Pour the curds into the cheesecloth.

Let the curds drain for 15 to 20 minutes. Then tie the edges of the cheesecloth together and hang this improvised bag of curds over a bowl in a warm spot to let more of the whey drain out. After an hour or two of draining, break up the curds in a sterilized bowl and mix in the salt. Pack the curds into a sterilized two-pound cheese mold lined with cheesecloth.

Fold the cheesecloth over the curds and place in a cheese press. (If you don't have a cheese press, you can improvise by using a "follower," a pressing lid for a cheese mold, topped with a board and weights. This is, however, not as easy to use or as reliable as a cheese press.) Press at 10 lbs. pressure for 15 minutes. Flip the cheese, increase the pressure to 20 lbs., and press for another 15 minutes. Remove the cheese and wrap it in a clean, dry cheesecloth. Invert it and place it back in the press. Increase the pressure to 50 lbs. and press for three days, inverting the cheese

Continued on next page

Continued from previous page

twice a day. After three full days of pressing, remove the cheese and rub the outside with salt. Allow it to air dry for two to three days, turning it frequently to keep moisture from accumulating on the bottom.

Wax the cheese by dipping it in melted cheese wax or by brushing melted cheese wax on its surface. If brushing the wax on, do one surface at a time and allow this coat to harden before waxing another section. Give the cheese two or three coats of wax. Then store the cheese for one month to two years at 46°F to 60°F and 75 to 95 percent humidity.

❀ RAMAQUINS OF CHEESE ❀

(Briggs)

"She was just sitting down to supper, Ma'am."

"And what had she got for Supper?" "I did not observe." "Bread & Cheese I suppose." "I should never wish for a better supper," said Ellen. "You have never any reason" replied her Mother, "as a better is always provided for you." (*Col Let, MW* 156–57)

I am usually at the fire cooking some little delicacy for the unhappy invalid—Perhaps hashing up the remains of an old Duck, toasting some cheese or making a Curry which are the favourite dishes of our poor friend. (*Beaut Desc, MW* 72)

. . . Betsey had finished her cry at being allowed to sit up only one hour extraordinary in honour of her sister, . . . leaving all below in confusion and noise again, the boys begging for toasted cheese, her father calling out for his rum and water, and Rebecca never where she ought to be. (*MP* 387)

It is impossible to do justice to the hospitality of his attentions towards me; he made a point of ordering toasted cheese for supper entirely on my account. (Letter from Jane Austen, August 27, 1805)

Bread and cheese, in some combination, were a mainstay of the English diet. Middlesex laborers in 1795 ate bread, cheese, and pork for breakfast, and the same for supper, and while one suspects that the gentry often ate fancier fare, Austen herself, as the above quotation demonstrates, was quite fond of homely toasted cheese. In its simplest form, toasted cheese was simply grated or sliced cheese placed on toast and browned. In the eighteenth century the browning would have been done at the fire or, in homes equipped with such an implement, with a salamander. Briggs's version, for which he provided two recipes (one with toast, one without), is more complex and, we think, tastier. This recipe earned huge raves from the entire tasting crew. Cheesy—cheesy— oh, so cheesy. . . .

Grate half a pound of Cheshire and half a pound of thin Gloucester cheese, put it into a stew-pan, with a gill of white wine, and keep it stirring over the fire till it is melted; then put in a spoonful of mustard, a little butter, and the yolks of four eggs beat up, stir it round till it is thick, and set it by to get cold; butter some small patty-pans, put it in, and bake it in a gentle oven till it is brown; then put it in a very hot dish, and send it away quick: or have a large pan of fat boiling, and drop it in with a spoon in drops, fry them quick and brown, put them on a sieve to drain, and then dish them up.

You may make them of Parmazan cheese if you have it.

Ramaquins on Toast

Prepare your cheese as before; toast some thin toasts, and cut them in what shape you please, put them in the dish, and while your cheese is hot put it on the toasts, and brown it with a hot iron or salamander, or put it in the oven a quarter of an hour, and send it to table hot and quick, as it soon gets cold.

MODERN RECIPE

1 lb. Parmesan, grated	2 tsp. Dijon mustard
½ lb. mild cheddar, grated	3 T butter
½ lb. Gouda, grated	8 egg yolks
1 cup white wine	8 slices of good-quality white bread

Using something slightly smaller than your ramekin as a template, cut circles of white bread that will fit inside your ramekins. Toast these either in the toaster or under a broiler. When the bread is toasted, put one slice in the bottom of each ramekin. Preheat oven to 400°F.

Place the wine in double boiler and add the cheeses. Stir occasionally until all the cheese is melted. (Stir continuously if your double boiler is not nonstick.) Add the mustard and butter and stir until they are fully incorporated. Add the egg yolks and stir continuously until the mixture thickens and becomes uniform. Immediately spoon the mixture over the toast slice in each ramekin, distributing the cheese mixture evenly. (If the cheese separates, spoon the solid cheese first, then evenly distribute the buttery remainder.) Bake in a 400°F oven for 5 to 10 minutes or until the cheese starts to bubble. Then turn on the broiler just until the tops begin to brown.

10

VEGETABLES

Vegetables (*Sand, MW* 380) in general were far less popular in Austen's day than they are now. To some extent, this was the result of seasonal availability. Not all vegetables could be preserved beyond their natural season, and most were far less palatable in their preserved state than when fresh. To some extent, the blame lay with the tendency of the English, noted by foreign observers, to overcook their vegetables and to smother them in butter sauce. But primarily, the relative absence of vegetables in the diet was due to the primitive under-standing of medicine and diet. No one even knew what a vitamin was, let alone where it might be found or what its impact on health might be. Novelist Frances Burney D'Arblay and her husband were unusual in being "people who make it a rule to owe a third of their sustenance to the Garden."

This is not to say that vegetables were not eaten, merely that they were over-whelmed in quantity by the vast piles of meat consumed on the average upper-class or middle-class table. Vegetables—though they were more commonly referred to at the time as "potherbs" or "garden stuff" (*Sand, MW* 380)—appeared on their own as side dishes or as accompaniments to meat or eggs. Al-most every country home had a kitchen garden, which in the case of large estates might run to several acres. Jane's mother was an avid gardener well into her old age and grew not only flowers but also herbs, fruit, potatoes, peas, and other vegetables. She had a fascination for new plants, judging from the fact that at Steventon she was considered trendy for growing potatoes, and at Chaw-ton, in 1813, she grew tomatoes for eating long before they were considered edible by most of the rest of the nation. A wide variety of vegetables was either grown at home or sold by shops or street vendors. In an 1819 letter to *The Gen-tleman's Magazine*, a correspondent catalogues the cries of some of London's street vendors, in which he mentions potatoes, "spinage," watercress, salad, and radishes for sale; the radishes sold for "twenty a penny."

Within the image: *Parting of the Loaves & Fishes*; *The Triumph of Benevolence*; *The Fall of MANNA*; *Table of Interest 5 ₚ Cent*; *Munificence*; *AQUA Regis*; *J.G.ᵗ design. et fecit*; *Queen Charlotte*; *TEMPERANCE enjoying a Frugal Meal*; *George III*; *Pub. July 28ᵗʰ 1792. by H. Humphry, Old Bond Street*

Temperance enjoying a Frugal Meal, 1792. The king and queen dine on boiled eggs and salad. Cruets for oil and vinegar can be seen between them. (Courtesy of the Lewis Walpole Library, Yale University. 792.7.28.1.)

Parson Woodforde's diary confirms that the full variety of vegetables was only available for part of the year. The majority of his references to eating vegetables are in the spring and summer, particular June to August, while his references to eating vegetables out of those seasons are to the sorts of vegetables that "kept" well for long periods of time. In the spring and summer, he ate green peas, artichokes, beans, asparagus, morels, truffles, stewed mushrooms, radishes, cucumbers, and new potatoes. In the fall and winter he was confined to root vegetables like onions (*Visit, MW* 53) and turnips that could be stored in a cool place and to items like olives (*S&S* 193) and peas that could be pickled or dried.

Storage methods varied according to the vegetable in question. Parsnips, for example, could simply be left in the ground over the winter, where their starch would convert to sugar as they froze. Potatoes could be stored in a cool, dark room such as a cellar. Cookbook author Charles Millington advised keeping beans in jars, alternating layers of beans and salt; peas, he said, should be boiled in salt water and dried. To reconstitute them, the cook should boil them in wa-

Old Times Returned, 1802. A balanced meal, at the turn of the nineteenth century: a bowl of salad, a large loaf of bread, a plate of potatoes, an enormous piece of roast beef, and, of course, wine both on the table and in the cooling tub at bottom right. (Courtesy of the Lewis Walpole Library, Yale University. 802.5.18.1.)

ter with salt, sugar, and butter, then drain them and serve them hot with butter. Mushrooms, according to Elizabeth Raffald and others, should be steeped in salt for a while, then drained, baked in an oven at very low temperature, then sealed in jars with the liquid that was yielded by the baking, capped with a layer of suet and a "bladder." They were to be stewed in milk and other ingredients for serving, with the steeping liquid set aside to give mushroom flavor to various made dishes.

❁ BOILED ARTICHOKES ❁
(Raffald)

. . . we have in fact all the comfort of an excellent Kitchen Garden, without the constant Eyesore of its formalities; or the yearly nuisance of its decaying vegetation. . . . We are quite as well off for Gardenstuff as ever we were—for if it is forgot to be brought at any time, we can always buy what we want at Sanditon-House.—The Gardiner there, is glad enough to supply us—. (*Sand, MW* 380)

Cooks of Austen's time also blanched, floured, and butter-fried artichokes, serving them with "melted butter" sauce or a sauce of butter, red wine, nutmeg, pepper, and salt. They tended to preserve artichokes not by pickling them but by drying them. Modern cooks would add lemon juice to the soaking water to prevent the artichokes from turning brown, and you may do so if you like.

If they are young ones leave about an inch of the stalks, put them in a strong salt and water for an hour or two. Then put them in a pan of cold water, set them over the fire, but don't cover them, it will take off their colour. When you dish them up put rich melted butter in small cups or pots, like rabbits. Put them in the dish with your artichokes and send them up.

❧ MODERN RECIPE

8 small artichokes	1 recipe **melted butter**
salt	

Heavily salt a large bowl of water. Trim the stems of the artichokes so that they are about 1" long. Soak the artichokes in the salted water for 1 to 2 hours. Then transfer them to a pot of plain water and boil until tender, about 30 minutes, or until stems are tender and leaves peel away easily. Serve with melted butter.

BOILED ASPARAGUS

(The French Family Cook)

The baked apples and biscuits, excellent in their way, you know; but there was a delicate fricassee of sweetbread and some asparagus brought in at first, and good Mr. Woodhouse, not thinking the asparagus quite boiled enough, sent it all out again. *(E 329)*

The principal cookbook authors of Austen's time recommended scraping off the tough outer skin of the asparagus stalks, sometimes until the stalks were white. Then they served them on toast dipped in boiling water, with melted butter either poured on top or served on the side. Asparagus could also be served pickled or in a ragout.

Boil it in salt and water, and dish it, serving a sauce over it. To be well done, it should be crisp: half a quarter of an hour will be sufficient to boil it. Take some good cullis, and put into it a little butter, salt and pepper; thicken it over the fire, and serve it, if you will, over the asparagus, or, if you like it better, serve a white sauce over it. Asparagus, when boiled and cold, is good eating with pepper, salt, oil, and vinegar.

 MODERN RECIPE

1 large bunch asparagus	salt
½ cup beef **broth**, **gravy**, or **white sauce**	pepper
1½ T butter	

Bring a pot of salted water to a boil. Add the asparagus and boil till crisp-tender, about 5 minutes. Meanwhile, heat the broth, butter, salt, and pepper in a small saucepan. Pour the sauce over the drained asparagus and serve.

ASPARAGUS FORCED IN FRENCH ROLLS

(Glasse)

At Devizes we had comfortable rooms, & a good dinner to which we sat down about 5; amongst other things we had Asparagus & a Lobster which made me wish for you, & some cheesecakes on which the children made so

delightful a supper as to endear the Town of Devizes to them for a long
time. (Letter from Jane to Cassandra, May 17, 1799)

Some of the best asparagus in England was grown on 260 acres in London, at the approximate site of today's Battersea Park.

This particular recipe was well received by all taste-testers, particularly the vegetarians. The children who taste-tested it also enjoyed it, though they compared the odd presentation to "Oompa-Loompa heads."

Take three French rolls, take out all the crumb, by first cutting a piece of the top-crust off; but be careful that the crust fits again the same place; fry the rolls brown in fresh butter; then take a pint of cream, the yolks of six eggs beat fine, a little salt and nutmeg, stir them well together over a slow fire till it begins to be thick; have ready a hundred of small grass boiled; then save tops enough to stick the rolls with, the rest cut small and put into the cream, fill the loaves with them: before you fry the rolls make holes thick in the top crust and stick the grass in; then lay on the piece of crust and stick the grass in, that it may look as if it were growing. It makes a pretty side-dish at a second course.

MODERN RECIPE

2 large white rolls	3 egg yolks
melted butter	½ tsp. salt
2 bunches asparagus (about 2 lbs.)	pinch of ground nutmeg
1 cup heavy cream	

Preheat the oven to 400°F. Have a bowl of cold water ready.

Trim off the tough ends of the asparagus and cut the stalks in half crosswise. Bring a pot of water to boil and boil the asparagus just until tender, about 3 to 5 minutes. Remove the asparagus from the boiling water and place in the bowl of cold water immediately to stop them from cooking further.

Slice the top third off each roll. Remove the soft inside from each bottom section, leaving a crust about ½" thick. Brush the insides of the bottoms of the rolls with butter. Brush the tops of the top crusts with butter as well. Place all the roll sections, butter side up, on a baking sheet and toast in the oven at 400°F until golden brown, about 5 to 8 minutes.

Meanwhile, on the stovetop, gently heat the cream, egg yolks, salt, and nutmeg. Do not allow this mixture to boil or scald on the bottom.

Continued on next page

Continued from previous page

As soon as the rolls are ready, arrange the bottom sections on a serving platter. In each top section, make several holes (the wide end of a chopstick works pretty well for this). Trim and insert one asparagus tip in each hole. Depending on the size of your rolls, you should be able to poke six to ten asparagus tips in each top section.

Slice the remaining asparagus stalks crosswise in ¼" sections, reserving a few more good-looking tips for garnish. Add the chopped asparagus to the cream sauce and stir until just heated through. Spoon the asparagus into the hollowed-out rolls and cover with the decorated roll tops. Spoon any remaining asparagus and cream around the rolls and garnish with the reserved asparagus tips. Serve immediately.

❈ SALAD OF ASPARAGUS ❈

(Millington)

Scale and cut off the heads of large asparagus, boil them till nearly done, strain, and put them into cold water for five minutes, and drain them dry; lay them in rows on a dish, put slices of lemon round the rim, and mix well together a little mustard, oil, vinegar, Cayenne pepper, and salt, and put it over the asparagus just before they are to be eaten.

MODERN RECIPE

2 lbs. asparagus	2 T white vinegar
bowl of ice water	pinch of cayenne pepper
1 T Dijon mustard	pinch of salt
1 T olive oil	lemon slices (optional)

Set a large pot of water on the stove to boil. Meanwhile, trim the woody ends off the asparagus stalks and use a vegetable peeler to peel off the skins on the lower half of the stalks. Boil 5 to 7 minutes or until beginning to grow tender but still mostly crisp. While the asparagus is boiling, mix the mustard, oil, vinegar, cayenne, and salt thoroughly and place in a small dish in the middle of a serving platter.

Remove the stalks to the bowl of ice water for 5 minutes and then arrange in neat rows on the serving platter. Garnish with lemon slices, if desired.

French Beans Ragooed

(Farley)

> His kindness was not confined to words; for within an hour after he left them, a large basket full of garden stuff and fruit arrived from the park, which was followed before the end of the day by a present of game. (*S&S* 30)

The eighteenth century saw two innovations in the European approach to planting and eating beans. The first was that climbing varieties of beans (the vines that gave rise to the story "Jack and the Beanstalk") were supplemented by beans that grew on bushes. The second innovation was the consumption of the entire bean, pod and all; until the eighteenth century green beans had been shelled like peas. In this recipe, it is clear that the pod is meant to be eaten. This recipe also uses onion for a hint of flavor and then removes it before serving, a common tactic of English cooks at the time, who had to cater to their employers' taste for the bland. I have retained the onion to appeal to a more modern palate, but you may follow Farley's procedure if you prefer.

String a quarter of a peck of French beans, but do not split them. Cut them across in three parts, and lay them in salt and water. Then take them out, and dry them in a coarse cloth; then fry them brown, pour out all the fat, and put in a quarter of a pint of hot water. Stir it into the pan by degrees, and let it boil. Then take a quarter of a pound of fresh butter rolled in a little flour, two spoonfuls of ketchup, a spoonful of mushroom pickle, four spoonfuls of white wine, an onion stuck with six cloves, two or three blades of mace beaten, half a nutmeg grated, and a little pepper and salt. Stir it all together for a few minutes, and then throw in the beans. Shake the pan for a minute or two, take out the onions, and pour all into your dish. This is a pretty side dish, which you may garnish with what you fancy, particularly pickles.

Modern Recipe

1 lb. green beans, trimmed and cut crosswise into thirds

salt

5 T butter, *in all*

2 T **walnut ketchup**

1 T **mushroom ketchup**

Continued on next page

Continued from previous page

4 T white wine

pinch of ground mace

pinch of ground cloves

¼ tsp. black pepper

½ tsp. ground nutmeg

½ tsp. salt

¼ of an onion, sliced

2 tsp. flour

Soak the beans for 1 hour in salted water. Remove them from the water, pat them dry, and melt 1 T of the butter in a skillet over medium heat. Add the beans and cook them until they begin to brown. Remove the beans, wipe the pan clean, and add ½ cup water.

Bring the water to a boil. Roll 4 T butter in the 2 tsp. of flour, pinching the lump of butter if necessary in order to incorporate the flour.* Add to the boiling water the butter and flour, ketchups, wine, mace, cloves, pepper, nutmeg, and salt. Heat for 1 minute, then add the beans and warm them for 1 more minute.

Serve immediately. Farley advised garnishing with "pickles," by which he meant any sort of pickled vegetables, not necessarily pickled cucumbers.

See Appendix 1: "What's with All the Butter?"

PICKLED BEET-ROOT

(Raffald)

. . . he was only giving his fair companion an account of the yesterday's party at his friend Cole's, and . . . she was come in herself for the Stilton cheese, the north Wiltshire, the butter, the cellery, the beet-root and all the dessert. (*E* 88–89)

Beets had once been a pottage vegetable—that is, they had been stewed into a kind of thick porridge. By Austen's time, however, this method of preparation had fallen out of favor, replaced by the methods of baking, boiling, and pickling. Eighteenth-century canning directions usually order the cook to pickle the vegetables in undiluted vinegar, which results in a very tasty product if eaten within a few days, but an inedibly sour mess if allowed to remain on the shelf for a few months. My recipe uses half vinegar and half water, which cuts the acidity somewhat.

Take red beetroots and boil them till they are tender. Then take the skins off and cut them in slices and gimp them in the shape of wheels, flowers, or what form you please, and put them into a jar. Then take as much vinegar as you think will cover them and boil it with a little mace, a race of ginger sliced, and a few slices of horseradish. Pour it hot upon your roots and tie them down.

They are a very pretty garnish for made dishes.

MODERN RECIPE

10 beets	1 tsp. mace
3 cups water	2" peeled and sliced fresh ginger
3 cups white vinegar	1½ T prepared horseradish

Boil the beets till tender. Remove the skins and slice ¼" thick. Prepare canning jars and a canner according to the manufacturer's directions. Add beets to the jars.

Boil the remaining ingredients together for 1 minute and pour over the beets, covering the beets but leaving the recommended air space at the top of the jar. Slide a sterilized spatula between the beets and the edges of the jar to remove any trapped air.

Can according to the jar manufacturer's directions.

BROCCOLI AS A SALAD

(Glasse)

> These two girls had been above an hour in the place, happily employed in visiting an opposite milliner, watching the sentinel on guard, and dressing a sallad and cucumber. (*P&P* 219)

Broccoli is a pretty dish by way of salad in the middle of a table; boil it like asparagus . . . lay it in your dish, beat up with oil and vinegar and a little salt. Garnish with nastertium-buds.

Or boil it, and have plain butter in a cup. . . .

MODERN RECIPE:

1 head broccoli	2 T vinegar
3 T olive oil	½ tsp. salt

Bring a pot of water to a boil over high heat. Cut up the broccoli and add it to the water. Return the water to a boil and cook for about 5 minutes, or until the broccoli is tender-crisp and bright green. Drain the broccoli and run cold water over it.

Whisk the oil, vinegar, and salt together. Toss this vinaigrette over the broccoli and serve at room temperature.

STEWED CABBAGE

(The French Family Cook)

Donwell was famous for its strawberry-beds, which seemed a plea for the invitation: but no plea was necessary; cabbage-beds would have been enough to tempt the lady. . . . (*E* 354)

In the following recipe, the cabbage is quartered, but it was also common to boil the head whole. The French Family Cook, however, includes another recipe for cabbage which lies at the opposite end of the spectrum of complexity. In that recipe, each leaf is separated from its neighbors by layers of forcemeat.

Cut a cabbage into four; boil it a quarter of an hour in water, and put in a bit of streaked bacon, cut into bits, with the rind on. Shift it afterwards into cold water; squeeze it well, and tie each quarter, that it may keep its form. Then stew it with some broth, salt, pepper, a bunch of parsley, scallions, cloves, a little nutmeg, and two or three roots, and the meat you intend to serve with it: when the meat and cabbage are done, wipe off the grease, and dish it for table, the streaked bacon upon it, and serve it with a sauce of good cullis, agreeably seasoned.

MODERN RECIPE

3 slices bacon, cut into bits	¼ tsp. cloves
1 head of cabbage	¼ tsp. nutmeg
1 cup chicken stock or beef stock	1 carrot, coarsely chopped
5 sprigs of parsley	1 cup **gravy**
3 scallions, chopped	

Quarter the cabbage, leaving a portion of the stem attached to each quarter. Cover it with water in a pot, add the bacon, and bring the water to a boil. Boil for 5 minutes. Strain off the liquid and reserve the cabbage and bacon.

Return the cabbage and bacon pieces to the pot and add the stock, parsley, scallions, cloves, nutmeg, and carrot. Stew over medium-high heat until the cabbage is fork-tender, about 5 to 10 minutes. Serve the cabbage on a platter with the gravy drizzled over it.

BOILED CABBAGE

(Farley)

Who can endure a Cabbage Bed in October? (*Sand, MW* 380)

Farley, like the author of The French Family Cook, *includes a recipe for "forced" (stuffed) cabbage. In that recipe, he boils a whole cabbage, removes the interior leaves, and stuffs the center with a "forcemeat" (a meatball-like stuffing) made principally of egg, chopped fish, and parsley. Then he ties the cabbage closed and stews it. The recipe below is much simpler and much more characteristic of how the English prepared cabbage; the foreign visitor Carl Moritz complained of the average English dinner in 1782, "To persons in my situation [it] generally consists of a piece of half-boiled or half-roasted meat; and a few cabbage-leaves boiled in plain water; on which they pour a sauce made of flour and butter, the usual method of dressing vegetables in England."*

All sorts of cabbages and young sprouts must have plenty of water allowed them to boil in, and when the stalks become tender, or fall to the bottom, it is a proof of their being sufficiently boiled. Then take them off before they lose their colour; but remember always to throw some salt into your water before you put in your greens. You must send your young sprouts to table whole as they come out of the pot; but many people think cabbage is best chopped, and put into a saucepan, with a piece of butter, stirring it about for five or and serve it up.

 MODERN RECIPE
_____

1 cabbage   1 recipe **melted butter**

Bring a large pot of salted water to a boil. Quarter the cabbage and boil till it is tender, about 10 to 15 minutes. Chop it coarsely and serve with melted butter.

✿ RAGOO'D CARROTS AND PARSNIPS ✿

(The French Family Cook)

That's right, my dear, very right. . . . They must not over-salt the leg; and then, if it is not over-salted, and if it is very thoroughly boiled, just as Serle boils our's, and eaten very moderately of, with a boiled turnip, and a little carrot or parsnip, I do not consider it unwholesome. (*E* 172)

Carrots and parsnips were both immensely useful vegetables, as they had a long shelf life when stored properly. Parsnips in particular were easy to store; they could remain in the ground all winter if necessary, as their starch would simply convert to sugar when it froze. Both vegetables could be added to boiling, stewing, or roasting meat or, as in the recipe below, prepared as a separate dish.

Cut them about the length of two fingers, shaping them round; boil them a quarter of an hour in water, and then put them into a stew-pan, with good broth, a glass of white wine, a bunch of herbs, and a little salt: when they are done, add a little cullis to thicken the sauce, and serve them with any thing you think proper.

MODERN RECIPE

3 large parsnips

4 large carrots

½ cup vegetable broth

1 cup white wine

1 T dried or 2 T fresh parsley

½ tsp. salt

2 T **cullis** or ½ T flour

Peel the vegetables and cut them crosswise in 1½" sections. At the thicker end of each root, cut these sections in half. Bring a pot of water to a boil and boil the roots for 15 minutes. Meanwhile, add the remaining ingredients, except for the cullis or flour, to a saucepan. Warm the sauce over medium-low heat while the roots are boiling, then drain the carrots and parsnips and put them in the saucepan as well. Cover the pot and continue cooking until the vegetables are fork-tender. Just before serving, add the cullis or flour, stir, and warm the vegetables for 1 more minute.

BOILED CARROTS

(Farley)

Scrape your carrots very clean, put them into the pot, and when they be enough take them out, and rub them in a clean cloth. Then slice them into a plate, and pour some melted butter over them. If they be young spring carrots, half an hour will boil them sufficiently; if they be large, they will require an hour; and old Sandwich carrots will take two hours boiling.

MODERN RECIPE

5 to 6 carrots, peeled and cut crosswise ¼" thick

1 recipe **melted butter**

Bring a saucepan of water to a boil. Add the carrots and boil until just tender, about 5 minutes. Serve with melted butter.

❧ RAGOO'D CELERY ❧

(Glasse)

. . . he was only giving his fair companion an account of the yesterday's party at his friend Cole's, and . . . she was come in herself for the Stilton cheese, the north Wiltshire, the butter, the cellery, the beet-root and all the dessert. (*E* 88–89)

The Coles' celery dish might have been this ragout, a simpler ragout, or another recipe given by Glasse, which involves boiling three-inch-long pieces of celery and smothering them in a béchamel sauce. It might also have been a batter-fried celery made by taking the base of a head of celery, dipping it in a coating of white wine, egg yolk, salt, and nutmeg, and frying it in—what else?—butter.

Wash and make a bunch of celery very clean, cut it in pieces about too inches long, put it into a stew-pan with just as much water as will cover it, tie three or four blades of mace, two or three cloves, about twenty corns of whole pepper in a muslin rag loose, put it into a stew-pan, a little onion, a little bundle of sweet herbs; cover it close, and let it stew softly till tender; then take out the spice, onion, and sweet herbs, put in half an ounce of truffles and morels, two spoonfuls of catchup, a gill of red wine, a piece of butter as big as an egg, rolled in flour, six farthing French rolls, season with salt to your palate, stir it all together, cover it close, and let it stew till the sauce is thick and good; take care that the rolls do not break, shake your pan often; when it is enough dish it up, and garnish with lemon. The yolks of six hard eggs, or more, put in with the rolls, will make it a fine dish. This for a first course.

If you would have it white, put in white wine instead of red, and some cream for a second course.

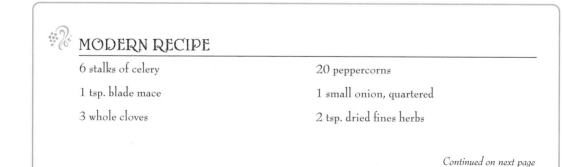

❧ MODERN RECIPE

6 stalks of celery

1 tsp. blade mace

3 whole cloves

20 peppercorns

1 small onion, quartered

2 tsp. dried fines herbs

Continued on next page

Continued from previous page

½ oz. truffles or morels

3 T butter rolled in 1 T flour*

2 T **walnut ketchup**

salt to taste

½ cup red wine (or ½ cup white wine and ½ cup cream)

small white rolls, lemons, or hard-boiled egg yolks for garnish (optional)

Cut the celery stalks crosswise into 2"-long pieces. Place the pieces in a pot and cover them with water. Add the mace, cloves, and peppercorns, tied in a square of cheesecloth, the onion, and the fines herbs. Simmer over medium-low heat until the celery is tender, about 15 minutes. Remove the celery from the water, pour out all the water and other ingredients, and return the celery to the pot along with the truffles or morels, ketchup, red wine (or white wine and cream), butter, flour, and salt. Cover and cook until the sauce is thick, 5 to 10 minutes. Serve warm, garnishing the platter with rolls, lemon wedges, or hard-boiled egg yolks.

*See *Appendix 1: "What's with All the Butter?"*

 ## STEWED CUCUMBERS

(Raffald)

Look at that Grove of Firs—I see a Leg of Mutton—They told me Edward was not Dead; but they deceived me—they took him for a Cucumber—. (*L&F, MW* 100)

Many eighteenth- and nineteenth-century recipes closely resemble those made today. A Regency salad, for example, is very similar to a modern one, and vegetables were often served in ways we would recognize. The most common methods of presentation were to serve the vegetables at room temperature, tossed in a vinaigrette, or to serve them hot with a side-dish of sauce, the most popular sauces being melted butter and water thickened with flour. Raffald's recipe for stewed cucumbers, however, is one of those recipes so far removed from our modern gustatory expectations that it seems truly alien. My nine-year-old son, who will eat almost anything, including smoked fish, raw oysters, whole jalapeños, and seaweed, found this dish beyond the pale. And my mother, always kind, commented, "Let's just say I'm glad I didn't live in the eighteenth century."

Why include it in this book, then? Well, it's an easy way to experience the great divide, in time and taste, that separates us from Austen's world. And unlike some of the other common dishes of the time that vastly differ from those we eat today, such as an-

imal heads and whole boiled turkeys, its ingredients are easy to find, easy and quick to prepare, and not so expensive that you'll feel a pang at throwing them out once you've tasted the weird combination of flavors and textures.

Peel off the out rind, slice the cucumbers pretty thick, fry them in fresh butter, and lay them on a sieve to drain. Put them into a tossing pan with a large glass of red wine, the same of strong gravy, a blade or two of mace. Make it pretty thick with flour and butter and when it boils up put in your cucumbers. Keep shaking them and let them boil five minutes, be careful you don't break them. Pour them into a dish and serve them up.

❧ MODERN RECIPE

2 large cucumbers, peeled and sliced crosswise ½" thick

5 T butter

1 cup red wine

1 cup beef broth

¼ tsp. mace

⅛ cup flour

Melt 2 T butter over medium-high heat and add the cucumber slices in a single layer. If they will not fit in the pan, fry them in two batches. Cook until they begin to brown on one side; then flip them and brown on the other side. Drain in a colander. (The cucumbers can be prepared up to this point and set aside until the rest of the meal is nearly ready.)

Heat the wine and broth in a large skillet over medium-high heat. Bring to a boil and reduce slightly; then add the flour, mix thoroughly, and add the butter. Continue stirring until you feel the sauce thickening. Add the cucumber slices and stir frequently for 5 minutes. Pour into a heated dish and serve.

❀ RAW CUCUMBERS ❀

(Ellis)

The cucumber will I beleive be a very acceptable present, as my Uncle talks of having enquired the price of one lately, when he was told a shilling. (Letter from Jane to Cassandra, May 5, 1801)

When you have pared and sliced cucumers, put a little water and some salt over them, and let them stand so about ten minutes; then drain that from them, and just wash them with a little vinegar, throwing that away likewise, before you put oil and vinegar upon them. This will make them eat much crisper and finer than without such management.—The addition of a few green nasturtian pods fresh gathered and eat with them, correct them, and make them much wholesomer as well as pleasanter, especially to such as do not chuse to eat onions with them.

MODERN RECIPE

2 cucumbers, peeled and sliced crosswise ¼" thick

salt

4 T white vinegar, *in all*

2 T olive oil

Place the cucumber slices in cold salted water for about 10 minutes. Drain the slices and toss them with 2 T of the vinegar. Just before serving, mix the remaining oil and vinegar, drain the cucumbers again, and toss them with the oil and vinegar.

RAGOUT OF CHAMPIGNONS, MUSHROOMS, AND MORELS

(*The French Family Cook*)

Put some champignons into a stew-pan, with a bit of butter, and a bunch of parsley and scallions; turn them a few times over the fire, shake in some flour, and moisten them with a glass of broth, half a glass of white wine, and as much gravy; let them boil a full hour; take the fat off, and add a little cullis; if you have none, add a little more flour when you put it over the fire; season it with salt and whole pepper. A ragout of mushrooms and morels is made in the same manner; but they should be washed in several waters.

MODERN RECIPE

8 oz. button mushrooms	1 cup **broth**
8 oz. other mushrooms of your choice	½ cup white wine
5 T butter	½ cup **cullis**
3 T chopped parsley	salt and pepper to taste
2 scallions, chopped	8 to 10 dried morels, soaked in warm water for 30 minutes
1½ T flour	

Melt the butter in a large saucepan over medium-high heat. Sauté the mushrooms, parsley, and scallions in the butter for 2 to 3 minutes, stirring constantly.

Sprinkle the flour into the pan and cook, stirring, for about half a minute. Pour in the broth, white wine, and cullis, reduce heat to low, and cook for 20 minutes. Add the morels and cook for 20 more minutes.

Add salt and pepper to taste and serve warm.

FRICASSEED MUSHROOMS

(Farley)

Having peeled and scraped the inside of your mushrooms, throw them into salt and water; but if they be buttons, rub them with flannel. Take them out and boil them in water, with some salt in it, and when they be tender, put in a little shred parsley, and an onion stuck with cloves. Toss them up, with a good piece of butter rolled in flour, and put in three spoonfuls of thick cream, and a little nutmeg cut in pieces; but both the nutmeg and the onion must be taken out before you send your mushrooms to table. Instead of the parsley, you may, if you choose it, put in a glass of wine.

MODERN RECIPE

salt

2 lbs. white button mushrooms, stems re-moved

¼ cup parsley, chopped

10 whole cloves

1 small onion

2 T butter rolled in and mixed with 1 T flour*

3 T cream

1 whole nutmeg, cut in half, or ½ tsp. ground nutmeg

Bring a pot of salted water to boil. Add the mushrooms and boil for 5 minutes. Remove the mushrooms, drain them, and put them in a saucepan with the parsley. Stick the whole cloves into the surface of the peeled whole onion and add it to the saucepan as well.

Place the saucepan over medium-low heat and add the floured butter, cream, and nutmeg. Simmer 15 minutes. Remove the onion and the nutmeg (if using a halved whole nutmeg).

*See *Appendix 1: "What's with All the Butter?"*

RAGOUT OF ONIONS

(Glasse)

What's not to love? Onions and butter! This recipe got big thumbs-up from all onion-worshipping tasters.

Take a pint of little young onions, peel them, and take four large ones, peel them, and cut them very small; put a quarter of a pound of good butter into a stew-pan, when it is melted and done making a noise, throw in your onions, and fry them till they begin to look a little brown; then shake in a little flour, and shake them round till they are thick; throw in a little salt, a little beaten pepper, a quarter of a pint of good gravy, and a tea-spoonful of mustard; stir all to-gether, and when it is well-tasted and of a good thickness pour it into your dish, and garnish it with fried crumbs of bread. They make a pretty little dish, and are very good. You may stew raspings in the room of flour, if you please.

MODERN RECIPE

1 lb. small boiling onions, peeled	½ tsp. salt
4 large yellow onions, peeled and chopped into ¼" dice	¼ tsp. pepper
	½ cup beef broth
¼ lb. (one stick) butter	1 tsp. Dijon mustard
¼ cup flour	¼ cup bread crumbs

Melt the butter in a large skillet over medium-high heat. As it begins to sizzle, add all the onions and stir occasionally until they brown and the brown coloring is uniformly distributed through the onions. (You can reduce the heat and let them continue to brown slowly if the rest of dinner is taking longer than you'd like.)

Add the flour and stir until the mixture thickens (about 1 minute). Add the salt, pepper, broth, and mustard and stir until thoroughly incorporated (1 to 2 minutes). Turn off the heat. (The onions can be prepared up to this point and reheated whenever it is convenient.)

In a skillet, heat a small amount of oil or butter and toss some plain bread crumbs in it. Toast the bread crumbs over medium-low heat until they are nicely browned. Remove them from the heat.

When you are ready to serve the dish, reheat the onions on the stove and warm a serving dish. Spoon the onion ragout into the dish and sprinkle the bread crumbs on top.

 BOILED GREEN PEAS

(Glasse)

We began Pease on Sunday, but our gatherings are very small,—not at all like the Gathering in the Lady of the Lake. (Letter from Jane to Cassandra, June 6, 1811)

The Austens apparently got an early start on their pea harvest in 1811; the traditional day to begin picking peas was the king's birthday, June 4. Peas were valued for their sweetness when fresh and for their ability to be dried and kept for long periods of time; a favorite method of preparation, other than simple boiling, was stewing them with lettuce. Austen's "Gathering" in the above allusion to Sir Walter Scott's "Lady of the Lake" is not a gathering of peas but a gathering of men, a clan gathering:

> *Till rose in arms each man might claim*
> *A portion in Clan-Alpine's name,*

From the gray sire, whose trembling hand
Could hardly buckle on his brand,
To the raw boy, whose shaft and bow
Were yet scarce terror to the crow.
Each valley, each sequestered glen,
Mustered its little horde of men
That met as torrents from the height
In Highland dales their streams unite
Still gathering, as they pour along,
A voice more loud, a tide more strong. . . .

(Canto III, Stanza XXIV, Lines 14–25)

Shell your pease just before you want them, put them into a very small quantity of boiling water, with a little salt and a lump of loaf sugar, when they begin to dent in the middle they are enough, strain them in a sieve, put a good lump of butter into a mug or small dish, and send them to table. Boil a sprig of mint in another water, chop it fine, and lay it in lumps round the edge of your dish.

 MODERN RECIPE

3 cups frozen peas	1 tsp. brown sugar
1 tsp. salt	3 T butter
½ T sugar	3 T fresh mint

Bring a saucepan of water to a boil. Add the salt, sugars, and peas. Return the water to a boil and boil the peas just until done, about three to four minutes. Drain the peas, keeping the water at a boil, and put them in a serving bowl. Top with the butter, tossing the peas with the butter to melt it and distribute it evenly. Add the mint to the water in which the peas were boiled and boil it for one minute. Remove the mint from the boiling water, chop it finely, and place little mounds of mint around the edge of the serving bowl, if it has a lip—or one mound in the center of the dish, if it does not.

 POTATOES

(Millington)

"Sir, it is a moor park, we bought it as a moor park, and it cost us—that is, it was a present from Sir Thomas, but I saw the bill, and I know it cost seven shillings, and was charged as a moor park."

"You were imposed on, ma'am," replied Dr. Grant, "these potatoes have as much the flavour of a moor park apricot, as the fruit from that tree. It is an insipid fruit at the best; but a good apricot is eatable, which none from my garden are." (*MP* 54)

Potatoes must not be boiled in more water than will keep them from burning. Let them be close covered, and as soon as the skins crack, they are done. Drain out all the water, let them stand covered for a minute or two, and serve them with the skins on, or peeled, on a plate with melted butter in a boat; otherwise peel and broil them on a gridiron till of a fine brown, and then send them to the table. Another method is, to put them in a saucepan, with good beef dripping, covered close, frequently shake the saucepan: and as soon of a fine brown, and crisp, take them up, drain off the fat, and serve them on a plate, with butter in a boat.

MODERN RECIPE (Boiled Potatoes)

2 lbs. small potatoes   1 recipe **melted butter**

Bring a large pot of salted water to a boil. Add the washed potatoes and boil until they can be easily pierced by a fork (the exact time will vary depending on the size of your potatoes). Meanwhile, make the melted butter.

When the potatoes are tender, drain them. At this point, you can serve them as they are with the melted butter sauce, peel off the skins and serve them with the melted butter, or remove the skins and briefly grill them before serving them with the melted butter.

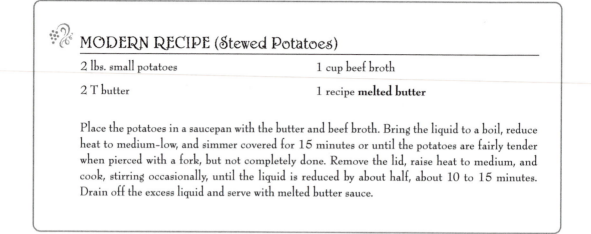

MODERN RECIPE (Stewed Potatoes)

2 lbs. small potatoes	1 cup beef broth
2 T butter	1 recipe **melted butter**

Place the potatoes in a saucepan with the butter and beef broth. Bring the liquid to a boil, reduce heat to medium-low, and simmer covered for 15 minutes or until the potatoes are fairly tender when pierced with a fork, but not completely done. Remove the lid, raise heat to medium, and cook, stirring occasionally, until the liquid is reduced by about half, about 10 to 15 minutes. Drain off the excess liquid and serve with melted butter sauce.

FRIED POTATOES

(Glasse)

The Board takes the liberty of desiring the Clergy, in their several parishes, to have the goodness . . . to encourage, as much as they can, the farmers and cottagers to plant potatoes this spring, in order that the kingdom may experience no scarcity, if the next harvest should prove either very late, or not sufficiently productive in bread corn. (Board of Agriculture, *Hints Respecting the Culture and Use of Potatoes*, 1795)

Glasse's cookbook was first written in 1745, though the edition from which this recipe is taken was published in 1796. Either way, crown pieces varied between about 1¼" and 1½" in diameter. Small potatoes, therefore, work best. Ordinary sugar works just fine for the sauce, but I use turbinado sugar, a less processed variety that retains some of the natural molasses; it more closely approximates what Glasse would have used in this dish.

Cut them into thin slices as big as a crown-piece, fry them brown, lay them in the plate or dish, pour melted butter and sack and sugar over them. These are a pretty corner-plate.

MODERN RECIPE

2 lbs. small potatoes, cut crosswise into ⅛"
slices

7 T butter, *in all*

1 tsp. sugar

1½ tsp. sherry

Melt 3 T butter in a large frying pan over medium heat. Add the potatoes and stir, turning frequently, until they are nicely browned. (They have a tendency to stick together, so a good plan is to fry them in multiple batches, in a single layer, flipping them like pancakes as each side browns.) Then place them in a warm oven until all the potatoes are finished.

Meanwhile, melt the remaining 4 T butter in a small saucepan. Add the sugar, stir, and add the sherry. Shake or stir the pan until the sauce is thoroughly mixed.

Place the potato slices on a warm platter and drizzle the sauce over them.

✿ SCOLLOPED POTATOES ✿

(Millington)

Millington recommends these potatoes as a supper dish. Similar recipes appear in many other cookbooks of the time. Parson Woodforde records eating this dish on at least one occasion, August 25, 1794, when he ate "Mashed Potatoes in 3. Scollop Shells brown'd over."

Boil them, beat them fine in a bowl, with cream, a large piece of butter, and a little salt. Put them into scollop-shells, smooth them, score them with a knife, lay thin slices of butter on the top, and put them into a Dutch oven to brown before the fire.

MODERN RECIPE

3 lbs. potatoes, peeled and quartered

1 c. heavy whipping cream

4 T butter

1 tsp. kosher salt

3 to 4 T butter, thinly sliced

Continued on next page

Continued from previous page

Preheat oven to 400°F. Boil the potatoes until fork-tender. Remove to a bowl and mash with the cream, 4 T butter, and salt. Spoon into ramekins and smooth the tops with the back of the spoon, then make a few slash marks in the tops with a sharp knife. Lay a thin slice of butter on top of each dish of potatoes. Bake 10 to 15 minutes, then place under the broiler until nicely browned (about 2 minutes).

SALAD

(Bradley)

These two girls had been above an hour in the place, happily employed in visiting an opposite milliner, watching the sentinel on guard, and dressing a sallad and cucumber. (*P&P* 219)

This Season [May] affords us great variety of Necessaries for Food, in the Farm and garden . . . [including] Cucumbers for stewing and in raw Sallads: however, in this Season all raw Sallads should yet partake of some warm Herbs. . . . The Method which I most approve of for dressing a Sallad, is, after we have duly proportion'd the Herbs, to take two thirds Oil Olive, one third true Vinegar, some hard Eggs cut small, both the Whites and Yolks, a little Salt and some Mustard, all which must be well mix'd and pour'd over the Sallad, having first cut the large Herbs, such as Sallery, Endive, or Cabbage-Lettuce, but none of the small ones; then mix all these well together, that it may be ready just when you want to use it, for the Oil will make it presently soften, and lose its briskness.

MODERN RECIPE

1 head lettuce, or an equal quantity of mixed baby lettuces, large leaves shredded into bite-size pieces

2 stalks celery, sliced ⅛" thick crosswise

1 endive, separated into individual leaves, and each leaf cut crosswise in half

¼ head cabbage, thinly sliced

1 cucumber, peeled and sliced ¼" thick crosswise

Continued on next page

Continued from previous page

Dressing
⅔ cup olive oil

⅓ cup red wine vinegar

1 hard boiled egg, finely minced

½ tsp. salt

1 T Dijon mustard

Mix the greens in a salad bowl. If you like, you may take Bradley's suggestion about "warm herbs" and wilt the celery and cabbage, heating it in a skillet over low heat for 5 to 10 minutes. Meanwhile, mix all the dressing ingredients and blend thoroughly; this is a good job for the food processor. Toss the dressing over the salad just before serving.

✾ BOILED TURNIPS ✾

(Farley)

That's right, my dear, very right. . . . They must not over-salt the leg; and then, if it is not over-salted, and if it is very thoroughly boiled, just as Serle boils our's, and eaten very moderately of, with a boiled turnip, and a little carrot or parsnip, I do not consider it unwholesome. (*E* 172)

The plan of a drain, the change of a fence, the felling of a tree, and the destination of every acre for wheat, turnips, or spring corn, was entered into with as much equality of interest by John, as his cooler manners rendered possible . . . . (*E* 100)

Turnips were one of the foods eaten by both humans and animals. Popularized by the agricultural reformer Lord Townshend in the 1730s—his enthusiasm earned him the nickname "Turnip" Townshend—they provided winter fodder that helped keep livestock alive through the lean winter months. The manure of those animals then provided extra fertilizer for the fields, which in turn produced better crops, allowing more animals to survive the winters, and so on. By Austen's day the turnip was firmly established as an agricultural mainstay, and though it was never a sought-after root vegetable for the table, its ubiquity meant that cooks had to prepare it sooner or later.

Turnips may be boiled in the pot with the meat, and indeed eat best when so done. When they be enough, take them out, put them into a pan, mash them with butter and a little salt, and in that state send them to table. Another method of boiling them, is as follows: Pare your turnips, and cut them into little square pieces of the size of dice, or as big as the top of your finger. Then put them into a saucepan, and just cover them over with water. As soon as they be enough, take them off the fire, and throw them into a sieve to drain. Put them into a saucepan, with a good piece of butter, stir them over the fire for a few minutes, and they will then be fit for the table.

MODERN RECIPE

1 lb. turnips	1 tsp. salt
3 T butter	

Wash and peel the turnips and trim off the tops and bottoms. Cut them into 1" dice. Bring a pot of salted water to a boil and add the turnips, boiling them until fork-tender, about 15 minutes. Mash the turnips with the butter and salt and serve immediately.

11

FRUIT, NUTS, AND FRUIT DESSERTS

Though the English were not wild about vegetables, they were quite enthusiastic about fruit (*Evelyn, MW* 182; *Sand, MW* 380; *S&S* 30). The cultivation of orchards had been a hobby of the well-to-do for centuries, and landowners took pride in locating and nurturing the best varieties. Parson Woodforde was at least as delighted with his Anson Apricot as Mrs. Norris was with her husband's Moor Park. (In fact, according to R. W. Chapman's notes to *Mansfield Park*, these were actually the same variety of tree, which was also called Temple's apricot or Dunmore's Breda.) The ingredients of desserts tended to reflect this pride. Fruit-based confections were quite popular, as were unadorned seasonal fruit and fruit that had been preserved in some way. Fruit found its way into puddings, cakes, jams, marmalades, jellies, dumplings, fritters, wines, pies, tarts, creams, and distilled waters. Preserving, drying, and pickling kept many fruits available (in some form, at least) year-round. For a nation that had not yet fully exploited chocolate as a confection, fruit provided a reasonable substitute for those with a sweet tooth, and cookbooks reflect this. To judge by the number of recipes available, English cooks took their fruit almost as seriously as they took their meat.

Parson Woodforde, once again, provides us with a window into what the gentry actually ate, as opposed to what was printed in contemporary cookbooks. His diaries record fruit as part of pastries and jellies, fruit in sauces to accompany meat, and fruit eaten on its own, almost always as part of a dessert course after dinner. On various days between 1780 and 1795, he ate "Currant Jelly Sauce" as an accompaniment to roast swan; a "Damson Cheese," which was a kind of fruit jelly made with damsons and sugar; applesauce as an accompaniment to pork; apple, currant, gooseberry, raspberry, and grape tarts; apple fritters; strawberry and raspberry creams; apple and raspberry puffs; baked apples; brandied cherries; apple, apricot, and gooseberry pies; and apricot dumplings.

Youth and Age, Dighton, 1788. The sleeping fruit-seller's goods include apples, strawberries, and possibly grapes and oranges. (Courtesy of the Lewis Walpole Library, Yale University. 788.1.3.1.)

Fruit he ate by itself included raisins, pippins, oranges, apricots, strawberries, black grapes, plums, mulberries, melons, currants, cherries, "Peaches, Nectarines and Grapes"—the last grouping identical in kind, and almost identical in wording, to the assortment of fruit served at Pemberley.

As extensive as his catalogue of fruit was, it was not exhaustive. Contemporary cookbooks also list recipes for desserts based on pears, peaches, pineapples, lemons, mangoes, cranberries, quinces, citrons, barberries, and blackberries. Austen mentions only some of the fruits and fruit dishes in the cook's repertoire, but these provide a good cross-section of the types of fruit used and the types of dishes in which they appeared. It should be remembered that a great deal of fruit, including the pyramids of fruit at Pemberley, would have been eaten fresh, with little or no accompaniment. Its sheer abundance and beauty was its chief attraction.

In the case of General Tilney's prized pineapples (*NA* 178), the appeal lay not only in the flavor and exotic appearance of the fruit, but also in its rarity and high cultivation cost. Pineapples required a series of specially designed hothouses and then needed years of attention before they began to produce fruit. The difficulty of growing them, the large numbers of servants needed to tend them, and their consequent value, made them the ultimate symbol of hospitality. Offering pineapple was not quite the equivalent of offering a guest gold, but it carried the same connotations of extravagant generosity. Pineapples could be preserved—John Farley, for example, offers an odd recipe for steeping whole pineapples in brine, artificially coloring them green, and storing them in sugar syrup—but as they were forced to produce at various times of year, there was no special need to serve them any way but fresh. Pineapples were destined to lose their extremely high value after shipping times from the tropics, but their lingering symbolism persists until the present day; the pineapple as a design motif emblematic of hospitality appears on household items from cabinet knobs and shortbread molds to cookware and textiles.

Fruit tended to be eaten after meat and its accompaniments. If there was only one course at dinner, the fruit tarts or other fruit dish would be placed on the table at the same time as the other food, but if there were a second course, the tarts and such would usually make their appearance then. Dessert was composed mostly of "finger foods" and often had a fruit component, usually something like raisins or fresh fruit that could be eaten easily without silverware.

TART PASTE

(Glasse)

Half a pound of butter, half a pound of flour, and half a pound of sugar; mix it well together, and beat it with a rolling-pin well, then roll it out thin.

MODERN RECIPE

½ lb. flour   ½ lb. sugar

½ lb. butter

Mix the flour and sugar together thoroughly. Cut the butter into small pieces and blend it into the dry mixture with your fingers, a food processor, or a pastry blender. The dough will be brittle, so if you are making a full-size pie or tart with it, roll it between two sheets of plastic wrap. Remove one sheet of wrap and invert the pie pan on top of the crust, then flip the pan over with the crust on top and remove the other sheet of plastic wrap.

This dough does not need to be pricked before baking, as the melting butter will leave a natural network of tiny holes in the crust. However, the melting butter also means that the sides of the crust will tend to shrink downward as it bakes. You can alleviate this problem somewhat by making an aluminum-foil "wall" around the outside of your pie pan and building the crust about an inch higher than you really want it to be. Place the pie pan on a baking sheet to catch any dripping butter, and remove the foil after baking.

This is pretty much the world's most decadent crust. Think thin, ultra-buttery, crunchy-chewy shortbread, and you're just about there. It has absolutely no redeeming nutritive value, and your guests will never, ever forget it and worship you forever as the Regency goddess (or god) that you are.

✿ PUFF PASTE ✿

(Glasse)

Take a quarter of a peck of flour, rub in a pound of butter very fine, make it up in a light paste with cold water, just stiff enough to work it up; then roll it up about as thick as a crown-piece, put a layer of butter all over; sprinkle on a little flour, double it up, and roll it out again; double it, and roll it three times; then it is fit for all sorts of pies and tarts that require a puff-paste.

MODERN RECIPE

8 cups flour

about 2 to 2¼ cups cold water

1 lb. plus 1½ sticks (12 T) butter

Measure the flour into a bowl. Cut up 1 lb. of butter into small pieces and blend it thoroughly into the flour with a pastry blender or your hands until it resembles cornmeal in texture. Pour 1 cup of the water into the butter-flour mixture and stir it into much of the dry mixture. Move the moistened dough to one side of the bowl and pour in another cup of water. Use this water to moisten most of the rest of the dough, then add about ¼ cup more water, if necessary, to moisten the rest of the dough. Stir with a spoon, then mix in the bowl with your hands to combine all the flour and butter with the moistened parts of the dough. The dough should be evenly moistened and not too damp or sticky. You may need a little more or a little less than 2¼ cups, depending on the moisture content of the local air and therefore your flour.

Flour a large flat surface. If you have a flat, clean countertop, this works best. If you have to use a wooden or marble board, you will need to divide the dough into about four parts and roll each individually. (The remainder of this recipe assumes that your are rolling out all the dough at once.)

Turn the dough out onto the floured surface. Roll it out ¼" thick, using flour as necessary to keep the dough from sticking to the rolling surface or rolling pin. Cut up ½ stick (4 T) butter into thin slices and lay them over half the surface of the dough. Sprinkle a little flour over the dough and fold the unbuttered half over the buttered half.

Roll the dough out again ¼" thick and repeat the process, buttering and flouring half the dough, folding it, and rolling it out again. Repeat once more with the last 4 T butter and roll out to the thickness prescribed in whatever recipe you're using.

This dough refrigerates well and can be made up to 3 days in advance.

A GOOD CRUST FOR GREAT PIES

(Glasse)

To a peck of flour add the yolks of three eggs, then boil some water, and put in
half a pound of fried suet, and a pound and a half of butter; skim off the butter
and suet, and as much of the liquor as will make a light good crust; work it up
well, and roll it out.

MODERN RECIPE

16 cups flour	¼ lb lard or suet
2 egg yolks	¾ lb. butter
3 to 4 cups water, *in all*	

Measure the flour into a very large bowl. Add the egg yolks and crumble the yolks into the flour
with your fingers until the liquid is very well distributed through the flour. In a saucepan, heat 2
cups water, the lard or suet, and the butter until all the fats are melted. Remove the saucepan from
the stove and allow the mixture to cool slightly, about 5 minutes.

Pour the liquid into the bowl of flour in stages. Pour about a cup in, stir it into the top of the
flour, and incorporate more flour with your hands to make a sturdy but not overly stiff dough. Set
that portion of the dough aside and add more of the warm liquid. Continue in this manner until
all of the liquid has been added to the flour. Then return all the pieces of dough to the bowl, mix
with the remaining flour, and add up to 2 cups of cold water, a little at a time, until all the flour
has been moistened and the dough is evenly mixed. The pastry should be thick and not sticky but
not too hard to roll or shape.

 APPLE TARTS

(Glasse)

Miss Bates, let Emma help you to a *little* bit of tart—a *very* little bit. Ours
are all apple tarts. You need not be afraid of unwholesome preserves here. (*E*
24–25)

. . . the very same evening William Larkins came over with a large basket of
apples, the same sort of apples, a bushel at least, and I was very much
obliged, and went down and spoke to William Larkins and every thing. . . .

But, however, I found afterwards from Patty, that William said it was all the apples of *that* sort his master had; he had brought them all—and now his master had not one left to bake or boil. William did not seem to mind it himself, he was so pleased to think his master had sold so many; for William, you know, thinks more of his master's profit than any thing; but Mrs. Hodges, he said, was quite displeased at their being all sent away. She could not bear that her master should not be able to have another apple-tart this spring. (*E* 239)

Mde Bigeon was below dressing us a most comfortable dinner of Soup, Fish, Bouillee, Partridges & an apple Tart. . . . (Letter from Jane to Cassandra, September 15, 1813)

If you bake in tin patties butter them, and you must put a little crust all over, because of the taking them out; if in China or glass, no crust but the top one; lay fine sugar at the bottom, then your plums, cherries, or any other sort of fruit, and sugar at top; then put on your lid, and bake them in a slack oven. Mince-pies must be baked in tin patties, because of taking them out, and puff-paste is best for them; for sweet tarts the beaten crust is best; but as you fancy. Apple, pear, apricot, &c. make thus: apples and pears, pare them, cut them into quarters, and core them; cut the quarters across again, set them on in a sauce-pan with just as much water as will barely cover them, let them simmer on a slow fire just till the fruit is tender; put a good piece of lemon-peel in the water with the fruit, then have your patties ready; lay fine sugar at bottom, then your fruit, and a little sugar at top; that you must put in at you discretion; pour over each tart a tea-spoonful of lemon-juice, and three tea-spoonfuls of the liquor they were boiled in; put on your lid, and bake them in a slack oven. Apricots so the same way, only do not use lemon.

MODERN RECIPE

8 small to medium-sized apples	8 T sugar
1 recipe **tart paste**	8 tsp. lemon juice
zest of 1 lemon	

Preheat the oven to 350°F.

Peel and core the apples and cut them into eighths. Put the apples into a saucepan with the lemon zest and just enough water to cover them, and simmer till tender, about 10 min-

Continued on next page

Continued from previous page

utes. Meanwhile, sprinkle ½ T sugar in the bottom of each of 8 ramekins and make the tart paste.

When the apples are done cooking, drain them and divide them equally between the 8 ramekins. Sprinkle ½ T sugar and 1 tsp. lemon juice over each.

Roll the Tart Paste out ¼" thick and cut 8 circles just a little larger than the top diameter of each ramekin. Lay on the crusts, allowing them to drape loosely over the apple filling and making sure that they cover the filling completely without extending beyond the rims of the ramekins.

Set the ramekins on baking sheets and put them into the oven. Cook for 20 minutes, then raise the heat to 450° F to brown the crust. As soon as the crusts turn golden brown, remove the tarts from the oven.

The tarts may be served hot or cold.

BAKED APPLES

(Glasse)

Oh! said I, Patty do not come with your bad news to me. Here is the rivet of your mistress's spectacles out. Then the baked apples came home, Mrs. Wallis sent them by her boy. . . . [D]ear Jane . . . really eats nothing—makes such a shocking breakfast, you would be quite frightened if you saw it. . . . But about the middle of the day she gets hungry, and there is nothing she likes so well as these baked apples, and they are extremely wholesome, for I took the opportunity the other day of asking Mr. Perry; I happened to meet him in the street. . . . I have so often heard Mr. Woodhouse recommend a baked apple. I believe it is the only way that Mr. Woodhouse thinks the fruit thoroughly wholesome. (*E* 236–37)

He contrived that she should be seated by him; and was sufficiently employed in looking out the best baked apple for her, and trying to make her help or advise him in his work, till Jane Fairfax was quite ready to sit down to the pianoforté again. (*E* 240)

And when I brought out the baked apples from the closet, and hoped our friends would be so very obliging as to take some, "Oh!" said he directly, "there is nothing in the way of fruit half so good, and these are the finest looking home-baked apples I ever saw in my life." . . . Indeed they are very delightful apples, and Mrs. Wallis does them full justice—only we do not have them baked more than twice, and Mr. Woodhouse made us promise to have them done three times. . . . The apples themselves are the very finest sort for baking, beyond a doubt; all from Donwell—some of Mr. Knightley's most liberal supply. (*E* 328)

Tea was made down stairs, biscuits and baked apples and wine before she came away. . . . (*E* 329)

The baked apples and biscuits, excellent in their way, you know. . . . (*E* 329)

Baked apples could be made in a "quick oven," as below, or slowly in an oven that was cooling after being used for other purposes. The Bateses, who are too poor to own an oven of their own, send their apples (and, no doubt, their bread as well) to be baked by the local baker, Mrs. Wallis, who probably charges them a small fee to use her oven. Since the apples are cooked as the oven is cooling, it takes two to three sessions to get them soft enough; Mr. Woodhouse, always careful of his digestion, prefers them cooked three times.

Put your apples into an earthen pan with a few cloves, a little lemon-peel, some coarse sugar, a glass of red wine; put them in a quick oven, and they will take an hour baking.

 ## MODERN RECIPE

5 small apples, cored

zest of one lemon

½ tsp. white sugar

½ tsp. brown sugar

1 cup red wine

Preheat oven to 300°F. Place the apples in a small pan such as a pie pan or loaf pan. Mix the lemon zest, sugars, and wine, and pour this mixture over the apples. Cover the pan with aluminum foil and bake until the apples are tender, about 30 minutes to 1 hour, depending on the size of the apples. Before serving, spoon a little of the sauce over the tops of the apples.

APPLE DUMPLINGS

(Raffald)

We have apple dumplings, however, very often. Patty makes an excellent apple-dumpling. (*E* 237)

Hannah Glasse makes apple dumplings as well. She omits the marmalade but adds a sprinkling of sugar at the end, setting the melted butter on the side. She also flours her hands when shaping the dumplings and flours the cloths before tying them up for boiling. The following recipe makes use of her suggestions.

Pare your apples, take out the core with an apple scraper, fill the hole with quince or orange marmalade or sugar, which suits you. Then take a piece of cold paste and make a hole in it as if you were going to make a pie. Lay in your apple, and put another piece of paste in the same form, and close it up round the side of your apple, it is much better than gathering it in a lump at one end. Tie it in a cloth and boil it three quarters of an hour. Pour melted butter over them and serve them up. Five is enough for a dish.

 ## MODERN RECIPE

5 apples, peeled and cored	½ recipe **puff paste**
5 T orange marmalade or 5 T brown sugar	½ recipe **melted butter**

Roll out the puff paste a little less than ¼" thick. Cut 10 circles, each about 3" wider in diameter than your apples. Place an apple on a pastry circle and fill the core with 1 T marmalade or sugar. Bring the edges of the pastry up around the apple to its "equator." Then place another pastry circle on top of the apple and pinch the two pieces of pastry together, sealing the apple into a layer of pastry. Repeat for the other four apples.

Dip a piece of cheesecloth, about 12" to 18" inches square, in a bowl of flour. Wrap it around an apple dumpling and tie it at the top with a length of kitchen twine. Repeat for the other 4 apples.

Bring a large pot of water to a boil. Put the apple dumplings into the boiling water and boil 45 minutes. Remove the dumplings from the water and untie the cloths. Carefully peel the cloths away from the dumplings. Serve with melted butter sauce.

APPLE PUDDING

(Farley)

The apples themselves are the very finest sort for baking, beyond a doubt; all from Donwell—some of Mr. Knightley's most liberal supply. He sends us a sack every year; and certainly there never was such a keeping apple any where as one of his trees—I believe there is two of them. My mother says the orchard was always famous in her younger days. (*E* 238)

Loaf sugar, which is called for in Farley's recipe, was a coarser and browner variety of sugar than the double- or triple-refined white sugar used in many other recipes.

Pare twelve large pippins, and take out the cores. Put them into a saucepan, with four or five spoonfuls of water, and boil them till they be soft and thick. Then beat them well, stir in a pound of loaf sugar, the juice of three lemons, and the peels of two cut thin and beat fine in a mortar, and the yolks of eight eggs beaten. Mix all well together, and bake it in a slack oven. When it be nearly done, throw over it a little fine sugar. If you please you may bake it in a puff paste at the bottom of the dish, and round the edges of it.

MODERN RECIPE

12 apples, peeled, cored, and cut into eighths	3 lemons
¾ lb. white sugar	8 egg yolks, lightly beaten
¼ lb. light brown sugar	

Place the apples in a large saucepan with about 2 cups of water. Bring to a boil, lower the heat to medium, cover, and boil 30 minutes. Remove lid and reduce heat to medium-low, cooking until the apples are very soft and the water is mostly evaporated, about 10 to 15 minutes (though the exact time will vary depending on the amount of moisture left in the pot). Stir and crush the apples as they cook uncovered. When cooking is done, they should form a thick applesauce. Cool the applesauce somewhat.

Preheat the oven to 300°F.

Add the sugars to the applesauce. Zest two of the lemons and juice all three. Strain the seeds from the juice and add the juice and zest to the applesauce. Add the egg yolks and stir thoroughly.

Place a folded dishtowel in the bottom of a large pan and fill the pan 1" deep with water. Pour the apple mixture into a ceramic casserole or soufflé dish and set the dish on top of the towel in the pan. Put the pan in the oven and cook until the center of the pudding turns a deep yellow and looks firm, about 1 hour and 5 minutes to 1 hour and 10 minutes. Serve hot or cold.

❈ APPLE PIE ❈

(Farley)

In the late eighteenth century, apple pie became an increasingly popular dish in the north of England, as coal barges returning from the south filled up with loads of apples and plums. In Kent, where Austen's brother Edward Knight lived and where apples were a principal crop, the apples were either turned into pies and tarts or pressed and processed into cider.

Farley recommends boiling the peels as well as the cores of the apples to make the apple syrup for this pie. Given the widespread use of pesticides in farming today, and the fact that pesticides tend to be most concentrated in the peels of fruits and vegetables, I would recommend against using the peels unless you are certain that your apples have been grown organically.

Another of Farley's recommendations is a cream sauce added to the pie just before serving. I found that this made the pie a little too moist and have made it optional. If you want the same flavors and are willing to sacrifice a little authenticity, you might merely make a little whipped cream with the addition of some sugar and nutmeg.

Having put a good puff paste crust round the edge of your dish, pare and quarter your apples, and take out the cores. Then lay a thick row of apples, and throw in half the sugar you intend to put into your pie. Mince a little lemon-peel fine, spread it over the sugar and apples, and squeeze a little lemon over them. Then scatter a few cloves over it, and lay on the rest of your apples and sugar. Sweeten to your palate, and squeeze a little more lemon. Boil the peeling of the apples and cores in some fair water, with a blade of mace, till it has a pleasing taste. Strain it, and boil the syrup with a little sugar, till there be but a small quantity left. Then pour it into your pie, put on your upper crust, and bake it. If you choose it, you may put in a little quince or marmalade. In the same manner you may make a *pear pie*; but in that you must omit the quince. You may butter them when they come out of the oven, or beat up the yolks of two eggs, and half a pint of cream, with a little nutmeg, sweetened with sugar. Put it over a slow fire, and keep it stirring till it begins to boil; then take off the lid, and pour in the cream. Cut the crust in little three corner pieces, and stick them about the pie.

MODERN RECIPE

½ recipe **puff paste**

1 lemon

6 to 8 apples

¼ cup plus 2 T sugar, *in all*

½ tsp. ground cloves

pinch of mace

Nutmeg Cream (optional)

2 egg yolks

1 cup heavy whipping cream

½ tsp. ground nutmeg

1 T sugar

Preheat the oven to 400°F.

Make the puff paste, roll it out ¼" thick, and lay it in a pie pan, cutting it so that it extends about ½" beyond the top edge of the pie pan.

Peel, core, and quarter the apples. Place the cores with 2 cups of water in a small saucepan with the cloves and mace and heat over medium heat. Meanwhile, lay a single layer of apple quarters, cut side down, in the pastry-lined pie pan. Sprinkle with half the ¼ cup sugar.

Zest and juice the lemon and sprinkle the lemon zest over the layer of apples. Sprinkle half the lemon juice over the apples. Add another layer of apples and sprinkle the remaining portion of the ¼ cup sugar and the remainder of the lemon juice.

Boil the apple cores, cloves, and mace for about 10 minutes. Strain the cores out of the liquid and return the liquid to the saucepan. Add 2 T sugar. Return to a gentle boil and cook until the syrup begins to thicken and about ¼ cup is left, about 5 to 10 minutes. Pour the syrup over the apples.

Roll out a top crust for the pie and place it on top of the pan. Trim the crust so that it extends about ½" beyond the edge of the pan.

If you are making the pie without the nutmeg cream, pinch the bottom and top edges of the crust together and fold the bottom crust over the top crust, rolling it in toward the pie to make an edge all the way around.

If you are making the pie with the nutmeg cream, leave the edges loose and do not pinch them together.

Bake the pie at 400°F until the pastry is golden brown, about 25 minutes.

If you are using the nutmeg cream, make it while the pie is baking. Place all the ingredients in a saucepan and place over medium heat until the mixture begins to bubble. Then remove the pan from the heat. When the pie is done, carefully lift the upper crust and pour in enough of the cream to fill the pan about halfway.

COMPOTE OF APPLES

(The French Family Cook)

"Oh! Mr. Knightley, one moment more; something of consequence—so shocked!—Jane and I are both so shocked about the apples!"

"What is the matter now?"

"To think of your sending us all your store apples. You said you had a great many, and now you have not one left. . . ." (*E* 245)

Apples picked in the fall could keep through most of the winter if they were stored carefully. They needed to be laid out in a cool place in a single layer, not touching each other; an attic, garret, or loft was frequently assigned for this purpose. Some varieties of apples "kept" better than others, but all varieties could grow a little soft toward the end of their shelf life. No doubt by the time the old year's apples were gone, people were already looking forward eagerly to the next crop.

Cut six large pippins in half, take off the rind, and throw the pippins, as you have pared them, into cold water; afterwards stew them, with a large glass of wine, the juice of half a lemon, and a bit of sugar; when they are done, put them upon your dessert-plate, reduce the syrup till it sticks to the fingers, and dish it upon the apples.

MODERN RECIPE

6 large apples

1¼ cups white wine

1 T lemon juice

1½ T sugar

Peel, halve, and core the apples. Place them in a saucepan or a wide, deep skillet with a lid. Add the wine, lemon juice, and sugar, cover tightly, and cook over medium heat until the apples have begun to soften, about 15 minutes. Place the apples on a serving plate (in a warm oven, if you plan to serve them warm) and cook the remaining liquid for a few more minutes, uncovered, until it thickens. Pour it over the apples and serve hot or cold.

APRICOT, CURRANT, CHERRY, OR GOOSEBERRY TART

(Millington)

"The truth is, ma'am," said Mrs. Grant . . . , "that Dr. Grant hardly knows what the natural taste of our apricot is; he is scarcely ever indulged with one, for it is so valuable a fruit, with a little assistance, and ours in such a remarkably large, fair sort, that what with early tarts and preserves, my cook contrives to get them all." (*MP* 54–55)

The fatigue, too, of so long a journey, became soon no trifling evil. In vain were the well-meant condescensions of Sir Thomas, and all the officious prognostications of Mrs. Norris that she would be a good girl; in vain did Lady Bertram smile and make her sit on the sofa with herself and pug, and vain was even the sight of a gooseberry tart towards giving her comfort; she could scarcely swallow two mouthfuls before tears interrupted her, and sleep seeming to be her likeliest friend, she was taken to finish her sorrows in bed. (*MP* 13)

There are more Gooseberries & fewer Currants than I thought at first.—We must buy currants for our Wine. (Letter from Jane to Cassandra, June 6, 1811)

Cook) Here is the bill of fare.
Chloe reads) 2 Ducks, a leg of beef, a stinking partridge, & a tart.
(*Scraps, MW* 173)

Cherries take but little baking. Gooseberries, to look red, must stand a good while in the oven. Apricots, if green, require more baking than when ripe. Fruit preserved high, should not be baked at all, but the crust should be baked first upon a tin the size of the tart. It may be cut out with a marking iron; when cold lay it one the fruit.

MODERN RECIPE

1 recipe **tart paste**

1 T sugar

Continued on next page

Continued from previous page

Filling

4 300g cans gooseberries

or

2½ cups pitted cherries

or

2½ cups pitted and halved apricots

or

2½ cups currants (if dried, soaked in water for ½ hour before baking, then drained)

Preheat oven to 400°F.

Roll out the crust ¼" thick and lay it in a pie pan. The crust will shrink a good deal in baking, so if you want it to remain as high as the sides of the pie pan, artificially extend the height of the pie pan by lining the rim with parchment paper.

Lay out the fruit in the tart crust and sprinkle it with the sugar. Bake until the fruit is tender and the tart crust is browned, about 20 minutes.

DRIED CHERRIES

(Millington)

And I declare if she is not gone away without finishing her wine! And the dried cherries too! (*S&S* 194)

Millington's version of this fruit dessert is artificially sweetened; The French Family Cook's author simply dries the cherries, unsweetened, in a cool oven, replacing them "again when the oven is at the same degree of heat, that is to say, after you have drawn your bread," and repeating as necessary until the fruit is fully dry.

Stone Morello cherries; sift over every pound of them a pound and a quarter of fine beaten sugar. The next day take them out of the sugar, and to every pound of sugar put two tablespoonfuls of water, and boil and skim it well, then put in the cherries, let the sugar boil over them; the next morning strain them, and to every pound of sirup put half a pound more of sugar. Let it boil a little thicker, then put in the cherries, to boil gently, and the next day strain them, put them into a stove, and turn them every day till dry.

MODERN RECIPE

1 lb. fresh cherries, pitted   2 T water

1¼ lb. sugar plus 6 oz.

Place the cherries in a lidded storage container and cover with 1¼ lb. sugar. Cover and leave overnight.

In the morning, remove the cherries from the sugar and shake off any excess. Place the sugar in a nonstick saucepan with 2 T water and stir over medium heat until the sugar is melted. Add the cherries; if the sugar recystallizes, just keep stirring and heating until the sugar melts again. Continue heating, stirring occasionally, until the sugar syrup comes to a full boil, with the bubbles reaching the center of the pot and the liquid becoming very frothy, inflated in volume, and pink. Boil 1 minute at this stage and remove the pot from the heat. Cool the cherries and syrup and store overnight.

The next morning, remove the cherries with a slotted spoon. Place the syrup in a saucepan and add 6 oz. sugar. Bring to a boil over medium heat and boil for 5 minutes, stirring constantly to keep the liquid from boiling over. Add the cherries and boil for 1 more minute. Turn off the heat and continue to stir the cherries occasionally as they cool.

Preheat oven to 175°F. Line a baking sheet with parchment paper, lift the individual cherries out of the syrup, and spread the cherries over the parchment paper in a single layer. Place them in the oven until they have dried to the consistency of a raisin, about 4 to 5 hours.

 CHERRY COMPOTE

(*The French Family Cook*)

> ...delicious fruit—only too rich to be eaten much of—inferior to cherries—(*E* 359)

Cut the end of the stalks, and put your cherries into a sauce-pan, with half a glass of water and a quarter of a pound of sugar: set them upon the fire and let them boil up two or three times; arrange them upon your dessert-plate, with the stalks upward; pour the syrup over, and serve them cold.

MODERN RECIPE

2½ lbs. cherries   ¼ lb. sugar

½ cup water

There are two theories regarding the initial preparation of the cherries. If you wish to prepare them just as *The French Family Cook* did, which admittedly makes for a prettier presentation, do not pit them, and leave the stems on. If you wish to make things a bit easier on your guests, remove the stems and pit the cherries.

Place the cherries, sugar, and water in a wide skillet over medium heat. Heat until the sugar melts, raise the heat to medium-high, and bring the liquid to a boil. Boil the liquid gently for 2 minutes, then remove the cherries to a serving platter or bowl with a slotted spoon. If you have left the stems on, arrange the cherries with the stems pointing upward.

Heat the remaining pan liquid over medium heat until it is reduced by about half. Pour this over the cherries and serve the cherries either warm or at room temperature.

GOOSEBERRY CREAM

(Glasse)

We have a good appearance of Flowers in the Shrubbery and borders, & what is still better, a very good crop of small Fruit, even your Goosberry Tree does better than heretofore, when the Gooseberries are ripe I shall sit upon my Bench, eat them & think of you, tho I can do that without the assistance of ripe gooseberries. . . . (Letter from Jane to her niece Anna Austen, July 1814)

This would make an interesting accompaniment to the gooseberry tart, above. The Austens were fond of gooseberries and grew them both at Southampton and at Chawton. They were not the only fans of this small round fruit. The English put them in tarts, sauces, and pies; the fruit was turned into wine and the vinegar-like concoction "verjuice," bottled for winter use, and turned into medicinal soups. Periodic contests for gooseberry size were held in northern England for much of the eighteenth century, with the winning berries in 1786 weighing about a half ounce each.

Take two quarts of gooseberries, put to them as much water as will cover them, scald them, and then run them through a sieve with a spoon; to a quart of the pulp you must have six eggs well beaten; and when the pulp is hot, put in an ounce of fresh butter, sweeten it to your taste, put in your eggs, and stir them over a gentle fire till they grow thick, then set it by; and when it is almost cold, put into it two spoonfuls of juice of spinach, and a spoonful of orange-flower water or sack; stir it well together, and put it into your bason: when it is cold, serve it to table.

MODERN RECIPE

1 quart canned gooseberries, drained	3 T sugar or more to taste
3 beaten eggs	green food coloring
1 T butter	1 T orange-flower water

Crush and strain the gooseberries either by running them through a food mill or by mashing them and pressing them through a strainer. Put the pulp in a saucepan along with the eggs and heat through. Add the butter and sugar and continue to heat gently over medium-low heat. Cook for about 10 minutes and remove from the heat. Stir in a few drops of food coloring to make the cream greener. Add the orange-flower water, spoon into dessert glasses, and chill.

COMPOTE OF SOUR GRAPES

(*The French Family Cook*)

The next variation which their visit afforded was produced by the entrance of servants with cold meat, cake, and a variety of all the finest fruits in season; but this did not take place till after many a significant look and smile from Mrs. Annesley to Miss Darcy had been given, to remind her of her post. There was now employment for the whole party; for though they could not all talk, they could all eat; and the beautiful pyramids of grapes, nectarines, and peaches, soon collected them round the table. (*P&P* 268)

It is entirely in keeping with eighteenth-century custom to make a decorative pyramid out of seasonal fruit or, in winter, out of preserved or extremely well-stored fruit. Grapes could be turned into raisins, of course, and were often served as a dessert in that form; Charles Millington advises his readers that, for storage purposes, Frontignac grapes are the best, and should be hung in a dry room, stalks still attached, with each bunch separate from the others. Grapes could also be pickled or preserved.

In season, this recipe from The French Family Cook *would also make a tasty part of the second course. It caters to the developing hunger for sugar in England and has the added advantage, in modern times, of being even easier to make with seedless grapes. This recipe met with strong approval from my adult and child tasters alike.*

Take a pound of grapes which are not quite ripe, split each grape with the point of a knife, and take out the seeds: when they are well done, throw them into boiling water, and when they begin to shrivel, take them from the fire, throw in half a glass of cold water, and let them remain in the same water till cold, that they may have time to plump: then boil a gill of water with six ounces of sugar, and put in the grapes; let them boil up two or three times, skim the syrup and dish them into a dessert-plate, taking care before you put over the syrup to boil it till it be clear.

 ## MODERN RECIPE

1 lb. seedless grapes   6 oz. sugar

½ cup ice water

Bring a saucepan full of water to a boil. Meanwhile, wash the grapes and remove any stems. When the water boils, add the grapes, and allow them to boil until they begin to shrivel, about 10 or 15 minutes. Turn off the heat and throw in the ice water, which will stop the boiling. Allow the grapes to cool in the cooking water for about 10 minutes. Meanwhile, bring ½ cup of water and the sugar to a boil in another saucepan. Add the grapes and boil for 1 minute. Using a slotted spoon, transfer the grapes to a serving plate and continue boiling the sugar syrup for 2 more minutes without stirring. Pour the syrup over the grapes.

This compote can be served hot or cold.

SYRUP OF MULBERRIES

(Bradley)

Delaford is a nice place, I can tell you; exactly what I call a nice old fashioned place, full of comforts and conveniences; quite shut in with great garden walls that are covered with the best fruit-trees in the country: and such a mulberry tree in one corner! Lord! how Charlotte and I did stuff the only time we were there! (*S&S* 196–97)

Mulberries were usually eaten fresh, as indicated in the above passage from Sense and Sensibility. *However, one does run across the occasional recipe that uses mulberries as an ingredient.*

Press out the Juice of Mulberries with your Hands, and pass it through a Sieve; and when it has stood to settle, pour off the clear, and put to it, its Weight of fine Sugar; put this into a Gallypot, and set that Pot into a Kettle of hot Water, which should be kept simmering near two Hours: stir the Syrup every now and then with a Silver Spoon, and take off what Scum may rise at Times, upon it; when it is enough, let it stand till it is quite cold, and then put it into clear dry Bottles with large Mouths, and stop them close. Keep this in a dry Place.

It is to be remark'd, that besides this Syrup is very cooling; its use is to colour stew'd Apples, or Puddings, or any Sweet Preparation made with Flour or Fruit: for in itself it carries no Flavour that will be predominant over that of another Fruit.

MODERN RECIPE

2 quarts mulberries   2 lbs. white sugar

Place a strainer over a bowl. Over the strainer, squeeze the mulberries to expel the juice. You should have about 1 pint of juice.

Place the juice and sugar into a double boiler and keep the water in the lower level of the double boiler simmering for 2 hours, stirring the juice occasionally and adding water to the lower pot as necessary to keep it from running dry.

Cool the syrup and store it in the refrigerator. Cooks in Austen's day used it as an additive to color other fruit desserts, but it's also tasty, reduced and thickened, on pancakes, waffles, ice cream, and other modern foods.

PRESERVED NECTARINES OR PEACHES

(Raffald)

. . . the beautiful pyramids of grapes, nectarines, and peaches, soon collected them round the table. (*P&P* 268)

The recipe is for peaches, though it works for nectarines as well. Nectarines and peaches were also sometimes pickled in a brine similar to that used for cucumber pickles, complete, in some versions, with a hint of mustard and garlic. The French Family Cook suggests slicing peaches raw and serving them in a dish, with sugar sprinkled over and under them.

Get the largest peaches before they are too ripe, rub off the lint with a cloth, then run them down the seam with a pin skin deep. Cover them with French brandy, tie a bladder over them and let them stand a week. Then take them out and make a strong syrup for them, boil and skim it well, put in your peaches and boil them till they look clear. Then take them out and put them into pots or glasses, mix the syrup with the brandy. When it is cold pour it on your peaches, tie them close down with a bladder that the air cannot get in, or the peaches will turn black.

MODERN RECIPE

10 peaches or nectarines	3 lbs. white sugar
two bottles Madeira or brandy	4 cups water

Run a sharp knife around the peach, cutting just through the skin all the way around the seam. Marinate at least 24 hours and no more than 7 days in the Madeira or brandy.

Place the sugar in a saucepan with the water and bring to a boil. While it rises to a boil, remove the peaches from the brandy, reserving the brandy, and halve and pit the peaches.

Boil the peach halves in the sugar syrup for 6 minutes, turning them gently and removing any skins that loosen and slip off. At the end of the 6 minutes, the peaches should have a glossy look and a slightly translucent surface appearance. Remove them to a bowl, return the pot of sugar syrup to medium heat, and add 3 cups of the brandy or Madeira in which the peaches were soaked. Bring this liquid to a boil and boil for 5 minutes, being careful not to let the pot boil over.

Ladle the peaches into canning jars that have been washed and kept hot according to the manufacturer's directions. Pour the brandy syrup into the jars, leaving ½" headspace at the top of each jar. Run a knife or spatula around the inside edges of each jar to release any trapped air. Clean the rims with a clean, damp cloth.

Put the lids on the jars and screw on the bands until resistance is met. Lower the jars of peaches onto a rack in a canner half full of boiling water. Add boiling water to cover the jars by 2", avoiding pouring water directly onto the jars. Do not let the jars touch the bottom of the boiling-water bath, the sides of the pot, or each other. Cover the water bath and boil 25 minutes.

Set the jars aside to cool. As they cool, the "button" on the top of each jar should sink downward with a popping noise, indicating that the jar is properly sealed.

❧ STRAWBERRY PRESERVES ❧

(Farley)

"You had better explore to Donwell," replied Mr. Knightley. "That may be done without horses. Come, and eat my strawberries. They are ripening fast." (*E* 354)

". . . We are to walk about your gardens, and gather the strawberries ourselves, and sit under trees;—and whatever else you may like to provide, it is to be all out of doors—a table spread in the shade, you know. Every thing as natural and simple as possible. Is not that your idea?"

"Not quite. My idea of the simple and the natural will be to have the table spread in the dining-room. The nature and simplicity of gentlemen and ladies, with their servants and furniture, I think is best observed by meals within doors. When you are tired of eating strawberries in the garden, there shall be cold meat in the house." (*E* 355)

. . . strawberries, and only strawberries, could now be thought or spoken of.—"The best fruit in England—every body's favourite—always wholesome.—These the finest beds and finest sorts.—Delightful to gather for one's self—the only way of really enjoying them. . . . [E]very sort good—hautboy infinitely superior—no comparison—the others hardly eatable—hautboys very scarce—Chili preferred—white wood finest flavour of all—price of strawberries in London—abundance about / Bristol— Maple Grove—cultivation—beds when to be renewed—gardeners thinking exactly different—no general rule—gardeners never to be put out of their way—delicious fruit—only too rich to be eaten much of—inferior to cherries—currants more refreshing—only objection to gathering strawberries the stooping—glaring sun . . . ."(*E* 358–59)

Yes, you were very cross; and I do not know what about, except that you were too late for the best strawberries. I was a kinder friend than you deserved. (*E* 368)

*The strawberries eaten at Mr. Knightley's would, of course, have been eaten fresh from the garden. However, strawberries were often preserved or turned into jam. Jane would have been familiar with different varieties of strawberries, as they grew in the gardens at both Chawton and Steventon. Hautbois, chili, and white wood are all varieties of strawberries; hautbois (*Fragaria moschata*) is a small, wild berry with flowers that rise on long stems above the rest of the plant.*

Strawberries were quite small by modern standards until the mid-eighteenth century, when two American imports, Fragaria chiloensis *and* virginiana, *crossbred and produced a new self-sustaining hybrid,* ananassa. *By the late eighteenth cen-*

tury, substantially larger strawberries were being grown. The interest in strawberries in Emma, *then, is in a fruit that only a generation or two earlier had been far less exciting.*

On a dry day, gather the finest scarlet strawberries, with their stalks on, before they be too ripe. Lay them separately on a china dish, beat and sift twice their weight of double-refined sugar, and strew it over them. Then take a few ripe scarlet strawberries, crush them, and put them into a jar, with their weight of double-refined sugar beat small. Cover them close, and let them stand in a kettle of boiling water till they be soft, and the syrup be come out of them. Then strain them through a muslin rag into a tossing-pan, boil and skim it well, and when it be cold, put in your whole strawberries, and set them over the fire till they be milk warm. Then take them off, and let them stand till they be quite cold. Then set them on again, and make them a little hotter, and do so several times till they look clear; but do not let them boil, as that will bring off their stalks. When the strawberries be cold, put them into jelly-glasses, with the stalks downwards, and fill up your glasses with the syrup. Put over them paper dipped in brandy, and tie them down close.

 MODERN RECIPE

6 lbs. strawberries, *in all*	3 lbs. sugar

Take half of the strawberries, remove the stems, and puree them with a food processor or a food mill. Place them in a double boiler with the sugar and heat over medium heat until the sugar dissolves and the liquid looks fairly uniformly red, about 5 to 10 minutes. Strain this liquid and return it to the pan.

Add the remaining 1 lb. strawberries, with their stems still attached. Cook, without bringing to a boil, for about 10 minutes over medium-low to low heat.

Ladle the strawberries into canning jars that have been washed and kept hot according to the manufacturer's directions. Pour the strawberry syrup into the jars, leaving ½" headspace at the top of each jar. Run a knife or spatula around the inside edges of each jar to release any trapped air. Clean the rims with a clean, damp cloth.

Put the lids on the jars and screw on the bands until resistance is met. Lower the jars of strawberries onto a rack in a canner half full of boiling water. Add boiling water to cover the jars by 2", avoiding pouring water directly onto the jars. Do not let the jars touch the bottom of the boiling-water bath, the sides of the pot, or each other. Cover the water bath and boil 15 minutes.

Set the jars aside to cool. As they cool, the "button" on the top of each jar should sink downward with a popping noise, indicating that the jar is properly sealed.

❈ ALMOND PUDDING ❈

(Rundell)

He had gone three miles round one day, in order to bring her some walnuts, because she had said how fond she was of them. . . . (*E* 28)

. . . the girl who could be gratified by a Robert Martin's riding about the country to get walnuts for her, might very well be conquered by Mr. Elton's admiration. (*E* 35)

Louisa drew Captain Wentworth away, to try for a gleaning of nuts in an adjoining hedge-row. . . . (*P* 86)

". . . Here is a nut," said he, catching down one from an upper bough. "To exemplify,—a beautiful glossy nut, which, blessed with original strength, has outlived all the storms of autumn. Not a puncture, not a weak spot any where.—This nut," he continued, with playful solemnity,—"while so many of its brethren have fallen and been trodden under foot, is still in possession of all the happiness that a hazel-nut can be supposed capable of." (*P* 88)

Nuts were almost always eaten raw, with the fingers, as part of a dessert course. Recipes for nut-based desserts often turn up in contemporary cookbooks, however, especially desserts based on almonds.

Beat half a pound of sweet and a few bitter almonds with a spoonful of water; then mix four ounces of butter, four eggs, two spoonfuls of cream, warm with the butter, one of brandy, a little nutmeg, and sugar to taste. Butter some cups, half fill, and bake the puddings.
Serve with butter, wine, and sugar.

❧ MODERN RECIPE

2 cups blanched slivered almonds	2 T heavy whipping cream
1 T water	1 T brandy
¼ lb. butter	½ tsp. nutmeg
4 eggs	⅓ cup sugar

Continued on next page

Continued from previous page

Preheat oven to 300°F. Fill a roasting pan ½" full of water and lay a folded dishtowel in the water. Butter 6 ramekins and set them on top of the dishtowel.

In a food processor, blend the almonds and water until they form a granulated paste.

In a saucepan, melt the butter. In a bowl, mix the eggs, cream, brandy, nutmeg, and sugar. Slowly add the melted butter, and then stir in the almonds. Fill the ramekins halfway and bake for 50 minutes.

ALMOND KNOTS

(Glasse)

Biscuits might be dropped and baked separately, or baked in a single layer and then cut up. These were shaped, after a fashion, out of a marzipan-like dough, and resemble an almond macaroon. They are among my family's and friends' favorite recipes from this cookbook—crunchy and sweet outside, moist and almondy inside. I have made this recipe by heating the sugar and almonds separately, as Glasse suggests, and without that extra step. I find that the extra step is largely unnecessary and have left it out of this version.

Take two pounds of almonds and blanch them in hot water, beat them in a mortar to a very fine paste, with rose-water; do what you can to keep them from oiling; take a pound of double refined sugar, sifted through a lawn sieve, leave out

Almond knots. (KO)

some to make up your knots, put the rest into a pan upon the fire till it is scalding hot, and at the same time have your almonds scalding hot in another pan; then mix them together with the whites of three eggs beaten to froth, and let it stand till it is cold, then roll it with some of the sugar you left out, and lay them in platters of paper: they will not roll into any shape, but lay them as well as you can, and bake them in a cool oven; it must not be hot, neither must they be coloured.

MODERN RECIPE

1 lb. blanched almonds	½ lb. sugar
2 T rose-flower water	2 egg whites

Preheat oven to 250°F. In a food processor, blend the almonds with the rose-flower water until the almonds have been ground to a fine paste. Add the sugar and mix thoroughly.

In a separate bowl, beat the egg whites until soft peaks form. Stir them into the almond mixture.

Pick up pieces of the dough and roll them into ropes about ½" in diameter. These ropes will want to break; if they do, just pinch them back together. They should be about 4" to 6" long.

As you finish rolling each rope, roll it lightly in a dish of sugar. Then, on a parchment-paper-lined baking sheet, make a loose, stacked spiral out of each rope. Each rough spiral should be about 2" to 2½" across and 1½" to 2" high. It will be narrower at the top than at the bottom, like a pyramid, and should look rather as if a child had extruded a bit of clay or dough through a toy press with a circular hole—in other words, it should look casually swirled and heaped. Small cracks will form at the edges of the ropes as you loop them on the baking sheet, but do not worry about this. Only pinch the rope back together or start over if it actually breaks.

An alternative method of shaping the dough is to take one tablespoon of dough at a time, rolling each piece into a ball and then rolling it through the sugar. The ball of dough can then be placed on the parchment paper and flattened to a ¼" to ½" thickness with the bottom of a glass. This method is considerably easier but looks a little less distinctive, is less authentic, and is a bit less interesting to eat; one advantage of the looped and swirled almond knot is that it creates a series of contrasting textures—crispy, chewy, crispy, chewy—with each bite.

The almond knots can be spaced quite closely on the baking sheet, as they do not rise or spread during baking. Do not allow the cookies to brown; if they show any sign of doing so, remove them from the oven immediately. Cook until the outside is firm, about 25 to 30 minutes.

ALMOND BISCUITS

(*The French Family Cook*)

This recipe has the marvelous quality of allowing for low-risk experimentation. It can be used in a wide variety of containers. I've baked it in tiny 1" × 1" tartlet tins, in which case it turns uniformly brown and crisp and tastes like almond-flavored air, and in regular-sized muffin tins, which yield a chewy, spongy, moist biscuit that tastes great (but can't be stacked, lest the individual biscuits cling to each other). Tartlet tins of intermediate size create a third texture, reminiscent of a Chinese almond cookie.

. . . take a quarter of a pound of sweet almonds, pick, and pound them fine in a mortar, sprinkling them from time to time with a little fine sugar; then beat them a quarter of an hour with an ounce of flour, the yolks of three eggs, and four ounces of fine sugar, adding afterward the white of four eggs whipt to a froth: have ready some paper moulds, made like boxes, about the length of two fingers square; butter them within, and put in your biscuits, throwing over them equal quantities of flour and powdered sugar: bake them in a cool oven, and when done of a good colour, take them out of the papers.

 ## MODERN RECIPE

¼ lb. blanched almonds	3 egg yolks
¼ lb. sugar plus 1 T, *in all*	4 egg whites
1 oz. flour	

Preheat oven to 275°F.

In a food processor, blend the almonds and 1 T of the sugar until the almonds are finely ground. Add the flour and egg yolks and process until the ingredients are thoroughly mixed and form a yellowish mass that tends to stick together.

In a separate bowl, whip the egg whites until they form stiff peaks. Gradually add the yellow almond paste, mixing on low speed until the almonds are just combined, then on high speed for five minutes. Generously grease a number of small tartlet tins set on a baking sheet or paper muffin cups set in a muffin pan. (A size about 1½" to 2" long works best, but the recipe is very forgiving—see the note, above.) If using smaller containers, fill them about ⅔ full with batter; if using larger muffin cups, fill them only about ½" deep.

Continued on next page

Continued from previous page

Bake 30 minutes, rotating the trays top to bottom and front to back halfway through the baking time. Let the biscuits cool; if they resist coming out of the tins, use a toothpick to break their contact with the sides and ease them out.

12

BREAD AND PORRIDGE

Because potatoes were not yet a principal part of the English diet, and rice was consumed only rarely, most of the starch on the table came from wheat flour in the form of breads, puddings, pancakes, and fritters. That it was wheat flour, and, whenever possible, *white* flour was a relatively new development in English history. For centuries, white bread had been a delicacy enjoyed only by the upper class, with humbler levels of society dining on fine whole-wheat bread, coarse whole-wheat bread, bread made of mixed wheat and rye flours, or, at the very bottom of the economic scale, bread made of barley or of barley and peas. However, by Austen's time, the working class had lost its *"rye teeth,"* in the words of a description of Nottinghamshire laborers in 1796. A correspondent to *The Gentleman's Magazine* wrote much the same thing of the Herefordshire peasantry in 1819: "Barley bread they do not eat." A large loaf of white bread was considered the right of every man, woman, and child, and people grew extremely cranky when they were forced by necessity to eat anything else, as they were at times during the shortages caused by the Napoleonic Wars.

In many cases, white bread and weak tea were the only luxuries. Many of the poor lived on bread and cheese from day to day, with scarcely any meat or vegetables to enliven their monotonous meals. Sir Frederick Eden, in his 1797 survey of *The State of the Poor*, suggested that broths of vegetables, cheap meat, oatmeal, and barley would be more nutritious than the bread-and-cheese regimen. For meatless meals, he urged the poor to adopt oatmeal porridge, pease puddings, and frumenty (barley cooked in milk). Alternative grains such as oatmeal were more popular in the north of England than in the south, and the rural poor were more likely than the urban poor to settle for mixed-grain bread. But townsfolk of all classes demanded white bread.

They did not always bake it themselves. Not all homes had bread ovens, which used expensive wood as fuel. People without an oven either bought ready-made bread from a baker or else made up their loaves at home and took them to the baker to be baked. Making up one's own loaves was time-consuming, but at least it allowed control over the ingredients. Bakers were frequently accused of whitening their bread with additives, chiefly alum. Alum mixed with salt was known in the trade as "stuff," and it was routinely added to bread to make the product "white, light and relishing." Frederick Accum detailed the prevailing methods of whitening bread in his *A Treatise on Adulterations of Food and Culinary Poisons* (1820). He noted that the alum was either mixed 1:3 with salt as "stuff" or premixed with the flour and called "sharp whites." The difference between adulterated and unadulterated bread was obvious to the knowledgeable eye, he said:

> If the alum be omitted, the bread has a slight yellowish grey hue—as may be seen in the instance of what is called *home-made bread*, of private families. Such bread remains longer moist than bread made with alum; yet it is not so light, and full of eyes, or porous, and it has also a different taste.

Grumblers!!, Woodward, 1799. Many prints show enormous loaves of bread being sliced in this fashion, with the loaf held cut-end-up on the lap. (Courtesy of the Lewis Walpole Library, Yale University. 799.11.0.1.)

Accum made a detailed study of the methods of bread production, and his account is interesting to the food historian not only because of his accounts of adulteration but also because he walks his readers step by step through the commercial baking process. In the first place, he explains that only forty-eight pounds of usable flour was actually produced from each sixty-one-pound bushel of wheat; the rest was bran, "pollard," a lower-grade flour containing finely ground bran, and waste. Five bushels of ground wheat yielded a 240-pound sack of flour, which was then sent to the baker, who turned it into eighty "quartern" loaves. The quartern loaf was supposedly a loaf made from four pounds of flour, but by Accum's reckoning, it was actually made from three pounds.

The baker first sifted the sack of flour, then turned to a basin called a seasoning tub, into which he poured two ounces of alum, a quart of boiling water, four to five pounds of salt, and an additional pail full of hot water. He allowed the mixture to cool to about 84°F, then added three to four pints of yeast.* The mixture was strained, poured into the center of the mound of flour, and mixed into dough, which was sprinkled with flour, covered with cloths, and left to rise for about three hours. When the dough rose enough to break through the flour covering the surface, the baker added another ounce of alum dissolved in warm

---

*The yeast was brewer's ale yeast, different from the dry yeast currently sold for making bread. It was always a challenge for housewives to keep their yeast from going bad, and they had different expedients for doing so. In hot weather, they would dry out the yeast that remained after they had brewed beer, sometimes mixing it with salt and forming it into ropes, sometimes spreading it on a board to dry and scraping it off as needed. Others bottled it in wide-mouthed containers and kept it cool, according to William Ellis, in a "ditch, pond, river, or well." Yeast, according to Ellis, was not the only substance used to help bread rise. He gives an account of using a sort of starter that enabled the housewife to use half the normal quantity of yeast:

> I shall here observe the method a days-man's (as we call them in *Hertfordshire*) or labourer's wife took to make and keep her leaven from one baking to another. Her family was a husband and five children, seven in all, which obliged her about every ten days end to bake one bushel of flower; and as her money was short, and yeast sometimes scarce and dear, she always took care to save a piece of her leavened dough, at each baking, about the bigness of her fist, and making a little hole in the middle of it with her finger, ram'd it full of salt, and in a ball shape she let it lie covered over with salt in her salt-box till the next baking; by which time it got dry and hard enough to break into crumbles, for mixing them with half a pint of yeast and warm water. This, when put into the middle of the flower, as it lay in a tub or kneading-trough, was stirred with some of the meal, and left to ferment and rise, which in warm weather it would do in an hour or two's time. Not that time is a true indication when it has fermented or risen enough; for to know this, she would look now and then, and when she saw the place cracked over where the leaven lay, she knew it was enough, and accordingly mixed the rest of the flower, and kneaded all into a moderate stiffness. . . .

water, kneaded the mass again, and left it to rise for a few more hours. When it had risen, the dough was kneaded again "for upwards of an hour" and cut into pieces, which were again sprinkled with flour and allowed to rise for four hours. A half-hour final kneading was concluded by cutting and weighing pieces of the proper size, and the loaves were baked for two and a half hours.

Some bakers added potatoes to their dough, Accum said: "I have witness that five bushels of flour, three ounces of alum, six pounds of salt, one bushel of potatoes boiled into a stiff paste, and three quarts of yeast, with the requisite quantity of water, produce a white, light, and highly palatable bread." He acknowledged that there was nothing harmful in this practice, but he was miffed that bakers did not pass their savings along to the customers in the form of lower prices. He was more indignant about bakers who used carbonate of magnesia, gypsum, chalk, and even pipe clay in their bread—all without telling the customers what the loaf contained. Accum was ahead of his time; legislation against adulterants in bread would not be passed until 1872.

Those who had ovens of their own, of course, could save money and be sure of the quality of their bread by making it themselves. William Ellis provides a description of home bread baking in his *The Country Housewife's Family Companion* (1750), an invaluable resource because it not only prescribes what housewives *should* do but also provides anecdotes and recipes illustrating what actual housewives and servants *did*. He writes that Hertfordshire housewives would first heat some water, then pour a bushel of flour into the kneading-tub and sprinkle a handful of salt over it, then stir the dry mixture:

> . . . then she mixes a pint of yeast with some of the flower, and lets it lie a little while to rise; next she lades her warm water over the whole mass, and kneads away. Others mix the yeast with the hot water, and pour it over the flower, and then knead all into a dough moderately stiff; and as they begin this when the fuel is put into the oven, they get the bread ready against it is hot, which will be in about an hour's time; and to know when it is enough, there are many ovens that have a little stone fixed in the brick work, at the farthest end, opposite the oven's mouth, which when cold is of a blackish colour, but when it appears whitish, it is a mark or indication for knowing the oven is hot enough. Others regard the sparkles of the fire that fly up, on rubbing the bottom of the oven. If these then spread briskly about, they reckon the oven is hot enough to be swept, and the loaves put in and stopt up.

As Ellis makes clear, half the art of baking lay in preparing the bread, the other half in preparing the oven.

Baking, because it was so labor intensive, tended to be concentrated into as few days as possible. An entire household's bread for the week, for example, would be baked in just one day. The dough would be mixed in a trough using a wooden paddle. The loaves would be shaped—in some parts of the country the cook made a cross on each loaf "to let out the devil"—and loaded into the oven using a wide wooden paddle called a peel. Baking bread was a laborious process, not merely because of the muscular kneading but also because the oven fires had to be lit, consumed, and swept out before each session of baking, to warm the oven sufficiently to bake the bread. This is one reason for long baking times; the oven started off at its maximum heat and grew gradually cooler as the bread baked. Small wonder that some women chose to buy their bread ready-made, though not all were sympathetic to their desires. William Cobbett, in *Cottage Economy* (1821), complained, "How wasteful, and indeed how shameful for a labourer's wife to go to the baker's shop; and how negligent, how criminally careless of the welfare of his family must the labourer be who permits so scandalous a use of the proceeds of his labour!"

Whether store-bought or homemade, however, bread truly was the foundation of the meal. Many people could not afford to eat meat on a daily basis, but a family was considered truly destitute if it could not buy bread. People ate bread and butter, buttered toast, and rolls for breakfast; for luncheon they often ate sandwiches, named for John Montagu, fourth earl of Sandwich, who invented that handy snack in about 1760; for dinner there were starchy meat puddings and sweet fruit puddings, both of which had flour as a chief ingredient; for tea there was more bread or toast, or possibly muffins, the bread known today in America as "English muffins" and in England as "crumpets"; and for supper there might be more bread and butter, or bread and cheese, or pottage or gruel made from various types of grain. At each of these meals, the quality and quantity of the bread would vary depending on the means of the family. The comfortably well-off ate good-quality white bread at each of these meals, and the

Toasting Muffins, Gillray, 1791. A print poking fun at George III's finances shows him toasting his own muffins with a toasting fork beside a fire. (Courtesy of the Lewis Walpole Library, Yale University. 791.11.28.1.)

wealthy might substitute French bread—not a baguette but a rich bread made with milk, butter, and eggs—which was substantially more expensive to make.

Given how common bread was on the table, Parson Woodforde's diary contains surprisingly few references to it. Perhaps it was part of the "&c." with which he so often concludes his bills of fare, after specifying the all-important meat dishes. He does, however, mention "dried Toast" after a funeral, "Fritters and toasted Cheese" on a meatless Good Friday, "bread & Butter" for breakfast, "hot Rolls, dried Toast, [and] Bread & Butter" at another breakfast, and other similar servings of bread. In one particularly intriguing episode, he describes a bread dole in February 1795 in which the baker of the donated loaves was the father of one of his servants. Woodforde, curious, weighed the loaves that were being given away and found that "The Sixpenny Loaf weighed—4. Pound, 5. Ounces. The Threepenny Loaf—2. Pound, 2. Ounces." He also, on more than one occasion, notes eating a somewhat exotic starch: "Maccaroni," which had been popularized in England by young men returning from the Italian portions of the Grand Tour. (Some of these aristocratic young men, in the mid-eighteenth century, formed a club called the Macaroni Club, in which they met to reminisce about the Italian journeys and to calculate how best to shock their parents and the public at large. They adopted outrageous fashions designed to draw comment and succeeded admirably. They and their imitators were satirized and lionized in numerous series of prints, and "Macaroni" became a term for someone who was self-consciously fashionable or truly cutting edge. This is the reason that the song "Yankee Doodle" contains that odd, apparently nonsensical reference to macaroni. The song was originally sung by British soldiers to taunt the Americans: you are such bumpkins, the message ran, that you stick a stupid feather in your hats and think *that's* fashion.)

❧ ENGLISH BREAD ❧

(Millington)

"And what had she got for Supper?" "I did not observe." "Bread & Cheese I suppose." "I should never wish for a better supper," said Ellen. (*Col Let, MW* 157)

. . . could I bear to see her want, while I had a bit of bread to give her? (*MP* 7)

Miss Campbell . . . was eligibly and happily settled, while Jane Fairfax had yet her bread to earn. (*E* 165)

Sift a peck of the best white flour into a trough, make a cavity in the centre, and strain through a hair sieve a pint of good yeast and a pint of lukewarm water mixed together; mix up gently with this liquor some of the flour till of a light paste, set it in a warm place covered over to prove for an hour; then mix the whole with two quarts of lukewarm water and a little salt, knead it of a good stiffness, prove it an hour more, and knead it again; prove it another hour, mould it into loaves or batch two pieces together, and bake them in a brisk oven. A middling-sized loaf will require an hour and a half in baking.

 ## MODERN RECIPE

8 cups flour

2 pkgs. active dry yeast

½ cup plus 1 pint lukewarm water (about 105°F to 110°F)

2 tsp. salt

Mix the yeast into ½ cup warm water. Let it stand for 15 minutes to proof—that is, to turn light and foamy, indicating that the yeast is alive and active.

In a large mixing bowl, mix the salt into the flour. Add the pint of warm water plus the water containing the proofed yeast. Mix the dough thoroughly with a large wooden spoon and then, when it gets too stiff to stir, with your hands.

Knead the bread dough on a floured board or countertop for 10 minutes. Then place it in a greased bowl covered with plastic wrap or a damp, clean dishtowel, and set it in a warm place to rise.

When the dough has approximately doubled in size, punch it down and knead it briefly to release air.

Line a baking sheet with parchment paper. Shape the dough into a single large loaf on the baking sheet, keeping the loaf as high and cylindrical as possible. Cover it very loosely with plastic wrap and set it aside to rise again.

Preheat the oven to 400°F. When the loaf has expanded by at least 50 percent in volume, put the loaf in the oven and bake for 1½ hours.

❊ FRENCH BREAD ❊

(Glasse)

". . . I did not quite like, at breakfast, to hear you talk so much about the French-bread at Northanger."

"I am sure I do not care about the bread. It is all the same to me what I eat." (*NA* 241)

Most recipes for French bread indicate that the crust was chipped off after baking, using a file or a knife. I am frankly baffled as to the reason for this. Perhaps it was meant to distinguish the richer French bread from its humbler English cousin; perhaps it reduced crumbs or unsightly chewing through crust and was therefore more genteel. I prefer this bread with the crust left intact, but if you like, you may chip it off for the sake of authenticity.

Take three quarts of water, and one of milk; in winter scalding hot, in summer a little more than milk warm; season it well with salt, then take a pint and a half of good ale yeast not bitter, lay it in a gallon of water the night before, pour it off the water, stir in your yeast into the milk and water, then with your hand break in a little more than a quarter of a pound of butter, work it well till it is dissolved, then beat up two eggs in a bason, and stir them in; have about a peck and a half of flour, mix it with your liquor; in winter make your dough pretty stiff, in summer more slack: so that you may use a little more or less flour, according to the stiffness of your dough: mix it well, but the less you work the better: make it into rolls, and have a very quick oven. When they have lain about a quarter of an hour, turn them on the other side, let them lie about a quarter longer, and then take them out and chip all your French bread with a knife, which is better than rasping it, and make it look spungy and of a fine yellow, whereas the rasping takes off all that fine colour, and makes it look too smooth. You must stir your liquor into the flour as you do for the pie-crust. After your dough is made, cover it with a cloth, and let it lie to rise while the oven is heating.

MODERN RECIPE

16 cups flour	4 T butter
1 quart water	1 egg
2 packages active dry yeast	1 T kosher salt
1¼ cups skim milk	

Measure 15 cups of the flour into a large mixing bowl. Save the last cup to add toward the end of the mixing if the dough seems too wet.

Set aside ½ cup of water, warm it to between 105°F and 110°F, and add the yeast. Stir in the yeast and then set it aside for 15 minutes to proof; if the yeast is active, it will develop a light froth at the top.

In a saucepan, warm the remaining water and the milk to 105°F to 110°F. Beat the egg and, in a mixing bowl, combine the yeast water, the water-milk mixture, the egg, and the salt. Blend together and pour into the 15 cups of flour. Mix the dough well with a wooden spoon, then turn it out onto a floured board or countertop and gently knead it for up to 5 minutes to incorporate any loose flour. Add part or all of the reserved cup of flour if the dough seems overly sticky.

Grease a large bowl. Put the lump of dough into the bowl, greasing one side, and then turn it upside down. Cover the bowl with plastic wrap or a damp kitchen towel and set it in a warm place to rise.

When the dough has approximately doubled in volume, punch it down and knead it for a minute or two on a lightly floured surface. Then cut the dough into quarters. Each quarter will make either four rolls or one loaf. Shape these and place them on greased on nonstick baking sheets, covered loosely with plastic wrap. Set them in a warm place to rise.

Meanwhile, preheat the oven to 425°F. As soon as the oven is preheated and the rolls have risen visibly, place the trays in the oven. (Normally, one would let the bread rise a second time until they had nearly doubled in size again. However, the soft nature of this dough means that a second full rise is difficult. The dough tends to stick to the plastic wrap as it rises, meaning that it tears and deflates when the wrap is removed; also, the rolls tend to rise outward rather than upward. A full second rise is possible, but you will need to monitor the rolls very closely or bake them in a deep-sided pan such as a roasting pan.)

Bake until the rolls or loaves are a uniform golden brown, about 45 to 55 minutes.

As for "chipping" the bread afterward, it's up to you. If you're going for strict authenticity, have at it and chip or rasp off the crust. It only affects the texture, not the taste, of the bread, and a modern diner would not expect the crust to be removed.

EXCELLENT ROLLS

(Rundell)

Warm one ounce of butter in half a pint of milk, put to it a spoonful and a half of yeast of small beer, and a little salt. Put two pounds of flour into a pan, and mix in the above. Let it rise an hour; knead it well; make into seven rolls, and bake in a quick oven.

If made in cakes three inches thick, sliced and buttered, they resemble Sally Lunn's, as made at Bath.

The foregoing receipt, with the addition of a little saffron boiled in half a tea-cupful of milk, makes them remarkably good.

 ## MODERN RECIPE

1¼ cups milk, *in all*	2 lbs. flour
pinch of saffron threads, crumbled	1 tsp. kosher salt
2 T butter	up to 1 cup warm water, 105°F to 110°F
½ pkg. active dry yeast	

In a small saucepan, combine the saffron with ¼ cup of the milk. Heat over medium-low for 2 minutes, stirring to keep the milk from scalding. Remove from the heat, pour into a small bowl, and let cool.

Pour the other cup of milk into the saucepan and add the butter. Warm until the mixture is between 105°F and 110°F. Then remove from heat, add the yeast, and pour into the bowl with the saffron milk.

Measure the flour and salt into a large mixing bowl and combine. Add the liquid mixture and stir. Then, very gradually, add warm water as necessary to make a stiff dough. Knead the dough on a floured surface for 5 minutes.

Grease a bowl. Put the dough into the bowl, then turn the dough over to grease the top. Cover the bowl with plastic wrap or a damp kitchen towel and set it in a warm place to rise. When the dough has approximately doubled in size, punch it down and knead it briefly to release trapped air bubbles.

Cut the dough into 8 pieces of equal size. Roll each into a ball and pinch any loose or awkward edges together on the underside. Grease 2 baking sheets and place 4 rolls on each. Cover the rolls loosely with plastic wrap and set them in warm place to rise a second time.

Continued on next page

Continued from previous page

Preheat oven to 425°F. Bake the rolls for 15 minutes, then reverse the baking sheets top-to-bottom and front-to-back and bake another 15 minutes. The crusts will be very firm and a deep golden brown.

 # MUFFINS

(Collingwood)

Mr & Mrs Edwards always drank a dish extraordinary, & ate an additional muffin when they were going to sit up late. . . . (*Wat, MW* 326–27)

Mr. Collins seemed likely to sink into insignificance; to the young ladies he certainly was nothing; but he had still at intervals a kind listener in Mrs. Philips, and was, by her watchfulness, most abundantly supplied with coffee and muffin. (*P&P* 76)

. . . Lady Russell, not long afterwards, was entering Bath on a wet after-noon, and driving through the long course of streets from the Old Bridge to Camden-place, amidst the dash of other carriages, the heavy rumble of carts and drays, the bawling of newsmen, muffin-men and milk-men, and the ceaseless clink of pattens. . . . (*P* 135)

The muffin last night—if it had been handed round once, I think it would have been enough. (*E* 170)

Collingwood's proportions of ingredients result in small, extremely dense muffins that look like miniature versions of modern English muffins. The version below results in a muffin that more closely resembles both the modern English muffin and the versions seen in prints from Austen's time. However, if you want to make Collingwood's recipe as written, use half as much beer. Then, when the dough is mixed, knead it for 5 to 10 minutes or until it is smooth. Turn it into a buttered bowl to let it rise; cover; and let rise in a warm place until its volume increases by about 50 percent. Then pull off pieces about the size of a small egg, roll them into balls, flatten them into discs about 1/2" thick, and let them rise, covered, for at least 1 hour. Cook on a griddle as directed for the muffins below.

Put a bushel of Hertfordshire white flour into your trough, three gallons of milk-warm liquor, and mix in a quart of mild ale, or good small-beer yeast, and half a pound of salt. Stir it well about a quarter of an hour, then strain it into the flour, mix your dough as high as you can, and let it lie one hour to rise. Then with your hand roll it up, and pull it into little pieces as big as a large walnut. Roll them with your hand like a ball, lay them on a table, and as fast as you do them lay a flannel over them, and be sure to keep your dough covered with flannel. When you have rolled out all your dough, begin to bake the first, and by that time they will be spread out in the right form. Lay them on your plate, and as the bottom begins to change colour, turn them on the other side. Take great care that they do not burn. If the middle of your plate be too hot, put a brick or two in the middle of the fire to slacken the heat. The plate you bake on must be thus fixed. Build a place, as if you were going to build a copper, or a piece of cast iron, all over the top, fixed in form just the same as the bottom of a copper, or iron pot, and make your fire under with coal, as under a copper.

MODERN RECIPE

16 cups unbleached white flour plus extra flour for shaping the muffins

1 package dry yeast

1 oz. (by weight) kosher salt

3 cups whole milk at 105° to 110°F

3 cups water at 105° to 110°F

2 12-oz. bottles of beer, heated to about 100° to 105°F

Mix the yeast into ½ cup of the warm water and set it aside for 15 minutes. It should become bubbly, proving that the yeast is still active. Meanwhile, mix the salt thoroughly with the flour in a large bowl.

Add all the liquid to the flour and salt. Stir for about 5 minutes until the ingredients are completely incorporated and the dough becomes very stretchy; the dough will be sticky and very soft. Cover the bowl with plastic wrap or a damp kitchen towel and set it in a warm place for 1 hour.

Prepare some cookie sheets by lining them with nostick silicone liners or with wax paper generously sprinkled with flour. When the dough has risen, dip one hand into the sticky mixture and grab a small handful of dough. Drop it into a bowl of flour and use your other hand to cover the dough lump with flour. Dip your sticky hand into the flour and toss the dough ball lightly back and forth from hand to hand to shake off the excess flour. Then set it on one of the lined cookie sheets. Continue until the cookie sheet is full; then cover it loosely with plastic wrap and fill and cover the other cookie sheets in the same way. Cover any leftover dough. The muffins can be left to rise on their pans for up to 1 hour or can be cooked immediately. Just be sure that the plastic wrap covering them does not stick to the tops if you opt to let them rise for more than about 15 minutes.

When all the cookie sheets are full, heat a nonstick griddle or large skillet at medium to medium-low heat. (The exact setting, just as with pancakes, takes a little experiment and depends on the performance of your individual stovetop.) Using a spatula, remove the muffins from the

Continued on next page

Continued from previous page

first tray you assembled and place them on the griddle. The dough will still be very soft, so try not to squish or roll the muffins as you remove them from the tray. It is sometimes helpful to sprinkle some flour around the muffin, using the spatula to slide the flour under the muffin from all sides before attempting to lift it.

Cook the muffins for 2 to 5 minutes on the first side, then flip, press lightly with a spatula, and cook for 2 to 5 minutes on the second side; the exact time will depend on your griddle. Ideally, you want to adjust the temperature so that each side takes closer to 5 than to 2 minutes to cook. When done, the first side will have a generous scattering of medium-brown spots. The second side will usually have a larger area of browning toward the middle of the muffin.

To serve, split the muffins with a fork in the following manner: Insert the tines of a fork into the edge of the muffin and pry it slightly apart. Remove the fork and continue the same procedure all the way around the circumference of the muffin. When you have gone all the way around, you can insert the fork more deeply and pry the two halves completely apart. Toast the muffins and spread them with butter. They can be toasted in a toaster, although in Austen's day the muffins would have been speared on a toasting fork and toasted at the drawing-room fire.

PLUMB PORRIDGE

(Glasse)

There is a fine old saying, which every body here is of course familiar with—"Keep your breath to cool your porridge,"—and I shall keep mine to swell my song. (*P&P* 24)

Like the barley gruel below, this recipe pairs barley and wine, a combination that does not readily spring to mind today.

Take a gallon of water, half a pound of barley, a quarter of a pound of raisins clean washed, a quarter of a pound of currants clean washed and picked: boil these till above half the water is wasted, with two or three blades of mace; then sweeten it to your palate, and add half a pint of white wine.

MODERN RECIPE

2 quarts water	¾ tsp. mace
¼ lb. barley	sugar to taste
2 oz. raisins	½ cup sweet white wine
2 oz. currants	

Bring the water to a boil over high heat. Add the barley, raisins, currants, and mace, and boil, stirring occasionally, until the water is reduced by half, about 25 minutes. Add the wine and sweeten to taste.

BUTTERED TOAST

When we arrived at the town where we were to Breakfast, I was determined to speak with Philander & Gustavus, & to that purpose as soon as I left the Carriage, I went to the Basket. . . . they desired me to step into the Basket as we might there converse with greater ease. Accordingly I entered & whilst the rest of the party were devouring Green tea & buttered toast, we feasted ourselves . . . by a confidential conversation. (*L&F, MW* 106)

He took his own Cocoa from the Tray,—which seemed provided with almost as many Teapots &c as there were persons in company, Miss P. drinking one sort of Herb-Tea & Miss Diana another, & turning completely to the Fire, sat coddling and cooling it to his own satisfaction & toasting some Slices of Bread, brought up ready-prepared in the Toast-rack. . . . When his Toils were over however, he moved back his Chair into as gallant a Line as ever, & proved that he had not been working only for himself, by his earnest invitation to her to take both Cocoa & Toast. (*Sand, MW* 416)

He was certainly very happy to turn the conversation on dry Toast, & hear no more of his sisters.—"I hope you will eat some of this Toast, said he, I reckon myself a very good Toaster; I never burn my Toasts—I never put them too near the Fire at first—& yet, you see, there is not a Corner but what is well browned.—I hope you like dry Toast."—"With a reasonable quantity of Butter spread over it, very much—said Charlotte—but not otherwise.—" "No more do I—said he exceedingly pleased—We think quite alike there.—So far from dry Toast being wholesome, I think it a very bad thing for the Stomach. Without a little butter to soften it, it hurts the Coats of the Stomach. . . ." (*Sand, MW* 417)

"She had been into the kitchen," she said, "to hurry Sally and help make the toast, and spread the bread and butter—or she did not know when they should have got tea. . . ." (*MP* 383)

Buttered toast was a staple for both breakfast and tea. It can simply be made in the toaster or, if you prefer, using a modern-day toasting fork over an open fire. A toasting fork can be made in a few minutes out of a wire coat hanger; it is important that the bread fit snugly into the tines of the fork so that it does not fall out when the bread is being turned. Cooks of Austen's day had single toasting forks at their disposal, as well as toasting racks that browned multiple slices of bread at once.

❀ BARLEY GRUEL ❀

(Collingwood)

Upon such occasions Mr. Woodhouse's feelings were in sad warfare. He loved to have the cloth laid, because it had been the fashion of his youth; but his conviction of suppers being very unwholesome made him rather sorry to see any thing put on it. . . .

Such another small basin of thin gruel as his own, was all that he could, with thorough self-approbation, recommend. . . . (*E* 24)

You must go to bed early, my dear—and I recommend a little gruel to you before you go.—You and I will have a nice basin of gruel together. My dear Emma, suppose we all have a little gruel. (*E* 100)

Gruel was considered a wholesome food for invalids. Frankly, however, the only reason I can offer for its popularity with invalids was that the invalids were too feeble to fight back. This is really a fairly nasty dish, which might be made more palatable by the use of a sweet white wine rather than red wine, or by the omission of the wine altogether. Maria Rundell uses port wine, which is sweeter and pairs somewhat better with the barley, but the dish is still less than delectable.

Put a quarter of a pound of pearl barley, and a stick of cinnamon, into two quarts of water, and let it boil till it be reduced to one quart. Add a pint of red wine and sugar to your taste. You may add two or three ounces of currants, if you please.

MODERN RECIPE

1 to 2 quarts water*	2 cups red wine (preferably port)
¼ lb. barley*	1 T sugar
1 cinnamon stick	2 oz. currants

Place the water in a large saucepan over high heat. Add the barley and cinnamon, bring to a boil, reduce the heat slightly, and cook the specified time.*

Stir in the red wine, sugar, and currants. Heat over medium to medium-low for 5 minutes.

*If you are using ordinary pearl barley, use two quarts of water and boil until the liquid is reduced by half. If you are using "instant" or quick-cook barley, use one quart of water and cook 10 minutes only.

 # WATER GRUEL

(Collingwood)

The gruel came and supplied a great deal to be said—much praise and many comments—undoubting decision of its wholesomeness for every constitution, and pretty severe Philippics upon the many houses where it was never met with tolerable;—but, unfortunately, among the failures which the daughter had to instance, the most recent, and therefore most prominent, was in her own cook at South End, a young woman hired for the time, who never had been able to understand what she meant by a basin of nice smooth gruel, thin, but not too thin. (*E* 104–5)

Mr. John Knightley, ashamed of his ill-humour, was now all kindness and attention; and so particularly solicitous for the comfort of her father, as to seem—if not quite ready to join him in a basin of gruel—perfectly sensible of its being exceedingly wholesome . . . (*E* 133)

This is an entirely different sort of gruel from the above. It doesn't taste actively bad, but it's about as bland as food can possibly be. It is a barely thickened buttered water, hence the name.

Put a large spoonful of oatmeal to a pint of water, stir them well together, and let it boil up three or four times, stirring it often; but take care not to let it boil over. Then strain it through a sieve, salt it to your palate, put in a good piece of fresh butter, brew it with a spoon till the butter be all melted, and it will be fine and smooth.

MODERN RECIPE

2 cups water	2 T butter
2 T oatmeal	

Place the water and oatmeal in a saucepan and bring to a boil. Boil gently for 10 minutes, uncovered. Pass the mixture through a strainer and return the liquid to the saucepan. Add the butter and stir until it is melted.

✿ BREAD AND BUTTER ✿

. . . her eyes could only wander from the walls marked by her father's head, to the table cut and knotched by her brothers, where stood the tea-board never thoroughly cleaned, the cups and saucers wiped in streaks, the milk a mixtures of motes floating in thin blue, and the bread and butter growing every minute more greasy than even Rebecca's hands had first produced it. (*MP* 439)

The next opening of the door brought something more welcome; it was for the tea-things, which she had begun almost to despair of seeing that evening. Susan and an attendant girl, whose inferior appearance informed Fanny, to her great surprise, that she had previously seen the upper servant, brought in every thing necessary for the meal; Susan looking as she put the kettle on the fire and glanced at her sister, as if divided between the agreeable triumph of shewing her activity and usefulness, and the dread of being thought to demean herself by such an office. "She had been into the kitchen," she said, "to hurry Sally and help make the toast, and spread the bread and butter—or she did not know when they should have got tea . . . (*MP* 383)

. . . they had to listen to the description of exactly how little bread and butter she ate for breakfast, and how small a slice of mutton for dinner . . . (*E* 168)

Bread and butter appeared at breakfast and at tea. It might take the form of slices of untoasted bread or of either hot or cold rolls. Rolls were usually made of the brioche-like French bread rather than the plain flour-and-salt English bread.

 SANDWICHES

(Hunter)

. . . as every thing will turn to account when love is once set going, even the sandwich tray, and Dr. Grant doing the honours of it, were worth looking at. (*MP* 65)

Bring up some Chocolate immediately; Spread a Cloth in the dining Parlour, and carry in the venison pasty—. In the mean time let the Gentleman have some sandwiches, and bring in a Basket of Fruit—Send up some Ices and a bason of Soup, and do not forget some Jellies and Cakes. . . . The Chocolate, The Sandwiches, the Jellies, the Cakes, the Ice, and the Soup soon made their appearance, and Mr. Gower having tasted something of all, and pocketed the rest, was conducted into the dining parlour, where he eat a most excellent Dinner & partook of the most exquisite Wines, while Mr. and Mrs. Webb stood by him still pressing him to eat and drink a little more. (*Evelyn, MW* 182)

Mrs. Weston proposed having no regular supper; merely sandwiches, &c. set out in the little room; but that was scouted as a wretched suggestion. A private dance, without sitting down to supper, was pronounced an infamous fraud upon the rights of men and women; and Mrs. Weston must not speak of it again. (*E* 254)

At Oakley Hall we did a great deal—eat some sandwiches all over mustard, admired Mr Bramston's & Mrs Bramston's Transparencies, & gained a promise from the latter of two roots of hearts-ease . . . for you. (Letter from Jane to Cassandra, October 25, 1800)

Hunter recommends using potted meat for sandwiches; other sources suggested thinly sliced veal or ham.

Put a layer of potted shrimps between two pieces of white bread and butter, and after pressing the sandwich gently down, cut it with a sharp knife, neatly round the edges. It is usual, before closing in, to spread a little made mustard over the meat.

OBS[ervation].

Potted meats of every kind make elegant sandwiches. These, when cut into mouthfuls, look better than when sent up in large pieces, as in that reduced shape, they may be taken up with a fork, and conveyed to the mouth of the fair one, without soiling her fingers or gloves.

MODERN RECIPE

8 slices white bread (preferably **English bread**)

thin slices of roast beef, roast veal, or ham or

potted meat such as potted shrimp

butter

prepared mustard

Spread butter over the insides of the slices of bread. Spread a little mustard over the butter and cover the mustard with a thin layer of sliced or potted meat. Cover the fillings with another slice of buttered bread and cut off the crusts.

BUNS

(Glasse)

She was so little equal to Rebecca's puddings, and Rebecca's hashes, brought to table as they all were, with such accompaniments of half-cleaned plates, and not half-cleaned knives and forks, that she was very often constrained to defer her heartiest meal, till she could send her brothers in the evenings for biscuits and buns. (*MP* 413)

Take two pounds of fine flour, a pint of good ale-yeast, put a little sack in the yeast, and three eggs beaten, knead all these together with a little warm milk, a little nutmeg, and a little salt; and lay it before the fire till it rises very light, then knead in a pound of fresh butter, a pound of rough caraway-comfits, and bake them in a quick oven, in what shape you please, on floured paper.

MODERN RECIPE

2 lb. flour

1 lb. butter, softened

1 package active dry yeast

¼ cup sherry

3 eggs, beaten

¼ cup milk, about 110°F

Continued on next page

Continued from previous page

½ tsp. ground nutmeg

½ tsp. salt

1 lb. **caraway comfits***

2 T caraway seeds

Measure the flour into a bowl. Blend in the softened butter with a pastry blender or your hands. In a separate bowl, mix the yeast, sherry, eggs, nutmeg, salt, and milk. Stir the wet mixture into the flour and butter mixture and combine into a single, cohesive ball of dough.

Scatter about ¼ cup of flour on a smooth, clean countertop or board. Knead the dough briefly (about 5 minutes) to ensure a uniform texture. Place the dough in a large, greased bowl and cover the top of the bowl with plastic wrap or a damp, clean dishtowel. Place the bowl in a warm place to allow the dough to rise.

When the dough has risen, preheat the oven to 400°F. Scatter the counter or board with flour again and turn the dough out onto the floured surface. Punch the dough down and knead it briefly, incorporating the caraway comfits, and shape it into rolls, using about ⅓ to ½ cup of dough for each. Set the rolls on parchment-paper-lined baking sheets and bake for 20 to 25 minutes.

*If you make the caraway comfits at home especially for this recipe, set aside the smallest fragments of caraway, the ones barely encrusted with sugar. Then use these, along with a little of the caraway-flavored sugar crystals, as a topping instead of ordinary caraway seeds.

❧ BOILED SAGO ❧

(Glasse)

Emma, on reaching home, called the housekeeper directly, to an examination of her stores; and some arrow-root of very superior quality was speedily despatched to Miss Bates with a most friendly note. In half an hour the arrow-root was returned. . . . (*E* 391)

An airing in the Hartfield carriage would have been the rack, and arrow-root from the Hartfield storeroom must have been poison. (*E* 403)

Arrowroot is a starch derived from the tubers of Maranta arundinacea; *similar starches can be extracted from other members of the genus* Maranta. *Along with its close relatives, sago, salop, and tapioca, arrowroot was considered an appropriate, nourishing food for invalids, so Emma naturally offers some to the ill and weak Jane Fairfax. It also makes sense that Hartfield would have plenty of arrowroot on hand, since Mr. Woodhouse's digestive system is so sensitive.*

Put a large spoonful of sago into three quarters of a pint of water, stir it, and boil it softly till it is as thick as you would have it; then put in wine and sugar, with a little nutmeg to your palate.

MODERN RECIPE

2½ T tapioca

1½ cups water

2 T white wine

2 T sugar

pinch nutmeg

Put the tapioca and water in a small saucepan and bring to a boil. Reduce heat to medium or medium-high and simmer for about 10 minutes or until the mixture is smooth and glutinous. Add the wine, sugar, and nutmeg, and serve.

❧ SUET PUDDING ❧

(Rundell)

MISS F. Take away the Liver & Crow & bring in the suet pudding.
          (*a short Pause.*)
MISS F. Sir Arthur shant I send you a bit of pudding?
LADY H. Sir Arthur never eats suet pudding Ma'am. It is too high a Dish
        for him.
MISS F. Will no one allow me the honour of helping them? Then John take
        away the Pudding & bring the Wine. (*Visit, MW* 53)

*I've made this a half-size pudding, just to give a taste of what one was like. For a full-size pudding, see **boiled plum pudding**, or double this recipe and follow Rundell's original recommendation of boiling for four hours. I've also taken the liberty of including this with the desserts, even though it was a savory rather than a sweet pudding and would not really have been considered a dessert. John Farley included a ½ tablespoon of ground ginger with his suet pudding, which makes it a little closer to a dessert pudding, but it was still more of a starch to accompany meat than a sweet.*

Shred a pound of suet; mix with a pound and a quarter of flour; two eggs beaten separately, a little salt, and as little milk as will make it. Boil four hours. It east well next day, cut in slices and broiled.

MODERN RECIPE

1 cup plus 1 T flour

½ lb. suet, finely chopped

1 egg, beaten

½ tsp. salt

3 T milk

Bring a large pot of water to a boil. In a mixing bowl, combine all the ingredients. Pour them out into a square of buttercloth or several stacked layers of cheesecloth and gather the loose ends, tying the cheesecloth into a bag with kitchen twine. (Unlike the plum pudding, which requires a fair amount of room for the expansion of the raisins and currants, this pudding bag can be a fairly snug fit.) Place the bag into the boiling water and boil for 2½ hours.

13

PASTRIES AND SWEETS

Few aspects of eighteenth-century cooking seem more alien to modern cooks than its approach to confectionery and pastry. It was, after all, the first age in which sugar was abundantly available in Europe, thanks to rapidly multiplying colonies in the West Indies. It was also an age without widespread refrigeration—only the wealthiest people, and commercial enterprises such as pastry shops (*NA* 44), could afford to keep icehouses for making chilled desserts. Both these influences had their effect on sweet dishes.

The relative novelty of large quantities of sugar made it the principal flavoring in many dishes. Jellies, for example, which were thickened with isinglass, hartshorn, or calf's-foot gelatin, often had little flavoring, because the beauty of the apparently frozen liquid was half the fun, and anything sweet was the other half. Cookbooks instructed readers in constructing gelatin models of moons, stars, fish ponds, islands, and temples, using specially designed molds and filling them with appropriate colors of "jelly." The lack of refrigeration meant that puddings, cakes, tarts, and biscuits dominated the national sweet tooth. Ices, jellies, and other desserts that needed to be cooled were consumed at the homes of the rich, at specialized shops, or during cold weather, when nature could be enlisted as *sous chef*.

Terminology is also somewhat surprising to the modern cook, especially to American cooks who are often unfamiliar with present-day British usage. "Pudding" in America means a specific kind of dessert, a thick, creamy substance in various flavors. In Britain, it can simply mean "dessert" in any shape and form. In Austen's time, it meant neither of these things. Pudding was a specific kind of dish that was by no means always a dessert. It might be a floury confection with fruit and suet, tied in a pudding bag and boiled; a meaty center surrounded by pastry, tied in the same bag and boiled; or a custardy mass baked in the dripping tray below a joint of roasting meat. There were lemon puddings

J. G. ad vivam. fec. *Hero's recruiting at Kelsey's; _ or _ Guard-Day at St James's.* *Pub.d June 9th 1797 by H. Humphrey. St James's Street*

Hero's recruiting at Kelsey's, Gillray, 1797. Uniformed army officers enjoy sugar plums and ices at a confectioner's. (Courtesy of the Lewis Walpole Library, Yale University. 797.6.9.2.)

and almond puddings, chestnut puddings and carrot puddings, spinach puddings and rabbit puddings. The starch in them most often came from flour, but there were also oat, millet, and barley puddings.

Savory puddings were often served with the meat in the first course, while sweet puddings followed in the second course; this distinction was, however, meaningless at dinners that had only one course. At such dinners, it is usually impossible to tell from contemporary documents what type of pudding was served. Parson Woodforde often records eating pudding and sometimes specifies the kind; "Batter Pudding," "apple Pudding," and "plumb Pudding" appear to have been the types he ate most frequently. Some of his puddings were baked, while others were boiled.

"Biscuits" in Austen's time were also not quite what might be expected. Biscuits, to current-day Americans, are flaky, not-at-all-sweet breads the size of dinner

Desire (No. 1), 1800. Desire is represented as "a Hungry Boy—and a Plumb Pudding." (Courtesy of the Lewis Walpole Library, Yale University. 800.1.20.3.)

rolls. In Britain, they are cookies. To Austen, they were small baked treats that usually contained flour, sugar, and eggs, but rarely butter. They might even be as simple as Hannah Glasse's orange biscuits, composed of dried sheets of orange peel and sugar. The common denominator between all biscuits was that they were baked—the root of "biscuit" means "cooked twice"—until they were dry.

Cakes, likewise, differed from their modern counterparts. They might be very small, for eating with tea, or they might be enormous, as they were for special occasions like weddings and Twelfth Night. These gigantic cakes were not cooked in pans, but instead with a large hoop around the dough to keep it roughly in shape. The idea of a specific sort of cake for weddings was just evolving. In general, wedding cakes were made with a rich batter, into which the cook placed candied citrus peel, nuts, raisins or currants, and some sort of alcohol—wine, brandy, or rum. The gigantic cake was baked, then covered with an almond icing, baked again to brown the icing, then coated with a very white icing to serve as a contrast to the almond layer beneath.

Pastry, too, was sometimes what we imagine and sometimes not. Tarts and

We'll make a Feast, H. Singleton and C. Knight, 1795. Two girls enjoy an apple, a pear, and some flower-shaped biscuits. (Courtesy of the Lewis Walpole Library, Yale University. 795.0.5.)

small pies often had a crust that is similar to what we use today and were not baked all that differently. But savory pies could be enormous and were baked without pans, in a crust so thick and stiff that it stood alone. Shaped like clay and filled with meat, they were completed in one of two ways. Either the "gravy" would be added before baking, in which case the top crust would be pinched into place atop the pie, or the top crust (the "lid") would be baked without attaching it to the bottom, and the liquid would be poured in after baking.

Parson Woodforde's diet included all these forms of pastry and confectionery. At various dinners and suppers, he records eating "a nice Batter Pudding with Currant Jelly," "plenty of plumb Puddings," raspberry and strawberry creams, tarts, cheesecakes, trifle, custards, "black Caps set into Custard," mince pies, jelly, and "blamange." One particularly sweet supper in 1783 included "Tarts, Italian Flummery-Blamanche black Caps and sweet-Meat"; blancmange was a kind of jelly, flummery was a stiff confection made with almonds and gelatin, and black caps were roasted halves of apples. The sweets served in his own house were made by his niece and housekeeper, Nancy Woodforde; on January 30, 1782, he writes that "Nancy [was] very busy all the morning in making Cakes, Tarts, Custards and Jellies for to Morrow." However, he also bought sweets in town; on May 12, 1790, he notes an expenditure of one shilling for "some Cakes at a Confectioners." On several occasions, he speaks of eating cake after a wedding. In April 1783 he calls this confection a "bride-Cake," and in June 1795 he calls it a "Wedding Cake" and notes the "Very curious devices on the Top of the Cake."

The Regency Twelfth Cake not cut up, Sayers, 1789. A mammoth cake in the style of those made for Twelfth Night, weddings, and other festivities. (Courtesy of the Lewis Walpole Library, Yale University. 789.2.19.1.)

ICE CREAM

(Briggs)

She then proceeded to a Pastry-cooks where she devoured six ices, refused to pay for them, knocked down the Pastry Cook & walked away. (*Cass, MW* 45)

". . . Send up some Ices and a bason of Soup, and do not forget some Jellies and Cakes." . . . The Chocolate, The Sandwiches, the Jellies, the Cakes, the Ice, and the Soup soon made their appearance. . . . (*Evelyn, MW* 182)

. . . they had driven directly to the York Hotel, ate some soup, and bespoke an early dinner, walked down to the Pump-room, tasted the water, and laid out some shillings in purses and spars; thence adjourned to eat ice at a pastry-cook's, and hurrying back to the Hotel, swallowed their dinner in haste. . . . (*NA* 116)

She was a little shocked at the want of two drawing-rooms, at the poor attempt at rout-cakes, and there being no ice in the Highbury card parties. (*E* 290)

Briggs's is the standard ice cream recipe, taken most likely from Hannah Glasse. It appears in John Farley as well. This can be made in an old-fashioned, crank-handled ice-cream maker, or more easily in a modern electric ice-cream maker, as you please. Briggs's recipe describes a still more old-fashioned method, a covered tin pot for the sweetened cream set in a tub of ice; confectioners late in the eighteenth century would have made it in a pair of pewter basins, one inside the other with a space between them for the ice and salt. The most popular recipes for ice cream involved fruit, but some people enjoyed brown bread ice, a frozen confection made of half a pint of brown bread crumbs, one and a half pints of cream, and sugar.

 This ice cream has a very delicate flavor. It can be eaten immediately or packed into a mold and later unmolded on a decorative dish.

Take a dozen ripe apricots, pare them very thin and stone them, scald them and put them into a mortar, and beat them fine; put to them six ounces of double-refined sugar, a pint of scalded cream, and rub it through a sieve with the back of a spoon; then put it into a tin with a close cover, and set it in a tub of ice broken small, with four handfuls of salt mixed among the ice; when you see your cream get thick round the edges of your tin, stir it well, and put it in again till it becomes quite thick; when the cream is all froze up, take it out of the tin, and put it into the mould you intend to turn it out of: mind that you put a piece of paper on each end, between the lids and the ice-cream, put on the top lid, and have another tub of ice ready, as before, put the mould in the middle, with the ice under and over it; let it stand four hours, and do not turn it out before you want it; then dip the mould into cold spring-water, take off the lids and paper, and turn it into a plate. You may do any sort of fruit the same way.

MODERN RECIPE

12 ripe apricots	2 cups heavy whipping cream
2 cups sugar	

Halve the apricots and remove the pits. Slice the halves thinly and put them in a nonstick saucepan over medium heat until they become soft and juicy (about 5 to 7 minutes). Meanwhile, heat the cream in another saucepan over medium-low heat. Add the sugar to the cream as it heats, stirring until the sugar dissolves. Do not let the cream boil.

When the apricots have softened, mash them through a strainer or run them through a food mill. Add the thick liquid that results to your cream mixture, mix thoroughly, and refrigerate until cold. Freeze according to the directions for your ice-cream maker.

❀ BOILED PLUM PUDDING ❀

(Glasse)

She was so little equal to Rebecca's puddings, and Rebecca's hashes, brought to table as they all were, with such accompaniments of half-cleaned plates, and not half-cleaned knives and forks, that she was very often constrained to defer her heartiest meal, till she could send her brothers in the evenings for biscuits and buns. (*MP* 413)

First take 2 lbs of bread
Be the crumb only weigh'd,
For the crust the good housewife refuses.
The proportions you'll guess
May be made more or less
To the size the family chuses.

Then its sweetness to make;
Some currants you take,
And sugar, of each half a pound
Be not butter forgot.
And the quantity sought
Must the same with your currants be found.

(from Mrs. Austen's "Receipt for a Pudding," collected by Martha Lloyd)

Plum puddings were already popular at Christmas time, though at this period they rarely had the alcoholic content they would later acquire. This version is a good-sized pudding that strongly resembles the ones seen in Regency illustrations. It browns very nicely in the boiling process and serves twelve to twenty people, depending on their appetites. Just be sure you turn it during the boiling and keep the water level high enough so that it doesn't burn.

Take a pound of suet cut in little pieces, not too fine, a pound of currants, and a pound of raisins stoned, eight eggs, half the whites, half a nutmeg grated, and a tea-spoonful of beaten ginger, a pound of flour, a pint of milk; beat the eggs first, then half the milk, beat them together, and by degrees stir in the flour, then the suet, spice, and fruit, and as much milk as will mix it well together very thick. Boil it five hours.

MODERN RECIPE

4 egg yolks	1 lb. suet, finely chopped (or rendered*)
4 eggs	1 lb. currants
1 to 2 cups milk	1 lb. raisins
1 tsp. ground or freshly grated nutmeg	1 lb. flour
1 tsp. ground ginger or freshly grated ginger	

Bring a large pot of water to a boil.

While it is heating, beat the eggs and egg yolks. Add 1 cup of the milk and mix thoroughly. Add the nutmeg and ginger.

In a separate bowl, mix the suet, currants, raisins, and flour. Add the wet mixture to the raisin and suet mixture and stir until thoroughly combined. If the mixture is not holding together as a thick, sticky batter, add up to one more cup of milk, ¼ cup at a time, to bring it to the right consistency.

Pour the batter into a large square of cheesecloth. Bring the ends of the cheesecloth together and tie the pudding into a ball with kitchen twine, leaving a little extra room in the bag to allow for the expansion of the fruit. Place the pudding bag in the boiling water, reduce the heat to medium, and cover the pot. Boil for 5 hours, making sure that the pudding is always covered in water.

*To render suet, place beef trimmings with fat into a large pot of water and boil gently for 1 to 2 hours. Remove the chunks of beef, discard any that have very little fat remaining on them, and cool the liquid in the pot. (Adding ice cubes works quickly.) The white fat—suet—will congeal on the top and can be skimmed off and refrigerated. Any chunks of beef with large quantities of fat still remaining on them can be returned to the pot and reboiled until most of the suet has been extracted. This method of obtaining suet takes longer than simply chopping up beef fat but results in a smoother and more consistent product.

ORANGE PUDDING

(Farley)

Not all puddings were loaded into a pudding bag and boiled. This one gets a puff-paste crust and bakes in the oven.

Beat sixteen yolks fine, mix them with half a pound of fresh butter melted, half a pound of white sugar, half a pint of cream, a little rose water, and a little nutmeg. Cut the peel of a large Seville orange so thin that none of the white may appear, beat it fine in a mortar till they be like a paste, and by degrees mix in the ingredients. Then lay a puff paste all over the dish, pour in the ingredients, and bake it.

MODERN RECIPE

16 egg yolks	½ tsp. rose-flower water
½ lb. butter, melted	½ tsp. ground nutmeg
½ lb. sugar	zest of one orange
1 cup heavy whipping cream	⅓ recipe **puff paste**

Preheat oven to 275°F. Pound the orange zest into a paste in a mortar and add it to other ingredients, except the puff paste, in a mixing bowl. Roll out the pastry ¼" thick and use it to line a soufflé or casserole dish. Pour the pudding into the crust and bake.

This pudding takes a long time to bake. The exact time will vary depending on the shape and size of your soufflé dish, but it will be at least 1 hour. The pudding will form a skin on top fairly early in the baking and will brown nicely, but it will need more baking before it is completely done. To tell whether the pudding is done, give the dish a very gentle shake. If the center undulates vigorously under the browned skin, the pudding is not yet done. When fully baked, the center will move very little when shaken.

This pudding can be eaten warm, but my family and friends prefer it chilled.

RICE PUDDING

(Millington)

. . . they were overtaken by Mr. John Knightley returning from the daily visit to Donwell, with his two eldest boys, whose healthy, glowing faces shewed all the benefit of a country run, and seemed to ensure a quick dispatch of the roast mutton and rice pudding they were hastening home for. (*E* 109)

Boil four ounces of ground rice till it is soft, beat up the yolks of four eggs, and add a pint of cream, four ounces of sugar, and a quarter of a pound of butter. Mix the whole together, and either boil or bake it.

MODERN RECIPE

1 cup arborio rice	½ cup sugar
4 egg yolks	¼ lb. butter, melted and cooled slightly
2 cups cream	

Preheat oven to 350°F. Bring a saucepan of water to a boil and add the rice. Cover and cook, stirring occasionally, until soft, about 20 minutes. Add more water if necessary to keep the rice from scalding.

Drain the rice and add the remaining ingredients. Pour into a 9" × 9" baking pan and bake for 30 minutes.

CALF'S FEET JELLY

(Farley, Rundell)

We brought a cold Pigeon pye, a cold turkey, a cold tongue, and half a dozen Jellies with us. . . . (*Lesley, MW* 119)

Susannah Carter gives a very similar recipe for calf's-foot jelly, though some of her terminology differs. Instead of "flannel bag" she says "jelly bag," and instead of "mountain wine" she says "Rhenish." She also adds her lemon peel, and a bit of rosemary, to the jelly bag itself, and strains the jelly a second time, giving it the flavor of rosemary and lemon as it is strained. Most jellies began with either isinglass or gelatin-rich calves' feet and had long cooking times to extract the gelatin. Modern packaged gelatin renders the long boiling times and use of egg whites unnecessary.

Farley's Recipe

Take two calfs feet, and boil them in a gallon of water till it comes to a quart. When it be cold, skim off all the fat, and take the jelly up clean. Leave what settling may remain at the bottom, and put the jelly into a saucepan, with a pint of mountain wine, half a pound of loaf sugar, and the juice of four lemons. Beat up six or eight whites of eggs with a whisk, then put them into the saucepan, stir all well together till it boils, and let it boil a few minutes. Pour it into a large flannel bag, and repeat it till it runs clear. Then have ready a large china bason, and put into it lemon-peel cut as thin as possible. Let the jelly run into the bason, and the lemon-peel will give it an amber colour and a fine flavour. Then fill your glasses.

Rundell's Recipe

Boil four quarts of water with three calf's-feet, or two cow-heels, that have been only scalded, till half wasted: take the jelly from the fat and sediment, mix it with the juice of a Seville orange and twelve lemons, the peels of three ditto, the whites and shells of twelve eggs, brown sugar to taste, near a pint of raisin wine, one ounce of coriander seeds, a quarter of an ounce of allspice, a bit of cinnamon, and six cloves, all bruised, after having previously mixed them cold. The jelly should boil fifteen minutes without stirring; then clear it through a flannel bag. While running take a little jelly, and mix with a tea-cupful of water, in which a bit of beet-root has been boiled, and run it through the bag when all the rest is run out; and this is to garnish the other jelly, being cooled on a plate; but this is a matter of choice. This jelly has a very fine high colour and flavour.

 MODERN RECIPE (Farley)

2 packets unflavored gelatin (½ oz. total)	1½ cups water
½ cup sweet dessert wine	juice and thinly peeled outer skin of 2 lemons

Bring the wine and water to a boil in a saucepan. Remove it from the heat. Stir in the gelatin, lemon juice, and lemon peel and let stand for 10 minutes. Remove the pieces of lemon peel and pour into dessert glasses. Chill until firm and serve cold.

 MODERN RECIPE (Rundell)

6 lemons	½ cup brown sugar
1 quart water	1 cup sweet wine
juice of one orange	1 tsp. ground coriander

Continued on next page

Continued from previous page

½ tsp. allspice

pinch of cinnamon

¼ tsp. ground cloves

5 packets unflavored gelatin, 1¼ oz. total weight

red food coloring (optional)

Pare off the yellow skin of 2 of the lemons with a small, sharp knife, being careful not to cut off the bitter white pith. Juice all 6 lemons.

Place the lemon peel, lemon juice, and all the other ingredients except the gelatin and the optional food coloring in a saucepan and bring to a boil over high heat. Reduce the heat to medium-low and simmer 15 minutes. Remove the lemon peel, stir in the gelatin until it dissolves, and add the food coloring if you are using it. Cool until lukewarm. Pour the gelatin into dessert glasses and chill until firm. Serve cold.

Made with 6 packets of gelatin, this is a *very* firm gelatin—which is probably about right, given that the cooks of Austen's era didn't have refrigerators. Modern diners may, however, like a slightly less springy version.

FRUIT IN JELLY

(Farley)

". . . Bring up some Chocolate immediately; Spread a Cloth in the dining Parlour, and carry in the venison pasty—. In the mean time let the Gentleman have some sandwiches, and bring in a Basket of Fruit—Send up some Ices and a bason of Soup, and do not forget some Jellies and Cakes." . . . The Chocolate, The Sandwiches, the Jellies, the Cakes, the Ice, and the Soup soon made their appearance, and Mr. Gower having tasted something of all, and pocketed the rest, was conducted into the dining parlour, where he eat a most excellent Dinner & partook of the most exquisite Wines, while Mr. and Mrs. Webb stood by him still pressing him to eat and drink a little more. (*Evelyn, MW* 182)

Jellies were used as centerpieces at "grand entertainments," as the cookbook authors of Austen's time would have phrased it. Large dinner parties might feature a central decorative jelly designed to look like something in particular. An often-printed recipe calls for fish molded of flummery (an opaque almond-based gelatin) and suspended in clear calves' feet jelly so that they looked as if they were swimming in a pond. Another used star and moon-shaped molds to keep spaces in a basin clear and filled the background in with colored flummery. Then the molds were removed and the star and moon shapes filled with calf's-feet jelly. The recipe for fruit in jelly is a bit simpler, requiring only a delicate touch in arranging the fruit.

Take a bason, put into it half a pint of clear stiff calfs feet jelly, and when it be set and stiff, lay in three fine ripe peaches, and a bunch of grapes with the stalk upwards. Put over them a few vine-leaves, and then fill up your bowl with jelly. Let it stand till the next day, and then set your bason to the brim in hot water. As soon as you perceive it gives way from the bason, lay your dish over it, and turn your jelly carefully upon it. You may use flowers for your garnish.

MODERN RECIPE

2 to 2½ recipes **calf's feet jelly**   1 small bunch grapes

3 peaches, quartered and pitted

Prepare ½ recipe calf's-feet jelly and pour it into a bowl or gelatin mold. Put it in the refrigerator to chill and set.

Break wooden skewers so that they can pierce the peach slices near one end, on the flesh side rather than the skin side, and maintain pressure between the peach slice (skin side toward the outside of the bowl or mold) and the inside of the mold (if using a mold), or the peach slice at the opposite end of the bowl (if using a bowl). The idea is to pin the peach slices in place, using just barely enough pressure to keep them standing upright. They should be arranged at even intervals around the bowl or mold, with the skewers piercing them at the higher end. Use more skewers, or skewers and string, to suspend a bunch of grapes in the bowl. All the fruit should fit inside the bowl, with no bits extending beyond the rim.

Prepare a full recipe of calf's-feet jelly. Pour into the bowl or mold, filling it until the gelatin is about ½" below the lowest skewer. Refrigerate until the jelly is firm.

Prepare ½ to 1 recipe of calf's feet jelly. Carefully remove the skewers (and string, if you used it) pinning the fruit in place. Pour in jelly to fill the bowl and refrigerate until firm.

To unmold, let the bowl or mold rest in a bowl of hot water until the gelatin around the edges softens. Place a plate on top of the mold and invert it, allowing the jelly to slip out onto the plate.

BUTTER CAKE

(Glasse)

I believe Mrs. Charles is not quite pleased with my not inviting them of-
tener; but you know it is very bad to have children with one, that one is
obliged to be checking every moment; "don't do this, and don't do that;"—
or that one can only keep in tolerable order by more cake than is good for
them. (*P* 45)

The next variation which their visit afforded was produced by the entrance
of servants with cold meat, cake, and a variety of all the finest fruits in season. . . . (*P&P* 268)

*Small tea cakes could be baked in a box oven next to the coal fire, but large cakes like
this one had to be baked in the bread oven. There was no huge cake pan; instead, the
housewife or cook used a round or oval wooden hoop called a garth, lined at the bottom
with buttered paper that was tied up around the sides of the garth. Tin hoops later replaced the wooden ones, and cake sizes were reduced, though even small cakes were gigantic in comparison to the ones we bake today.*

*This is a sizable cake with a bready texture and an appealing, delicate flavor. It was
very well received by people who appreciate less-sweet cakes, and those who like a little
more sweetness found it to be very good when spread with apricot jam. Our tasters also
suspected that slices of it would toast nicely.*

*Though by no means the largest cake in the eighteenth-century cookbooks, it is too
big for a conventional cake pan. A 12" springform pan works well, though you can also
make it in a 12" deep-dish pizza pan. To make it in a pizza pan, spray the pan with
cooking spray and tear off a long piece of parchment paper, long enough so that if you
stand it on edge, you can wrap it all the way around the pan and have five or six inches
to spare. Cut the parchment paper in half lengthwise and save one half for later. Fold
the remaining part in half lengthwise and stand it around the inside of the pan, pressing it against the sprayed edges of the pan so that it sticks fairly smoothly to the sides
of the pan. Spray the interior of the parchment paper with more cooking spray. The
batter will fill your pan, and as the cake rises, it will follow the parchment-paper extensions rather than spilling out of the pan.*

*I reduced the number of egg yolks by two in this recipe in order to account, at least
in part, for the fact that eighteenth-century chicken eggs were sometimes smaller than
the extra-large eggs available today. If your mixer bowl is small, you may have to make
the egg-butter-sugar mixture in two batches. Save this recipe for a big gathering—it's
truly cake on steroids.*

You must take a dish of butter, and beat it like cream with your hands, two pounds of fine sugar and well beat, three pounds of flour well dried, and mix them in with the butter, twenty-four eggs, leave out half the whites, and then beat all together for an hour: just as you are going to put it into the oven, put in a quarter of an ounce of mace, a nutmeg beat, a little sack or brandy, and seeds or currants, just as you please.

MODERN RECIPE

5 sticks butter (1¼ lbs.)	¼ oz. mace
2 lbs. sugar (about 4½ cups)	1½ oz. ground nutmeg
3 lbs. flour	2 cups currants
12 eggs	½ cup sherry
10 egg yolks	

Preheat oven to 300°F. Cream the butter and add the sugar, blending thoroughly. Add the eggs and egg yolks and beat until the mixture is smooth; then add 2 cups of the flour and continue to beat until the mixture is creamy and free of lumps. Turn the batter into a large bowl and add the rest of the flour, 2 cups at a time, stirring each time until the batter is smooth and uniform. It will be a stiff and sticky dough.

Stir in the mace, nutmeg, currants, and sherry. Pour into a large, greased pan (see notes above) and bake in the center of a 300°F oven for 2 hours. Reduce heat to 250°F and bake until the top is golden brown and the center of the cake is firm, about 45 minutes. (Monitor the cake as it bakes. In the last hour or so, the center of the cake will go from being slightly indented and wet-looking to being gently convex, dry, and golden brown, with networks of small cracks on the surface.)

CAKE À LA DUCHESSE

(The French Family Cook)

The solemn procession, headed by Baddeley, of tea-board, urn, and cake-bearers, made its appearance, and delivered her from a grievous imprisonment of body and mind. (*MP* 344)

This is a rather odd cake in that there is no sugar in the actual cake itself, only in the icing.

Knead half a pound of flour with a gill of water, half a pound of butter, half a spoonful of orange-flower water, some green lemon-peel shread very fine, four eggs and a little salt; let the paste rest two hours, and then beat it with the rolling pin, and form a cake. When baked, put a white ice over it, made with half the white of an egg, beat with powdered sugar and some drops of lemon juice. Put the cake into the oven a moment, to dry the ice.

MODERN RECIPE

½ lb. butter, softened

4 eggs

½ cup water

½ T orange-flower water

zest of one lemon

½ tsp. salt

½ lb. flour

Icing

1 egg white

2 cups powdered sugar

½ tsp. lemon juice

Preheat the oven to 350°F.

Cream the butter with a mixer. Add the eggs and blend well. Add the orange-flower water, lemon zest, and salt and mix well again. Then add the flour and stir until just combined.

Spread the cake batter in a cake pan. Bake until the top begins to turn golden brown and looks solid, about 45 to 50 minutes. Set the cake aside to cool, reduce the oven heat to 300°F, and make the icing. Mix the egg white, lemon juice, and powdered sugar slowly at first until the sugar is combined, then on high speed for 5 minutes.

As soon as the cake is cool to the touch, place it on a baking sheet on a sheet of parchment paper. Spread the icing evenly over the cake and place it in the oven at 300°F for 5 minutes.

Remove the cake from the oven and set it aside until it is cool again. Remove the parchment paper from the bottom, taking any excess icing with it, and transfer the cake to a cake stand or platter.

FINE LITTLE CAKES

(Glasse)

. . . her more active, talking daughter, almost ready to overpower them with care and kindness, thanks for their visit, solicitude for their shoes, anxious inquiries after Mr. Woodhouse's health, cheerful communications about her mother's, and sweet-cake from the beaufet—"Mrs. Cole had just been there, just called in for ten minutes, and had been so good as to sit an hour with them, and she had taken a piece of cake and been so kind as to say she liked it very much; and therefore she hoped Miss Woodhouse and Miss Smith would do them the favour to eat a piece too. . . ."(*E* 156)

Some cakes were giant wheels of dense, currant-laden dough. Others, like John Farley's "Cream Cakes," were very light; the cream cakes were essentially baked meringues delicately flavored with lemon zest and sometimes made into little sandwiches with a layer of jam or preserved fruit in the middle. Hannah Glasse's "Fine Little Cakes" are midway between the two types of cakes. They contain many of the same ingredients as large currant cakes, but they are small enough to be eaten daintily with the fingers.

One pound of butter beaten to cream, a pound and a quarter of flour, a pound of fine sugar beat fine, a pound of currants clean washed and picked, six eggs, two whites left out, beat them fine; mix the flour, sugar, and eggs by degrees into the batter, beat it all well with both hands; either make into little cakes, or bake it in one.

 ## MODERN RECIPE

1 lb. butter, at room temperature	1 lb. currants
1¼ lbs. flour	6 egg yolks
1 lb. sugar	4 egg whites

Preheat the oven to 350°F.

Cream the butter. Add the sugar, combine completely, and then add the egg yolks and whites. Stir in the flour until just combined, then add the currants.

Line cookie sheets with greased parchment paper or ungreased silicone baking liners.

Continued on next page

Continued from previous page

The batter will be quite sticky. Flouring your hands, take ½ cup of the dough at a time and pat the dough into rounds ½" tall. Bake 30 to 35 minutes or until brown at the edges and firm in the middle.

The batter can also be made up into large cakes. Grease a cake pan and firm it ¾" to 1" thick with batter. Bake 40 to 45 minutes.

SAFFRON CAKE

(Farley)

Her father's comfort was amply secured, Mrs. Bates as well as Mrs. Goddard being able to come; and her last pleasing duty, before she left the house, was to pay her respects to them as they sat together after dinner; and while her father was fondly noticing the beauty of her dress, to make the ladies all the amends in her power, by helping them to large slices of cake and full glasses of wine, for whatever unwilling self-denial his care of their constitution might have obliged them to practise during the meal. (*E* 213)

Take a quartern of fine flour, a pound and a half of butter, three ounces of carraway seeds, six eggs well beaten, a quarter of an ounce of cloves and mace finely beaten together, a little cinnamon pounded, a pound of sugar, a little rose-water and saffron, a pint and a half of yeast, and a quart of milk. Mix all together lightly with your hands in this manner: First boil your milk and butter, then skim off the butter, and mix it with your flour and a little of the milk. Stir the yeast into the rest, and strain it. Mix it with the flour, put in your seeds and spice, rose-water, tincture of saffron, sugar, and eggs. Beat it all well up lightly with your hands, and bake it in a hoop or pan well buttered. It will take an hour and a half in a quick oven. If you choose it, you may leave out the seeds; and some think the cake is better without them.

MODERN RECIPE

1 quart milk	½ tsp. saffron threads
1½ lbs. butter, room temperature	6 eggs, beaten
1 pkg. active dry yeast	½ oz. ground cloves
4 lbs. flour	½ oz. ground nutmeg
3 oz. caraway seeds (optional)	1 tsp. ground cinnamon
1 T rose-flower water	1 lb. sugar

Preheat the oven to 400°F. Butter a large round pan at least 2" deep (I used a 13" × 2" deep-dish pizza pan). If your pan is less than 3" tall, cut a long strip of parchment paper, fold it in half, and run it around the inside rim of the pan to extend the height of the sides. Then butter the inside of these parchment-paper walls.

In a saucepan, heat the milk and butter over medium heat until the butter is melted. Let the mixture cool to about 110°F and add the yeast, rose-flower water, saffron, and eggs.

In a large mixing bowl, mix the flour with the caraway seeds, cloves, nutmeg, cinnamon, and sugar. Add the liquid mixture to the dry mixture, combining the two thoroughly. Turn the batter into the prepared pan and bake for one hour at 400°F. Then reduce the heat to 350°F and bake until the cake is lightly browned on top and no longer doughy in the center, about 30 to 45 minutes more.

CAKE À LA ROYALE

(The French Family Cook)

Cake baking became a more widespread activity in the beginning of the nineteenth century, as more and more kitchen fireplaces included a little side oven, heated by its contact with the main fire. This small oven was insufficient for serious bread baking, but it could cook pies, tarts, and small cakes such as these. At this time, the small sweets that would become known in America as "cookies" were still being called either cakes or biscuits.

Put a little green lemon-peel, shred fine, into a stew-pan, two ounces of sugar, a little salt, a bit of butter half the size of an egg, and a glass of water, with four or five spoonfuls of flour: stir it over the fire till the paste becomes thick, and begins to stick to the stew-pan; then take it off the fire and put in an egg, stirring it in the paste, till it be well mixed; then add another, and continue to add one egg at a time, till the paste softens without becoming liquid; then put in some crisped orange flowers and two bitter almond biscuits, the whole shred fine: make the paste into little cakes, about half the circumference of an egg; put them upon buttered paper, gild them over with the yolk of an egg beat, and put them for half an hour in an oven moderately hot.

MODERN RECIPE

zest of one lemon	5 T flour
2 oz. sugar	1 egg
½ tsp. salt	1 small almond biscotti or 2 to 3 crisp almond macaroons, finely crumbled
1½ T butter	
1 cup water	1 egg yolk

Preheat oven to 375°F. Line a baking sheet with greased parchment paper or an ungreased silicone baking liner.

In a small saucepan, heat the water, lemon zest, sugar, salt, butter, and flour until the butter has melted and the paste becomes uniform. Remove from heat and stir in the egg until it is well mixed. Add the crumbled cookie(s) and drop by teaspoonfuls onto the baking sheet. Brush the cakes lightly with egg yolk and bake for 20 minutes.

POUND CAKE

(Glasse)

> At nine in the morning we meet and say our prayers in a handsome Chapel, the pulpit, etc., now hung with black. Then follows breakfast consisting of chocolate, coffee and tea, plum cake, pound cake, hot rolls, cold rolls, bread and butter, and dry toast for me. (Letter from Mrs. Austen while visiting Stoneleigh, August 13, 1806)

Take a pound of butter, beat it in an earthen pan with your hand one way till it is like a fine thick cream; then have ready twelve eggs, but half the whites, beat them well, and beat them up with the butter, a pound of flour beat in it, a pound of sugar, and a few carraways; beat all well together for an hour with your hand, or a great wooden spoon, butter a pan and put it in, and then bake it an hour in a quick oven.

For change, you may put in a pound of currants, clean washed and picked.

MODERN RECIPE

1 lb. butter, softened	1 lb. flour
6 eggs	1 lb. sugar
6 egg yolks	1 T caraway seeds

Preheat oven to 400°F.

Cream the butter in a mixing bowl. Add the eggs and egg yolks and blend well. In a separate bowl, mix the flour, sugar, and caraway seeds, and then add these dry ingredients to the butter and egg mixture. Stir until just combined. Pour the batter into a greased bundt pan and bake for 30 minutes. Then reduce the oven heat to 350°F and bake 30 minutes more or until the cake is well browned and a toothpick comes out clean.

BRIDE-CAKE

(Raffald)

. . . the wedding-cake, which had been a great distress to him, was all eat up. His own stomach could bear nothing rich, and he could never believe other people to be different from himself. . . . He had been at the pains of consulting Mr. Perry, the apothecary, on the subject. Mr. Perry was an intelligent, gentlemanlike man . . . ; and, upon being applied to, he could not but acknowledge . . . that wedding-cake might certainly disagree with many— perhaps with most people, unless taken moderately. . . . (*E* 19)

The breakfast was such as best breakfasts then were: some variety of bread, hot rolls, buttered toast, tongue or ham and eggs. The addition of chocolate at one end of the table, and the wedding cake in the middle, marked the speciality of the day. (Caroline Austen, describing the wedding breakfast of Anna Austen and Ben Lefroy, 1814)

The wedding cake was, during Austen's lifetime, undergoing a serious metamorphosis. For centuries, "cakes" had been bready, yeast-risen concoctions, but shortly be-

fore Austen's birth, there was a drift toward butter and sugar and away from yeast. Cakes became denser and more like the dessert we call cake today. For special occasions, such as Twelfth Night and weddings, there was an increasingly widespread tradition of serving a special kind of cake, immense in size, heavily laden with fruit and spices, and enriched with alcohol, usually brandy. Such a cake was sweet, decorative, and enduring; the dried fruit and alcohol content meant that it "kept" for a long time and could thus be distributed, sometimes over great distances, to family and friends who could thus partake of the celebration from afar. When I made this cake, I was able to confirm its extraordinary longevity; a month after its baking, acceptable pieces could still be carved from it by trimming off the dry outer edges.

Icings for cakes, including bride cakes, ranged from soft meringues to thick fondants. Part of its purpose was flavor and texture, but chiefly it served as a show of consumer power: the whiteness of the icing displayed the fact that the family could afford the whitest, most highly refined sugar. Elizabeth Raffald, a professional confectioner, used a double icing on her bride cake. First she iced the cake with an almond icing, a derivative of the medieval marchpane or marzipan, and then she iced it with a white sugar icing. The almond icing was browned in the oven to make a greater contrast with the white layer, and the white layer was put on the cake while it was still warm, but not returned to the oven for drying, as so many other icings were.

By 1806, some cakes at least were being ornamented with crowns, shells, flowers, and leaves made of colored sugar paste. By 1809, commercial bakers in Edinburgh were using "spangles, gold and silver leaf, drague, mottoes, nonpareils, rock candies, etc., according to fancy. . . . Cakes are also ornamented with gum paste in flowers, festoons, trophies, etc., etc." These decorations were not explicitly associated with wedding cakes, which were frequently a simple, plain white, but at least some wedding cakes were decorated. Parson Woodforde recorded receiving a slice of wedding cake in June 1795 with "Very curious devices on the Top of the Cake."

Special notes for this recipe: *This cake uses a phenomenal quantity of ingredients. Those for the cake alone, not counting the two types of icing, weigh over twenty pounds, making it not only a tasty dessert but also a decent weight-lifting accessory or lethal weapon. Accordingly, it is easiest for home bakers to divide the ingredients into two equal batches and mix it in two very large mixing bowls. Home bakers might wish to halve the recipe and make a smaller version, as well; in this case, baking times should be reduced.*

Baking such a large cake presents additional difficulties for the home cook. I used a 16" × 3" commercial cake pan and found that it was just a hair too large for the larger of my ovens. I was able to work around this difficulty by keeping the oven door slightly ajar and draping fire-proof insulating materials over the gap, but not everyone will find this a workable solution. Slightly smaller pans are available online and from specialty stores in some areas. I suspect that a 14" × 3" pan would work very well, but it would

A freshly-baked bride cake, weighing in at a whopping 22 pounds. (KO)

Bride-cake cross-section, showing the contrast between the royal icing and the filling. (KO)

definitely require the parchment-paper side extensions described in the directions below. Pans wider than 16" are not recommended, as the layering of batter and candied fruit becomes difficult beyond that diameter.

The fortunate aspect of baking this cake is that, like most cakes of the period, it is a hardy and forgiving recipe. Cakes of the day were, after all, designed for sooty ovens with inaccurate temperature controls and no timers. The cake was done when it was done, and since the cake was baked at a relatively low temperature, it could be left alone for the first part of its stay in the oven with almost no supervision. Only toward the end of the baking time did the housekeeper or pastry-cook need to keep a close eye on its progress. A little experience of a particular oven and its quirks would soon have given the servant in charge of baking this cake a good sense of when it would be done.

For the less-experienced kitchen maid, it will suffice to know that the cake is done when the top is nicely browned and the cake is firm all the way into the center. It should not be noticeably moister or doughier in the center than at the edges, and it should form a very shallow dome. If the center of the cake is lower than the sides, the cake is not done. The toothpick test, inserting a toothpick in the center to ensure that no large crumbs or wet bits cling to the wood, is a useful tool in gauging doneness, but it should not be relied upon exclusively. This cake, because of the density of the batter, will pass the toothpick test comparatively early in the baking process. Doneness should be judged by a combination of toothpick testing, rising, brownness, and texture.

This sounds complicated, but it's actually not. The cake will pass these tests for as much as twenty or thirty minutes of its baking time, since the baking temperature is so low and the volume of the cake is so vast. Anything within that window will be pretty edible—a fact that Austen's kitchen-maid contemporaries no doubt relied upon. Baking times below are for a 16" × 3" pan, but don't panic if you don't have such a pan or if your oven won't accommodate one. Just use a smaller pan, take a deep breath, trust your ability to judge doneness, and—when in doubt—rely on the fact that most of your guests have never eaten an eighteenth-century wedding cake before and, unlike the wedding guests in Emma, *will have no basis for comparison. If they think it's overdone or underdone (gasp), chide them for their lack of knowledge of Regency cooking, and tell them that Jane would be very, very disappointed in them.*

As to Plumb-cake, Seed-cake, or Rice-cake, it is best to bake them in Wood Garths, for if you bake them in either Pot or Tin, they burn the Out-side of the Cakes, and confine them so that the heat cannot penetrate into the Middle of your Cake, and prevents it from rising. . . .

To make a BRIDE CAKE

Take four Pounds of fine Flour well dried, four Pounds of fresh Butter, two Pounds of loaf Sugar, pound and sift fine a quarter of an Ounce of Mace, the same of Nutmegs, to every Pound of Flour put eight Eggs, wash four Pounds of Currants, pick them well and dry them before the Fire, blanch a Pound of sweet Almonds (and cut them length-ways very thin), a Pound of Citron, one Pound of candied Orange, the same of candied Lemon, half a Pint of Brandy; first work the Butter with your Hand to a Cream, then beat in your Sugar a quarter of an Hour, beat the Whites of your Eggs to a very strong Froth, mix them with your Sugar and Butter, beat your Yolks half an Hour at least, and mix them with your Cake, then put in your Flour, Mace and Nutmeg, keep beating it well 'till your Oven is ready, put in your Brandy, and beat your Currants and Almonds lightly in, tie three Sheets of Paper round the Bottom of your Hoop to keep it from running out, rub it well with Butter, put in your Cake, and lay your Sweet-meats in three Lays, with Cake betwixt every Lay, after it is risen and coloured, cover it with paper before your Oven is stopped up; it will take three hours baking.

To make ALMOND ICEING for the BRIDE CAKE

Beat the whites of three Eggs to a strong Froth, beat a Pound of Jordan Almonds very fine with Rose Water, mix your Almonds with the Eggs lightly together, a Pound of common Loaf Sugar beat fine, and put in by Degrees, when your Cake is enough, take it out and lay your Iceing on, and put it in to Brown.

To make SUGAR ICEING for the BRIDE CAKE

Beat two pounds of double refined Sugar, with two ounces of fine Starch, sift it through a Gawze Sieve, then beat the Whites of five Eggs with a Knife upon a Pewter Dish half an Hour, beat in your Sugar a little at a Time, or it will make the Eggs fall, and will not be so good a colour, when you have put in all your Sugar, beat it half an Hour longer, then lay it on your Almond Iceing, and spread it even with a Knife; if it be put on as soon as the Cake comes out of the Oven, it will be hard by that Time the Cake is cold.

MODERN RECIPE

Cake
4 lbs. flour

4 lbs. butter, softened

1½ lbs. white sugar

½ lb. brown sugar

¼ oz. ground mace

¼ oz. ground nutmeg

32 eggs, separated

4 lbs. currants

1 lb. blanched slivered almonds

3 lbs. assorted **sweetmeats** (candied citrus peel)

1 cup brandy

Almond Icing
6 egg whites

3 tubes marzipan

1 T rosewater

Sugar Icing
5 egg whites

2 lbs. white sugar

2 ounces cornstarch

Continued on next page

Continued from previous page

Preheat the oven to 300°F. Place one rack in or near the bottom third of the oven and one rack just below it. Prepare your baking pan(s): Grease the bottom and sides. (This recipe assumes you are using one large pan.) Then tear off a piece of parchment paper a few inches longer than the circumference of your pan. Fold the paper in half lengthwise and wrap it around the inside walls of the pan, thereby extending the height of the pan's sides. Grease the inside of the parchment paper and the inside of the overlap to help it stick to the pan's sides while you make the cake batter.

In a mixer, cream the butter. Add the sugars and mix until creamy and light. Remove to a large mixing bowl (or bowls—see special notes, above. The remainder of the recipe will assume you are using two separate mixing bowls and dividing the ingredients equally between them).

Clean out the mixer bowl and add 8 egg whites. Beat them to stiff peaks and empty them into one of your batter bowls. Repeat and add the next 8 egg whites to the same bowl. Repeat the process for the other mixing bowl, beating 2 batches of 8 egg whites each and adding them to the butter–sugar mixture. In each bowl, fold in the egg whites.

Place 16 egg yolks in the mixer bowl and mix on medium speed for 3 to 4 minutes. Add the yolks to one of the bowls. Repeat for the other bowl.

In one or more large mixing bowls, blend the flour, mace, and nutmeg. Add the dry ingredients to the batter bowls, 2 cups at a time, stirring each time until the dry ingredients are just incorporated.

Add the brandy, almonds, and currants, and stir until just combined.

Pour ¼ of the total amount of batter into the prepared pan and spread it out into an even layer. (In my 16" × 3" pan, this works out to a layer about ¾" to 1" thick.) Sprinkle ⅓ of the candied citrus peel evenly across the surface of the batter. Repeat with another quarter of the batter and another third of the peel. Repeat with the third quarter of the batter and the last of the peel. Then spread the last quarter of the batter across the top.

Put the cake in the oven—a good workout if ever there was one—and place one or more pans underneath it. (These are to catch dripping batter.) Bake 1½ hours. Reduce heat to 250°F and bake until top is browned, a toothpick inserted into the center comes out clean, and the center is generally firm and higher than the edges—about another 1½ hours. Cover the top of the cake loosely with parchment paper if it seems to be browning too quickly.

Remove the cake from the oven and let it cool. As it cools, slide the parchment paper out from between the pan walls and the cake. Leave the oven on at 250°F.

Next, make the almond icing. Beat the egg whites stiff. Crumble the marzipan and add it to the mixer along with the stiff egg whites and the rosewater.

Place a layer of parchment paper on top of the cake, and a baking sheet on top of the parchment paper. Invert the cake onto the baking sheet. Spread the almond icing thinly over the top and sides of the cake. Return the cake to the oven, turning it occasionally, until the almond icing is firm to the touch and evenly browned (about 20 minutes).

Continued on next page

Continued from previous page

While the almond icing browns, make the sugar icing. Beat 5 egg whites stiff in a mixer. Stir the sugar and cornstarch together in a mixing bowl and add them gradually to the egg whites at low speed.

Remove the cake from the oven and immediately spread the sugar icing over the almond icing. Do this gently, but if the almond icing is adequately browned, it will not pull away from the cake as it is covered by the sugar icing. If the sugar icing drips off the sides, keep scooping it up and re-spreading it. Ice the cake one section at a time, being sure you are done with one section before moving on; by the time you work your way around the cake, the first sections will already be setting and stiffening, and any further work on those sections will make them rough-looking.

When most of the sugar icing has partially set, run a knife around the base of the cake to trim away any excess sugar icing that may have dripped down the sides and pooled at the bottom.

Finding a stand for a cake this large can be tricky. I generally wash out the 16" × 3" cake pan used for baking the cake, invert it, cover it with decorative paper or cloth, and set the finished cake on the upturned bottom of the cake pan. Uneaten pieces of the cake will keep for a relatively long time at room temperature but can be refrigerated or frozen for an even longer life.

PLUM CAKE

(Rundell)

This cake can be made, like many of the others in this chapter, in a very large pan with its sides artificially heightened with parchment paper. It will also make two 10" or 12" cakes baked in springform pans or six conventional 9" cake layers.

Mix thoroughly a quarter of a peck of fine flour, well dried, with a pound of dry and sifted loaf sugar, three pounds of currants washed and very dry, half a pound of raisins stoned and chopped, a quarter of an ounce of mace and cloves, twenty Jamaica peppers, a grated nutmeg, the peel of a lemon cut as fine as possible, and half a pound of almonds blanched and beaten with orange-flower water. Melt two pounds of butter in a pint and a quarter of cream, but not hot; put to it a pint of sweet wine, a glass of brandy, the whites and yolks of twelve eggs beaten apart, and half a pint of good yeast. Strain this liquid by degrees into the dry ingredients, beating them together a full hour, then butter the hoop, or pan, throw in plenty of citron, lemon, and orange-candy.

If you ice the cake, take half a pound of double-refined sugar sifted, and put a little with the white of an egg, beat it well, and by degrees pour in the remainder. It must be whisked near an hour, with the addition of a little orange-flower water, but mind not to put too much. When the cake is done, pour the iceing over, and return it to the oven for fifteen minutes; but if the oven be warm, keep it near the mouth, and the door open, lest the colour be spoiled.

MODERN RECIPE

8 cups flour	2 lbs. butter
¾ lb. white sugar	1½ cups heavy whipping cream
¼ lb. brown sugar	2 cups sweet white dessert wine
3 lbs. currants	1 cup brandy
½ lb. raisins	12 eggs
zest of one lemon	1 pkg. active dry yeast
½ lb. blanched almonds	1½ lb. **sweetmeats** (optional)
1 T orange-flower water	

Preheat oven to 300°F.

In a very large bowl (or evenly divided between two bowls), mix the flour, sugars, currants, raisins, and lemon zest. Your hands will actually work better for evenly mixing the raisins and currants than a spoon will. Make sure the raisins and currants do separate and get coated with the flour, leaving no large clumps.

In a food processor, blend the almonds and orange-flower water until the almonds are finely ground. Add them to the dry ingredients and mix thoroughly.

In a saucepan, melt the butter with the cream over medium-low heat. Do not allow the cream to boil. Meanwhile, whisk the eggs in a large mixing bowl and add the wine, brandy, and yeast. When the butter is just melted, add the cream and butter mixture to the wine and egg mixture and whisk thoroughly.

Stir the wet ingredients into the dry ones. Pour the batter into a large (14" or 16") cake pan with its sides made taller by a rim of parchment paper; two 10" to 12" springform pans; or six 9" cake pans. Your may, if you like, pour half the batter into each pan, then add a sprinkling of sweetmeats, and then pour in the other half of the batter.

Bake the cakes until the tops are evenly browned, the centers are gently domed and no longer moist-looking, and a toothpick inserted into the center of the cake comes out clean. This will take about 60 to 70 minutes for a 9" cake pan, about 2 hours for a 12" springform pan, and about 2½ hours for a 16" cake pan. Cooking times can vary a great deal based on the size of the pan and the quirks of your oven, so the best test is the appearance of the cake.

✸ LEMON CUSTARD ✸

(Glasse)

I do not advise the custard. (*E 25*)

This is a delicious, surprisingly tart and lemony dessert very much like a lemon curd. I do advise the custard.

Take a pint of white wine, half a pound of double-refined sugar, the juice of two lemons, the out-rind of one pared very thin, the inner-rind of one boiled tender and rubbed through a sieve, let them boil a good while, then take out the peel and a little of the liquor, set it to cool, pour the rest into the dish you intend for it; beat four yolks and two whites of eggs, mix them with your cool liquor, strain them into your dish, stir them well up together, set them on a slow fire, or boiling water to bake as a custard; when it is enough, grate the rind of a lemon all over the top; you may brown it over with a hot salamander. It may be eat either hot or cold.

MODERN RECIPE

2 cups white wine	4 egg yolks
½ lb. sugar	2 egg whites
2 lemons	

Preheat oven to 300°F. Lay a dishtowel, folded in half, in the bottom of a large roasting pan, and fill the roasting pan ½" deep with water.

Zest one of the lemons and set the zest aside. Zest the other lemon and set it aside in a separate place. Then, with a small sharp knife, cut off the thick white inner rind of one lemon. Juice this lemon and the other lemon, strain the seeds from the juice, and set the juice aside. Cut the white lemon pith into ¼"-wide strips and place them in a small saucepan with 2 cups of water. Bring the water to a boil and boil the pith for 25 minutes. Drain away the water and run the pith through a food mill or strainer. Then measure out 2 teaspoons of the pith pulp.

In a medium saucepan, bring the wine, sugar, zest of one of the lemons, lemon pith, and lemon juice to a boil. Boil these ingredients for 15 minutes, then set the pan aside to cool slightly.

Continued on next page

Continued from previous page

In a heatproof mixing bowl, beat the egg yolks and whites together until they are well blended. Add ¼ cup of the hot lemon liquid and mix well. Add another ¼ cup at a time, stirring constantly, until all the hot liquid has been added to the eggs. (Do not add the eggs to the hot liquid, or you will end up, not with a custard, but with a lemon syrup sprinkled with scrambled eggs.)

Strain the liquid and pour it into 6 ramekins. Place the ramekins on top of the towel in the roasting pan and set the pan in the oven for 50 minutes. Remove the custards from the oven and sprinkle with the reserved lemon zest. Serve hot or cold.

❀ SWEETMEATS ❀

(Collingwood)

Had not Elinor, in the sad countenance of her sister, seen a check to all mirth, she could have been entertained by Mrs. Jennings's endeavours to cure a disappointment in love, by a variety of sweetmeats and olives, and a good fire. (*S&S* 193)

"Sweetmeats" were not a single type of food but a category comprising a range of foods. The French Family Cook *includes marmalades, jams, preserved fruits, and nuts in this category. Maria Rundell, similarly, includes actual candies as well as the marmalade and preserves mentioned in* Sense and Sensibility *and* Mansfield Park:

But unfortunately in bestowing these embraces, a pin in her ladyship's head dress slightly scratching the child's neck, produced from this pattern of gentleness, such violent screams, as could hardly be outdone by any creature professedly noisy. . . . She was seated in her mother's lap, covered with kisses, her wound bathed with lavender-water, by one of the Miss Steeles, who was on her knees to attend her, and her mouth stuffed with sugar plums by the other. . . . all their united soothings were ineffectual till lady Middleton luckily remembering that in a scene of similar distress last week, some apricot marmalade had been successfully applied for a bruised temple, the same remedy was eagerly proposed for this unfortunate scratch. . . . (S&S 121)

"The truth is, ma'am," said Mrs. Grant . . . , "that Dr. Grant hardly knows what the natural taste of our apricot is; he is scarcely ever indulged with one, for it is so valuable a fruit, with a little assistance, and ours in such a remarkably large, fair sort, that what with early tarts and preserves, my cook contrives to get them all." (MP 54–55)

*Another good example of a sweetmeat is the **dried cherries** in Chapter 11.*

One common meaning of "sweetmeats" was candied citrus peel, usually the candied peels of lemons, oranges, or, less commonly, citrons. Modern chunks of candied citrus peel tend to be sticky and syrupy, but Collingwood seems to intend that these be a good deal drier, with the sugar visibly "candied."

Cut your oranges or lemons lengthways, and take out all the pulp and inside skins. Put the peels into hard water and strong salt for six days, and then boil them in spring water till they are tender. Take them out, and lay them on a sieve to drain. Make a thin syrup with a pound of loaf sugar to a quart of water, and boil them in it for half an hour, or till they look clear. Make a thick syrup of double-refined sugar, with as much water as will wet it. Put in your peels and boil them over a slow fire till you see the syrup candy about the pan and peels. Then take them out, and sprinkle fine sugar over them. Lay them on a sieve, and dry them before the fire, or in a cool oven.

 ## MODERN RECIPE

8 lemons, oranges, or citrons	2 T salt
water	3 cups plus 2 T sugar, *in all*

Peel the oranges or lemons. Mix 4 cups of water with the salt, and set the peels to steep in the salt water. Refrigerate for 5 days, changing the salt water twice during this period.

Drain the peels and rinse them. Place them in a large pot of water and bring to a boil. Boil until they are tender and slightly translucent. Drain and cool them and cut them lengthwise into strips about ¼" wide. Then cut these crosswise about ½" long.

On the stove, bring 1 pound of sugar (about 2 cups plus 2 tablespoons) to a boil with 4 cups of water. Put the peels into the sugar water and boil for 30 minutes.

Preheat oven to 200°F and line a baking sheet with parchment paper.

Meanwhile, in another saucepan, place 1 cup of sugar and ¼ cup of water and heat over medium-low until the sugar is well dissolved. Drain the boiled peels and add them to this sugar syrup, stirring once. Do not stir once the sugar begins to boil. Boil the peels for 15 minutes, then stir, scraping the crystals off the sides of the pan, and keep stirring; this will cause the rest of the sugar to crystallize rapidly around the peels. The sugar will boil up very white and light and will noticeably change texture. Once it becomes thick and grainy, which happens very

Continued on next page

Continued from previous page

quickly, dump the entire mass onto the parchment paper. Separate the peels with a spoon until they cool a little, at which point you can easily separate them with your fingers, making a single layer.

Bake the peels at 200°F for 20 to 40 minutes or until they are dry to the touch. Put the peels into an airtight container, and save any leftover sugar crystals from the pan; they will have a delicate citrus flavor and can be used in desserts, tea, coffee, etc.

✲ GINGERBREAD ✲

(Glasse)

. . . her eyes fell only on the butcher with his tray, a tidy old woman travelling homewards from shop with her full basket, two curs quarrelling over a dirty bone, and a string of dawdling children round the baker's little bow-window eyeing the gingerbread . . . . (*E* 233)

Gingerbread had long been a special treat among the English, and by Austen's time it had evolved from its medieval roots as a dish made with bread crumbs and wine. It could be made as a breadlike loaf or as bite-size gingerbread "nuts." Large cakes of gingerbread were sometimes baked, then pressed into detailed wooden molds, such as molds of kings and queens, and occasionally gilded. Contemporary prints often show rows of such gingerbread hanging from booths at fairs. Gingerbread also appears to have been used at fairs as a target. A piece of gingerbread was spiked on a post, and people paid to throw sticks at it, trying to knock it off in order to win a prize.

Take three pounds of flour, one pound of sugar, one pound of butter rubbed in very fine, two ounces of ginger beat fine, a large nutmeg grated; then take a pound of treacle, a quarter of a pint of cream, make them warm together, and make up the bread stiff; roll it out, and make it up in thin cakes, cut them out with a tea-cup, or small glass; or roll them round like nuts, and bake them on tin plates in a slack oven.

MODERN RECIPE

1½ lbs. flour (about 5¼ cups)

11 oz. sugar

½ lb. butter

1½ tsp. ground ginger

½ tsp. nutmeg

8 oz. (about ¾ cup) molasses

¼ cup cream

Preheat oven to 300°F. Mix the flour, sugar, ginger, and nutmeg thoroughly and blend in the butter finely with your fingers or a pastry blender. Heat the molasses and cream together over medium-low heat for about 5 minutes; then add them to the dry ingredients and stir till evenly mixed. The dough will be thick and somewhat dry.

Roll "nuts" about 1" in diameter with your hands (the dough will soften as it is worked) and place them an inch apart on an ungreased cookie sheet. Bake 20 minutes, rotating the pan once from front to back and from top to bottom midway during the cooking time.

If you like, you may roll the dough out ¼" thick and cut out circles with a teacup or round cookie cutter. These should be cooked for less time than the nuts, about 12 to 15 minutes.

ROUT-CAKES

(Rundell)

She was a little shocked at the want of two drawing-rooms, at the poor attempt at rout-cakes, and there being no ice in the Highbury card parties. (*E* 290)

"A large spoonful"—a measurement that occurs in many a Regency recipe—is an imprecise quantity. In most of the recipes in this book, it has been interpreted as one tablespoon. But there is no guarantee that this is precisely what the cookbook authors meant, or that this is precisely the quantity that every kitchen maid used. Since Mrs. Elton is so shocked by the inadequacy of Highbury rout-cakes, I made this recipe two ways, both of which were tasty. They simply had different textures. The first version, a drier, denser "cake," is reproduced below. To make the second version, simply triple the quantities of the orange-flower water, rose water, wine, and brandy.

Mix two pounds of flour, one ditto butter, one ditto sugar, one ditto currants, clean and dry; then wet into a stiff paste, with two eggs, a large spoonful of orange-flower water, ditto rose-water, ditto sweet wine, ditto brandy; drop on a tin plate floured, a very short time bakes them.

MODERN RECIPE

3½ cups flour	1 T orange-flower water
1 lb. butter	1 T rose-flower water
1 lb. sugar	1 T sweet dessert wine
1 lb. (1¾ cups) currants	1 T brandy
2 eggs	

Preheat oven to 350°F. Cream the butter and sugar. Add the eggs, orange-flower water, rose-flower water, wine, and brandy, and mix well. Stir in the flour just until evenly mixed, then stir in the currants until they, too, are evenly mixed.

Grease a baking sheet or line it with parchment paper or a silicone baking liner. Take pieces of batter about a tablespoon at a time, roll them round (using flour on your hands if the mixture sticks),* drop them onto the baking sheet about 1½" apart, and flatten them slightly with the bottom of a glass or cup so that they are about ½" thick. They will not spread appreciably in baking. Bake 25 minutes or until lightly browned.

*If you are making the second, moister version of the recipe, you will find it harder to shape the cakes. Just make them as round as possible.

DROP BISCUITS

(Glasse)

She was so little equal to Rebecca's puddings, and Rebecca's hashes, brought to table as they all were, with such accompaniments of half-cleaned plates, and not half-cleaned knives and forks, that she was very often constrained to defer her heartiest meal, till she could send her brothers in the evenings for biscuits and buns. (*MP* 413)

These are biscuits in the British sense—that is, cookies—rather than in the American sense. They are spongy and delicately flavored, much like a cookie version of the sponge-cake base of a strawberry shortcake.

Take eight eggs, and one pound of double-refined sugar beaten fine, twelve ounces of fine flour well dried, beat your eggs very well, then put in your sugar and beat it, and then your flour by degrees, beat it all very well together without ceasing; your oven must be as hot as for halfpenny bread; then flour some sheets of tin, and drop your biscuits of what bigness you please, put them in the oven as fast as you can, and when you see them rise, watch them; if they begin to colour, take them out, and put in more; and if the first is not enough, put them in again: if they are right done, they will have a white ice on them: you may, if you choose, put in a few carraways; when they are all baked, put them in the oven again to dry, then keep them in a very dry place.

 MODERN RECIPE

8 eggs   ¾ lb. flour

1 lb. sugar

Preheat oven to 425°F.

Beat the eggs well; add the sugar and then gently stir in the flour. The batter will be quite moist. Cover some baking sheets with parchment paper. (It helps to grease the parchment paper as well, but it is not strictly necessary.) Drop tablespoonsfuls of batter on the parchment paper, 2" apart, and bake until the cookie rims have turned golden brown, about 10 to 12 minutes. If you are baking 2 or more sheets of biscuits at once, reverse the positions of the sheets midway through baking to ensure even browning. Let the biscuits cool almost completely before removing them from the parchment paper, which will help to keep the bottoms intact.

CHOCOLATE BISCUITS

(The French Family Cook)

Tea was made down stairs, biscuits and baked apples and wine before she came away: amazing luck in some of her throws . . . . (*E* 329)

Take six eggs, and put the yolks of four into one pan, and the whites of the whole six into another; add to the yolks and ounce and a half of chocolate, bruised very fine, with six ounces of fine sugar; beat the whole together well, and then put in the whites of your eggs whipt to a froth: when they are well mingled, stir in by little and little six ounces of flour, and put your biscuits upon white paper, like spoon biscuits . . . or in little paper moulds buttered: throw over a little fine sugar, and bake them in an oven moderately heated.

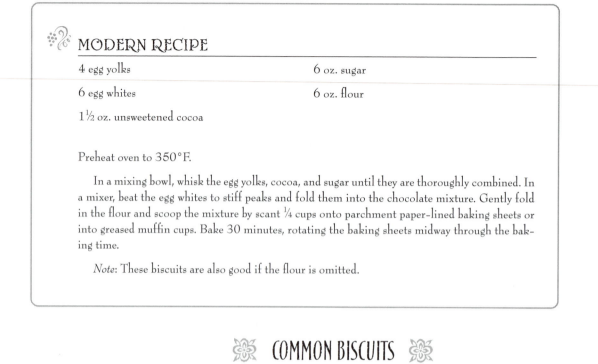

MODERN RECIPE

4 egg yolks	6 oz. sugar
6 egg whites	6 oz. flour
1½ oz. unsweetened cocoa	

Preheat oven to 350°F.

In a mixing bowl, whisk the egg yolks, cocoa, and sugar until they are thoroughly combined. In a mixer, beat the egg whites to stiff peaks and fold them into the chocolate mixture. Gently fold in the flour and scoop the mixture by scant ¼ cups onto parchment paper-lined baking sheets or into greased muffin cups. Bake 30 minutes, rotating the baking sheets midway through the baking time.

Note: These biscuits are also good if the flour is omitted.

COMMON BISCUITS

(*The French Family Cook*)

The baked apples and biscuits, excellent in their way, you know . . . . (*E* 329)

Take the weight of eight eggs in fine sugar, and of four in flour, and put them separately upon a plate; break the eight eggs, and beat the yolks half an hour with the sugar, and a little green lemon-peel; then beat the white, and when they are well frothed, mix them with the sugar, and stir in the flour by degrees: have ready some tin or paper moulds, buttered within; put in your paste, filling the moulds but a little more than half; throw some powdered sugar over, and set your biscuits in an oven half an hour; when they are of a fine gilt colour, and half cold, take them out of the moulds.

MODERN RECIPE

8 eggs, separated

1 lb. sugar

zest of one lemon

½ lb. flour

confectioner's sugar

Preheat oven to 350°F.

With a mixer, beat the egg yolks, sugar, and lemon zest on high speed until the mixture is frothy and light, about 2 minutes.

In a separate bowl, beat the egg whites until they form stiff peaks. Fold them into the yolk mixture. Gently fold in the flour and pour the batter into greased paper muffin cups, filling each cup just a little more than halfway. Sprinkle the biscuits with powdered sugar.

Bake 30 minutes. Remove the biscuits when they are golden brown. Let them cool and remove the muffin cups.

ORANGE BISCUITS

(Glasse)

Pare your oranges, not very thick, put them into water, but first weigh your peels, let it stand over the fire, and let it boil till it be very tender; then beat it in a marble mortar, till it be very fine smooth paste; to every ounce of peels put two ounces and a half of double-refined sugar well searced, mix them well together with a spoon in the mortar, then spread it with a knife upon pie-plates, and set it in an oven a little warm, or before the fire; when it feels dry upon the top, cut it into what fashion you please, and turn them into another plate, and set them in a stove till they are dry; where the edges look rough, when it is dry, they must be cut with a pair of scissars.

MODERN RECIPE

4 to 5 oranges

7½ oz. sugar

Continued on next page

Continued from previous page

Preheat oven to 200°F.

Peel the oranges with a small sharp knife, avoiding as much of the white pith as possible. You should have about 3 ounces of peel.

Bring a small pot of water to a boil and add the peels. Boil for 15 minutes. Drain the peels and place them, along with the sugar, in a food processor. Process to a smooth paste.

Line a baking sheet with parchment paper or a nonstick silicone baking liner. Spread the paste in circles, a tablespoon or two at a time, across the paper, about ⅛" thick.

Bake at 200°F for 1 hour to 1 hour 30 minutes, or until the biscuits appear light in color and feel dry to the touch.

 FINE CHEESECAKES

(Farley)

> At Devizes we had comfortable rooms, & a good dinner to which we sat down about 5; amongst other things we had Asparagus & a Lobster which made me wish for you, & some cheesecakes on which the children made so delightful a supper as to endear the Town of Devizes to them for a long time. (Letter from Jane to Cassandra, May 17, 1799)

These cheesecakes are nothing like a modern cheesecake. They have a relatively small proportion of cheese and taste somewhat more like a bread pudding than a creamy New York cheesecake.

Warm a pint of cream, and put to it five quarts of milk warm from the cow. Then put to it rennet, give it a stir about, and when it be turned, put the curd into a linen cloth or bag. Let it drain well away from the whey, but do not squeeze it too much. Then put it into a mortar, and break the curd as fine as butter. Put to the curd half a pound of sweet almonds blanched and beat exceedingly fine, and half a pound of macaroons beat very fine, but if you have no macaroons, use Naples biscuits. Then add to it the yolks of nine eggs beaten, a nutmeg grated, two perfumed plumbs dissolved in rose or orange-flower water, and half a pound of fine sugar. Mix all well together, then melt a pound and a quarter of butter, and stir it well in. Then make a puff paste in this manner; Take a pound of fine flour, wet it with cold water, roll it out, put into it by degrees a pound of fresh butter, and shake a little flour on each coat as you roll it.

Then proceed to finish your cake in the manner before directed. If you have any dislike to the perfumed plumbs, you may leave them out.

MODERN RECIPE

1 cup cream*

2½ quarts of milk*

½ tablet rennet dissolved in ¼ cup distilled water*

¼ lb. blanched almonds

¼ lb. macaroons or bicotti

5 egg yolks

½ tsp. grated nutmeg

1 T rose-flower or orange-flower water

¼ lb. sugar

½ lb. plus 4 T butter

½ recipe **puff paste**

In a large pot, bring the cream and milk to between 80°F and 90°F. Add the dissolved rennet and let the milk sit, remaining warm, for 30 minutes. The milk will form a thick curd.

Line a colander with a double layer of cheesecloth and set it over a bowl. Ladle the curds into the cheesecloth, tie the loose ends together, and suspend the cheesecloth bag over the bowl to drain. Let the whey (the thin liquid) drip away from the curds in the bag for 30 minutes. You should have about 2 to 2½ cups of curd.*

Preheat oven to 350°F.

In a food processor, grind the almonds and macaroons finely. Put them in a mixing bowl along with the drained curd, egg yolks, nutmeg, rose- or orange-flower water, and sugar.

Melt the butter, let it cool for a few minutes, and blend it into the rest of the batter.

Line a pie pan with the puff paste, rolled between ⅛" and ¼" thick. Pour the batter into the crust and bake for 45 minutes, or until they are nicely browned on top.

*You can substitute 16 oz. of soft cream cheese for this step.

CARAWAY COMFITS

She was seated in her mother's lap, covered with kisses, her wound bathed with lavender-water, by one of the Miss Steeles, who was on her knees to attend her, and her mouth stuffed with sugar plums by the other. (S&S 121)

Sugar plums could be any kind of small sweet made with boiled sugar; caraway comfits were a popular type of sugar plum. There were smooth comfits, which were individually dipped dozens of times in sugar, and rough comfits which were simply mixed with hot sugar syrup and cooled. These are the rough kind, which are considerably easier to make.

MODERN RECIPE

½ cup caraway seeds

3 cups sugar

1⅓ cup water

Prepare a large baking sheet by lining it with parchment paper.

Mix the sugar and water together in a saucepan. Bring to a boil over medium heat and boil at about 240°F to 250°F for 25 minutes. The mixture will start by being very light and foamy—be sure not to let it boil over. It will then darken and thicken, and the caraway seeds will be more easily visible. Stir nearly constantly.

Pour the mixture out onto the parchment paper-lined baking sheet and spread it thinly. Let it cool, then break it into small chunks, each containing one to three caraway seeds. (Pressing the heel of your hand against a wooden spoon and the back of the spoon against a clump of seeds and sugar works well for breaking up the comfits.)

14

SOUPS, STEWS, AND CURRIES

Soup was the quintessentially cheap meal, the means by which the poor could turn a lump of unappetizing meat, a few handfuls of grain, and some vegetables into a tasty and nutritious meal. It was a source of unfailing exasperation to reformer Sir Frederick Eden that the poor insisted upon roasting their meat, or boiling it in a mass, rather than chopping it up for soup, which would have been, to his mind, more economical. Yet soup could be dressed up quite a bit beyond this modest presentation. On the tables of the gentry, it might be the sea in which swam a French roll, a fowl, or a piece of veal. It was certainly, if nothing else, an opportunity to display the huge and decorative tureens that formed an essential part of a good china service.

Soups usually started with a broth, to which the cook added herbs, vegetables, and usually some sort of meat. Sometimes it was beef, but it might also be fish, oysters, or eels. Turtle soup was considered highly desirable, but it was also prohibitively expensive, and most people made do with mock turtle soup made from gravy, Madeira, and calf's head. To complete the illusion, it was suggested that the cook serve this soup in a turtle's shell. (The phenomenon of veal masquerading as turtle is

A General Fast in Consequence of the War!!, 1794. This detail clearly shows the soup tureen. (Courtesy of the Lewis Walpole Library, Yale University. 794.2.14.1.)

why the Mock Turtle in *Alice in Wonderland* has a turtle's flippers and a calf's head.)

Generally served as part of the first course, if the meal was grand enough to be divided into courses, the soup was served right away. Once it was finished, its tureen—which usually occupied a place of honor at either the top or the bottom of the table—was removed and replaced with another showy dish. Thus, Jane Austen's uncle James Leigh Perrot wrote of his dinner on July 4, 1806, that he ate "Mackerell at Top, Soup at Bottom removed for a Neck of Venison." Soup was also considered appropriate for suppers at private balls and for people returning from an outing, such as a trip to the theater. Austen does not usually specify what type of soup was served, but she does make a reference to "white soup" (*P&P* 55), which was the most elegant type of soup, based on veal broth, cream, and almonds. Its lofty reputation stands in contrast to the humble, everyday "pease-soup" served at Steventon on November 30, 1798. Pease-soup was ubiquitous and without pretensions, a thinner descendant of the centuries-old "pease porridge hot, pease porridge cold, pease porridge in the pot, nine days old." Of course, just because pea soup was plain did not make it unpopular, even among the gentry; Parson Woodforde often mentions eating "Peas Soup."

Stews were thicker and more generally full of meat; like soups, they had the advantage of needing little attention from the cook. Once in the pot, they could be left to cook themselves, with only occasional stirring required. Curry was the stew's exotic cousin, which, with "pillau" or "pillaw" made its way into cookbooks via Britain's possessions in the East Indies. Curry is not an individual spice but a mixture of several spices, and by the 1780s this mélange, premixed and ready for use, had found its way into English groceries and kitchens. No doubt its spicing was too strong for some palates—it is hard, for example, to imagine the digestively timid Mr. Woodhouse asking for seconds—but it appealed to many, especially to Britons back in England after military or civil service in India.

❧ WHITE SOUP ❧

(Carter, Millington)

"By the bye, Charles, are you really serious in meditating a dance at Netherfield?—I would advise you, before you determine on it, to consult the wishes of the present party; I am much mistaken if there are not some among us to whom a ball would be rather a punishment than a pleasure."

"If you mean Darcy," cried her brother, "he may go to bed, if he chuses, before it begins—but as for the ball, it is quite a settled thing; and as soon as Nicholls has made white soup enough I shall send round my cards." (*P&P* 55)

Millington's recipe is the more conventional version, almost identical to that given by London Tavern cook John Farley. Carter's recipe, however, is worth reading, if only to see that the same term, "white soup," could mean very different things to different authors.

Carter's Recipe

Put in a clean sauce-pan two or three quarts of water, the crum of a two-penny loaf with a bundle of herbs, some whole pepper, two or three cloves, an onion or two cut across, and a little salt: let it boil covered till it is quite smooth; take celery, endive, and lettuce only the white parts, cut them in pieces, not too small, and boil them till they are very tender, strain your soup off into a clean stew-pan; put your herbs in, with a good piece of butter stirred in it till the butter is melted, and let it boil for some time, till it is very smooth. If any scum arises, take it off very clean: soak a small French roll, nicely rasped, in some of the soup; put it in the middle of the dish, pour in your soup, and send it to table.

Millington's Recipe

Put a knuckle of veal, a large fowl, and a pound of lean bacon into a saucepan with six quarts of water, half a pound of rice, two anchovies, a few pepper-corns, a bundle of sweet herbs, two or three onions, and three or four heads of celery, cut in slices, and stew them till the soup is as strong as you wish, and then strain it through a hair sieve into an earthen pan. Let it stand all night; the next day skim it clean, and pour it into a stewpan. Put in half a pound of sweet almonds, beat fine, boil it a quarter of an hour, and strain it through a lawn sieve. Then put in a pint of cream and the yolk of an egg, stir all together, boil it a few minutes, then pour it into the tureen, and serve it.

MODERN RECIPE (Carter)

3 quarts water	1 tsp. kosher salt
2 cups bread crumbs	4 stalks celery, cut crosswise into 1" pieces
¼ cup chopped fresh herbs—parsley, sage, and oregano work nicely	2 heads endive, coarsely chopped
1 tsp. black peppercorns	½ head iceberg lettuce, coarsely chopped
3 whole cloves	3 T butter
2 medium onions, peeled and halved	1 roll of **French bread**

In a stock pot, bring the water, bread crumbs, herbs, peppercorns, cloves, onions, and salt to a boil. Reduce the heat to medium-low, cover, and simmer 30 minutes. Strain the soup through a fine strainer or a colander lined with cheesecloth; in the latter case, you may need to make a bag of the cheesecloth and squeeze it to extract most of the moisture.

Meanwhile, bring a large pot of water to a boil. Add the celery and boil 5 minutes. Add the endive and lettuce and boil till tender, about 5 minutes more. Drain the vegetables and add them to the strained bread broth. Add the butter and stir until the butter is melted.

Pour the soup into a tureen. Place a French roll in the center and serve hot.

MODERN RECIPE (Millington)

6 quarts water	3 sprigs fresh sage
1 veal or beef soup bone	3 sprigs fresh parsley
1 chicken (or 2 to 4 lbs. miscellaneous left-over poultry bits)	3 onions, peeled and halved
1 lb. Canadian bacon or ham	2 heads celery, sliced crosswise into 1" pieces
½ lb. rice	½ lb. blanched almonds
2 anchovy filets	2 cups heavy whipping cream
1 tsp. whole black peppercorns	1 egg yolk

Continued on next page

Continued from previous page

Place all ingredients except the almonds, cream, and egg yolk in a large stock pot and bring to a boil. Reduce heat to a simmer, cover, and cook for at least 3 hours. Strain the broth through a cheesecloth-lined colander and refrigerate overnight.

The next day, skim off the congealed fat. Return the broth to a stock pot and warm over medium heat. Meanwhile, grind the almonds to a fine powder in a food processor. Add the almonds to the broth and simmer 30 minutes. Mix the egg yolk into the cream, add the egg-cream mixture, and warm until the soup just begins to bubble again. Pour into a tureen and serve immediately.

❀ ASPARAGUS SOUP ❀

(Farley)

I shall be able to manage the Sir-loin myself; my Mother will eat the Soup,
and You and the Doctor must finish the rest. (*Lesley, MW* 113)

My tasters found this soup edible, but very different from what they expected from an asparagus soup. The pea soup that appears later in this chapter was received much more warmly.

Cut four or five pounds of beef to pieces; set it over a fire, with an onion or two, a few cloves, and some whole black pepper, a calfs foot or two, a head or two of celery, and a very little bit of butter. Let it draw at a distance from the fire; put in a quart of warm beer, three quarts of warm beef broth, or water. Let these stew till enough; strain it, take off the fat very clean, put in some asparagus heads cut small (palates* may be added, boiled very tender) and a toasted French roll, the crumb taken out.

*The soft palate (fleshy part of the upper mouth) of a cow.

MODERN RECIPE

3 lbs. beef stew meat	1 T butter
2 medium onions, peeled and quartered	1 quart beer
4 whole cloves	3 quarts beef broth
10 black peppercorns	1 lb. asparagus, cut crosswise into 1" pieces
8 celery stalks, washed and chopped into 1" long pieces	1 roll of **french bread**
	melted butter (about 1 or 2 T)

In a large stock pot, melt the butter over medium heat. Add the stew beef, onions, spices, and celery, and cook, stirring occasionally, for 10 to 15 minutes or until the meat is evenly browned. Add the beer and broth; cover and simmer until the meat is tender (about 1 hour). Meanwhile, in a saucepan, boil the asparagus until bright green and still crisp, about 5 minutes. Immerse the asparagus immediately in hot water to stop the cooking process. Excavate a French roll from the bottom, removing the soft inner bread and leaving a shell about 1" thick around the top and sides. Brush this inside and out with butter and toast under the broiler just until a deep golden brown.

Remove the soup from the heat and skim off the fat. Return the soup to the heat and add the asparagus, heating just until the asparagus sections are warm, about 1 minute. Pour soup into a tureen and float the hollowed-out French roll in the middle, right side up.

SOUP AND BOUILLIE

(Farley)

Mde Bigeon was below dressing us a most comfortable dinner of Soup, Fish, Bouillee, Partridges & an apple Tart . . . . (Letter from Jane to Cassandra, September 15, 1813)

Soup and bouillie was an easy dish for the cook to prepare because the actual time cutting and chopping was negligible compared to the cooking time. She could set it near the fire and leave it to cook itself while she prepared multiple vegetable garnishes. In addition, the dish yielded two separate parts of a dinner: the "bouillie," a very tender slow-cooked brisket, and the soup, made of the broth in which the brisket had been stewed. With Farley's suggested additions, and perhaps a little bread, this dish makes an entire meal for several people.

To make the bouillie, roll five pounds of brisket of beef tight with a tape; put it into a stewpot, with four pounds of the leg-of-mutton piece of beef, and about seven or eight quarts of water. Boil these up as quick as possible, and skim it very clean; add one large onion, six or seven cloves, some whole pepper, two or three carrots, or a turnip or two, a leek and two heads of celery. Stew these very gently, closely covered for six or seven hours. About an hour before dinner, strain the soup through a piece of dimity that has been dipped in cold water; put the rough side upwards. Have ready boiled carrots cut like wheels, turnips cut in balls, spinach, a little chervil and sorrel, two heads of endive and one or two of celery cut into pieces. Put these into a tureen, with a Dutch loaf or a French roll dried, after the crumb is taken out. Pour the soup to these boiling hot, and add a little salt and chyan. Take the tape from the bouillie, and serve it in a square dish, with mashed turnips and sliced carrots in two little dishes. The turnips and carrots should be cut with an instrument that may be bought for that purpose.

 ## MODERN RECIPE

1 beef brisket	6 carrots
3 lbs. stew beef	2 large turnips
1 large onion, peeled and quartered	1 cup fresh spinach
7 whole cloves	½ cup chervil or sorrel
1 tsp. black peppercorns	2 heads Belgian endive
3 carrots, peeled and cut crosswise into 2" sections	4 stalks celery
2 small turnips, peeled and quartered	1 large white roll
1 leek, white and green parts, cut crosswise into 2" sections	butter
9 stalks celery, cut crosswise into 2" sections	salt and cayenne pepper to taste
	1 recipe **boiled turnips**

Using three pieces of kitchen twine, tie the brisket in a tight roll. In a large stock pot, place the brisket, stew beef, onion, cloves, peppercorns, carrots cut in 2" sections, the 2 quartered turnips, leek, and celery cut in 2" sections. Fill the pot the rest of the way with water, leaving enough space at the top to allow for boiling. Bring the water to a boil, reduce to a simmer, and cover tightly, cooking over low heat for 5 to 7 hours.

Continued on next page

Continued from previous page

Remove the brisket and stew beef from the water and set aside. Strain the liquid that remains in the pot, skim off the fat, return the beef and brisket to the pot, cover, and keep warm. Add salt and cayenne to taste.

(*Note:* The recipe can be prepared a day ahead up to this point, which makes the soup easier to strain. Refrigerate the broth and meat separately. The next day, skim the broth, add the meat, and reheat both together.)

Prepare the boiled turnips.

Meanwhile, bring a smaller pot of water to a boil. Peel the remaining carrots and turnips. Cut the carrots crosswise ¼" thick and dice the turnips into 1" cubes. Add the carrots and turnips to the boiling water and boil till tender. While they are boiling, roughly chop the spinach, chervil or sorrel, and endive into bite-size pieces. Cut the remaining 4 stalks of celery crosswise into ¼" slices.

Cut the top off the white roll. Pull out the soft interior of the bread, leaving a crust about ½" thick. Brush the crust with butter and toast under the broiler just until golden brown.

Place the boiled turnips, spinach, chervil or sorrel, endive, celery, and half the boiled carrots into a soup tureen. Pour in the hot broth, place the toasted roll in the center, and cover the tureen.

Untie the brisket and place it on a large platter, surrounded by the chunks of stew beef.

Set the brisket in the center of the table and the soup at the top. At the bottom of the table, put a dish containing the remaining boiled and sliced carrots and a dish containing the boiled turnips.

CHESTNUT SOUP

(Glasse)

If Mr E. does not lose his money at cards, you will stay as late as you can wish for; if he does, he will hurry you home perhaps—but you are sure of some comfortable soup. (*Wat, MW* 315)

. . . she had only to rise and, with Mr. Crawford's very cordial adieus, pass quietly away; stopping at the entrance door, like the Lady of Branxholm Hall, "one moment and no more," to view the happy scene, and take a last look at the five or six determined couple, who were still hard at work—and then, creeping slowly up the principal staircase, feverish with hopes and fears, soup and negus, sore-footed and fatigued, restless and agitated, yet feeling, in spite of every thing, that a ball was indeed delightful. (*MP* 280–81)

Take half an hundred of chesnuts, pick them, put them in an earthen pan, and set them in the oven half an hour, or roast them gently over a slow fire, but take care they do not burn; then peel them, and set them to stew in a quart of good beef, veal, or mutton broth, till they are quite tender; in the mean time, take a piece or slice of ham, or bacon, a pound of veal, a pigeon beat to pieces, a bundle of sweet herbs, an onion, a little pepper and mace, and a piece of carrot; lay the bacon at the bottom of a stew-pan, and lay the meat and ingredients at top; set it over a slow fire till it begins to stick to the pan, then put in a crust of bread, and pour in two quarts of broth; let it boil softly till one third is wasted, then strain it off, and add to it the chesnuts; season it with salt, and let it boil till it is well tasted, stew to pigeons in it, and fry a French roll crisp; lay the roll in the middle of the dish, and the pigeons on each side; pour in the soup, and send it away hot.

MODERN RECIPE

4 slices bacon	1 quart broth
1 lb. stew beef	½ cup bread crust or dried bread
1 chicken breast, sliced	1 or 2 pigeons, washed and patted dry
several sprigs of fresh thyme and marjoram	1 tsp. salt
1 onion, quartered	50 chestnuts; fresh, roasted, and peeled; or canned
1 tsp. black pepper	
½ tsp. ground mace	1 roll of **French bread** or 1 **excellent roll**
half a carrot, peeled	butter

Place the bacon at the bottom of a soup pot. Lay the stew beef on top of the bacon and the sliced chicken on top of the beef. Add the thyme, marjoram, onion, pepper, mace, and carrot. Heat over medium-low for 15 minutes.

Add the broth and bread and raise the heat to medium. Cook until reduced by a third, about 30 minutes. Strain the broth and return it to the pot along with the pigeon(s), salt, and chestnuts. Cover and cook over medium-low heat for 1 hour; then reduce the heat to low, turn the pigeon(s) upside-down in the liquid, and cook for 30 more minutes.

Toward the end of the cooking time, melt some butter in a skillet over medium heat. When it sizzles and begins to turn brown, add the roll and fry it golden brown on all sides in the butter. Pour the soup into a tureen and set the roll in the center. Hannah Glasse advised serving the pigeon(s) in the soup as well, which is fine if you're striving for authenticity, but I find that modern diners avoid hacking off bits of a whole bird in serving themselves soup. I generally remove the pigeon(s) to a separate platter and simply explain that the birds would originally have been served as part of the soup.

 CRAWFISH SOUP

(Glasse)

... after having laboured both Night and Day, in order to get the Wedding
dinner ready by the time appointed, after having roasted Beef, Broiled Mut-
ton, and Stewed Soup enough to last the new-married couple through the
Honey-moon, I had the mortification of finding that I had been Roasting,
Broiling, and Stewing both the Meat and Myself to no purpose .... (*Lesley,
MW* 112–13)

At 7 we set off in a Coach for the Lyceum—were at home again in about 4
hours and ½—had Soup & wine & water, & then went to our Holes. (Letter
from Jane to Cassandra, September 15, 1813)

Take a gallon of water and set it a-boiling; put in it a bunch of sweet herbs, three
or four blades of mace, an onion stuck with cloves, pepper and salt; then have
about two hundred craw-fish, save about twenty, then pick the rest from the
shells, save the tails whole; beat the body and shells in a mortar with a pint of
peas (green or dry), first boiled tender in fair water; put your boiling water to it
and strain it boiling hot through a cloth till you have all the goodness out of it;
set it over a slow fire or stew-hole, have ready a French roll cut very thin, and let
it be very dry, put it to your soup, let it stew till half is wasted, then put a piece
of butter as big as an egg into a sauce-pan, let it simmer till it is done making a
noise, shake in two tea-spoonfuls of flour, give them a shake round, put to them
a pint of good gravy, let it boil four or five minutes softly, take out the onion,
and put to it a pint of the soup, stir it well together, and let it simmer very softly
a quarter of an hour; fry a French roll very nice and brown, and the twenty
craw-fish; pour your soup into the dish, and lay the roll in the middle and the
craw-fish round the dish.

Fine cooks boil a brace of carp and tench, and perhaps a lobster or two, and
many more rich things, to make a craw-fish soup; but the above is full as good,
and wants no addition.

MODERN RECIPE

2 quarts water

2 sprigs each fresh thyme, fresh marjoram, and fresh oregano

1 tsp. mace

half an onion

1 tsp. whole cloves

pepper and salt to taste

2 lbs. peeled crawfish meat or 50 live crawfish

1 cup fresh or frozen peas

half a roll of **French bread**, thinly sliced*

2 T butter plus some for frying the roll

1 tsp. flour

1 cup **gravy** or **cullis**

1 whole roll of **French bread**

If using live crawfish, bring a large pot of salted water to a boil. Add the crawfish, return to a boil, and boil for 5 to 7 minutes. You will need to cook the crawfish in several batches. Reserve a few of the best-looking for garnish and peel the rest.

In a soup pot, bring the 2 quarts of water to a boil and add the fresh herbs, mace, onion, cloves, pepper, salt, crawfish meat, peas, and thinly sliced roll. Reduce heat to medium-low and simmer gently, uncovered, for 90 minutes, or until the liquid is reduced by half.

In a small saucepan, heat the 2 T butter until it begins to brown and add the flour. Remove from the heat.

Remove the onion from the soup and add the butter and flour to the soup. Heat some additional butter in a pan over medium heat and fry the whole French roll until it is golden brown on all sides. Pour the sauce into a tureen and set the fried roll in the center. Serve immediately.

*A roll, in Austen's day, appears to have been bigger than a standard dinner roll today—it was about the size of a large man's fist.

GIBLET SOUP

(Farley)

In comparison with his brother, Edmund would have nothing to say. The soup would be sent round in a most spiritless manner, wine drank without any smiles, or agreeable trifling, and the venison cut up without supplying one pleasant anecdote of any former haunch. (*MP* 52)

Not choosing to fast so long, I made a good Luncheon here upon some exceeding good giblet soup. (Jane's uncle James Leigh Perrot, in a letter of July 4, 1806)

To four pounds of gravy beef, put two pounds of scrag of mutton, and two pounds of scrag of veal. Put to this meat two gallons of water, and let it stew very softly till it is a strong broth. Let it stand to be cold, and then skim off the fat. Take two pair of giblets, well scalded and cleaned, put them into the broth, and let them simmer till they are very tender. Take out the giblets, and strain the soup through a cloth. Put a piece of butter rolled in flour into a stewpan, and make it of a light brown. Have ready chopped small some parsley, chives, a little penny-royal, and a little sweet marjoram. Put the soup over a very slow fire; put in the giblets, fried butter, herbs, a little Madeira wine, some salt, and some chyan pepper. Let them simmer till the herbs are tender, and then send the soup to table with the giblets in it.

MODERN RECIPE

2 lbs. stew beef	½ cup finely chopped parsley
2 lbs. stew lamb or lamb neck	¼ cup finely chopped chives
1 gallon water	1 sprig fresh marjoram
giblets of 2 chickens	⅓ cup Madeira
3 T butter rolled in and mixed with 1½ T flour*	1½ tsp. salt
	¼ tsp. cayenne pepper

Place the beef, lamb, and water in a large stock pot and bring to a boil. Reduce heat to a simmer and cook, covered, for 90 minutes. Add the giblets, cover, and cook for an additional 30 minutes. Remove the giblets and set aside. Strain the broth and skim off the fat.

In a small saucepan, brown the butter and flour over medium heat.

Return the broth to the stock pot and add the remaining ingredients, including the browned butter and the reserved giblets. Cook over medium heat for 10 minutes and serve.

*See *Appendix 1: "What's with All the Butter?"*

MOCK TURTLE SOUP

(Farley)

". . . Send up some Ices and a bason of Soup, and do not forget some Jellies and Cakes." . . . The Chocolate, The Sandwiches, the Jellies, the Cakes, the Ice, and the Soup soon made their appearance . . . . (*Evelyn, MW* 182)

... they had driven directly to the York Hotel, ate some soup, and bespoke an early dinner, walked down to the Pump-room, tasted the water, and laid out some shillings in purses and spars .... (*NA* 116)

Scald a calfs head with the skin on, and pull off the horny part, which must be cut into pieces about two inches square. Wash and clean these well, dry them in a cloth, and put them into a stewpan, with four quarts of broth made in the following manner: Take six or seven pounds of beef, a calfs foot or two, an onion, two carrots, a turnip, a shank of ham, a head of celery, some cloves and whole pepper, a bunch of sweet herbs, a little lemon-peel, a few truffles and eight quarts of water. Stew these well till the broth be reduced to four quarts, then strain it, and put it in as above directed. Then add to It some knotted marjoram, a little savory, thyme, and parsley, and chop all together. Then add some cloves, and mace pounded, a little chyan pepper, some green onions, and a shalot chopped; a few mushrooms also chopped, and half a pint of Madeira. Stew all these together gently, till they be reduced to two quarts. Then heat a little broth, mix some flour smooth in it, with the yolks of two eggs, and keep these stirring over a gentle fire till near boiling. Then add this to the soup, stirring it as it is pouring in, and let them all stew together for an hour or more. When you take it off the fire, squeeze in the juice of half a lemon and half an orange, and throw in boiled forcemeat balls. The quantity of soup may be increased by adding more broth, with calfs feet and ox palates cut in pieces, and boiled tender.

MODERN RECIPE

3 lbs. stew beef	2 sprigs each fresh marjoram, fresh thyme, and fresh oregano
2 or 3 beef soup bones	
1 onion, trimmed, peeled, and quartered	zest of one lemon
1 carrot, peeled and halved crosswise	2 truffles
¼ lb. ham	1 tsp. dried marjoram
4 stalks celery, cleaned and sliced crosswise into quarters	1 tsp. dried savory
	1 tsp. dried thyme
1 tsp. whole cloves	1 tsp. dried parsley
1 tsp. black peppercorns	½ tsp. ground cloves

Continued on next page

Continued from previous page

½ tsp. ground mace	½ cup broth
½ tsp. cayenne pepper	2 T flour
2 sliced scallions	2 egg yolks
1 minced shallot	juice of half a lemon
5 or 6 mushrooms, finely diced	juice of half an orange
1 cup Madeira	12 **force-meat balls** (optional)

Place all the ingredients down to the Madeira in a large stock pot and cover them with 4 quarts of water. Bring to a boil, reduce heat to medium, and cook until the liquid is reduced by half (about 1 hour). If the liquid seems to be reducing in volume too fast, add a little more water and lower the heat to medium-low.

In a small saucepan, heat the broth, flour, and egg yolks over medium-low, stirring constantly, until they begin to steam. Remove this mixture from the heat and pour it into the soup slowly, stirring the soup constantly as you do so. Cover the soup and cook for another hour.

Just before serving, stir in the lemon juice, orange juice, and (if using them) the force-meat balls.

ONION SOUP

(Raffald)

The soup was fifty times better than what we had at the Lucas's last week . . . . (*P&P* 342)

M[r] J. Plumptre joined us in the latter part of the Even[g]—walked home with us, ate some soup, & is very earnest for our going to Cov[ent] Gar[den] again to night to se Miss Stephens in the Farmers Wife. (Letter from Jane to Cassandra, March 1814)

Boil eight or ten large Spanish onions in milk and water, change it three times, when they are quite soft rub them through a hair sieve. Cut an old cock in pieces and boil it for gravy with one blade of mace, strain it and pour it upon the pulp of the onions. Boil it gently with the crumb of an old penny loaf grated into half a pint of cream; add Chyan pepper and salt to your taste. A few heads of asparagus or stewed spinach both make it eat well and look very pretty. Grate a crust of brown bread round the edge of the dish.

MODERN RECIPE

8 large yellow onions	1 cup heavy whipping cream
3 cups milk	1 tsp. cayenne pepper
2 cups chicken broth	1 T salt
¼ tsp. mace	2 cups fresh spinach
1½ cups bread crumbs, *in all*	1 T butter

Peel and quarter the onions. Place them in a stock pot with the milk and enough water to cover them. Bring the pot to a boil, reduce the heat to a simmer, and cook until the onions are very tender, about 30 minutes. Add water as necessary to keep the onions covered. When the onions are thoroughly cooked, drain off the water and milk. In a food processor, puree the onions.

In a large pot, heat the broth, mace, and onion puree over medium heat. Add 1 cup of the bread crumbs, the cream, the cayenne, and the salt. When the soup boils, reduce the heat to a gentle simmer and keep it warm until you are ready to serve it.

Meanwhile, bring a small pot of water to a boil. Add the spinach leaves and boil them for 1 minute. Remove them from the water, and drain them on paper towels.

In a small skillet, melt the butter over medium heat. Add the remaining ½ cup of bread crumbs and stir them constantly until they turn golden brown, about 3 minutes. Remove the skillet from the heat.

To serve, pour the soup into a tureen. Lay the spinach leaves in clumps across the top of the soup and sprinkle the browned bread crumbs around the edge of the tureen.

MACARONI SOUP

(Glasse)

Still Mrs. Norris was at intervals urging something different, and in the most interesting moment of his passage to England, when the alarm of a French privateer was at the height, she burst through his recital with the proposal of soup. "Sure, my dear Sir Thomas, a basin of soup would be a much better thing for you than tea. Do have a basin of soup." (*MP* 180)

Take three quarts of the strong broth and one of the gravy mixed together; take half a pound of small pipe macaroni and boil it in three quarts of water, with a little butter in it, till it is tender; then strain it through a sieve, cut it in pieces of about two inches long, put it in your soup, and boil it up for ten minutes, and then send it to table in a tureen, with the crust of a French roll toasted.

MODERN RECIPE

¼ lb. elbow macaroni	2 cups **gravy**
1 T butter	salt and pepper to taste
6 cups **broth**	a slice of **French bread**, toasted

Bring a medium-sized pot of water to a boil with the butter. Add the elbow macaroni and cook for 7 minutes. Drain the macaroni and add it to a saucepan with the broth, gravy, salt, and pepper. Bring the broth to a boil, reduce to a simmer, and cook for 10 minutes. Toast a slice of French bread and float it on the surface of the soup.

BROTH

(The French Family Cook)

. . . by the time she judged it reasonable to have done with her boot, she had the comfort of further delay in her power, being overtaken by a child from the cottage, setting out, according to orders, with her pitcher, to fetch broth from Hartfield. (*E* 88)

Choose the meat found and fresh killed: skim your broth, salt it, and put into it different sorts of vegetables, well picked, scraped, and washed; as celery, onions, carrots, parsnips, leeks, and cabbage: let your broth boil gently till the meat be done, and then strain it through a sieve or napkin, to use as you think proper. A piece of beef weighing six pounds will require six hours boiling, one of twelve or fourteen, eight. Take care to tie the vegetables you put in together, that you may take them out of the pot entire, and they will serve to put into your soups.

MODERN RECIPE

4 lbs. stew beef, lamb, or chicken

1 head celery, stalks washed and cut crosswise in quarters

3 onions, trimmed, peeled, and quartered

4 carrots, peeled, trimmed, and cut crosswise into thirds

3 parsnips, peeled, trimmed, and cut crosswise into thirds

1 large leek, trimmed, thoroughly washed, and cut crosswise into 2" pieces

1 small cabbage, quartered

Place all the ingredients in a large stock pot and cover with water. Bring to a boil over high heat; then reduce heat to medium low or low, cover, and simmer gently for 6 hours, adding water as necessary to keep the ingredients covered with water. Strain the liquid, skim off the fat, and store it in the refrigerator or freezer. It will keep for a few days in the refrigerator and a few months in the freezer.

PEASE SOUP

(Farley)

Dear Jane, how shall we ever recollect half the dishes for grandmamma? Soup too! Bless me! I should not be helped so soon, but it smells most excellent, and I cannot help beginning. (*E* 330)

Mr Lyford was here yesterday; he came while we were at dinner, and partook of our elegant entertainment. I was not ashamed at asking him to sit down to table, for we had some pease-soup, a sparerib, and a pudding. (Letter from Jane to Cassandra, December 1, 1798)

Take a peck of green peas, shell and boil them in spring water till they be soft, and then work them through a hair sieve. Take the water your peas were boiled in, and put into it three slices of ham, a knuckle of veal, a few beet-leaves shred small, a turnip, two carrots, and add a little more water to the meat. Set it over the fire, and let it boil an hour and an half; then strain the gravy into a bowl, and mix it with the pulp. Then put in a little juice of spinach, which must be beat and squeezed through a cloth, and put in as much as will make it look of a pretty colour. Then give it a gentle boil, to take off the taste of the spinach, and slice in the whitest part of a head of celery. Put in a lump of sugar of the size of a walnut, take a slice of bread, and cut it into little square pieces; cut a little bacon in the same manner, and fry them of a light brown in fresh butter. Cut a large cabbage-lettuce in slices, fry it after the other, and put it into the tureen, with fried bread and bacon. Have ready boiled, as for eating, a pint of young peas, put them into the soup, and pour all into your tureen. If you choose, you may put a little chopped mint.

MODERN RECIPE

4 quarts frozen peas	½ T white sugar
¼ lb. sliced ham	½ T brown sugar
1 beef soup bone	1 large slice **English bread**
greens of 3 beets, rinsed and coarsely chopped	4 to 6 T butter for frying
1 turnip, trimmed and peeled	1 head cabbage
2 carrots, trimmed, peeled, and halved crosswise	4 slices bacon
2 stalks celery, sliced ¼" thick crosswise	1 T chopped mint for garnish (optional)

Prepare the peas according to the package directions. Reserve 2 cups of the peas and puree the rest in a food processor. Set the peas and the pea puree aside in the refrigerator.

Measure three quarts of water into a pot and add the ham, soup bone, beet greens, turnip, and carrots. Bring the water to a boil, reduce the heat slightly, and boil gently for 1½ hours.

Strain the liquid, return it to the pot, and add the pea puree. Add the celery and simmer over medium-low heat for 5 minutes. Add the sugar and reserved whole peas and simmer for 5 minutes more.

Meanwhile, melt the butter in a large skillet over medium heat. Cut the slice of bread into 1" to 2" squares and fry both sides of the squares briefly in the butter, about 2 minutes per side. Quarter the cabbage, cut it crosswise into ½" slices, and fry these in the butter, about 6 to 8 minutes in all. Set both the bread squares and the cabbage aside on paper towels to drain. Cut the bacon crosswise into 1" to 2" slices and fry these until they are well browned.

To serve, place the fried cabbage in a tureen. Pour in the pea soup, then garnish with the bacon and bread squares. If you decide to use the mint, place a mound of it in the center of the soup.

❁ STEWED BEEF-GOBBETS ❁

(Glasse)

How little one minds
If a company dines
On the best that the Season affords!
How short is one's muse
O'er the Sauces and Stews,
Or the Guests, be they Beggars or Lords. (Headache, MW 448)

"Stewing" frequently meant cooking a large chunk of meat in liquid, rather than prepar-
ing a chunky, thick-sauced soup. Glasse's recipe is more like what we would consider a
stew today, and it is quite tasty, despite its unappetizing name.

Get any piece of beef except the leg, cut it in pieces about the bigness of a pullet's egg, put them in a stew-pan, cover them with water, let them stew, skim
them clean, and when they have stewed an hour, take mace, cloves, and whole
pepper tied in a muslin rag loose, some celery cut small, put them into the pan
with some salt, turnips and carrots pared and cut in slices, a little parsley, a bundle of sweet herbs, and a large crust of bread. You may put in an ounce of barley
or rice, if you like it. Cover it close, and let it stew till it is tender; take out the
herbs, spices, and bread, and have ready fried a French roll cut in four. Dish up
all together, and send it to table.

❧ MODERN RECIPE

2 lbs. stew beef

1 tsp. mace

1 tsp. whole cloves

2 tsp. black peppercorns

4 stalks celery sliced crosswise ¼" thick

1 tsp. salt

4 to 5 small turnips or potatoes, cut into 1"
dice

4 carrots, peeled and sliced crosswise ¼" thick

a few sprigs of parsley

1 tsp. dried or 2 tsp. fresh chopped thyme

1 tsp. dried or 2 tsp. fresh chopped oregano

1 tsp. dried or 2 tsp. fresh chopped marjoram

Continued on next page

Continued from previous page

1 oz. pearl barley or rice (optional)   1 roll of **french bread**

large bread crust   butter for frying

Place the beef in a stock pot and add water to just cover the beef. Bring the water to a boil, reduce to a simmer, and cover. Simmer 1 hour. Meanwhile, cut a small square of cheesecloth (about 6" square) and measure the mace, cloves, and peppercorns into the center. Gather the corners and tie the cheesecloth closed with kitchen twine. Add the cheesecloth bag, celery, salt, turnips or potatoes, carrots, parsley, thyme, oregano, marjoram, and the barley or rice, if you are adding it. Cover the pot again and simmer until the beef is tender, about 1 hour.

Meanwhile, melt some butter in a skillet over medium heat. Cut the French roll in quarters and fry the cut sides until they are golden brown, about 2 minutes per side.

Remove the cheesecloth bag and the remains of the bread crust. Pour the stew into a tureen and arrange the fried quarters of the roll in the tureen. Serve immediately.

CURRY

(Glasse)

We spent a very pleasant Day, and had a very good Dinner, tho' to be sure the Veal was terribly underdone, and the Curry had no seasoning. I could not help wishing all dinner-time that I had been at the dressing it—. (*Lesley, MW* 121)

This is a very mild curry, as spicy food had yet to make any inroads on the British table. Glasse's quantities have been halved.

Take two small chickens, skin them and cut them as for a fricassee, wash them clean, and stew them in about a quart of water for about five minutes, then strain off the liquor and put the chickens in a clean dish; take three large onions, chop them small and fry them in about two ounces of butter, then put in the chickens and fry them together till they are brown; take a quarter of an ounce of turmeric, a large spoonful of ginger and beaten pepper together, and a little salt to your palate, stew all these ingredients over the chickens whilst frying, then pour in the liquor and let it stew about half an hour, then put in a quarter of a pint of cream and the juice of two lemons, and serve it up. The ginger, pepper, and turmeric must be beat very fine.

MODERN RECIPE

1 small chicken (about 4 lbs.), skinned and cut up	1 T finely chopped fresh ginger, pounded to a paste in a mortar, or ½ T ground ginger
1 quart water	½ T black pepper
3 large onions, finely chopped	salt to taste
4 T butter	½ cup heavy whipping cream
1 T turmeric	juice of 2 lemons

Pour the water into a stock pot and bring it to a boil. Add the chicken parts and parboil them for 5 minutes. Remove the pot from the heat, drain off the water and reserve it for later, and remove the chicken pieces to a plate.

Melt the butter in a wide, deep, lidded skillet over medium heat. When it begins to sizzle, add the chopped onions and the chicken parts. Turn the chicken parts until they are browned on all sides. Then add the turmeric, ginger, black pepper, and salt. Add 1 cup of the reserved boiling liquid, cover, and reduce heat to a gentle simmer. Simmer 30 minutes.

Remove the lid, simmer for 5 minutes, and add the cream. Warm completely through, then add the lemon juice. Simmer for 5 more minutes, then serve.

15

SAUCES AND SPICES

It has been claimed that the English of Austen's day had only one sauce, or perhaps only two sauces—brown and white. This is a vast oversimplification. While it is true that the most common sauce for meat was its own juices thickened into a seasoned gravy, and that the most common sauce for vegetables was "melted butter" (a combination of butter and flour), there were plenty of other sauces (*Headache, MW* 448). There were oyster sauces that were popular with turkey, onion sauces for poultry and rabbit, celery sauce, applesauce, sorrel sauce, and sauces made with hard-boiled eggs. Most sauces were based on either gravy or cullis, strong broths based on browned beef, veal knuckles, fish, or vegetables. Then there were condiments, either homemade or store-bought, that added to the depth of simple sauces: lemon pickle, mushroom ketchup, walnut ketchup, and mum (beer) ketchup (but not tomato ketchup).

The use of spices had declined since the seventeenth century, but Georgian cooks had a wide range of spices available to them, thanks to England's far-flung commercial empire. A well-stocked pantry might have salt, black and white pepper, mustard, nutmeg, mace, cloves, cayenne pepper, Jamaica pepper (allspice), cinnamon, caraway seeds, saffron, and even curry powder. Vanilla was prohibitively expensive, but its place was supplied by rose-water and orange-flower-water, which lent a subtle flavor to fruit dishes and pastries.

These spices, generally acquired from grocers, were not always thoroughly pure. Frederick Accum's *A Treatise on Adulterations of Food and Culinary Poisons* (1820) reveals the sorts of deceptions that were practiced only a few years after Austen's death; one may assume that most of these stratagems were also being employed during her lifetime, as Accum often supplies anecdotal evidence from earlier dates. Mustard, he wrote, was adulterated with capsicum to increase its shelf life and improve its color, or with radish seed and pea flour to save money; both black and white pepper were about 16 percent "false pepper," "made up of oil cakes (the residue of linseed, from which the oil has been pressed,) common clay, and a portion of Cayenne pepper, formed in a mass, and granulated by being first pressed through a sieve, and then rolled in a cask." Pepper was perhaps the most adulterated spice. Ground pepper was extended with sweepings from the floors of pepper warehouses, while so-called white pepper was in fact merely black pepper that had been steeped in sea water and urine to remove the dark skin of the peppercorns. As with all food products in an age before protective legislation, the buyer had to be extremely cautious.

APPLE SAUCE

(Farley)

Applesauce was commonly served with pork and goose.

Pare, core, and slice some apples, and put them with a little water into the saucepan, to keep them from burning, and put in a bit of lemon-peel, bruise the apples, and add a piece of butter, and a little sugar.

 ## MODERN RECIPE

5 apples, peeled, cored, and quartered   1 T sugar

2 T butter

Place the apples in a saucepan with enough water to cover them, and bring the water to a boil over high heat. Reduce the heat to a gentle simmer, cover the saucepan, and stew the apples until they are very tender and mash easily, about 1 hour.

Mash the apples by pressing them against the inside of the saucepan with a wooden spoon. Continue cooking them as you do this. When all the apples are mashed, simmer uncovered until some of the water evaporates and the applesauce thickens. The texture should resemble commercial applesauce but be a little chunkier and thinner. Add the butter and sugar, stir thoroughly, heat for another minute or two, and serve.

This sauce can be made the day before serving and reheated.

BROWNING

(Farley)

Take four ounces of treble-refined sugar, and beat it small. Put it in an iron frying-pan, with an ounce of butter, and set it over a clear fire. Mix it well together all the time, and when it begins to be frothy, the sugar will be dissolving. Hold it higher over the fire, and when the sugar and butter be of a deep brown, pour in a little red wine. Stir them well together, then add more wine, and keep stirring it all the time. Put in the outer rind of a lemon, a little salt, three spoonfuls of mushroom ketchup, two or three blades of mace, six cloves, four shalots peeled, and half an ounce of Jamaica pepper. Boil them slowly for ten minutes, pour it into a bason, and when cold, bottle it up for use, having first carefully skimmed it. This is a very useful article, and such as the cook should never be without, it being almost of general use.

 ## MODERN RECIPE

1 cup plus 2 T sugar	6 T mushroom ketchup
4 T butter	¼ tsp. mace
zest of two lemons	12 whole cloves
½ cup red wine	4 large or 8 small shallots, peeled and halved
½ tsp. kosher salt	¼ cup whole allspice

In a nonstick saucepan, heat the sugar and butter over medium heat, stirring constantly, until both are completely melted, about 7 to 8 minutes.

Reduce heat to medium-low and continue stirring until the sugar froths high, steams a good deal, and turns a medium-dark brown, about 2 to 3 minutes. Carefully and slowly pour in half the red wine, being careful not to let the hot mixture splatter and stirring constantly. Stir for about a minute and add the rest of the wine. Reduce heat to low.

Add the remaining ingredients and simmer 10 minutes, stirring occasionally. Remove from the heat and allow the sauce to cool to room temperature.

Strain the liquid through a strainer and bottle. Browning will keep for several months in the refrigerator and can be canned according to the directions for your particular canner and jars.

 CELERY SAUCE

(Glasse)

Celery sauce was commonly served with poultry. Glasse actually offers three different ways of making this sauce: the way I've made it here, the same way but with the addition of a little cream, and as a "brown" celery sauce with red wine, ketchup, and gravy. In the version below, it's a flavorful and pleasant-looking pale green sauce that can be garnished nicely with lemon slices or wedges. Glasse makes no mention of crushing or mashing the celery once it is stewed, but I find that the sauce benefits from pureeing.

Take a large bunch of celery, wash and pare it very clean, cut it into little thin bits, and boil it softly in a little water till it is tender; then add a little beaten mace, some nutmeg, pepper, and salt, thickened with a good piece of butter rolled in flour; then boil it up and pour in your dish.

 ## MODERN RECIPE

2 cups water	¼ tsp. black pepper
2 cups celery, sliced crosswise ⅛" to ¼" thick	½ tsp. salt
¼ tsp. ground mace	2 T butter rolled in and mixed with 1 T flour*
¼ tsp. ground nutmeg	

Bring the water to a boil in a saucepan and add the celery. Return the water to a boil over high heat, reduce the heat to medium or medium-high, and cook, uncovered, for 15 minutes.

Puree the remaining water and celery together in a blender or a food processor. Return the puree to the saucepan over low heat and add the remaining ingredients, stirring constantly until the butter is melted and the sauce is warmed through.

*See *Appendix 1: "What's with All the Butter?"*

CULLIS, OR A THICK GRAVY

(Millington)

Put into a pan, with one quart of water, slices of ham, veal, celery, carrots, turnips, onions, leeks, a small bunch of sweet herbs, some allspice, black pepper, mace, a piece of lemon-peel, and two bay-leaves, and draw these till of a light brown, (but do not let it burn) and discharge it with beef stock. When it boils, skim it clear from fat, and thicken it with flour and water, or flour and butter passed. Boil it gently for three quarters of an hour; season it with Cayenne-pepper, lemon-juice, and salt; strain it, and add a little of the following liquid.

MODERN RECIPE

1 quart water

1 thick slice of ham

2 lbs. veal

3 stalks celery, cut crosswise into 3" long pieces

3 carrots, peeled, trimmed, and cut crosswise into 3" long pieces

2 turnips, peeled and cut in 1" dice

1 onion, peeled and quartered

1 leek, washed, trimmed, and cut crosswise into 3" long pieces

6 sprigs mixed fresh herbs such as sage, oregano, thyme, rosemary, or parsley

1 tsp. whole allspice

1 tsp. black peppercorns

½ tsp. blade mace

zest and juice of one lemon

2 bay leaves

1 quart beef stock

¼ cup flour

¼ cup water or 4 T butter

½ tsp. cayenne pepper

1 tsp. kosher salt

In a stock pot, place the water, ham, veal, celery, carrots, turnips, onion, leek, herbs, allspice, pepper-corns, mace, lemon zest, and bay leaves. Heat over medium heat until most of the liquid is consumed.

Add the beef stock and bring to a boil. Thicken it with either ¼ cup of flour mixed with ¼ cup water or ¼ cup flour mixed with 4 T butter, stirring until the flour is thoroughly combined. Cover the pot and simmer for 45 minutes.

Remove the lid, stir the cullis, and add the cayenne, lemon juice, and salt. Strain off the solids and let the liquid cool to room temperature, then refrigerate or freeze.

EGG SAUCE

(Farley)

Glasse's version of this recipe uses the yolks of the hard-boiled eggs as well as the whites. Raffald partially chops the whites, then adds the yolks and chops the mixture coarsely.

Take two eggs, and boil them hard. First chop the whites, then put them into a quarter of a pound of good melted butter, and stir them well together.

 ## MODERN RECIPE

2 eggs   ¼ lb. butter

Hard-boil the eggs and separate the whites from the yolks. Melt the butter in a small saucepan over medium-low heat and add the yolks, stirring until the yolks are thoroughly blended. Finely chop the whites, add them to the butter, and stir until warm, about 1 minute.

GRAVY

(Glasse)

Glasse describes her version of brown gravy as appropriate for turkey, fowl, or "Ragoo." Today, the gravy that accompanies a meat dish tends to be made from the same type of meat; not so in the eighteenth century, when poultry was often accompanied by a beef-based gravy.

Take a pound of lean beef, cut and hack it well, then flour it well, put a piece of butter as big as a hen's egg in a stew-pan; when it is melted, put in your beef, fry it on all sides a little brown, then pour in three pints of boiling water and a bundle of sweet herbs, two or three blades of mace, three or four cloves, twelve whole pepper-corns, a little bit of carrot, a little piece of crust of bread toasted brown; cover it close, and let it boil till there is about a pint or less; then season it with salt, and strain it off.

MODERN RECIPE

1 lb. beef, thinly sliced	4 whole cloves
flour	12 black peppercorns
4 T butter	2" peeled carrot or parsnip
6 cups hot water	1 oz. hard bread crust
2 sprigs each fresh marjoram, thyme, oregano	salt to taste
½ tsp. ground or blade mace	

Melt the butter in a large saucepan over medium-high heat. Dredge the beef slices in flour and brown them on all sides, about 2 minutes per side. Carefully add the hot water, herbs, cloves, peppercorns, carrot or parsnip, and bread crust, and bring to a boil. Cover, reduce heat to medium, and boil until reduced by about ⅔, about 2 hours. Strain and season to taste with salt.

LEMON PICKLE

(Glasse)

Take two dozen of lemons, grate off the out-rinds very thin, cut them in four quarters, but leave the bottoms whole, rub on them equally half a pound of bay salt, and spread them on a large pewter dish, put them in a cool oven, or let them dry gradually by the fire till all the juice is dried into the peels, then put them into a pitcher well glazed; with one ounce of mace, half an ounce of cloves beat fine, one ounce of nutmeg cut in thin slices, four ounces of garlic peeled, half a pint of mustard-seed bruised a little, and tied in a muslin bag; pour two quarts of boiling white wine and vinegar upon them, close the pitcher well up, and let it stand five or six days by the fire; shake it well up every day, then tie it up, and let it stand for three months to take off the bitter; when you bottle it, put the pickle and lemon in a hair sieve, press them well to get out the liquor, and let it stand still another day, then pour off the fine, and bottle it; let the other stand three or four days, and it will refine itself, pour it off and bottle it, let it stand again and bottle it, till the whole is refined. It may be put in any white sauce, and will not hurt the colour. It is very good for fish-sauce and made-dishes; a tea-spoonful is enough for white, and two for brown sauce for a fowl; it is a most useful pickle, and gives a pleasant flavour. Be sure you put it in before you thicken the sauce or put any cream in, lest the sharpness make it curdle.

MODERN RECIPE

24 lemons	2 medium heads garlic
½ lb. kosher salt	1 cup mustard seed
1 oz. mace	4 cups white wine
½ oz. ground cloves	4 cups white vinegar
½ oz. ground nutmeg	

Preheat oven to 200°F. With a paring knife, cut off the lemon peels, leaving a thin white rind on each lemon. The peels can be set aside and used for making **sweetmeats**. Quarter the lemons and, in a large bowl, toss the lemon quarters with the salt.

Spread the lemons out on 2 large nonreactive baking sheets or in glass or ceramic baking dishes such as pie plates and casseroles. The lemons should be in a single layer with the rinds on the bottom. Place the lemons in the oven and bake until they are dry. This can take an entire day, sometimes two. If the top side is entirely dry, you may turn the lemons over to dry the underside.

When the lemons are dry, mix the remaining ingredients in a pot over the lowest possible heat. Shake off excess salt from the lemons (it doesn't matter if some still clings to them), add the lemons to the pot, and cover, cooking as gently as possible for 2 hours and adding more vinegar if necessary to maintain the same level of liquid. Cool the lemon mixture and place in a lidded plastic container. Refrigerate for 2 to 4 weeks, tightly covered. Then strain the mixture, squeezing the lemons well and reserving the strained liquid. If you like, you can put the remaining solids into a food processor for just a few seconds, then heat them over low heat, and strain this pulp a second time, adding it to the first strained liquid.

Lemon pickle can be kept in the refrigerator almost indefinitely, as it is highly acidic. It will keep as long there as, say, that jar of mango chutney you bought for making one recipe two years ago and haven't touched since. Lemon pickle can also be canned for storage at room temperature; follow the manufacturer's directions on your canning jars and canner.

❋ MELTED BUTTER ❋

(Farley)

She could not but observe that the abundance of the dinner did not seem to create the smallest astonishment in the General; nay, that he was even looking at the side-table for cold meat which was not there. His son and daughter's observations were of a different kind. They had seldom seen him eat so heartily at any table but his own; and never before known him so little disconcerted by the melted butter's being oiled. (*NA* 214–15)

The poorer the household, the greater the proportion of flour to butter. Melted butter sauce could be flavored with various condiments, such as anchovy and mustard, depending on the dish it was intended to accompany. It was typically served in a separate sauce boat. The phenomenon of "oiling" had to do with the method of preparation; if the butter is heated too much, it will separate and the sauce will not be pleasingly thick and uniform. Hannah Glasse, in her version of this recipe, attributes "oiling" to the cook's failure to shake the pan in one direction during the melting of the butter.

Keep a plated or tin saucepan for the purpose only of melting butter. Put a little water at the bottom, and a dust of flour. Shake them together, and cut the butter in slices. As it melts, shake it one way; let it boil up, and it will be smooth and thick.

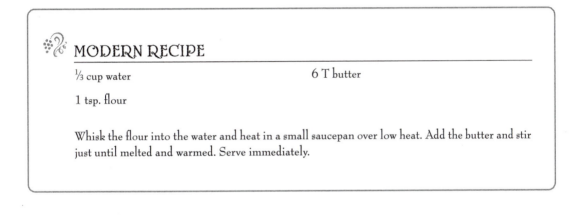

MODERN RECIPE

⅓ cup water

1 tsp. flour

6 T butter

Whisk the flour into the water and heat in a small saucepan over low heat. Add the butter and stir just until melted and warmed. Serve immediately.

 ## MUSHROOM KETCHUP

(Raffald)

To a Quart Bottle of nice Mushrooms . . . paid 0.6.0. To a Quart Bottle of Mushroom Catchup 0.3.6. (Diary of Parson James Woodforde)

This recipe turned out to be incredibly frustrating. It begins well enough—the mushrooms and salt react with each other in a most satisfying manner—but the cooking part proves to be nearly impossible according to Raffald's instructions. The "quick oven for twelve hours," or a quick oven for any appreciable length of time at all, results in mushrooms that resemble charcoal briquets. Reducing the heat doesn't break down the mushrooms very much, with the result that the "ketchup" is more like a broth. So I did what any sensible cook would do; I cheated. Read on.

Take the full grown flaps of mushrooms, crush them with your hands, throw a handful of salt into every peck of mushrooms and let them stand all night. Then put them into stewpans and set them in a quick oven for twelve hours, and strain them through a hair sieve. To every gallon of liquor put of cloves, Jamaica, black pepper, and ginger, one ounce each, and half a pound of common salt. Set it on a slow fire and let it boil till half the liquor is wasted away, then put it in a clean pot. When cold bottle it for use.

 ## MODERN RECIPE

40 oz. Portobello mushrooms	1½ tsp. cloves
¼ cup kosher salt	1½ tsp. allspice
Seasoning (add 1 batch of seasoning mix to every 2 cups of prepared mushrooms, as described below)	1½ tsp. black pepper
	1½ tsp. ground ginger

Crush the mushrooms into large chunks with your hands. Toss the salt over them and let them stand overnight. They will settle, shrink, and ooze a good deal of liquid. In the morning, pour the mushrooms and their liquid into a food processor and process until fairly smooth, with just a few small chunks of mushroom left. Depending on your food processor, you may need to do this in two batches.

Pass the mushrooms through a strainer, discarding any pieces that won't go through the strainer, and measure the amount of resulting liquid and pulp. To every two cups of liquid and pulp, add 1½ tsp. of each of the spices listed above. Place the mixture in a large saucepan and simmer for ½ hour or until the liquid begins to thicken.

The mushroom ketchup can be refrigerated for up to two months or canned according to the manufacturer's directions for your canning jars and canner.

 # MUSHROOM POWDER

(Raffald)

Take the thickest large buttons you can get, peel them, cut off the root end but don't wash them. Spread them seperately on pewter dishes and set them in a slow oven to dry. Let the liquor dry up into the mushrooms, it makes the powder stronger, and let them continue in the oven till you find they will powder. Then beat them in a marble mortar and sift them through a fine sieve with a little Chyan pepper and pounded mace. Bottle it and keep it in a dry closet.

 MODERN RECIPE

40 oz. white mushrooms   ¼ tsp. ground mace

¼ tsp. cayenne pepper

Preheat the oven to 200°F. Lay the mushrooms in a single layer on baking sheets and keep them in the oven until they are fully dry. (This will take several hours.) Place them in a food processor with the mace and cayenne and process to a powder.

ONION SAUCE

(Raffald)

This is also an appropriate sauce for rabbit; Glasse makes a similar sauce, but serves it in a sauce boat garnished with lemon.

Boil eight or ten large onions, change the water two or three times when they are boiling. When enough, chop them on a board to keep them from going a bad colour. Put them in a saucepan with a quarter of a pound of butter, two spoonfuls of thick cream, boil it a little and pour it over the ducks.

 MODERN RECIPE

8 large onions   2 T heavy whipping cream

¼ lb. butter

Bring a large pot of salted water to a boil. Peel, trim, and quarter the onions. Boil them until they are very tender, about 30 minutes. Drain the onions and puree them in a food processor. Pour them into a saucepan along with the butter and cream and heat just until it begins to bubble.

❀ OYSTER SAUCE ❀

(Farley)

Some flavors seem so well paired that one item seems incomplete without its traditional accompaniment. Fish and chips, turkey and bread-based stuffing, and popcorn with butter and salt come to mind. However, many supposedly essential unions have not always been constant. Cooks of Austen's day often considered a red wine sauce particularly appropriate for such mild-tasting vegetables as cucumbers and celery, and this combination tastes odd or even actively unpleasant to our changed palates. The pairing of pork or goose with applesauce has survived more successfully.

Somewhat more long-lived than cucumbers stewed in red wine, but a good deal less common today than pork and applesauce, is the pairing of turkey and oysters. A traditional turkey dinner in America almost always features a bread stuffing of some kind, perhaps enhanced with nuts or pork sausage. But in Austen's time, people rarely ate roast turkey without oyster sauce, and oyster-based sauces were also served with other foods, such as fish. Some cookbooks retained a bread sauce for turkey—not a stuffing, but a mild white sauce thickened with softened bread, a holdover from the middle ages. But by the Regency, it was oyster sauce that dominated, both in the cookbooks and in diary entries and letters that mentioned eating turkey.

Open a pint of oysters into a bason, wash them out of their liquor, and put them into another bason. Pour the liquor, as soon as it be settled, into a saucepan, and put to it a little white gravy, and a teaspoonful of lemon-pickle. Thicken it with flour, and a large piece of butter, and then boil it three or four minutes. Put in a spoonful of thick cream, and then your oysters. Keep shaking them over the fire till they be quite hot, but do not let them boil.

❧ MODERN RECIPE

2 cups oysters, in the shell	3 T butter rolled in 1½ T flour*
¼ cup **white sauce**	1 T heavy whipping cream
1 tsp. **lemon pickle**	

Place a colander in a bowl and shuck the oysters over the colander, allowing any liquid to drain into the bowl. Discard the oyster shells and drain off the liquid from the bowl. Place the oyster

Continued on next page

Continued from previous page

liquid in a saucepan over medium heat. Add the white sauce and lemon pickle and stir to combine.

Add the floured butter and stir until it has melted and the flour is completely incorporated in the sauce. Bring to a boil and cook for 3 minutes, stirring constantly and making sure that the sauce does not boil over. Add the cream and the oysters, reduce the heat slightly, and continue to stir, without allowing the sauce to return to a boil, until the oysters are hot, about 1 to 2 minutes.

*See Appendix 1: "What's with All the Butter?"

 # SAUCE À LA ANGLOISE

(*The French Family Cook*)

Sauces based on hard-boiled eggs were uniquely English at this time period and widely popular, though they fell out favor during the Victorian era. Even The French Family Cook, *which was designed to introduce French cooking to English kitchens, includes a French-influenced version of this quintessentially English sauce.*

Mince the yolks of two eggs boiled hard, put half into a stew-pan, with an anchovy and some fine capers chopped, a glass of good broth, a little salt and whole pepper, and a bit of butter, half the size of an egg, rolled in flour: thicken it upon the fire, serve it over any thing you please, and strew the remainder of the egg upon the meat.

 ## MODERN RECIPE

2 hard-boiled egg yolks, *in all*

1 anchovy filet

2 tsp. minced capers

¾ cup broth

¼ tsp. salt

½ tsp. black peppercorns

2 T butter rolled in and mixed with 1 T flour*

Continued on next page

Continued from previous page

Mince both hard-boiled egg yolks and reserve one. Place the other in a small saucepan with the remaining ingredients and simmer for about 10 minutes. Pour the sauce over meat and scatter the remaining hard-boiled egg as a garnish.

See Appendix 1: "What's with All the Butter?"

SAUCE À LA ESPAGNOLE

(The French Family Cook)

> *How little one minds*
> *If a company dines*
> *On the best that the Season affords!*
> *How short is one's muse*
> *O'er the Sauces and Stews,*
> *Or the Guests, be they Beggars or Lords.* (Headache, MW 448)

Put a cullis in a stew-pan, with a good glass of white wine, the same quantity of broth, a bunch of parsley and scallions, two cloves of garlic, half a laurel-leaf, some coriander seed, two spoonfuls of oil, an onion sliced, any sort of root you choose to give it a flavour, and the half of a parsnip; let it boil nearly two hours over a very slow fire, take the fat off and strain the sauce, season it with salt and pepper.

MODERN RECIPE

1 cup gravy	2 clove garlic
1 cup broth	1 bay leaf
1 cup white wine	½ tsp. coriander seed
½ cup chopped fresh parsley	2 T olive oil
4 scallions, white and green parts, thinly sliced	1 small onion, peeled, halved, and thinly sliced

Continued on next page

Continued from previous page

1 carrot, peeled, trimmed, and sliced crosswise into 2"-long pieces

1 small parsnip, about 4" long, peeled,
trimmed, and halved crosswise

salt and pepper to taste

Place all the ingredients except the salt and pepper in a saucepan. Bring them to a boil, reduce the
heat to medium-low, and simmer 2 hours. Strain the sauce and season to taste with salt and pepper.

SAUCE À LA ITALIENNE

(The French Family Cook)

Put two spoonfuls of sweet oil into a stew-pan, some mushrooms cut small, a
bunch of parsley, scallions, and the half of a laurel-leaf, two cloves, and a clove
of garlic; turn the whole a few times over the fire and shake in a little flour:
moisten it with a glass of white wine, as much good broth, adding salt and whole
pepper; let it boil half an hour, skim away the fat, take out the bunch of herbs
and serve it. You may, if you please, make use of vegetable broth, and, in the
place of cullis, put in a little more flour and two spoonfuls of onion juice.

MODERN RECIPE

2 T olive oil

6 mushrooms, diced

½ cup parsley, not chopped but instead left on
the stem

3 scallions, trimmed and cut crosswise in half

2 whole cloves

1 garlic clove

1 T flour

1 cup white wine

1 cup vegetable or meat broth

½ tsp. kosher salt

½ tsp. black peppercorns

Heat the olive oil in a saucepan over medium heat. Add the mushrooms, parsley, scallions, bay
leaf, cloves, and garlic, and cook for one minute. Sprinkle the flour over the vegetables and cook
for another 30 seconds.

Continued on next page

Continued from previous page

Add the wine, broth, salt, and pepper. Bring to a boil, reduce the heat to medium-low, and simmer gently for 30 minutes. Strain and serve.

 SAUCE À LA RAVIGOTTE

(The French Family Cook)

Put a glass of excellent broth into a stew-pan, half a coffee spoonful of vinegar, salt, whole pepper, and a bit of butter about the size of a walnut, mixed with flour; some tarragon, civit, chervil, pimpernel, and garden cresses: boil these herbs in water, squeeze and cut them very small; put them into the sauce and thicken it over the fire, to serve with any thing you please: if the salad herbs be put into the sauce without being parboiled, half the quantity will be sufficient.

MODERN RECIPE

1 cup beef broth	2 tsp. tarragon leaves, finely minced
1 T vinegar	1 T watercress, finely minced
¼ tsp. kosher salt	1 T butter rolled in ½ T flour*
¼ tsp. black peppercorns	

Bring the broth, vinegar, salt, and pepper to a boil over medium heat. Reduce heat to low, add the tarragon, watercress, and floured butter, and simmer gently for 10 minutes.

See Appendix 1: "What's with All the Butter?"

 SAUCE À LA REINE

(The French Family Cook)

Put a bit of butter, with some mushrooms, an onion, a carrot, a parsnip, half a clove of garlic, parsley and scallions, into a stew-pan; turn it a few times over the fire and shake in a little flour; moisten it with a large glass of broth, and the same quantity of white wine; let it boil an hour, skim it, and strain it through a sieve: then boil a gill of milk with a bit of crumb of bread half the size of an egg, and when the bread has sucked up all the milk, squeeze it through a sieve with a spoon, and put it into your sauce, with salt and large pepper.

MODERN RECIPE

4 T butter	½ cup parsley, coarsely chopped
8 oz. mushrooms, finely diced	2 scallions, coarsely chopped
1 small onion, diced	1 cup broth
1 carrot, peeled, trimmed, and cut crosswise into ¼" pieces	1 cup white wine
	½ cup milk
1 parsnip, peeled, trimmed, and cut crosswise into ¼" pieces	piece of bread, approximately 2" × 2"
½ clove of garlic, peeled	salt and pepper to taste

Melt the butter in a large saucepan over medium heat.

Add the mushrooms, onion, carrot, parsnip, garlic, parsley, and scallions, and cook over medium-low heat for 5 minutes.

Sprinkle in the flour and stir in the broth and white wine. Simmer over low or medium-low heat for 1 hour.

Turn off the heat. Strain the sauce and return it to the saucepan. In a separate small saucepan, bring the milk and bread to a boil for 2 minutes. Run the bread through the finest holes of a food mill, scrape it through a strainer with the back of a spoon, or put it in a food processor. Add the milk and the finely ground bread to the sauce and gently heat. Season with salt and pepper to taste.

 SAUCE À LA SULTANE

(The French Family Cook)

Put a pint of broth into a stew-pan, with a glass of white wine, two slices of peeled lemons, two cloves, a clove of garlic, half a laurel-leaf, parsley, scallions, onion, and the flavour of any root you please: boil it an hour and a half over a slow fire, and reduce it to the consistence of a sauce; strain it through a sieve, and then add salt, large pepper, the yolk of an egg boiled hard and chopped, and a little boiled parsley shred fine.

MODERN RECIPE

2 cups broth	2 scallions, sliced
1 cup white wine	1 small onion, diced
1 lemon	1 carrot or parsnip, peeled, trimmed, and sliced crosswise ¼" thick
2 whole cloves	
1 clove garlic, peeled and bruised	¼ tsp. salt
1 bay leaf	⅛ tsp. white pepper
½ cup plus 1 T chopped parsley, *in all*	1 hard-boiled egg

Peel the lemon and quarter it. In a saucepan, over medium heat, heat the broth, wine, 2 of the lemon quarters, cloves, garlic, bay leaf, ½ cup parsley, scallions, onion, and carrot or parsnip. Bring the liquid to a boil, reduce to a simmer, and cook for 90 minutes.

Strain the sauce. Return it to the saucepan over medium-low heat and add the remaining 1 T parsley. Cook for 2 minutes. Add the salt, white pepper, and the yolk of the hard-boiled egg, crumbling the egg yolk as you add it. Whisk the sauce to combine the egg yolk and cook for 3 more minutes. Serve warm.

WALNUT KETCHUP

(Raffald)

Walnut ketchup was one of the most common cooking condiments of the eighteenth century. Long before there was tomato ketchup, there was this all-purpose seasoning, which shows up in many sauces. Its closest modern equivalent is probably Worcester-shire sauce, and if you have to substitute something for it in a recipe, Worcestershire's probably the way to go. But walnut ketchup is thicker, spicier, and far more flavorful. There were numerous ways to make it; my version is a close modern equivalent for those of us who don't want to marinate our walnuts for a full year before using them. Alegar was vinegar made from ale; my recipe uses a combination of unspoiled beer and vinegar to approximate the taste.

Put your walnuts in jars, cover them with cold strong ale alegar, tie them close for twelve months. Then take the walnuts out from the alegar and put to every gallon of the liquor two heads of garlic, half a pound of anchovies, one quart of red wine, one ounce of mace, one of cloves, one of long, one of black and one of Jamaica pepper, with one of ginger. Boil them all in the liquor till it is reduced to half the quantity, the next day bottle it for use. It is good in fish sauce or stewed beef. In my opinion it is an excellent catchup, for the longer it is kept the better it is. I have kept it five years and it was much better than when first made.

MODERN RECIPE

12 oz. beer	⅜ oz. ground mace
4 cups walnuts	⅜ oz. ground cloves
1 cup cider vinegar	⅜ oz. pink or green peppercorns
1 head of garlic	⅜ oz. black pepper
3 oz. anchovy filets	⅜ oz. allspice
12 oz. red wine	⅜ oz. ground ginger

In a food processor, grind the walnuts finely. Add them to the beer and the cider, cover tightly, and refrigerate for up to 3 days.

Peel and chop or press the garlic. Place all the ingredients, including the marinating walnuts and their liquid, into a large saucepan over medium heat. Cook for 30 minutes, stirring frequently. Cool to room temperature and refrigerate overnight. The next day, strain the liquid, discarding the solids, and bottle it. It will keep well in the refrigerator and can be canned according to the directions on your canning jars and canner.

WHITE FISH SAUCE

(Glasse)

It was said that the English had only two sauces—brown (gravy) and white ("melted butter," which was in reality a gravy made of butter, water, and flour). This version adds somewhat more flavor, but not a great deal. I've reduced the quantities of some of the ingredients to intensify the flavor a bit. To make the authentic version, double the quantities of wine, water, butter, and flour.

Wash two anchovies, put them into a sauce-pan with one glass of white wine and two of water, half a nutmeg grated, and a little lemon-peel; when it has boiled five or six minutes strain it through a sieve, add to it a spoonful of white wine vinegar, thicken it a little, then put in a pound of butter rolled in flour, boil it well and pour it hot upon your dish.

MODERN RECIPE

2 anchovy filets	zest of one lemon
½ cup white wine	1 T white wine vinegar
1 cup water	½ lb. butter mixed with ¼ cup flour*
1 tsp. grated nutmeg	

Place the anchovies, wine, water, nutmeg, and lemon zest in a saucepan over medium-high heat and bring to a boil. Keep the liquid at a boil for 5 minutes, then add the vinegar and boil for 2 more minutes. Reduce the heat to medium, add the floured butter, let it return to a boil, and serve immediately with seafood.

*See *Appendix 1: "What's with All the Butter?"*

WHITE SAUCE

(The French Family Cook)

Put some good meat, or, if you would make your sauce *en maigre*, vegetable broth into a stew-pan, with a good piece of crumb of bread, a bunch of parsley, scallions, garlic, shallots, thyme, laurel and basil, a clove, a little grated nutmeg, some whole mushrooms, a glass of white wine, salt and pepper: let the whole boil till half is consumed, strain it through a coarse sieve to draw from it a small cullis, and when you are ready to use it, put in the yolk of three eggs, beat up with some cream, and thicken it over the fire, taking care that the eggs do not curdle.

MODERN RECIPE

2 cups vegetable broth	½ tsp. dried basil or 1 sprig fresh basil
2 oz. stale bread, crumbled	one whole clove
½ cup chopped parsley	½ tsp. ground nutmeg
2 chopped scallions	5 to 6 mushrooms
2 cloves coarsely chopped garlic	1 cup white wine
2 chopped shallots	salt and pepper to taste
½ tsp. dried thyme or 1 sprig fresh thyme	3 egg yolks
1 bay leaf	½ cup cream

Place all the ingredients except the egg yolks and cream into a saucepan and bring them to a boil over high heat, stirring occasionally. Boil until reduced by half, about 15 to 20 minutes.

In a small heatproof bowl, combine the egg yolks and cream. Gradually add about ½ cup of the sauce to this mixture, working very slowly and stirring constantly to keep the egg yolks from accidentally cooking. Then reduce the heat on the stove to medium-low, add this mixture back to the pot, and cook, stirring, until the sauce thickens, about 5 minutes. Do not let the sauce boil again as it thickens; reduce the heat immediately if it appears ready to boil.

WHITE SAUCE FOR FOWLS

(Raffald)

Take a scrag of veal, the necks of the fowls or any odd bits of mutton or veal you have; put them in a saucepan with a blade or two of mace, a few black pepper-corns, one anchovy, a head of celery, a bunch of sweet herbs, a slice of the end of a lemon. Put in a quart of water, cover it close, let it boil till it is reduced to half a pint. Strain it and thicken it with a quarter of a pound of butter mixed with flour. Boil it five or six minutes, put in two spoonfuls of pickled mushrooms, mix the yolks of two eggs with a teacupful of good cream and a little nutmeg. Put it in your sauce, keep shaking it over the fire, but don't let it boil.

MODERN RECIPE

½ lb. veal	¼ lemon
½ lb. poultry scraps	1 quart water
¼ tsp. mace	¼ lb. butter rolled in and mixed with ¼ cup flour*
½ tsp. black peppercorns	
1 anchovy filet	2 T pickled or fresh mushrooms, finely chopped or sliced
the base of a head of celery after the stalks have been cut off, rinsed, and quartered	2 egg yolks
	¾ cup cream
1 sprig fresh rosemary	½ tsp. ground nutmeg
1 sprig fresh dill	
1 sprig fresh tarragon	

Place the veal, poultry, mace, peppercorns, anchovy, celery, herbs, lemon, and water in a saucepan and bring them to a boil over high heat. Cover, reduce the heat to medium, and boil until the liquid is reduced to about a cup, about 30 to 40 minutes.

Strain off the solids and return the liquid to the saucepan. Add the floured butter, keeping the heat at medium, and return to a boil. Boil for 5 minutes and then add the pickled mushrooms. Lower the heat and mix the egg yolks, cream, and nutmeg in a separate bowl. Gradually add about half the hot liquid to the bowl with the egg yolk mixture, stirring constantly and adding the liquid very slowly so that the egg yolks don't accidentally cook. Then pour the diluted egg yolks back into the saucepan and cook, stirring or shaking gently, for 3 to 5 minutes.

*See *Appendix 1: "What's with All the Butter?"*

WHITE SAUCE WITH CAPERS AND ANCHOVIES

(The French Family Cook)

Put a bit of butter about the size of an egg, rolled in flour, into a stew-pan; dilute it with a glass of broth, an anchovy cut fine, capers and scallions whole, salt and whole pepper: thicken it over the fire, and, before you serve it, take out the scallions.

MODERN RECIPE

4 T butter rolled in and mixed with 2 T flour*

1 cup **broth**

1 anchovy filet, chopped

2 T capers

2 scallions, halved crosswise

salt to taste

½ tsp. black peppercorns

Place all the ingredients in a saucepan over medium heat. Stir until it thickens noticeably, remove the scallions, and serve.

*See *Appendix 1: "What's with All the Butter?"*

16

BEVERAGES

The beverages drunk by Jane Austen's contemporaries fell into several categories, including milk, hot drinks, wines, beer, and hard liquor. On occasion, these categories overlapped, as in the case of the syllabub, a mixture of wine and milk, or as in the case of chocolate, which was a hot drink made with milk. Water is seldom mentioned as a drink on its own, though it was mixed with wine and heated to make tea and coffee. Water delivery to towns was improving after 1800, as entrepreneurs built piping systems, but prices were high and pipe maintenance erratic. Pollution of water by human, animal, and industrial waste made it often unsafe to drink from the local lake or river. There were places in the country where wells and streams could be trusted, but for the most part, when we hear of people in this era drinking water on its own, they are drinking mineral water in a spa as part of a medical cure.

Milk was drunk on its own and was very much appreciated when it came fresh from one's own farm's dairy. Town milk was far more suspect. Sometimes diluted with water, almost always thin, blue, and dirty, it was made even more unpalatable in places such as Bath by the methods of its production. The cows who yielded the local milk were kept in barn stalls rather than in grassy fields, and their inferior fodder yielded inferior milk. Still, for many people, it was the only option. It was sold in the streets by milkwomen, who carried two pails suspended from a pole across the shoulders, or directly from cows or asses who were milked at the door of each house. Some argued that the working class ought to drink less tea and more milk, but David Davies, in *The Case of the Labourers in Husbandry* (1795), responded that this, while desirable, was impossible:

> Were it true that poor people could everywhere procure so excellent an article as milk, there would be then just reason to reproach them for giving

preference to the miserable infusion of which they are so fond. But it is not
so. Wherever the poor can get milk, do they not gladly use it? And where
they cannot get it, would they not gladly exchange their tea for it?

The problem was not that people did not like milk, but that good milk was simply too expensive.

The poor often had milk only in their tea, but at the other end of the social
spectrum it was enjoyed in a variety of forms. For wealthy invalids, especially
those with tuberculosis, there was asses' milk (*Sand, MW* 393, 401), which had
fewer nutrients than cows' or goats' milk but also had less protein and fat and
was thus more easily digested. Mixed with cocoa, milk became "chocolate," a
luxurious breakfast drink enjoyed at the homes of the wealthy and on special
occasions. François de La Rochefoucauld, writing in 1784, explained that in
England, "Breakfast consists of tea and bread and butter in various forms. In
the houses of the rich, you have coffee, chocolate and so on." A correspondent
to *The Gentleman's Magazine* claimed, in 1819, that cocoa was drunk throughout the nation every morning in the homes of the gentry and nobility, but he
may have been overstating his case. Parson James Woodforde records drinking
coffee and tea on almost every evening social occasion, but chocolate makes a
much less frequent appearance in his diaries. It is associated with special occasions; on February 12, 1782, for example, it is served before and after a funeral, along with toast, cake, and wine. Chocolate was heated in special pots,
similar to coffeepots, but with an aperture at the top for a stirring rod or mill,
which acted like a whisk.

COFFEE

The two most popular hot beverages were coffee and tea. Coffee, a drink once
almost unknown outside the Middle East, became the beverage of choice in
much of Europe during the seventeenth century. It conquered England as well
in the late 1600s, and coffeehouses sprang up all over London to meet the demand. In 1700 there were about 2,000 of these establishments in London
alone, and in time each coffeehouse developed its own self-selected clientele—
lawyers, Whigs, Tories, actors, importer-exporters, stockbrokers, and so on. The
coffeehouse that attracted shipping merchants became the basis for the marine
insurance company Lloyd's of London; another house, patronized by stockbrokers, developed into the Stock Exchange.

However, a variety of factors combined to topple coffee from the throne of
fashion. Chief among these was the rise of the East India Company, which was

Telling Fortune in Coffee Grounds, 1790. A coffee set with its characteristic angled-handled pot. (Courtesy of the Lewis Walpole Library, Yale University. 790.4.10.1.)

the only licensed importer of tea. Furthermore, most of England's coffee came from the West Indies—in 1788 half the world's supply was grown in San Domingo alone—and the West Indies were inexorably moving to a monocultural economy based on sugar, the most profitable crop grown in the islands. On a smaller, more personal scale, tea was simply easier to make. It could be stored for longer than coffee without losing its flavor, did not need to be roasted or ground, was cheaper, and could be easily mixed by unscrupulous dealers with a long list of adulterants. Coffee lost its ascendancy, and most of the old coffeehouses were gone by 1730. In their place arose public gardens where people could drink their tea in three-sided, roofed cubicles before strolling the elaborately landscaped grounds in search of romance and panoramic views.

Coffee did not disappear from the English table, however. It merely moved into the home, where it could be enjoyed by men and women alike. It became a common drink at breakfast and at teatime (*NA* 215; *S&S* 233; *P&P* 37, 163, 173; *MP* 104), though never as popular as tea. Jane's mother, writing in 1806 of the lavish breakfasts at Stoneleigh, a relative's house, mentioned the appearance of "chocolate, coffee and tea, plum cake, pound cake, hot rolls, cold rolls, bread and butter, and dry toast for me." Among the immediate Austen family, it appears that Jane's brother Edward was fondest of coffee; Jane wrote that he would need the use of a coffee mill while visiting the family home at Steventon, because he was in the habit of taking coffee every day with his breakfast.

The coffee itself, like tea, sugar, citrus fruit, spices, and similar imported luxuries, would have been purchased from a grocer. The beverage was considered harder to adulterate than tea, though Frederick Accum noted that is was sometimes mixed with "pigeon's beans and pease," a practice banned by an act of 1803. Contemporary illustrations of people drinking coffee show a tall, tapered coffeepot with a narrow, curved spout and a long handle, with a wide, ridged grip, attached to the back of the coffeepot at an angle. The pot's lid is a shallow dome with a knob on top. Coffeepots were sometimes made of a layered metal called "Sheffield plate"—copper coated thinly with silver on the outside and with tin on the inside. Ceramic coffeepots, however, were rare. Cups (*P&P* 341) might or might not have handles. The coffee, once made and set on the table, was served by the hostess (*P&P* 76, 341). Afterward, fortunes were sometimes read in the leftover grounds, in much the same way that some people read tea leaves.

Though tea continued to reign supreme throughout Austen's lifetime (*E* 323), coffee was about to experience a resurgence in popularity. Import duties on coffee were lowered in 1808 and 1825, and coffeehouses began to make a comeback. There were only a dozen in London in 1815, but they multiplied rapidly in the 1820s, and there were almost 1,800 by 1840. Selling coffee, tea, spruce beer, and ginger beer, and providing access to a wide variety of newspapers, they became important gathering places once again.

TEA

Still, tea (*Wat*, *MW* 326, 356; *Sand*, *MW* 416; *NA* 238; *S&S* 198; *P&P* 100, 217, 299, 344, 346; *MP* 108, 324, 381; *E* 21, 22, 124, 255, 310, 323, 329, 344, 347, 434) reigned supreme, and Austen mentions it more than any other beverage. The only drink to rival it in popularity during the eighteenth century was beer, and beer was drunk in contexts that were at least one degree removed from Austen's genteel female world. Tea, however, was at the heart of the gentry's social life, providing occupation for the hands, a subject for discussion, and a means, even in the way it was bought and prepared, of maintaining class distinctions. It became a part of the ritual and pace of the day and reached from the royal family all the way down to the humblest laborers.

Sources vary as to the exact amount that was consumed. Peter Clark claims that in 1800 Britons consumed 23 million pounds of tea and that consumption rose slowly but steadily thereafter; Hoh-cheung Mui and Lorna Mui state that the annual retained imports averaged 16 million pounds from 1799 to 1801. In any case, it would be hard to calculate the exact amounts involved, because so much of the tea that came into the country was smuggled and thus avoided tabulation. Richard Twining, of the famous tea-selling family, commented in his *Observations on the Tea & Window Act and on the Tea Trade* (1785) that "the smuggler has become so formidable a rival [to the East India Company], that, upon the most moderate computation, they shared the Tea-trade equally between them; and according to some calculations, the smuggler had two thirds of it." Smugglers, who were paid in tea, were depicted as carrying the leaves into the country strapped around their midriffs and thighs, packed into the panniers of ladies' skirts, and stuffed in bundles under hats. Even quite respectable people bought smuggled tea; the comfort-loving diarist Parson Woodforde certainly did so. The reduction of the tea tax from 119 percent to 12.5 percent in 1784 may have diminished the trade somewhat—official consumption jumped from 5 million pounds in 1784 to 11 million in 1785—but Richard Twining was still disturbed by the problem a year after the tax cut, and tea remained one of the two most-smuggled items in the 1820s (the other was foreign liquor).

Another aspect of tea consumption that the official statistics do not reflect is the way tea made its way down the social scale. One fairly obvious measure of income, as reflected in tea drinking, is that the rich drank the better-quality and thus more expensive teas, while the less affluent purchased cheaper varieties. This comes as no surprise to modern readers, who understand perfectly well the difference between Lipton's, purchased prebagged in cartons at the grocery store, and a fancy, exotic variety of tea purchased by the pound in a coffee shop. Each caters to a different audience. Nor is it surprising that the rich drank more tea than the poor. The comfortably wealthy Edward Austen's household at Godmersham consumed forty-eight pounds of tea year, according to Jane's estimate, but their tea bill was dwarfed by the Earl of Stamford's, who in the 1790s ordered eighty-five to ninety-five pounds a year from Twining's. This, too, makes perfect sense to us: If you have more money, you can buy more tea. What does come as a surprise to modern readers is the *re-use* of tea. Used cars, used clothing, used books, used CDs we understand, but secondhand tea is quite another matter. Yet, in Austen's time, tea was a valuable enough commodity to be brewed as many as three times. In well-off households, the members of the family would drink the first brew. Then the leaves would pass to the servants, to be enjoyed a second time. Finally, a servant entitled to this perquisite (usually the cook or housekeeper) would sell the twice-used leaves to the poor and pocket the money. Even within a single social episode, the tea might be steeped several times; Susannah Blamire's poem "Stoklewath; or, the Cumbrian Village," written around 1776, describes women talking over tea:

Cup after cup sends steaming circles round,
And oft the weak tea's in the full pot drowned;
It matters not, for while their news they tell
The mind's content, and all things move on well.

For these women at least, the quality of the tea was less important than the ritual of drinking it.

Opinions varied as to whether the poor should be drinking tea at all. Even third-hand tea caused some reformers to recoil in horror at beggars' insistence

Anti-Saccharrites, Gillray, 1792. Tea without sugar is clearly not much of a treat for John Bull's pouting daughters. (Courtesy of the Lewis Walpole Library, Yale University. 792.3.27.1.)

on drinking it. Wholesome, traditional beer, they chided, was being forsaken for mere fashionable tea. The poor were aping their betters and wasting money on a frivolous luxury. As early as the mid-eighteenth century, a witness claimed that in Nottingham "almost every Seamer, Sizer and Winder will have her Tea in a morning . . . and even a common Washer woman thinks she has not had a proper Breakfast without Tea and hot buttered White Bread!" Jamaican sugar planter Edward Long, delighted by this turn of events, exulted that sugar was "so generally in use, and chiefly by the assistance of tea, that even the poor wretches living in almshouses will not be without it." By 1773, Richard Price was asserting that the "lower ranks of the people are altered in every respect for the worse, while tea, wheaten bread and other delicacies are necessaries which were formerly unknown to them." Frederick Eden, in the 1790s, bemoaned the change as bad for laborers' health, but by that time tea had been accepted as one of the necessities of life; in some parishes the very definition of poverty was the inability to buy tea and sugar. Roy Porter gives an example of one Oxfordshire laborer, near the turn of the century, who spent £2 10s., or about 20 percent of his total annual income of £31 8s., on tea and sugar. Clergyman David Davies regretted the state of affairs, but did not condemn the poor for their love of tea. After all, he wrote in *The Case of the Labourers in Husbandry* (1795), their tea was humble enough:

> Still you exclaim, Tea is a luxury. If you mean fine hyson tea, sweetened with refined sugar, and softened with cream, I readily admit it to be so. But this is not the tea of the poor. Spring water, just coloured with a few leaves of the lowest-priced tea, and sweetened with the brownest sugar . . . , is the luxury for which you reproach them.

Ironically, tea was wholesome in its own way: It forced workers to boil their often-contaminated water, thus sparing them many parasitic and bacterial illnesses.

Davies might have added adulteration to his list of the deficiencies of "the tea of the poor." Dust, twigs, sloe leaves, blackberry leaves, and "smouch" were all mixed into genuine tea by unscrupulous shopkeepers. Smouch was made by drying and baking ash tree leaves, then crushing them, steeping them in copperas and sheep's dung; Richard Twining estimated that the production of smouch in one small nine-mile area amounted to twenty tons annually. Nor were shopkeepers alone to blame. The Chinese, from whom all the tea of Austen's time was purchased, knew that people expected the best green teas to have a bluish cast, and they sometimes added Prussian blue and gypsum to their teas before shipping. There was a general perception among the tea-buying public that green teas were easier to adulterate, and over time, perhaps because of this perception, preference shifted to black teas.

Several types of both green and black teas were available in the late eighteenth and early nineteenth centuries. The black teas (which were distinguished from the green teas by being dried longer) included bohea, souchong, congo (or congou), and pekoe. Of these, bohea was the cheapest, and when duties were reduced and prices fell, it was scorned. Even the unfashionable word "bohea" was avoided by tradesmen, who began mixing it with low-quality congou and selling it as "congou kind." An anonymous 1773 poem, "Morning," expressed disdain for bohea, even before the 1784 tax cut:

> Gratefully mild, the fragrant hyson tea
> > Best pleases me, exotic teas among;
> With strong distaste I shun the harsh bohea,
> > Whose grating roughness much offends the tongue.

Pekoe was the best of the black teas, but it was not popular on its own. Rather, it was mixed with other black teas to produce tasty blends. The cheapest green tea was singlo, and other green teas (*Sand, MW* 418) included hyson, caper, Twankey, gunpowder, and bloom. Like the black teas, these were often combined in special blends. Gunpowder, for example, a high-quality tea with a rolled leaf, had too intense a flavor for many, and it was often mixed with hyson. The singlo variety bloom green, conversely, was thought to be too weak on its own and was typically mixed with other varieties of singlo. There were also some intermediate teas, dried for longer than the green teas but less than the black; these included Bing and Imperial.

The naming of teas tends to be complicated by the fact that a single tea may have several different names. As Eliot Jordan, tea buyer for Peet's Coffee and Tea, told me, "When a tea name becomes famous in China, all the producers will start using it across all different kinds of teas. . . . [E]very China tea has at least three names, and if you gather three identical teas together, they will invariably be named differently." He likens bohea to a modern Keemun black tea and says that congou is a name applied to a wide variety of Chinese black teas. Among the green teas, the name hyson still applies to a twisted, grey-green tea leaf from eastern China, while "bloom" is now not considered a specific type of tea at all. According to Mr. Jordan, it is

> a tea industry term describing the "down" or tiny fibers that form on a tea leaf bud when it is properly made. When tea is tumbled or blended the blooms comes off in a cloud of dust, sometimes resettling into little balls.

Green tea, in all its varieties, was the original tea that traveled to Europe. The origin of black tea lay in the length of the passage to England. Green tea stored in the damp holds of East India Company ships tended to grow moldy, but tea dried at hotter temperatures—black tea—kept better during transit. Mr. Jordan joked that those *really* committed to historical authenticity could simulate the effect of the voyage by "aging" the tea "in a damp basement for six months." In a more serious vein, he noted that black teas tend to have a smokier flavor, a consequence of the drying process that not all tea drinkers appreciate.

Within each kind of tea—bohea, gunpowder, and so on—there were nine different grades of quality recognized by the tea trade. A well-supplied tea dealer, then, might have as many choices as a fancy coffeehouse today. While a small village shop would have few choices on hand, a large city grocer might carry six, seven, or even nine different types of hyson, plus other varieties and a whole host of blends. In 1791, London's Brewster and Gillman carried nine grades of congou, ranging in price from 3s. 3d. to 5s. per pound; nine grades of singlo from 3s. 3d. to 9s. 6d.; and twelve types of hyson, costing from 5s. 3d. to 9s. 6d. This was a fairly typical price range. Other examples from the 1790s show prices per pound falling mostly between three and ten shillings.

Unlike many commodities, tea was never sold in the outdoor public markets. By law, it had to be sold in "entered places" such as grocers' shops or the Twinings tea shop in the Strand. China, glass, wine, and brandy merchants also sometimes sold tea. In the smaller towns and villages, a chandler's shop—which dealt in a variety of wares, including bacon and candles—might be the place where locals purchased their tea and sugar. (However, when they lived at Steventon, the Austens sent to Twinings in London for their tea.) Shops that dealt in tea needed to pay an annual fee of 5s. 6d. to be licensed by the government, so there is some record of the kinds and numbers of places that retailed tea. In the tax year 1783–84, for example, London had about 3,000 licensed tea dealers, the larger towns of England and Wales about 7,000 more, and the small towns and villages an additional 24,000. The total number of tea dealers in 1783 was 32,754, a figure that rose to 48,263 by 1787 and to 56,248 by 1801. Of course, there may have been many more individuals selling smuggled tea without paying the license fee.

Once purchased, tea was kept in a locked chest or closet, partly to prevent pilfering and partly to monitor the supply for fear of running out. It was drunk both at breakfast (*NA* 175) and at the close of the afternoon; the idea of "tea" as a distinct meal was yet to evolve, but already the ceremony of drinking tea and perhaps eating a little something was fully entrenched as a way of ending the afternoon and beginning the evening (*Wat, MW* 354; *NA* 118; *S&S* 99, 106, 166; *P&P* 68, 160, 166; *MP* 104, 177, 180, 227; *E* 8, 209, 210, 311, 382–83). Tea was "brought in" or "handed round" at a specified interval after the beginning of dinner, typically about three hours, which allowed plenty of time for a leisurely meal and either a walk or some after-dinner conversation (*Sand, MW* 390–91). The Edwardses, in *The Watsons*, drink their tea at 7:00 P.M. (*MW* 326); the Watsons appear to drink it at about the same time, as they are sitting at tea when a guest calls on his way "home to an 8 o'clock dinner" (*MW* 355). Tea might also be enjoyed at evening social events (*Wat, MW* 332; *NA* 21, 23, 25; *P* 189) such as parties, dances, and concerts; at a "fete" at Kingston Hall in 1791, the hostess, Frances Bankes, served orgeat (a barley or almond-based drink), lemonade, two types of negus, and tea. Though tea was usually drunk indoors, the great public gardens at Ranelagh and Vauxhall had given people a taste for taking their tea outside as well. Accordingly, people who could afford to indulge in landscaping often added little buildings to their gardens in which they could serve tea and partake of the surrounding scenery (*E* 27). By the 1810s, tearooms had sprung up in resort towns to free travelers from the necessity of preparing the beverage in their lodgings; like a good circulating library and a sizable ballroom, the tearoom became an indispensable attraction for a tourist town.

When tea was made at home, servants (*MP* 180) would bring in the "tea things" so often mentioned by Austen (*Wat, MW* 326, 355; *MP* 335, 379, 383). These included cups (*MP* 439), which for much of the eighteenth century had no handles—hence the expression "a dish of tea," which became a vulgarism by the end of Austen's life (*Wat, MW* 326; *MP* 379). Saucers (*MP* 439) and spoons were also provided; when a drinker had finished, he or she was supposed to place the spoon in or across the cup to signal that no more tea was desired. On occasion, the spoons themselves were numbered, so that the hostess could return the appropriate cup to each guest after refilling it. Lumps of sugar were retrieved from a bowl with a small set of tongs, and, in any household that could afford it, milk or cream would be offered as well. The hostess brewed the tea herself (*Wat, MW* 319; *S&S* 98, 163; *P&P* 341; *MP* 219, 335, 344), either in a teapot or in an urn (*MP* 344), a large metal container shaped rather like a Greek vase. The water inside the urn was kept hot either by a charcoal fire in the base or by inserting a red-hot cylindrical piece of metal. While lovely ceramic teapots figure in many engravings and oil paintings of the era, the urn was for many people of Austen's time the definitive symbol of tea.

OTHER HOT DRINKS

Like coffee, tea, and chocolate, other hot drinks were associated with specific purposes or times of day. For example, "caudle" was a warm drink composed of oatmeal, mild spices, water, and wine or ale; it was considered especially appropriate for invalids and for postpartum women. Negus, on the other hand, was associated with late-night parties, particularly balls held during the winter, when dancers might need a warming beverage between periods of activity,* It was made with white wine, red wine, or port mixed with lemon juice, and spices. Maggie Lane states that it was also made without sugar but with calf's-foot jelly and mixed about twenty minutes before serving to allow the jelly to melt; other recipes, such as Mrs. Beeton's from a half-century later, leave out the jelly and add the sugar.

WINE

Because wine grapes grew poorly in the English climate, almost all of the nation's grape-derived wine (*S&S* 185; *E* 130, 213, 329) was imported from the Continent. From France came Burgundies, claret (light red wines, specifically those of Bordeaux—see *J&A*, *MW* 18, 23; *MP* 47), champagne (which at this date might be either red or white and was likely to be bubble-free), and Frontignac (a sweet wine from southern France). Port (*P&P* 76) came from Portugal (hence its name), sherry and alicant from Spain, and Chian from the Greek island of Chios. The sweet, expensive Muscat known as Constantia (*S&S* 197) came from South Africa, while Canary sack and Madeira (*MP* 74; *E* 365) were named for the islands that produced them. "Mountain" was a sweet white wine from Malaga, while "Rhenish" hailed from the Rhine region. Many of the favorite wines were fortified with brandy for increased alcohol content. Port, for instance, had just undergone a revolution in the 1770s; new bottling technology allowed it to mature for ten to fifteen years, instead of the previous three or four, and the richer wines that resulted were extremely popular. Marsala, too, a sweet Sicilian wine, was fortified with brandy.†

However, though the English had to import their best grape wines, they themselves produced wines from other fruit, including gooseberries, currants, apricots, orange, elderberries, and quince; the Austens made gooseberry, orange, and currant wines, sometimes from homegrown, sometimes from purchased fruit. Their friend Alethea Bigg was well known for her orange wine, the recipe for which Jane requested in January 1817. Orange wine was typically made in

---

*Although Parson Woodforde drank white wine negus at an inn in Sherborne at 11:00 A.M. on August 3, 1789.

†Frederick Accum, in 1820, printed statistics on the alcohol content of various alcoholic beverages. Madeira, he said, averaged 22.27 percent alcohol by volume; port 22.96 percent; white Constantia 19.75 percent, red Constantia 18.92 percent, red Madeira 20.35 percent, Cape Madeira 20.51 percent, claret 15.1 percent, Malmsey Madeira 16.4 percent, gooseberry wine 11.84 percent, elder wine 9.87 percent, mead 7.82 percent, and brandy 53.39 percent.

John Bull and his Friends Commemorating the Peace, 1802. The Peace of Amiens was greeted with hopes that high prices would fall and food would once again be plentiful. John Bull celebrates with (roughly left to right) a sirloin, a mug of stout, a loaf of "The Best Wheaten Bread," mutton, hops, a potato, double Gloucester cheese, "Excellent Fresh Butter," rum, port, Cognac, and unadulterated flour. (Courtesy of the Lewis Walpole Library, Yale University. 802.3.0.1.)

the winter, when Seville oranges were in season, and shifted into casks in the summer. The English also created *faux* versions of Continental wines—a useful skill when enemy blockades disrupted supply. Contemporary cookbooks feature recipes for mountain wine, Cyprus wine, Frontignac, sack, and champagne, most of which involved steeping imported raisins for several days, then fermenting the strained liquid. Another home-brewed drink, mead, was made by fermenting honey. The Austens kept bees at both Steventon and Chawton, and they were fond of mead, despite the fact that it was losing favor in the nation as a whole. Recipes for mead varied widely; some included the sorts of spices we associate with mulled wine or cider, such as nutmeg, mace, and cloves, while others used green herbs such as marjoram, thyme, or rosemary.

Wine was most often served during dinner, especially during the dessert course (*Wat, MW* 325; *S&S* 355). Neighbors sitting near each other drank toasts together, and the men tended to pour the wine for the ladies. These ladies kept their consumption to a minimum and then retired and allowed the men to get down to the serious drinking, which concluded when they joined the women in the drawing room for tea and coffee. Austen also records in her letters drinking wine at parties and, mixed with water (*MP* 66; *E* 25, 365), after returning home from the theater. Her character Catherine Morland, imitating her creator, drinks "warm wine and water" at bedtime (*NA* 29).

It was the sunset of a hard-drinking age; Admiral Lord Thomas Cochrane, looking back on his youthful years in the Navy, remembered being a relatively sober youth among bibulous companions. He attempted to keep from getting drunk by tipping some of his wine down his sleeve, was detected, and narrowly escaped the standard punishment of having to drink a bottle all by himself. Men often measured their wine consumption in bottles rather than glasses (*NA* 63, 64; *P&P* 20), and wine—imported wine at least—was usually more alcoholic than it is today. Parson Woodforde records substantial consumption of alcohol at his annual tithe dinners, where he entertained parishioners on a fairly lavish scale in order to console them for having to give him a share of their produce. At a typical dinner, he might have fifteen or so farmers as his guests, who would drink, in the course of the evening, copious amounts of beer, plus four to six bottles of port wine and about eight bottles of rum. As for Woodforde himself, he recorded in August 1790 that he was reducing his personal consumption of port, for health reasons, from a pint a day to a mere "2. or 3. Glasses."

Austen was well aware of the bibulousness of her age. On November 20, 1800, she called her own overindulgence in wine at Hurstborne a "venial error" and mentioned it only because the aftereffects—was she hung over?—seemed to be affecting her handwriting. She also frequently comments in her novels and letters on the drunkenness of others. The most sustained example of drunkenness in her works is *Jack & Alice,* a humorous early work in which the main characters are nearly always three sheets to the wind. They are variously "Dead Drunk" (*MW* 14), "a little addicted to the Bottle" (13), "heated by wine (no uncommon case)" (15), "dead drunk" again (19), overly fond of claret (18, 23), or overly fond of liquor in general (23). Alice's brother Jack dies of drink (25), while her father is "a drunken old Dog to be sure" (25). Most of the humor of *Jack & Alice* comes from the ridiculousness of a family resorting quite so freely to the bottle—no one in Austen's own family could have supposed this a realistic portrait—but imagine a young woman in 1860 or 1880 drawing a light, comic portrayal of alcoholism and its fatal consequences. Such levity would not have been acceptable in Queen Victoria's day, and Austen's casual jocularity says a great deal about how much heavy drinking was tolerated in her own time. Indeed, even as a product of the rowdy Georgian age, she often voices disapproval of drinking (*MP* 426). Fanny Price's father comes in for some of her strongest condemnation; Fanny is "sadly pained by his language and his smell of spirits" (*MP* 380), and the narrator, not pained but simply disgusted, concludes, "he swore and he drank, he was dirty and gross" (*MP* 389).

Wine was sometimes bought in bottles (which were occasionally disguised with a false crust around the neck to simulate age), but it was also bought in large quantities and bottled at home. Parson Woodforde, for example, would buy a quarter of a pipe of port at a time from his wine merchant (*Col Let, MW* 158), Mr. Priest. (A pipe equaled 105 imperial gallons, or 131.25 U.S. gallons, so Woodforde was buying enough port to fill a sizable fish tank.) Then it was decanted into a decorative container, and a label made of silver, enamel, or ceramic was hung around the neck of the decanter to identify its contents. This method of labeling wine would last until the late nineteenth century and the advent of printed paper labels that identified the wine and its vintage. If there was a butler in the home, it would be his job to bottle, store, and serve the wine, as well as to care for the decanters and glasses.

Wine was used as an ingredient in food and in mixed drinks such as the caudle described above. Another mixed drink containing wine was the syllabub, a mixture of milk or cream and wine. Traditionally made with milk fresh from the cow and served on the spot, it was by Austen's time a drink prepared beforehand. The frothed milk or cream was separated and allowed to stand and drain, then replaced over the "thin." The contrast between the translucent mixture at the bottom of the glass and the stiff, long-lasting foam at the top was the chief attraction of a syllabub.

BEER

Beer and ale are less present in Austen's works than wine, although beer was, along with tea, one of England's most popular drinks. Historically, it had been brewed at home, supplying much the same place at the table that water would now; servants typically drank at least a quart a day. Mrs. Austen brewed beer at Steventon in the last years of the eighteenth century and at Chawton cottage many years later. But home brewing was slowly being overtaken by commercial brewing. In 1788, a total of nearly 5 million barrels were produced by common brewers and brewing victuallers such as innkeepers and publicans, and 9 million barrels were produced at home. By 1800, commercial and domestic brewers were producing roughly equal volumes, and by 1815 home brewing had fallen behind.

Several types of beer and ale were made. Ale and beer were divided into "strong," "table," and "small" varieties, differentiated from each other by alcohol content*; an 1806 letter written by Jane's mother at Stoneleigh describes the mansion's "strong beer" and "small beer" cellars. Pubs might offer a cheap brown ale, a more heavily hopped brown ale, and an expensive, high-quality pale ale; when the three types were mixed together in one glass, the resulting concoction was known as "three threads." A very dark, heavily hopped, bitter, high-alcohol beer was introduced in 1722; soon thereafter, it became known as "porter" because of its popularity with London porters. It was popular with brewers, too, because the dark color and strong taste hid impurities. They built enormous production vats; the Meux brewery, in 1795, had a vat that could hold 20,000 barrels (almost 750,000 gallons). Much to the brewers' chagrin, in the late eighteenth century, pale ales came back into fashion.

This is Your Sort!—Here's to ye, 1794. The foaming tankard of beer—every Englishman's birthright. (Courtesy of the Lewis Walpole Library, Yale University. 794.6.4.1.)

Brewing beer, like baking bread or making wine, was a delicate business subject to the vagaries of bacteria. Since the science of fermentation was poorly understood, brewers had few tools, such as the thermometer (in use by commercial brewers from the 1780s) and the saccharometer (which measured alcohol content and thus helped to demonstrate how much fermentation had taken place). However, things could and did go wrong, and most specialized brewing knowledge took the form of damage control. Was the beer cloudy? Add isinglass (a gelatin derived from fish) to "fine" it, that is, to remove impurities. Was the beer sour? Add six special compound balls to each barrel; their marble, oyster shells, or chalk would reduce acidity, while their isinglass and bean flour would act as refining agents. Did it taste bad in general? Add spices. Was it too pale? Toss in some tobacco, treacle, or licorice. Was the head not frothy enough? Add some "beer-heading," a combination of green vitriol, alum, and salt.

Some of these processes were benign. Others were truly dangerous, such as the addition of black extract. This was made by boiling *cocculus indicus* into, in

---

*Frederick Accum, writing in 1820, estimated the alcohol content of various beers and ales as Burton ale, 8.88 percent alcohol; Edinburgh ale, 6.2 percent, Dorchester ale, 5.5 percent; brown stout, 6.8 percent; London porter, 4.2 percent; and London small beer, 1.28 percent. Beer brewed in the countryside tended to be less alcoholic than beer brewed in London.

Frederick Accum's words, "a stiff black tenacious mass, possessing, in a high degree, the narcotic and intoxicating quality of the poisonous berry from which it is prepared"; *cocculus indicus* berries contain a convulsive poison called picrotoxin which can be used to stun fish and kill lice.

Opium, tobacco, poppy extract, and *nux vomica* were also used to make beer seem stronger; the last of these was a bitter tree seed that contained strychnine. Porter, the easiest of the beers to adulterate, was supposed to be made of browned malt and three pounds of hops to every thirty-six gallons of liquid. The hops added a bitter flavor and also acted as a preservative. However, hops were expensive, and pale malt was cheaper than brown, so commercial brewers made a paler, weaker brew and resorted to various stratagems to disguise it as genuine porter. To color the porter, brewers added caramelized sugar; to give it a bitter flavor, they added poisonous wormwood or quassia, the bitter, narcotic derivative of a Jamaican tree. Capsicum, grains of paradise, ginger, coriander, and orange peel were also used as flavorings. Sulphuric acid was added to "bring beer forward," that is, to simulate eighteen months' aging in much less time.

One form of beer was made neither with barley nor with hops but with spruce tree needles. This was the spruce beer, more similar in spirit to root beer than to ale, that Frank Churchill copied a recipe for. It was made from the tips of spruce branches, boiled in water, sweetened with molasses, and mixed with yeast.

SPIRITS

Gin, brandy, and rum were the most widely drunk types of hard liquor (*MP* 4); each, according to Frederick Accum in 1820, was more than 50 percent alcohol by volume. Gin, also known as "Hollands" or "Geneva," was made domestically and had acquired a fairly nasty reputation earlier in the century, when its low price and wide availability occasioned Britain's first major urban drug crisis. Dram shops had advertised that a person could get drunk for a penny and dead drunk for twopence; rooms with straw on the floor were provided for those who wanted to pay a little extra to have a place to sleep off their liquor. The crisis was eventually controlled by the imposition of taxes that raised the price of gin. Taxation made it harder to acquire cheap gin, but not impossible, as illegal distilleries were happy to supply their customers "by moonshine." Parson Woodforde was an avid customer; in 1781 he drank "some smuggled gin which I liked." On 1792 he noted that a local gin smuggler had received a light punishment from some excise officers, and on March 7, 1794, he "had 2. Tubbs of Geneva brought me this Evening by Moonshine, 4. Gallons each Tub."

Brandy came from abroad, principally from France, and was also a popular item with smugglers. On December 29, 1786, Woodforde recorded,

> Had another Tub of Gin and another of the best Coniac Brandy brought me this Evening ab^t 9. We heard a thump at the front Door about that time, but did not know what it was, till I went out and found the 2 Tubs— but nobody there.

Rum came from even further away. It was a by-product of the West Indian sugar industry, and since Britain had quite a number of sugar colonies, rum was fairly cheap. The liquor fermented from leftover molasses formed the basis of grog, the sailor's typical drink afloat, a mixture of rum, water, and lime juice. Ashore, rum was mixed up as punch, a popular drink at all festive occasions, but especially when men got together for club events. Woodforde typically used two bottles of rum to make each large bowl of punch. He also drank rum outside his house; a glass of rum and water (*MP* 387) cost him threepence at a local inn in May 1794.

Let us all be Unhappy together, Cruikshank, 1791. The punch bowl and ladle were essential elements of many celebrations and of the meetings of men's clubs. Scenes around punch bowls were common in eighteenth- and early nineteenth-century prints; what is unusual about this image is that it also shows a man on the left relieving himself in a chamber pot.

CHOCOLATE

(Raffald, Rundell)

At nine in the morning we meet and say our prayers in a handsome Chapel, the pulpit, etc., now hung with black. Then follows breakfast consisting of chocolate, coffee and tea, plum cake, pound cake, hot rolls, cold rolls, bread and butter, and dry toast for me. (Letter of Mrs. Austen, August 13, 1806, from the mansion at Stoneleigh)

The breakfast was such as best breakfasts then were: some variety of bread, hot rolls, buttered toast, tongue or ham and eggs. The addition of chocolate at one end of the table, and the wedding cake in the middle, marked the speciality of the day . . . . (from Caroline Austen's description of the wedding of Anna Austen and Ben Lefroy at Steventon, 1814)

Bring up some Chocolate immediately; Spread a Cloth in the dining Parlour, and carry in the venison pasty—. In the mean time let the Gentleman have some sandwiches, and bring in a Basket of Fruit—Send up some Ices and a bason of Soup, and do not forget some Jellies and Cakes. . . . The Chocolate, The Sandwiches, the Jellies, the Cakes, the Ice, and the Soup soon made their appearance . . . . (*Evelyn, MW* 182)

He took his own Cocoa from the Tray,— . . . & turning completely to the Fire, sat coddling and cooling it to his own satisfaction. . . . When his Toils were over however, he moved back his Chair into as gallant a Line as ever, & proved that he had not been working only for himself, by his earnest invitation to her to take both Cocoa & Toast.—She was already helped to Tea— which surprised him—so totally self-engrossed had he been.—"I thought I should have been in time, said he, but cocoa takes a great deal of Boiling."— "I am much obliged to you, replied Charlotte—but I prefer Tea." "Then I will help myself, said he.—A large Dish of rather weak Cocoa every evening, agrees with me better than any thing."—It struck her however, as he poured out this rather weak Cocoa, that it came forth in a very fine, dark coloured stream—and at the same moment, his Sisters both crying out—"Oh! Arthur, you get your Cocoa stronger & stronger every Even[s]"—(*Sand, MW* 416–17)

The General, between his cocoa and his newspaper, had luckily no leisure for noticing her. (*NA* 203)

Raffald's recipe for boiled cocoa can be made either with water, as she specifies, or with milk; during Austen's lifetime it might be made with either. For the simpler version, use unsweetened powdered cocoa. Hannah Glasse's recipes for turning cacao beans into solid chocolate, however, make use of anise, cinnamon, almonds, pistachios, achiote (for coloring), musk, ambergris, nutmeg, vanilla, and cardamom seed. To give your cocoa some of these flavors, try the optional ingredients.

Raffald's recipe results in an incredibly thick and fairly bitter beverage, more like a chocolate syrup than modern hot cocoa. Maria Rundell, writing several years after Raffald, adapts chocolate and makes it a more recognizable beverage, largely for the purpose of economy; Raffald's chocolate would have been quite expensive to enjoy on a regular basis. The synthesized modern recipe below allows you to adapt Raffald and Rundell to your own personal tastes.

Raffald's Recipe

Scrape four ounces of chocolate and pour a quart of boiling water upon it, mill it well with a chocolate mill and sweeten it to your taste. Give it a boil and let it stand all night, then mill it again very well. Boil it two minutes, then mill it till it will leave a froth upon the top of your cups.

Rundell's Recipe

Cut a cake of chocolate in very small bits; put a pint of water into the pot, and when it boils, put in the above; mill it off the fire until quite melted, then on a gentle fire till it boil; pour it into a basin, and it will keep in a cool place eight or ten days, or more.

When wanted, put a spoonful or two into milk, boil it with sugar, and mill it well.

This, if not made thick, is a very good breakfast or supper.

 ## MODERN RECIPE (Raffald)

⅓ cup unsweetened baking cocoa or 1 oz. unsweetened baking chocolate	**Spice mix (optional)** pinch anise seed
⅓ cup sugar	2 pinches cinnamon
1 to 1½ cups water or milk	3 blanched almond slivers
	pinch achiote
	2 pinches ground nutmeg
	¼ tsp. vanilla
	pinch ground cardamom

If you are using the solid baking chocolate, grate it finely and place it in a heatproof bowl.

Continued on next page

Continued from previous page

In a saucepan, bring the water or milk to a boil. Remove it from the heat and add the cocoa and sugar, whisking to combine the ingredients. Add the spice mix, if you are using it, and whisk that in as well.

Return the cocoa to the stove and boil gently for 2 minutes, stirring or whisking frequently. Do not let the cocoa boil over. Remove from heat, whisk again, and serve. If you are using it as an ingredient in Rundell's chocolate, you may either use it immediately or refrigerate for later use.

 ## MODERN RECIPE (Rundell)

1 recipe **chocolate** (Raffald recipe)   1 cup milk per serving

Heat the milk in a saucepan, stirring constantly to keep it from scalding. Add 2 to 3 T of Raffald's chocolate per serving. Serve as soon as the chocolate is hot. If you have an antique-style chocolate pot, you can use the wand in its lid to froth the chocolate before serving.

 # NEGUS

(Mrs. Beeton, *Book of Household Management*, 1861)

As Tom Musgrave was seen no more, we may suppose his plan to have succeeded, & imagine him mortifying with his Barrel of Oysters, in dreary solitude—or gladly assisting the Landlady in her Bar to make fresh Negus for the happy Dancers above. (*Wat, MW* 336)

. . . she had only to rise and, with Mr. Crawford's very cordial adieus, pass quietly away; stopping at the entrance door, like the Lady of Branxholm Hall, "one moment and no more," to view the happy scene, and take a last look at the five or six determined couple, who were still hard at work—and then, creeping slowly up the principal staircase, feverish with hopes and fears, soup and negus, sore-footed and fatigued, restless and agitated, yet feeling, in spite of every thing, that a ball was indeed delightful. (*MP* 280–81)

This is a recipe from 1861, certainly later than the period under consideration. However, most negus recipes are fairly consistent and vary only slightly in the spicing. The most surprising thing about this negus recipe is the expectation that this alcoholic beverage will be consumed primarily by children.

1 pint port wine
1 quart boiling water
¼ lb. sugar
1 lemon
grated nutmeg to taste

As this beverage is more usually drunk at children's parties than at any other, the wine need not be very old or expensive for the purpose, a new fruity wine answering very well for it. Put the wine into a jug, rub some lumps of sugar (equal to ¼ lb.) on the lemon-rind until all the yellow part of the skin is absorbed, then squeeze the juice, and strain it. Add the sugar and lemon-juice to the port wine, with the grated nutmeg; pour over it the boiling water, cover the jug, and, when the beverage has cooled a little, it will be fit for use. Negus may also be made of sherry, or any other sweet white wine, but is more usually made of port than of any other beverage.

MODERN RECIPE

Beeton's quantities may be used as written. Zest the lemon and finely chop the zest; then use a mortar and pestle, if you have one, to bruise it with 2 T of the sugar. In a bowl, mix the port, all the sugar, the lemon peel, and the grated nutmeg. Pour in the boiling water and serve when cool enough to drink.

WINE

Let me know when you begin the new Tea—& the new white wine. (Letter from Jane to Cassandra, September 23, 1813)

At 7 we set off in a Coach for the Lyceum—were at home again in about 4 hours and ½—had Soup & wine & water, & then went to our Holes. (Letter from Jane to Cassandra, September 15, 1813)

Henry desires Edward may know that he has just bought 3 dozen of Claret for him (Cheap) & ordered it to be sent down to Chawton. (Letter from Jane to Cassandra, May 24, 1813)

One evening, Alice finding herself somewhat heated by wine (no very un-common case) determined to seek a relief for her disordered Head & Love-sick Heart in the Conversation of the intelligent Lady Williams. (*J&A*, *MW* 15)

MISS F. Will no one allow me the honour of helping them? Then John take away the Pudding & bring the Wine.
[SERVANTS *take away the things and bring in the Bottles & Glasses*.]
LORD F. I wish we had any Desert to offer you. But my Grandmother in her Lifetime, destroyed the Hothouse in order to build a receptacle for the Turkies with it's materials; & we have never been able to raise another tolerable one.
LADY H. I beg you will make no apologies my Lord.
WILLOUGHBY. Come Girls, let us circulate the Bottle. (*Visit*, *MW* 53–54)

"He . . . has lived very well in his time, I dare say; he is not gouty for noth-ing. Does he drink his bottle a-day now?"

"His bottle a-day!—no. Why should you think such a thing? He is a very temperate man, and you could not fancy him in liquor last night?"

"Lord help you!—You women are always thinking of men's being in liquor. Why you do not suppose a man is overset by a bottle? I am sure of *this*—that if every body was to drink their bottle a-day, there would not be half the disorders in the world there are now. It would be a famous good thing for us all." (*NA* 63)

And yet I have heard that there is a great deal of wine drank in Oxford. (*NA* 64)

Let me call your maid. Is there nothing you could take, to give you present re-lief ?—A glass of wine;—shall I get you one ?—You are very ill. (*P&P* 276)

Mr. Crawford's being his guest was an excuse for drinking claret every day. (*MP* 47)

And I declare if she is not gone away without finishing her wine! And the dried cherries too! (*S&S* 194)

To say the truth Nerves are the worst part of my Complaints in *my* opinion. My Sisters think me Bilious, but I doubt it. . . . If I were Bilious, he contin-ued, you know Wine w^d disagree with me, but it always does me good. The more Wine I drink (in Moderation) the better I am.—I am always best of an Even^g.—(*Sand*, *MW* 415)

Mrs. Goddard, what say you to *half* a glass of wine? A small half glass—put into a tumbler of water? (*E* 25)

She believed he had been drinking too much of Mr. Weston's good wine, and felt sure he would want to be talking nonsense. (*E* 129)

If you are serving a breakfast, wine is not appropriate. At a luncheon or picnic, watered wine, or small quantities of fruit wine or mead may be served. For dinners, Madeira, claret, port, and the sweeter white wines are historically accurate; fruit wines are less common but not unknown. The quantity of wine drunk at supper, if supper was served, diminished, and wine was often merely an ingredient in a warm beverage such as a posset or caudle.

MEAD

(Woodforde)

I am so pleased that the Mead is brewed! (Letter from Jane to Cassandra, March 9, 1814)

> LADY H.   I assure you my Lord, Sir Arthur never touches wine; but Sophy will toss off a bumper I am sure to oblige your Lordship.
> LORD F.   Elder wine or mead, Miss Hampton? (*Visit, MW* 53)

The following recipe comes from Parson Woodforde's diary, October 20, 1794. Make sure to sterilize your fermenting container and utensils with a sterilizing solution (available at brewing shops) to prevent contamination by wild yeasts that can spoil the flavor of your mead.

Busy most part of the Afternoon in making some Mead Wine, to fourteen Pound of Honey, I put four Gallons of Water, boiled it more than an hour with Ginger and two handfulls of dried Elder-Flowers in it, and skimmed it well. Then put it into a small Tub to cool, and when almost cold I put in a large gravey-Spoon full of fresh Yeast, keeping it in a warm place, the Kitchen during night.

MODERN RECIPE

14 lbs. clover honey

4 gallons water

2 cups dried elder flowers

6" to 8" peeled fresh ginger, cut crosswise into $\frac{1}{2}$" sections

1 packet dried ale yeast

Continued on next page

Continued from previous page

In a six-gallon pot (or in multiple stock pots), boil the honey, water, elder flowers, and ginger for 1 hour. Turn off the heat on the stove. Fill a deep sink, cooler, galvanized tub, or other container with ice water, and set the pot(s) in the water to bring down the temperature of the honey mixture. Use a thermometer to monitor the temperature; brewing supply stores often carry floating thermometers that are very easy to use.

Fill a one-cup measuring cup half-full with warm (105°F to 110°F) water. Stir in the dry yeast and let it sit for about 15 minutes. If the yeast develops a light, foamy layer at the top, it is active and can be used.

When the honey mixture has reached a temperature of 72°F to 78°F, put the yeast into a six-gallon fermenting container such as a food-grade plastic bucket with an airlock lid. Pour in the honey mixture and stir gently for a minute or two. Then seal the lid, fill the airlock about half full with water, and set the bucket in a warm place to ferment.

Fermentation has begun when bubbles can be seen moving through the airlock. Leave the mead in the fermenter for 1 month. Then rack it off into another sanitized fermenter (see **gooseberry wine**, below, for the racking technique). Rack monthly until sediment stops forming and bubbling ceases entirely. This may take up to 6 months.

Sanitize bottles. I use large bottles with ceramic and rubber-gasket pressure seals, but you may wish to use wine-bottling equipment, wine bottles, and corks. Sanitize tubing and a bottle filler and fill the clean, dry bottles with mead. Cork or seal and store the mead in a cool, dark place until you are ready to drink it.

GOOSEBERRY WINE

(Glasse)

MISS F. This, Ladies & Gentlemen is some of my dear Grandmother's own manufacture. She excelled in Gooseberry Wine. (*Visit, MW* 54)

Home winemaking has come a long way since Glasse's day; this recipe makes use of some modern additives such as supplementary acids and Campden tablets and has a much higher chance of success than Glasse's.

Gather your gooseberries in dry weather, when they are half ripe, pick them, and bruise a peck in a tub, with a wooden mallet; then take a horse-hair cloth and press them as much as possible, without breaking the seeds; when you have pressed out all the juice, to every gallon of gooseberries put three pounds of fine dry powder sugar, stir it all together till the sugar is dissolved, then put it in a vessel or cask, which must be quite full: if ten or twelve gallons, let it stand a fortnight; if a twenty gallon cask, five weeks. Set it in a cool place, then draw it off from the lees, clear the vessel of the lees, and pour in the clear liquor again: if it be a ten gallon cask, let it stand three months; if a twenty gallon, four months; then bottle it off.

MODERN RECIPE

6 lbs. gooseberries, fresh or canned	¼ tsp. wine tannin
6 lbs. white sugar	1¼ tsp. pectic enzyme powder
2½ gallons warm water	3 Campden tablets, crushed
2½ tsp. winemakers' acid blend (citric, malic, and tartaric acids)	1 package Champagne yeast
2½ tsp. yeast nutrient	1½ tsp. potassium sorbate (stabilizer)

Sanitize all equipment: a primary fermenter, a fruit straining bag, a spoon, and a hydrometer. Let them air-dry.

Place a fruit-straining bag in the bottom of the fermenter, open it wide, and spoon in the gooseberries. If you are using fresh gooseberries, you will need to crush them to release their juice. Tie off the bag at the top.

Bring the sugar and water to a boil over high heat, making sure the sugar is fully dissolved. Remove the sugar-water from the heat and pour in into the fermenter over the fruit. Let the liquid cool to room temperature.

Add the acid blend, yeast nutrient, pectic enzyme powder, tannin, and Campden tablets. Stir to dissolve the additives. Cover the fermenter for 12 hours with a clean, damp cloth.

Add activated yeast and re-cover the fermenter. Every day for a week, stir the "must"—the fruit-sugar liquid—gently, being careful not to disturb the sediment forming at the bottom of the fermenter.

At the end of the week, pull the fruit straining bag out of the fermenter and allow the excess liquid to drain back into the fermenter. Do not squeeze the fruit. Remove the bag, re-cover the fermenter, and let the must rest for 12 hours.

Fill a sanitized siphon hose with water and hold your thumbs over the open ends. Place the primary fermenter on a shelf or counter above the secondary fermenter. Immerse one end of the siphon into the must and place the other end at the bottom of the secondary fermenter. Allow both ends of the siphon to open by removing your thumbs, and the must will begin to flow from one con-

Continued on next page

Continued from previous page

tainer to the other. This is called "racking." Rack most of the liquid, making sure not to capture any of the sediment at the bottom of the primary fermenter. Add water, if necessary, to bring the total liquid volume back up to 3 gallons. Cover the secondary fermenter with a sanitized lid and airlock.

Every 30 days thereafter, rack the wine. When no new sediment has formed in the previous month, the wine is nearly ready to bottle. Add the stabilizer and re-cover the fermenter for 10 days. When the 10 days have elapsed, sanitize a siphon and bottling wand, as well as the bottles you will be using. Bottle the wine and cork it. (Tools for this, as well as the other special tools and ingredients in the recipe, can be found at brewing and winemaking supply stores in many cities and online.)

ELDER WINE

(Carter)

LADY H. I assure you my Lord, Sir Arthur never touches wine; but Sophy
           will toss off a bumper I am sure to oblige your Lordship.
LORD F. Elder wine or mead, Miss Hampton?
SOPHY. If it is equal to you Sir, I should prefer some warm ale with a toast
           and nutmeg.
LORD F. Two glasses of warmed ale with a toast and nutmeg. (*Visit, MW*
           53)

An 1800 illustration reproduced by Dorothy Hartley shows street vendors selling cold ginger beer and hot elder wine. Modern recipes for elderberry wine often include spices or even raisins, but Carter's recipe is more bare-bones. The only modern touches are a few chemical additives designed to improve the outcome of the winemaking process.

When the elder-berries are ripe, pick them, and put them into a stone jar: set them in boiling water, or a slack oven, till the jar is as warm as you can well bear to touch it with your hands; then strain the fruit through a coarse cloth, squeezing them hard, and pour the liquor into a kettle. Put it on the fire, let it boil, and to every quart of liquor add a pound of Lisbon sugar, and skim it often. Then let it settle, pour it off into a jar, and cover it close.

MODERN RECIPE

1 lb. dried elderberries

2½ lbs. white sugar

1 gallon water

1 tsp. yeast nutrient

1½ tsp. winemakers' acid mix (citric, malic, and tartaric acids)

1 Campden tablet, crushed

½ tsp. pectic enzyme

1 package wine yeast

1½ tsp. stabilizer

Sanitize all utensils, including the primary fermenter, fruit straining bag, and rubber gloves for handling the berries. (The use of rubber gloves is advised to prevent the transfer of bacteria or wild yeasts from your hands to the wine.)

Place the berries in a large bowl with 3 quarts of water. Let them sit, covered, for at least 4 hours. Strain the liquid into the primary fermenter and place the fruit in the fruit straining bag. Tie the bag off and place it in the fermenter.

On the stove, bring the water and sugar to a boil. Pour this hot liquid into the fermenter over the fruit juice and bag. Cover with a damp, clean cloth, and let the liquid cool to room temperature. Add the yeast nutrient, acid mix, and Campden tablet powder. Re-cover and let the liquid sit for 12 hours.

Add the pectic enzyme powder. Re-cover and let sit for 12 more hours. Add the yeast, following the package directions for preparing the yeast. Re-cover.

Ferment for 2 weeks, stirring daily, being careful not to disturb the sediment at the bottom. Remove the fruit straining bag, allowing liquid to drip back into the fermenter (but not squeezing the bag). Seal with a sanitized lid and airlock and store in a cool, dark place.

Every 30 to 60 days, rack the wine, which means transferring it to a new, sanitized container, and leaving any sediment behind. (See **gooseberry wine** for method.) Top up the liquid volume by adding water. After 6 months of this, add stabilizer. Wait 10 days. Rack the wine one more time, add sugar to taste, and bottle. Store the bottles for six months to a year before drinking.

❀ WHIPT SYLLABUBS ❀

(Farley)

. . . my Sister came running to me in the Store-room with her face as White as a Whipt syllabub, and told me that Hervey had been thrown from his Horse, had fractured his Scull and was pronounced by his Surgeon to be in the most emminent Danger. (*Lesley, MW* 113)

His heart . . . was as delicate as sweet and as tender as a Whipt-syllabub. . . .
(*Lesley, MW* 117)

This recipe, to my mind, tastes better with white wine than with red, but eighteenth-century cooks couldn't resist an opportunity to present diners with a contrast of some kind. In this case, the creamy alcohol-scented topping contrasts with the thin wine beneath, and the glasses of white-wine syllabubs would have stood near their red-wine counterparts, offering a contrast of colors as well as textures. Modern whipping cream does not seem to require the straining specified by Farley and other cookbook authors, especially given the efficiency of electric mixers and food processors.

Rub a lump of loaf sugar on the outside of a lemon, put it into a pint of thin cream, and sweeten it to your taste. Then put in the juice of a lemon, and a glass of Madeira wine, or French brandy. Mill it to a froth with a chocolate mill, and take it off as it rises, and lay it into a hair sieve. Then fill one half of your posset-glasses a little more than half full with white wine, and the other half of your glasses a little more than half full with red wine. Then lay on your froth as high as you can; but take care that it be well drained on your sieve, otherwise it will mix with your wine, and your syllabub will be thereby spoiled.

 ## MODERN RECIPE

1 T white sugar	½ cup Madeira or brandy
½ T brown sugar	1 bottle white wine
zest of one lemon	1 bottle red wine
2 cups whipping cream	

With a mixer or a food processor's whisk attachment, whip the sugars, lemon zest, cream, and Madeira or brandy for about 3 to 5 minutes, or until the cream is well whipped and soft peaks form.

Pour the red and white wines into transparent glasses, to within about an inch of the top, and spoon about ¼ cup of the flavored whipped cream on top of each glass of wine. Use a second spoon to slide the cream off your spoon and into the glass, because otherwise you will be tempted to shake or tap the spoon to remove the cream, and either of these latter methods will result in the cream becoming partially mixed with the wine.

PORTER

(Millington)

"I understand you," he replied, with an expressive smile, and a voice perfectly calm, "yes, I am very drunk.—A pint of porter with my cold beef at
Marlborough was enough to over-set me." (*S&S* 318)

Perry tells me that Mr. Cole never touches malt liquor. You would not think
it to look at him, but he is bilious—Mr. Cole is very bilious. (*E* 210)

*Brewing beer was a laborious business. First, a huge kettle of water was set boiling.
Boiling water was poured into a tub along with ground malt, and the mixture was carefully stirred together to make a mash. The mash was steeped and its liquid content
drawn off to make strong beer; then more water was added for a second steeping to
make small beer or ale. "Twenty-four bushels of malt," wrote John Farley, "will make
two hogheads of as good strong beer as any in England, and also two hogsheads of very
pretty ale. This strong beer should be kept for two or three years, and the ale never less
than one, before tapped." Hops were added as needed.*

*In the recipe below, Farley lists Creolus Indian berry and copperas, both of which
were common beer additives at the time, and both of which are poisonous. Our modern
recipe, needless to say, leaves these ingredients out.*

To brew five barrels of porter use the following ingredients: one quarter of malt,
eight pounds of hops, nine pounds of treacle, eight pounds of liquorice-root,
eight pounds of essentia bina, eight pounds of colour, half an ounce of capsicum, two ounces of Spanish liquorice, quarter of an ounce of Creolus Indian
berry, two drachms of salt or tartar, a quarter of an ounce of powdered alum and
copperas in equal quantities, three ounces of ginger, four ounces of slacked
lime, one ounce of linseed, and two drachms of cinnamon. Essentia bina is
eight pounds of moist sugar boiled in an iron vessel to a thick sirup, quite black
and very bitter. Colour is made of 8 pounds of moist sugar, boiled till between
bitter and sweet, and which gives the porter a fine mellow colour.

MODERN RECIPE

4 oz. Fuggle hops	⅛ tsp. powdered ginger
10 lbs. British brown malt*	½ cinnamon stick
2 lbs. pale malt*	a bag of ice
1 lb. chocolate malt	one packet dry ale yeast
¼ oz. brewers' licorice stick	¼ to ⅓ lb. molasses
1 oz. licorice root	¼ lb. essentia bina
⅛ tsp. grains of paradise (paradise seeds)	¼ lb. color
⅛ tsp. cream of tartar	5 oz. corn sugar

Bring 2 quarts of water to 160°F. Place the hops in a hop bag and set them in this water to soak.

Bring 13 quarts of water to 156°F and add the malt. This is your mash. Keep the mash at 156°F for 1 hour, heating and stirring as needed to keep the mash warm. During this time, the starches in the barley will be converted into sugars. To test the success of the conversion, transfer about a tablespoon of the mash liquid to a white plate or bowl. Add a little iodine, or an iodine-based sanitizing concentrate. If the iodine does not change color, starch conversion is complete. Meanwhile, bring 3 gallons of water up to 170°F. This hotter water will stop the chemical processes going on in the mash.

Pour enough warm water into your lautering tun to raise the water level above the level of the false bottom by about an inch; this will help to keep the mash from clogging the holes in the false bottom. Bring this water, too, to 170°F. Ladle the mash into the lautering tun and add the 3 gallons of 170°F water. This is called "sparging."

Drain the liquid through the tap at the bottom of the lautering tun into a large kettle for boiling. If necessary, you can divide the liquid, called "wort," between two or more kettles. Add the hops and hop infusion. Place the licorice stick, licorice root, grains of paradise, and cinnamon stick in another hop bag and add this to the wort as well. Add the pinch of cream of tartar and the pinch of ginger to the wort.

Bring the wort to a boil and boil for 1 hour, being very careful not to let the wort boil over. Meanwhile, sanitize a primary fermenter (usually a food-grade plastic bucket with a lid and an airlock), the airlock and stopper, and any utensils, such as a plastic spoon, that you will be using to transfer the boiled wort to its fermenter. When the fermenter has air-dried after being sanitized, measure the molasses into the fermenter.

Next, make the essentia bina and color. For each, place ¼ lb. sugar in a pan with 1 oz. water. Heat over high heat. For the color, cook about 6 to 8 minutes, without stirring, until the mixture turns caramel-colored. Remove from the heat. For essentia bina, cook a total of 10 to 12 min-

Continued on next page

Continued from previous page

utes, without stirring, until the mixture turns black and begins to smoke slightly. Remove from the heat. Both the essentia bina and the color will need to be transferred to the primary fermenter as soon as they are cool enough not to damage the material of which the fermenter is made, because both additives will tend to solidify when completely cool. If they do solidify before you can transfer them, add ½ cup water to each and reheat until the sugars dissolve again. Then cool slightly and add to the fermenter.

When the wort is done boiling, drain it into the fermenter. The movement of the wort as it is added will tend to help the dispersal of the molasses, essentia bina, and color. Discard the bag of hops, but add the bag of spices to the primary fermenter. Add cold water as necessary to bring the total liquid volume to 5 to 6 gallons.

Immediately begin cooling the wort. The faster you accomplish this, the better. You can set the fermenter in a sink or tub full of ice water, or you can use a special tool called a wort chiller, available at brewing supply stores.

When the wort reaches about 72°F, add the yeast, following the package directions. Stir with a sanitized spoon for 1 or 2 minutes.

Seal the fermenter with a lid and an airlock half-filled with water. Set the fermenter in a cool, dark place. Fermentation should begin within a day and will be evident because bubbles will rise through the airlock. When the bubbling ceases, you can use isinglass to clarify the beer (the method typically used by Regency brewers). Dissolve ¼ tsp. of powdered isinglass in 1 cup of beer at 60°F, and after ½ hour add the solution to the rest of the beer and stir gently. You can instead siphon the beer off into a secondary fermenter, leaving the thick layer of yeast behind, and storing for up to 1 more week.

Sanitize a siphon tube, bottling wand, bottle caps, a long spoon, and bottles. Add the corn sugar and stir gently. Bottle the beer and store in a cool, dark place.

*If you can't find British brown malt, use 10 lbs. pale malt and 2 lbs. caramel malt in place of the 10 lbs. British brown malt and 2 lbs. pale malt.

 ## WARMED ALE WITH A TOAST AND NUTMEG

LADY H. I assure you my Lord, Sir Arthur never touches wine; but Sophy
        will toss off a bumper I am sure to oblige your Lordship.
LORD F. Elder wine or mead, Miss Hampton?
SOPHY. If it is equal to you Sir, I should prefer some warm ale with a toast
        and nutmeg.
LORD F. Two glasses of warmed ale with a toast and nutmeg. (*Visit, MW* 53)

Various types of heated and spiced (or "mulled") beer were served for centuries in England. Austen is not specific about which type of mulled ale she means. She might have meant, for example, "lambswool," which took its name from the puffy shapes of the burst roasted apples which were floated in it. Or she might have meant "wassail," an ale-based punch on which pieces of toast were sometimes set adrift. She might simply have meant literally what she said—warm ale with nutmeg and a piece of toast on top. I have chosen the coward's way out and listed a number of optional ingredients with which interested readers may experiment.

 MODERN RECIPE

1 pint ale	pinch of cinnamon (optional)
1 T light brown sugar	1 small apple (optional)
pinch of ground ginger	1 piece of thinly sliced white bread
2 pinches of ground nutmeg	

In a saucepan over medium heat, warm the ale for about 5 minutes. Meanwhile, place the sugar, ginger, nutmeg, and cinnamon (if you decide to use it) in a heatproof bowl. Pour the hot ale over the spices and sugar and set aside.

If you are adding the apple, preheat the oven to 450°F. Place the apple in a foil loaf pan and cover loosely with foil. Roast until the apple's skin splits.

Toast the slice of bread until it is well browned and no longer flexible at all.

When you are ready to serve, return the spiced ale to the saucepan and warm it for a few minutes over medium heat. Pour into a large heatproof mug or tankard and top with the apple, the toast, or both.

✿ SPRUCE BEER ✿

(1760 recipe from Journal of Jeffery Amherst, Governor-General of British North America)

> . . . he wanted to make a memorandum in his pocket-book; it was about spruce beer. Mr. Knightley had been telling him something about brewing spruce beer, and he wanted to put it down. . . . (*E* 339)

> It is you however in this instance, that have the little Children—& I that have the great cask—, for we are brewing Spruce Beer again. . . . (Letter from Jane to Cassandra, December 9, 1808)

Take 7 Pounds of good spruce & boil it well till the bark peels off, then take the spruce out & put three Gallons of Molasses to the Liquor & boil it again, scum it well as it boils, then take it out the kettle & put it into a cooler, boil the remained of the water sufficient for a Barrel of thirty Gallons, if the kettle is not large enough to boil it together, when milkwarm in the Cooler put a pint of Yest into it and mix well. Then put it into a Barrel and let it work for two or three days, keep filling it up as it works out. When done working, bung it up with a Tent Peg in the Barrel to give it vent every now and then. It may be used in up to two or three days after. If wanted to be bottled it should stand a fortnight in the Cask. It will keep a great while.

 ## MODERN RECIPE

½ lb. spruce twigs (clip from the outermost 6" of the branches)

3⅜ cups molasses

2½ gallons plus 1 cup of water

2 T ale yeast

Sterilize all utensils before brewing, using either hot water or a sterilizing solution, to keep wild yeast from ruining the beer.

Boil the spruce twigs for at least 1 hour in the 2 gallons of water, skimming off any foam that rises to the top of the pot. Remove the twigs and discard. Add the molasses and boil 30 minutes, skimming as needed. Meanwhile, proof the yeast by dissolving it in a cup of warm (105°F–110°F) water.

Strain the liquid through muslin into a food-safe plastic bowl or bucket. Allow the liquid to cool to between 105°F and 110°F; you can set the entire container in a pan or bucket of cool water to help the process along (remember to remove your container from the cool water once the mixture reaches the proper temperature). Add the proofed yeast and mix thoroughly. Cover with a cloth and allow to stand, unstirred, for 2 to 3 days. Skim off any foam that rises to the surface, but do not stir. When foam no longer rises from the liquid, strain again through muslin and drink immediately or bottle in sanitized bottles, leaving a 3" air gap at the top of each bottle. Let the bottles stand overnight, then cap.

 # PUNCH

Oh! here comes Hill. My dear Hill, have you heard the good news? Miss Lydia is going to be married; and you shall all have a bowl of punch, to make merry at her wedding. (*P&P* 307)

Punch recipes varied according to the preference of the host, but the five essential ingredients were water, rum, citrus juice, sugar, and spice. I like turbinado sugar, a less refined form of sugar that has some of the molasses left in, partly because of its depth of flavor, and partly because it approximates the sugar that Austen's contemporaries would have used in punch. Double- or triple-refined sugar, which was more costly, would have been reserved for baking and for use in tea, where appearance mattered. This is a very strong-tasting punch; if you like something a little milder, try the grog in the next recipe.

MODERN RECIPE

Hot Punch	Cold Punch
1 cup lemon or orange juice	1 cup lime juice
2 cups sugar	2 cups sugar
3 cups rum	3 cups rum
4 cups water	4 cups water
nutmeg to taste	nutmeg to taste

Mix all the ingredients together. For cold punch, chill the mixture until serving time. For hot punch, heat the ingredients in a pot over medium heat to the desired temperature. Transfer the cold or hot punch to a serving bowl. (If you are making hot punch, make sure your punch bowl will tolerate hot liquids without cracking.) Some of Austen's contemporaries floated thin slices of citrus fruits in the bowl.

GROG

. . . from six o'clock to half past nine, there was little intermission of noise or grog. (*MP* 413)

Grog served aboard ship was generally "three-water grog," that is, three parts water to one of rum, mixed as available with lemon or lime juice and sugar. The recipe below represents the most palatable presentation of the 3:1 ratio and assumes unlimited access to fruit juice and sugar and a standard daily ration of ½ pint of rum.

MODERN RECIPE

8 oz. (1 cup) dark rum

¼ cup lemon or lime juice

3 cups water

2 T sugar

Mix. Drink. Man the capstan.

17

SAMPLE MENUS

❧ AN INN BREAKFAST ❧

When we arrived at the town where we were to Breakfast, I was determined to speak with Philander & Gustavus, & to that purpose as soon as I left the Carriage, I went to the Basket. . . . [T]hey desired me to step into the Basket as we might there converse with greater ease. Accordingly I entered & whilst the rest of the party were devouring Green tea & buttered toast, we feasted ourselves . . . by a confidential conversation. (*L&F, MW* 106)

Chocolate	Dry toast
Green tea	Bread and butter
Black tea	Honey
Hot rolls	Shredded ham

❧ BREAKFAST IN MILSOM-STREET ❧

. . . never in her life before had she beheld half such variety on a breakfast-table. . . . (*NA* 154)

Chocolate	Excellent rolls (hot or cold)
Coffee	Neat's tongue
Tea	Bread and butter
Plum cake	Dry toast
Pound cake	

Bill of Fare for January, from Francis Collingwood's *The Universal Cook, and City and Country Housekeeper*, 1801. Soups are at the top and bottom of the first course, indicated by closed tureens. In the second, as was traditional, sweet dishes such as jellies and fruit desserts are served side-by-side with roast meats and vegetables. The use of a diagram to indicate placement of dishes on the table was common in contemporary cookbooks. (Library of Congress.)

❁ BREAKFAST AT ❁ MANSFIELD PARK

Hard-boiled eggs
Pork chops with mustard
Coffee
Tea
Chocolate
Rolls

❁ A HUNTING BREAKFAST ❁ AT CHARLES MUSGROVE'S COTTAGE

There had been music, singing, talking, laughing, all that was most agreeable; charming manners in Captain Wentworth, no shyness or reserve; they seemed all to know each other perfectly, and he was coming the very next morning to shoot with Charles. He was to come to breakfast. . . . (*P* 58–59)

Cold roast beef
Ale
Fried herrings
Hard-boiled eggs
Cheese
Pork chops
Fried beef steaks
Coffee

THE NICEST COLD LUNCHEON IN THE WORLD

... when we got to the George, I do think we behaved very handsomely, for we treated the other three with the nicest cold luncheon in the world, and if you would have gone, we would have treated you too. (*P&P* 222)

Raw cucumbers
Salad of asparagus

Porter, mead, or fruit wines

A COLD COLLATION AT PEMBERLEY

The next variation which their visit afforded was produced by the entrance of servants with cold meat, cake, and a variety of all the finest fruits in season; but this did not take place till after many a significant look and smile from Mrs. Annesley to Miss Darcy had been given, to remind her of her post. There was now employment for the whole party; for though they could not all talk, they could all eat; and the beautiful pyramids of grapes, nectarines, and peaches, soon collected them round the table. (*P&P* 268)

Butter cake
Cold roast beef
Cold roast ham
Pyramid of grapes
Pyramid of nectarines

Pyramid of peaches
Selection of gooseberries, raspberries,
   currants, figs, mulberries, pears,
   plums, muscadines, melons, and/or
   pineapples

A PICNIC WITH SIR JOHN BARTON

... in the summer he was for ever forming parties to eat cold ham and chicken out of doors, and in winter his private balls were numerous enough for any young lady who was not suffering under the insatiable appetite of fifteen. (*S&S* 33)

Ham pie
Potted ham and chicken
Roast chicken

Boiled fowls
Selection of summer fruits
Ale or mead

BOX HILL PICNIC

It was now the middle of June, and the weather fine; and Mrs. Elton was growing impatient to name the day, and settle with Mr. Weston as to pigeon-pies and cold lamb, when a lame carriage horse threw every thing into sad uncertainty. (*E* 353)

Pigeon pie
Split leg of mutton
Strawberries
Currants or cherries

Fine little cakes
Ale or porter
Spruce beer

MR. KNIGHTLEY'S STRAWBERRY PARTY

Go and eat and drink a little more, and you will do very well. Another slice of cold meat, another draught of Madeira and water, will make you nearly on a par with the rest of us. (*E* 365)

Strawberries
Broiled mutton chops
Boiled green peas

Fried potatoes
Madeira and water

DINNER AT THE WATSONS'

I do beg & entreat that no Turkey may be seen today. I am really frightened out of my wits with the number of dishes we have already. (*Wat, MW* 354)

Chicken surprize
Giblet soup
Suet pudding
Fricasseed tripe

Roast turkey
Boiled green peas
English bread

DINNER IN HARLEY STREET

The dinner was a grand one, the servants were numerous, and every thing bespoke the Mistress's inclination for shew, and the Master's ability to support it. . . . (*S&S* 233)

First Course

Pea soup
Roast chickens
Venison pasty
Veal cutlets
Haunch of venison
Crawfish soup

Turkey à la poele
Asparagus soup
Harrico of mutton
Roast ham
Tongue and turnips

Second Course

Peas
Stewed prawns
Lemon custard
Roast turkey or duck
Apricot tart
Cherry or gooseberry tart

Stewed hare
Jelly
Apple pie
Boiled artichokes
Partridge in Panes

 DINNER AT SOTHERTON

Dinner was soon followed by tea and coffee, a ten miles' drive home allowed no waste of hours, and from the time of their sitting down to table, it was a quick succession of busy nothings till the carriage came to the door. . . . (*MP* 104)

First Course

Beans
Shoulder of mutton surprised
Cod with onions
Mock turtle soup
Tongue

Beef rumps en matelotte
Fricando of veal
Leg of lamb
Roast leveret
Asparagus soup

Second Course

Vegetable racoo
Ducks or tartlets
Crawfish
Turkey or haunch of venison
Transparent pudding or currant pie

Cherry tart
Eggs and spinach
French beans
Cheese cake
Mushrooms

❀ DINNER AT WOODSTON ❀

She could not but observe that the abundance of the dinner did not seem to create the smallest astonishment in the General; nay, that he was even looking at the side-table for cold meat which was not there. His son and daughter's observations were of a different kind. They had seldom seen him eat so heartily at any table but his own; and never before known him so little disconcerted by the melted butter's being oiled. (*NA* 214–15)

Onion soup
Portugal beef
Pigeons with fine herbs
Fried sole

French rolls
Pickled beet-root
Potatoes
Macaroni soup

❀ A FAMILY DINNER AT CAMDEN-PLACE ❀

Her making a fourth, when they sat down to dinner, was noticed as an advantage. (*P* 137)

Rice soup
Salmon boiled in wine
Harrico of mutton
Roast beef

Asparagus forced in french rolls
Compote of apples
French rolls
Orange pudding

❀ DINNER AT MANSFIELD PARSONAGE ❀

The Dr. was very fond of eating, and would have a good dinner every day. . . . (*MP* 31)

. . . the dinner itself was elegant and plentiful, according to the usual style of the Grants, and too much according to the usual habits of all to raise any emotion except in Mrs. Norris, who could never behold either the wide table or the number of dishes on it with patience, and who always did contrive to experience some evil from the passing of the servants behind her chair, and to bring away some fresh conviction of its being impossible among so many dishes but that some must be cold. (*MP* 239)

First Course

Roast beef	Eggs en surtout
Rice pudding	Chestnut soup
Stewed oysters	Scotch collops à la françoise
Goose with mustard	Boiled cabbage

Second Course

Ragooed carrots and parnsips	Ducks à la mode
Radishes	Curry
Braised pheasant	Boiled turnips
Currant tart	Turkey pinions

TEA AT MANSFIELD PARK

The solemn procession, headed by Baddeley, of tea-board, urn, and cake-bearers, made its appearance, and delivered her from a grievous imprisonment of body and mind. Mr. Crawford was obliged to move. She was at liberty, she was busy, she was protected. (*MP* 344)

Tea	Chocolate biscuits
Coffee	Orange biscuits
Plum cake	Fine little cakes

TEA AT THE EDWARDSES'

The entrance of the Tea things at 7 o'clock was some relief—& luckily M^r & Mrs Edwards always drank a dish extraordinary, & ate an additional muffin when they were going to sit up late, which lengthened the ceremony almost to the wished for moment. (*Wat, MW* 326–27)

Tea	Muffins, with butter

🌸 TEA IN SANDITON 🌸

He took his own Cocoa from the Tray,—which seemed provided with almost as many Teapots &c as there were persons in company, Miss P. drinking one sort of Herb-Tea & Miss Diana another, & turning completely to
the Fire, sat coddling and cooling it to his own satisfaction & toasting some
Slices of Bread, brought up ready-prepared in the Toast-rack . . . (*Sand,
MW* 416)

Tea	Chocolate
Herbal teas	Buttered toast

🌸 A MODEST SUPPER 🌸

"And what had she got for Supper?" "I did not observe." "Bread & Cheese I
suppose." "I should never wish for a better supper," said Ellen. "You have
never any reason" replied her Mother, "as a better is always provided for
you." (*Col Let, MW* 156–57)

English Bread	Stilton cheese, North Wiltshire cheese, or cheddar cheese

🌸 A LITTLE BIT OF HOT SUPPER 🌸

This was agreed to, and Mrs. Philips protested that they would have a nice
comfortable noisy game of lottery tickets, and a little bit of hot supper afterwards. The prospect of such delights was very cheering, and they parted
in mutual good spirits. (*P&P* 74)

Boiled fowls	Veal cutlets
Scolloped oysters	Radishes
Fricasseed tripe	

SUPPER AT MANSFIELD PARK

Mrs. Norris . . . was cross because the house-keeper would have her own way
with the supper. . . . (*MP* 267)

Cold roast beef or roast mutton
Pickled mushrooms

Wild ducks hashed
Fine cheesecakes

SUPPER AT HARTFIELD

. . . the supper-table, which always closed such parties . . . was all set out and
ready, and moved forwards to the fire, before she was aware . . . [w]ith the
real good-will of a mind delighted with its own ideas, did she then do all
then honours of the meal, and help and recommend the minced chicken
and scalloped oysters with an urgency which she knew would be acceptable
to the early hours and civil scruples of their guests.

Upon such occasions Mr. Woodhouse's feelings were in sad warfare. He
loved to have the cloth laid, because it had been the fashion of his youth; but
his conviction of suppers being very unwholesome made him rather sorry to
see any thing put on it. . . .

Such another small basin of thin gruel as his own, was all that he could,
with thorough self-approbation, recommend. . . .

"Mrs. Bates, let me propose your venturing on one of these eggs. An egg
boiled very soft is not unwholesome. Serle understands boiling an egg better than any body. I would not recommend an egg boiled by any body else—
but you need not be afraid—they are very small, you see—one of our small
eggs will not hurt you. Miss Bates, let Emma help you to a *little* bit of tart—
a *very* little bit. Ours are all apple tarts. You need not be afraid of unwholesome preserves here. I do not advise the custard. Mrs. Goddard, what say
you to *half* a glass of wine? A small half glass—put into a tumbler of water? . . ." (*E* 24–25)

The baked apples and biscuits, excellent in their way, you know; but there
was a delicate fricassee of sweetbread and some asparagus brought in at first,
and good Mr. Woodhouse, not thinking the asparagus quite boiled enough,
sent it all out again. (*E* 329)

Soft-boiled eggs
Water gruel
Apple tarts
Lemon custard

Fricasseed sweetbreads
Salad of asparagus
Common biscuits
Wine

❀ A BALL SUPPER FOR EIGHTEEN COUPLE ❀

My dear Lady Elliott, do not be uneasy. The dining parlour will admit eighteen couple with ease; card-tables may be placed in the drawing-room; the library may be open for tea and other refreshments; and let the supper be set out in the saloon. (*S&S* 252)

Lady Lucas, who had been long yawning at the repetition of delights which she saw no likelihood of sharing, was left to the comforts of cold ham and chicken. (*P&P* 100)

Dear Jane, how shall we ever recollect half the dishes for grandmamma? Soup too! Bless me!(*E* 330)

Cold roast chicken
Cold roast ham
White soup
Fried patties
Scotch collops à la Françoise
Ducks à la mode
Roast leveret
Pigeon pie

Salad
Scolloped potatoes
Apple pie
Orange pudding
Sandwiches
Punch
Negus
Wine

APPENDIX 1:
WHAT'S WITH ALL THE BUTTER?

You will notice, as you read through the recipes included in this book, that butter is used in a majority of them. Olive oil—usually referred to in cookbooks of the time simply as "oil" or "sweet oil"—was rarely used for sautéing, as it had to be imported from Spain or Italy and was therefore expensive. It tended to be used only for vinaigrettes.

Butter, however, did not need to be imported. Many country dwellers had cows of their own and could make butter on a nearly daily basis. Those who did not, and their neighbors in towns, could buy butter at market from the many women who earned money by selling their surplus milk, butter, and cheese. Butter's ready availability, therefore, made it the most popular type of cooking fat.

As to why so much of it was used, there are several explanations. One is that there were obviously no nonstick pans in the Regency. In order to keep food from sticking, cooks had to use either a good deal of liquid or a good deal of fat, and sometimes both. Another is that people simply liked their food rich and had no modern concerns about cholesterol. They understood that obesity could lead to certain ailments, such as gout, but they showed little inclination to change their habits in order to avoid such ills.

A third reason for the generous use of butter had to do with servants' prerogatives. Servants were paid in a combination of wages, clothes, tips, and perquisites that varied by rank. The cook was entitled to used surplus fats, such as the butter and meat fat left over in the dripping tray after roasting a large piece of beef. The more butter used for basting, the more dripping was left in the pan, and the more fat the cook got to sell for her own benefit. Employers often complained that their cooks were deliberately wasting butter in order to increase their own profit at the expense of their employers.

Butter was used for frying, basting, baking, and the thickening of sauces. This last technique is seldom discussed in cookbooks of our own time. The theory is somewhat the same as a roux, with the body of a sauce coming from a mixture of flour and fat. With a roux, however, the fat and flour are cooked together first, and then other ingredients are added. In the eighteenth-century technique, the butter is mixed with the flour—usually described in cookbooks as "a lump of butter rolled in flour"—and then added to the nearly complete sauce, usually as the last step in its preparation. The distinct advantage of this technique over the mere sprinkling of flour into a sauce is that as the butter melts, it automatically distributes the flour evenly throughout the sauce, without lumps.

When you see this technique mentioned in a recipe, the theory is that you roll the butter in the flour, then pinch or squeeze the butter as necessary to incorporate more flour. When thickening a sauce this way, I usually take a lump of butter of the correct size, dunk it thoroughly in my flour canister, then squeeze it firmly in my fist three or four times, pushing more flour into the butter with each squeeze. In the recipes, I have usually given the amount of flour used as half that of the butter, but this is simply a rough approximation of the quantities involved. Roll and squeeze away, get your hands good and floury, and don't worry too much about exact proportions. (If precision were really important, Hannah Glasse et al. would have given us better instructions than "a lump of butter.")

APPENDIX 2:
INGREDIENTS AND SOURCES

BACON   There is more than one type of bacon, as anyone who has traveled or lived in both the United States and Britain knows. There is the fatty, heavily streaked meat that Americans know as bacon and the cured pork tenderloin that they call Canadian bacon, as well as the intermediate variety of cured meat that most English shoppers call bacon. This cookbook tends to assume that "bacon" means the fatty American variety, as late eighteenth- and early nineteenth-century cooks usually used bacon to provide fat content for basting and to prevent some foods from sticking to the pan.

BLUE MOLD   Also known as *Penicillum roqueforti*. Available from cheesemaking supply stores, including some that sell supplies online.

BROTH   You may use the broth recipe included in this cookbook or a broth from your local supermarket.

BROWNING   Easily the most useful sauce additive in the Regency cupboard. It adds instant depth and flavor to any meat sauce. There is no really good modern counterpart, but fortunately, browning is not hard to make and keeps for a long time if refrigerated.

CHEESE SALT   A noniodized salt designed specifically for cheesemaking. Available from cheesemaking supply stores, including some that sell supplies online.

CULLIS   A thick broth, somewhere between a broth and a gravy in consistency. Canned broth from the supermarket may be substituted, but genuine cullis adds a distinctive flavor that is worth pursuing.

FORCE-MEAT   The same sort of combination of ingredients found in meat-loaf or meatballs—some sort of ground meat, a starchy ingredient such as flour or bread crumbs, a binder like egg yolk, and various spices. It took its name from the fact that it was often "forced," or stuffed, into various other types of food, such as pies, birds, and hollowed-out vegetables.

GOOSEBERRIES   Americans will have a difficult time finding these unless they happen to grow them at home. Gooseberries are available online in cans, both in a form suitable for use in tarts and in a crushed form for winemaking. Some specialty British-goods stores have them, as does the occasional foreign-food aisle of a well-stocked grocery store.

GRAVY   You may use the gravy recipe included in this cookbook or a gravy from your local supermarket.

JAMAICA PEPPER   Allspice.

LEMON PICKLE   A truly distinctive condiment that adds a unique flavor and is, rather unfortunately, a pain in the butt to make. If you don't want to go to the trouble of making genuine lemon pickle, lemon juice is a (barely) acceptable substitute.

LEVERET   A young hare. Unless you have access to wild game (or an unusually adventurous butcher), you are unlikely to find this meat. Use rabbit instead, which can be found in good markets and online through specialty meat suppliers. (Watch out for shipping costs, though.)

LONG PEPPER   A relative of traditional pepper. It was not available during the time that I was test-cooking these recipes, but I have learned that it is now available online from Zingelman's.com. Those who wish to use it can reinsert it into the appropriate recipes.

MEAT CURING MIX   In Austen's time, this would have been a combination of saltpeter, bay salt, and common salt. Modern nitrate-nitrite mixes are available in some markets and online. The Morton salt company sells one variety, for example, and this is available in Morton's online store.

MESOPHILIC STARTER   A bacterial culture available from cheesemaking supply stores, including some that sell supplies online.

MOREL   A spongy, roughly conical fungus available fresh in some areas and dried in others.

MUSHROOM KETCHUP   An eighteenth-century condiment that is no longer commercially available. A thick steak sauce is the closest modern counterpart, but it's far too vinegary in taste. I highly recommend that you make your own mushroom ketchup; canned, it keeps for a very, very long time, so if you make a large batch, you won't have to do it often.

MUSHROOM POWDER   No commercially available modern counterpart, but you could crumble or food-process dry mushrooms to achieve the same effect—possibly with more flavor.

ORANGE-FLOWER WATER   Available online from specialty spice suppliers.

PHEASANT   Your source for this game bird will vary depending on your location. I'm fortunate enough to live near several markets that either carry pheasants routinely or will order them on short notice. My uncle-in-law, by contrast, is a hunter and simply shoots his own. For those who lack access to either source, there are several online purveyors of game meats who will ship overnight. The shipping costs can be steep, however.

PIGEON (SQUAB)   See pheasant.

RENNET   A thickening agent for cheese, originally derived from the stomachs of calves. Now available in liquid and tablet forms, as well as an all-vegetable form, from cheesemaking-supply stores, including some that sell supplies online.

ROSE-FLOWER WATER   A common flavoring before vanilla became more popular and widely available. Rose-flower water can be purchased now from online specialty spice suppliers.

SIPPETS   Slices of bread toasted or fried in butter.

SWEETBREADS   The thymus gland of certain immature mammals, principally calves. Generally available only in extremely well-stocked gourmet markets, Asian markets, and Latin American markets.

TONGUE   Usually, in modern markets (when you can find it), this will be beef tongue, though the tongues of other animals were prepared for the table in

Austen's day. Generally available only in extremely well-stocked gourmet markets, Asian markets, and Latin American markets.

TRIPE   The stomach lining of a cow. Generally available only in extremely well-stocked gourmet markets, Asian markets, and Latin American markets.

VENISON   Deer meat. Available at some well-stocked markets and online from specialty meat suppliers.

WALNUT KETCHUP   A tasty eighteenth-century condiment that cannot be found commercially and must be homemade. The closest widely available substitute is Worcestershire sauce.

APPENDIX 3:
SPECIAL TOOLS AND SOURCES

BUTTER MUSLIN/BUTTERCLOTH   A tightly woven version of cheesecloth. Available from cheesemaking supply stores, including some that sell online.

CHEESE MOLDS   Forms for draining, shaping, and pressing cheeses. Available from cheesemaking supply stores, including some that sell online.

CHEESE PRESS   A tool for pressing excess liquid out of hard cheeses such as cheddar and North Wiltshire. Available from cheesemaking supply stores, including some that sell online. Traditional wood varieties, as well as easily sanitized metal and plastic versions, can be obtained from many sources. Cheese pressing can be improvised with common kitchen items, but the results can be erratic. If you're just trying one cheese to see how it works, it's probably not worth investing in a cheese press. If, like me, you've tried a couple of cheeses and gotten hooked on cheesemaking, a cheese press makes life much, much easier.

PIE AND CAKE PANS   You can get by with normal-sized pie and cake pans by scaling down amounts and cooking times, but someone who wishes to impress his or her guests with the scope of Regency dinner parties will probably want to invest in one or more really big pans—the biggest that will fit in your oven. Fourteen-inch and sixteen-inch cake pans can be purchased from online suppliers and sometimes from local party-supply stores. Some communities even have stores devoted to supplies for cake baking and decorating, and these, too, will stock extra-large pans.

SALAMANDER   A piece of metal with a handle. One end was heated and passed over food to brown the top. The action of the salamander can be simulated either with the broiler element in an oven or a butane kitchen torch of the type used for browning crème brulée. The former works more quickly; the latter offers the cook more control.

SANITIZERS   These come in powder or liquid form and are diluted for washing utensils that come into contact with cheese, beer, wine, and mead. They can be purchased from brewing- and winemaking-supply stores, including many that sell online.

SCALE   A kitchen scale of some kind is essential for re-creating historical recipes, as measurements are often given in weight rather than volume.

BIBLIOGRAPHY

SOURCES OF ORIGINAL RECIPES

Bradley, Richard. *The Country Housewife and Lady's Director in the Management of a House, and the Delights and Profits of a Farm*. 1736. Reprint, London: Prospect Books, 1980.

Briggs, Richard. *The English Art of Cookery*. Dublin: P. Byrne, 1798.

Carter, Susannah. *The Frugal Housewife, or Complete Woman Cook*. London: E. Newbery, 1795.

Collingwood, Francis. *The Universal Cook, and City and Country Housekeeper*. 3rd ed. London: C. Whittingham, 1801.

Ellis, William. *The Country Housewife's Family Companion*. 1750. Reprint, Totnes, Devon: Prospect Books, 2000.

Farley, John. *The London Art of Cookery*. 1783. Reprint, Lewes, East Sussex: Southover Press, 1988.

The French Family Cook: Being a Complete System of French Cookery. London: J. Bell, 1793.

Glasse, Hannah. *The Art of Cookery Made Plain and Easy*. 1796, rev. ed. Reprint, Schenectady, NY: United States Historical Research Service, 1994.

Harrison, Sarah. *The House-keeper's Pocket-book; And Compleat Family Cook*. London: R. Ware, 1748.

Hunter, Alexander (using pseudonym Ignotus). *Culina Famulatrix Medicinae*. York: T. Wilson, 1805.

Millington, Charles. *The Housekeeper's Domestic Library; or, New Universal Family Instructor*. London: M. Jones, 1805.

Raffald, Elizabeth. *The Experienced English Housekeeper*. 1769. Reprint, Lewes, East Sussex: Southover Press, 1997.

Rundell, Maria. *A New System of Domestic Cookery*. 1816. Reprint, New York: Vantage Press, 1977.

Woodforde, James. *Passages from the Five Volumes of the Diary of a Country Parson 1758–1802*, selected and edited by John Beresford. New York: Oxford University Press, 1935.

OTHER RESOURCES

Accum, Frederick. *A Treatise on Adulterations of Food and Culinary Poisons*. 1820. Reprint, N.p.: Mallinckrodt Collection of Food Classics, 1966.

Ashley, William. *The Bread of Our Forefathers: An Inquiry in Economic History*. Oxford: Clarendon Press, 1928.

Beeton, Isabella. *The Book of Household Management*. 1861. Reprint, London: Cape, 1968.

Black, Maggie, and Deirdre Le Faye. *The Jane Austen Cookbook*. Chicago: Chicago Review Press, 1995.

Burnett, John. *Plenty and Want: A Social History of Diet in England from 1815 to the Present Day*. Rev. ed. London: Scolar Press, 1979.

Charsley, Simon R. *Wedding Cakes and Cultural History*. London: Routledge, 1992.

Cheke, Val. *The Story of Cheese-Making in Britain*. London: Routledge and Kegan Paul, 1959.

Clark, Peter. *The English Alehouse: A Social History 1200–1830*. London: Longman, 1983.

Gomme, George Laurence, ed. *The Gentleman's Magazine Library—Vol. 1: Manners and Customs*. 1883. Reprint, Detroit: Singing Tree Press, 1968.

Grossman, Anne Chotzinoff, and Lisa Grossman Thomas. *Lobscouse and Spotted Dog*. New York: W. W. Norton and Company, 1997.

Hackwood, Frederick W. *Inns, Ales, and Drinking Customs of Old England*. 1909. Reprint, London: Bracken Books, 1985.

Hartley, Dorothy. *Food in England*. 1954. Reprint, London: Little, Brown, and Company, 1999.

Lane, Maggie. *Jane Austen and Food*. London: The Hambledon Press, 1995.

Latham, Jean. *A Taste of the Past*. London: Adam and Charles Black, 1975.

Lonsdale, Roger, ed. *The New Oxford Book of Eighteenth-Century Verse*. 1984. Reprint, Oxford: Oxford University Press, 1987.

Mennell, Stephen. *All Manners of Food: Eating and Taste in England and France from the Middle Ages to the Present*. 2nd ed. Urbana, IL: University of Illinois Press, 1996.

The Mirror of the Graces. 1811. Reprint, Mendocino, CA: R. L. Shep, 1997.

Monckton, H. A. *A History of the English Public House*. London: The Bodley Head, 1969.

Mui, Hoh-Cheung, and Lorna H. Mui. *Shops and Shopkeeping in Eighteenth-Century England*. Montreal: McGill-Queen's University Press, 1989.

Olsen, Kirstin. *All Things Austen: An Encyclopedia of Austen's World*. Westport, CT: Greenwood Press, 2005.

Pendergrast, Mark. *Uncommon Grounds: The History of Coffee and How It Transformed the World*. New York: Basic Books, 1999.

Pettigrew, Jane, *A Social History of Tea*. London: National Trust, 2001.

Roberts, Jonathan. *The Origins of Fruit and Vegetables*. New York: Universe Publishing, 2001.

Simpson, Helen. *The London Ritz Book of Afternoon Tea: The Art and Pleasures of Taking Tea*. New York: Arbor House, 1986.

Wilson, C. Anne. *Food and Drink in Britain from the Stone Age to the 19th Century*. 1973. Reprint, London: Constable, 1991.

Index

Page numbers in **bold** type indicate recipes.

About the Author

KIRSTIN OLSEN is a freelance writer and the author of several reference works, including *All Things Shakespeare* (2002) and *All Things Austen* (2005), both available from Greenwood Press.